THAT TIME I GOT REINCARNATED AS A

SLIME

14

Author: **FUSE**

Artist: **TAIKI KAWAKAMI**

Character design: **MITZ VAH**

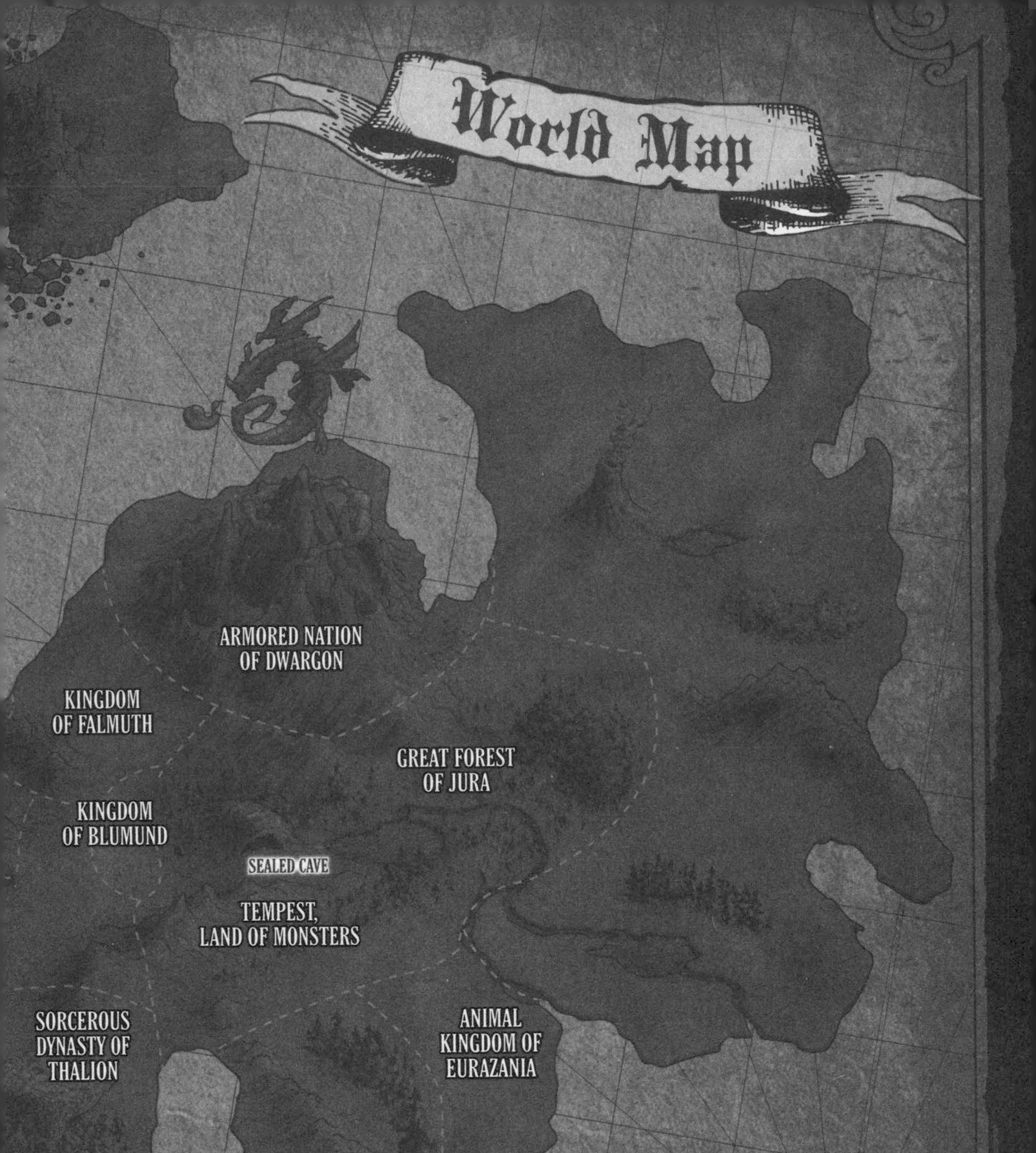
World Map
ARMORED NATION OF DWARGON
KINGDOM OF FALMUTH
GREAT FOREST OF JURA
KINGDOM OF BLUMUND
SEALED CAVE
TEMPEST, LAND OF MONSTERS
SORCEROUS DYNASTY OF THALION
ANIMAL KINGDOM OF EURAZANIA

PLOT SUMMARY

In Rimuru's absence, two barriers were erected over Tempest. One shuts off contact with the outside world by nullifying magic, and the other weakens all monsters. That delays Rimuru's return, and he arrives to find the town badly damaged. The worst tragedy, however, is the death of Shion and innocent residents. But when Eren claims to know a fairy tale about resurrecting the dead, Rimuru decides that he must evolve into a Demon Lord to save his companions. ▼

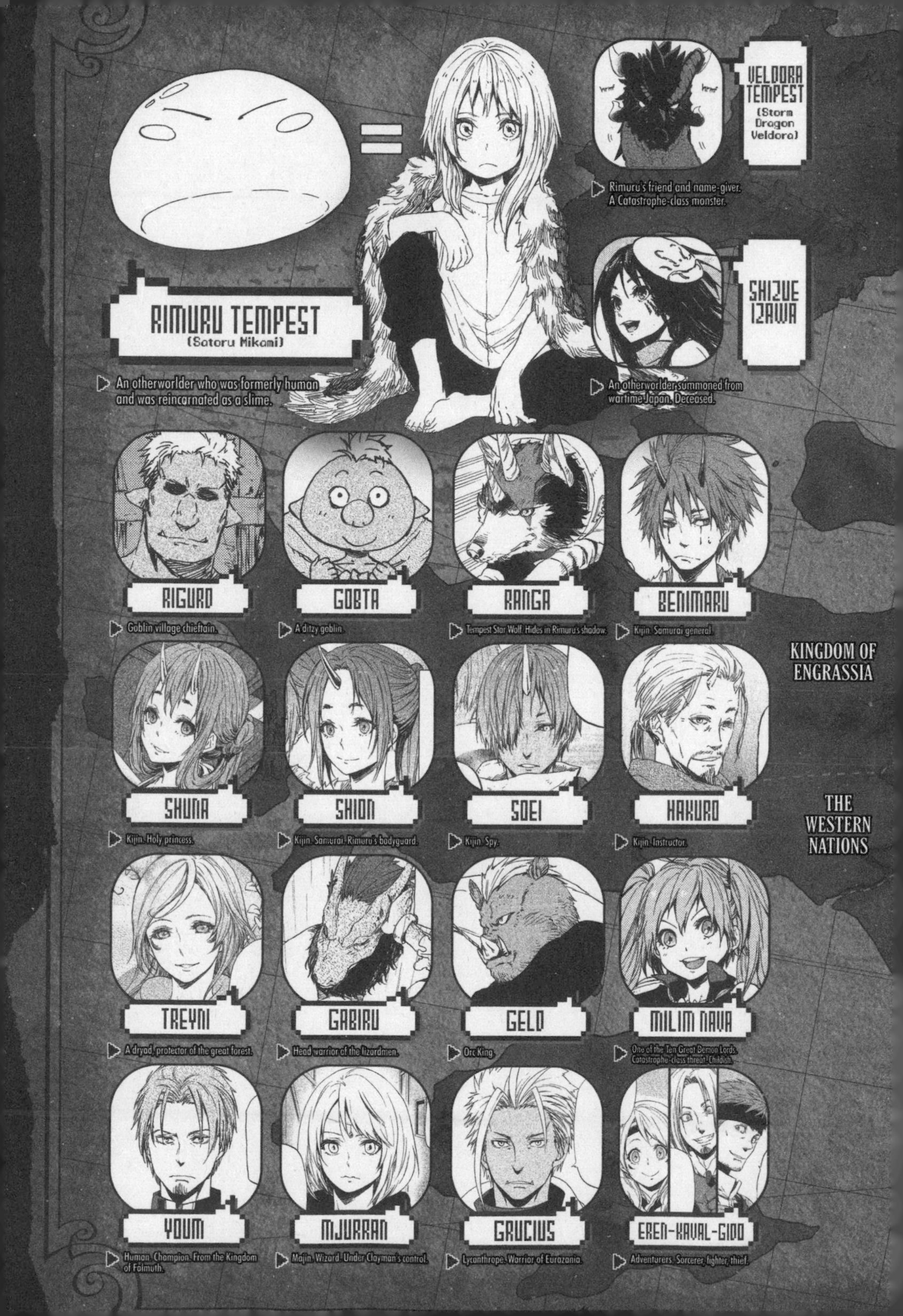
RIMURU TEMPEST
(Satoru Mikami)
An otherworlder who was formerly human and was reincarnated as a slime.
VELDORA TEMPEST
(Storm Dragon Veldora)
Rimuru's friend and name-giver. A Catastrophe-class monster.
SHIZUE IZAWA
An otherworlder summoned from wartime Japan. Deceased.
RIGURD
Goblin village chieftain.
GOBTA
A ditzy goblin.
RANGA
Tempest Star Wolf. Hides in Rimuru's shadow.
BENIMARU
Kijin. Samurai general.
KINGDOM OF ENGRASSIA
SHUNA
Kijin. Holy princess.
SHION
Kijin. Samurai. Rimuru's bodyguard.
SOEI
Kijin. Spy.
HAKURO
Kijin. Instructor.
THE WESTERN NATIONS
TREYNI
A dryad, protector of the great forest.
GABIRU
Head warrior of the lizardmen.
GELD
Orc King.
MILIM NAVA
One of the Ten Great Demon Lords. Catastrophe-class threat. Childish.
YOUM
Human. Champion. From the Kingdom of Falmuth.
MJURRAN
Majin. Wizard. Under Clayman's control.
GRUCIUS
Lycanthrope. Warrior of Eurazania.
EREN-KAVAL-GIDO
Adventurers. Sorcerer, fighter, thief.

CONTENTS

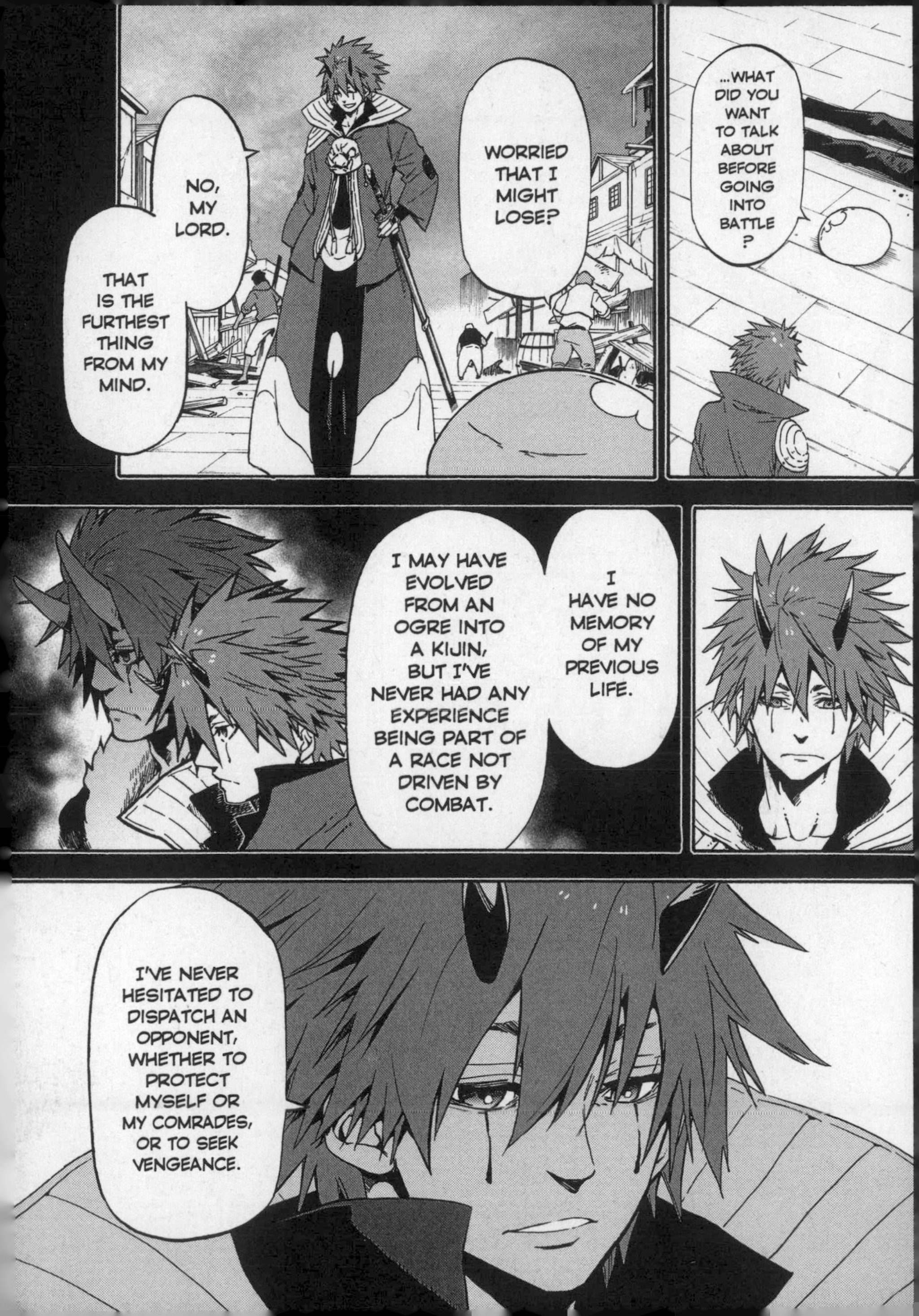
...WHAT DID YOU WANT TO TALK ABOUT BEFORE GOING INTO BATTLE?
WORRIED THAT I MIGHT LOSE?
NO, MY LORD.
THAT IS THE FURTHEST THING FROM MY MIND.
I HAVE NO MEMORY OF MY PREVIOUS LIFE.
I MAY HAVE EVOLVED FROM AN OGRE INTO A KIJIN, BUT I'VE NEVER HAD ANY EXPERIENCE BEING PART OF A RACE NOT DRIVEN BY COMBAT.
I'VE NEVER HESITATED TO DISPATCH AN OPPONENT, WHETHER TO PROTECT MYSELF OR MY COMRADES, OR TO SEEK VENGEANCE.

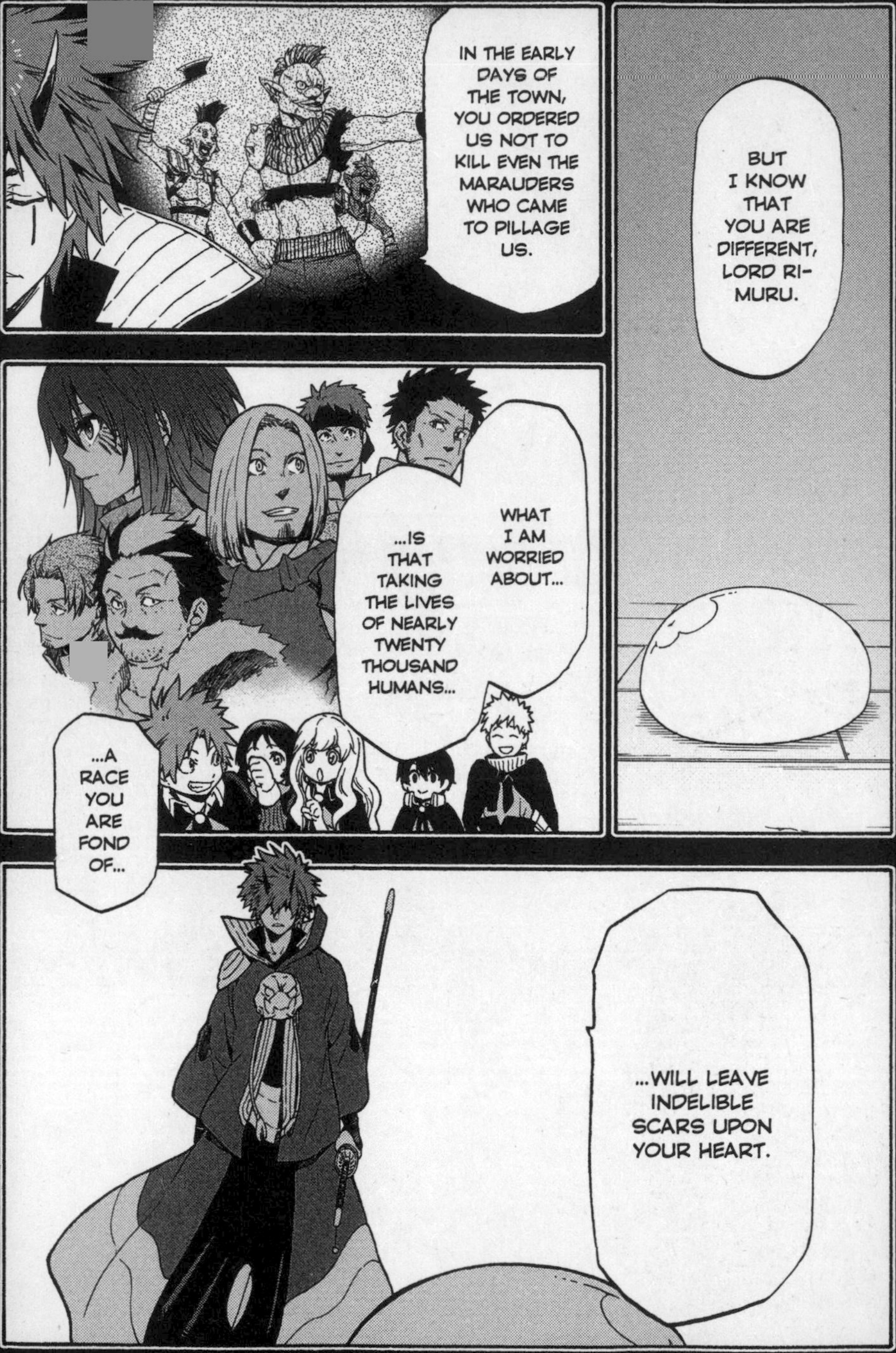
BUT I KNOW THAT YOU ARE DIFFERENT, LORD RI-MURU.
IN THE EARLY DAYS OF THE TOWN, YOU ORDERED US NOT TO KILL EVEN THE MARAUDERS WHO CAME TO PILLAGE US.
WHAT I AM WORRIED ABOUT...
...IS THAT TAKING THE LIVES OF NEARLY TWENTY THOUSAND HUMANS...
...A RACE YOU ARE FOND OF...
...WILL LEAVE INDELIBLE SCARS UPON YOUR HEART.

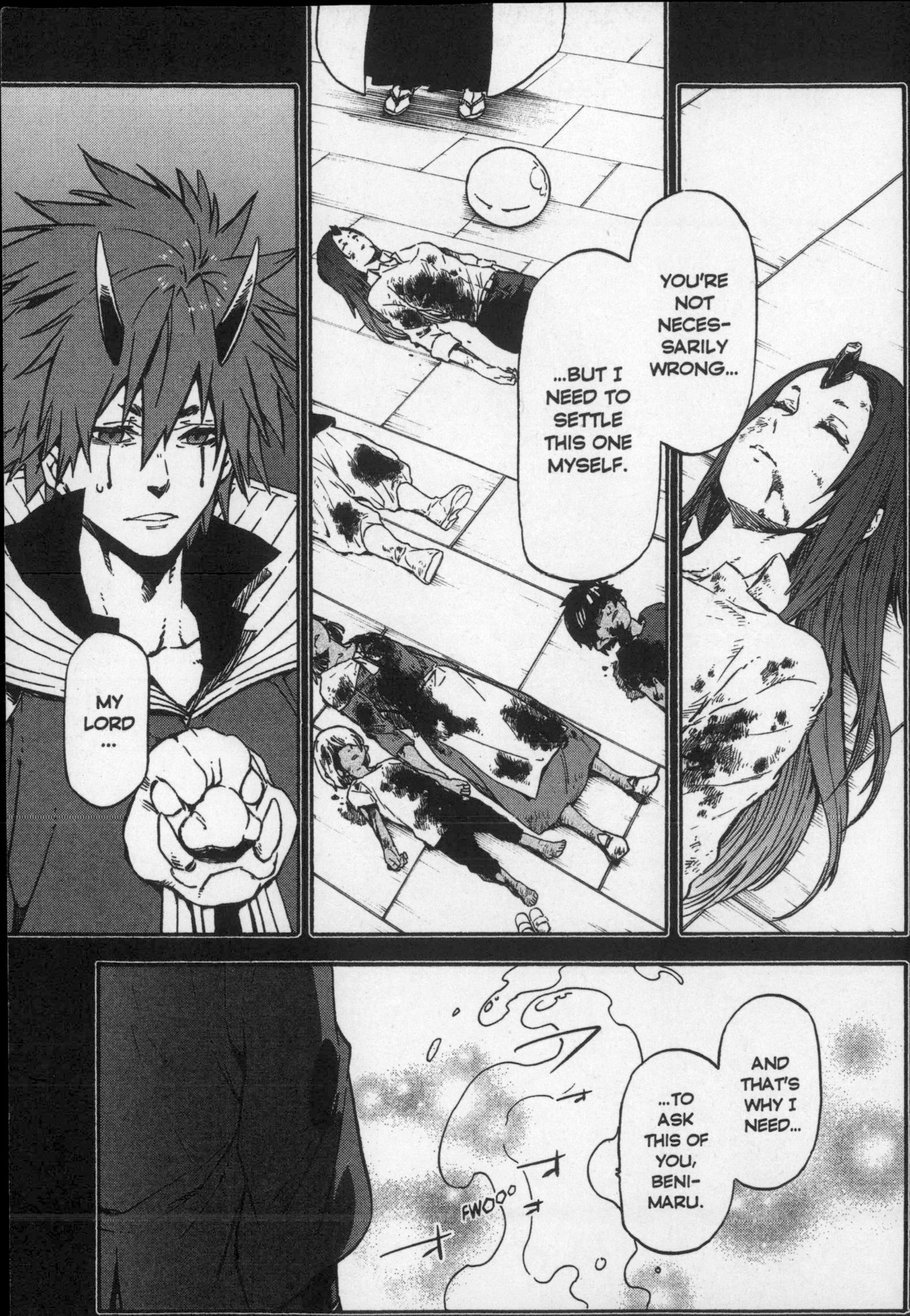
YOU'RE NOT NECES-SARILY WRONG...
...BUT I NEED TO SETTLE THIS ONE MYSELF.
MY LORD ...
AND THAT'S WHY I NEED...
...TO ASK THIS OF YOU, BENI-MARU.
FWOOO

CHAPTER 64 Difference in Class

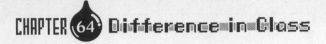

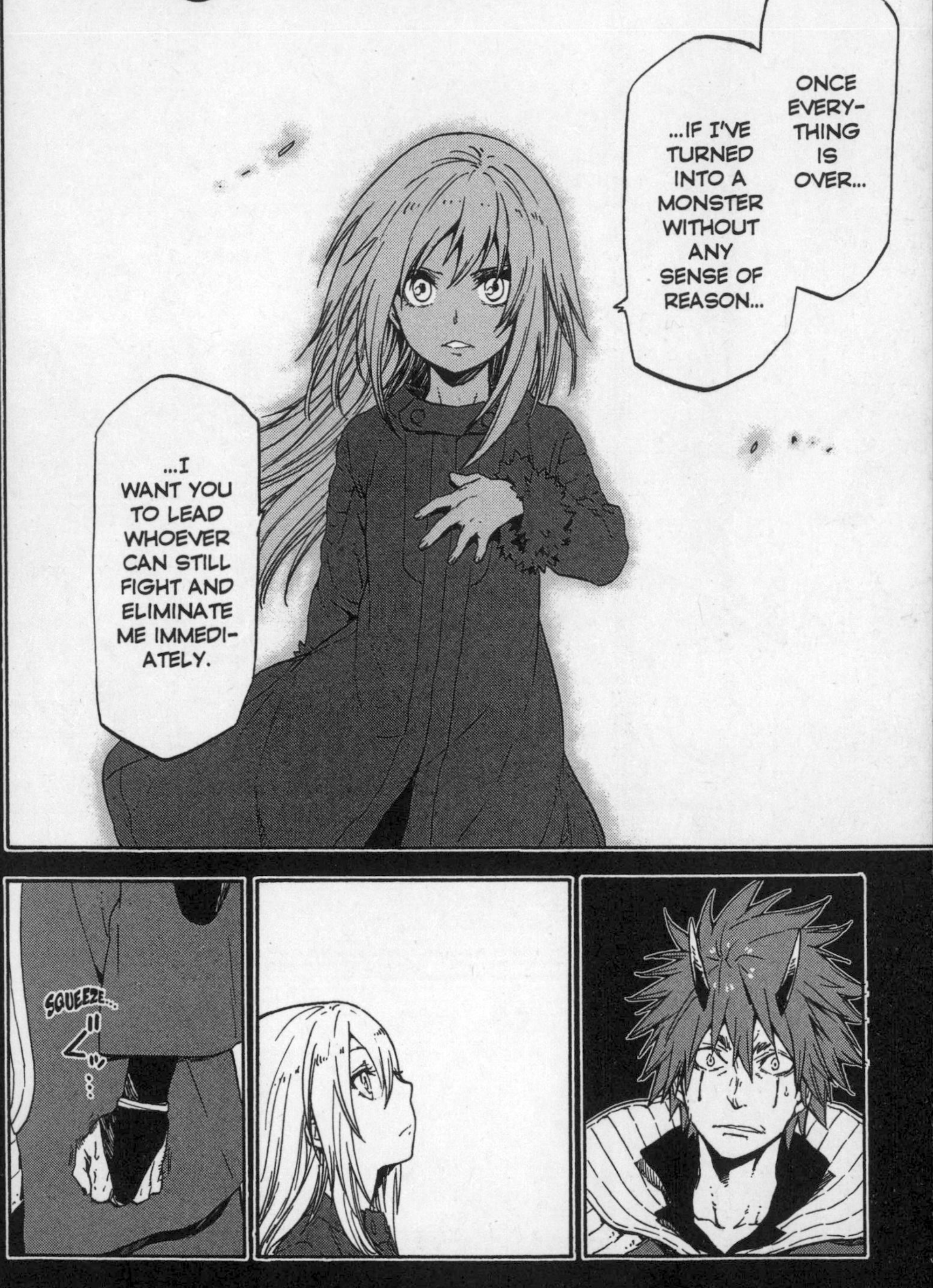
ONCE EVERY-THING IS OVER...
...IF I'VE TURNED INTO A MONSTER WITHOUT ANY SENSE OF REASON...
...I WANT YOU TO LEAD WHOEVER CAN STILL FIGHT AND ELIMINATE ME IMMEDI-ATELY.
SQUEEZE...

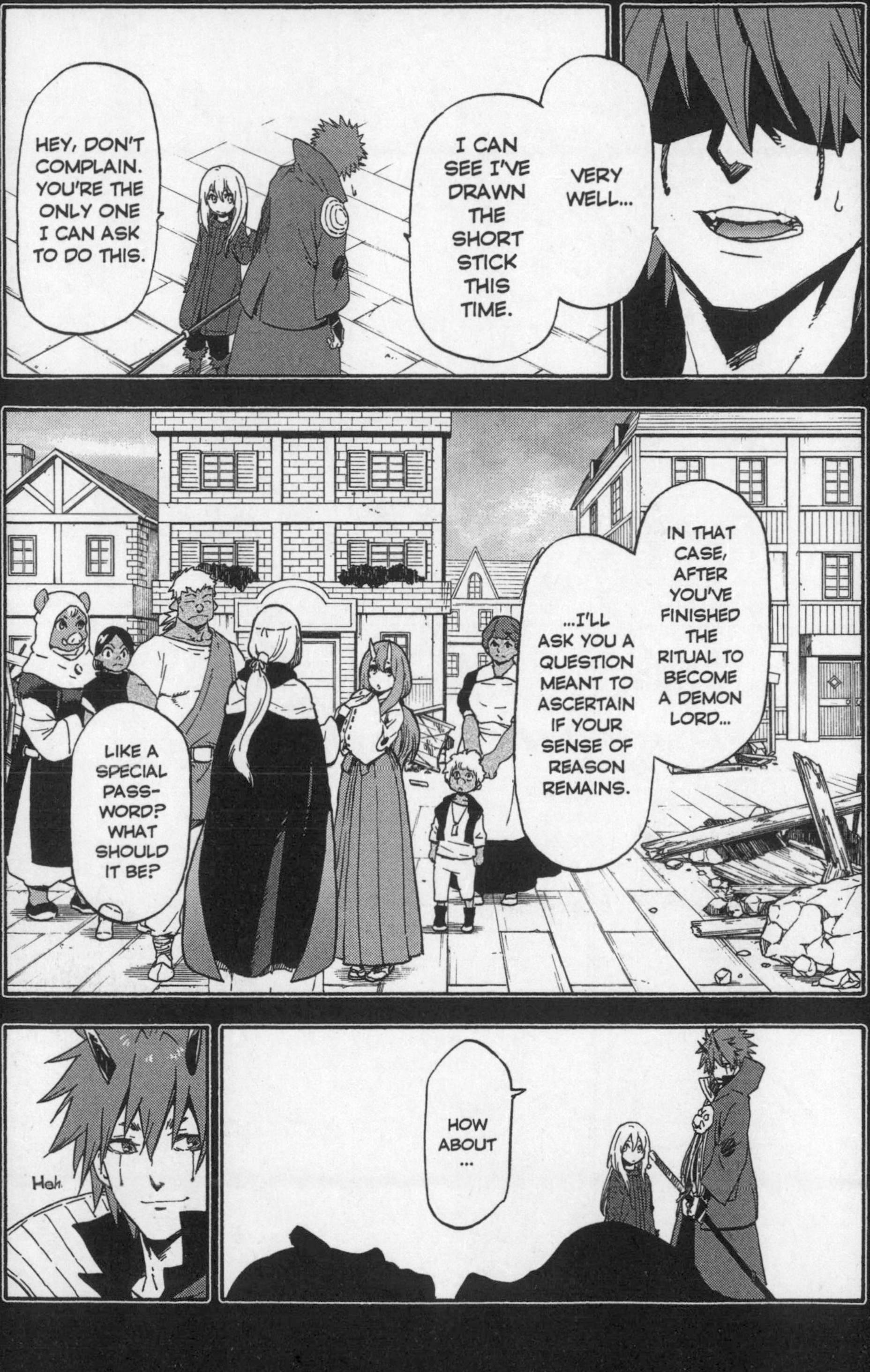
VERY WELL...
I CAN SEE I'VE DRAWN THE SHORT STICK THIS TIME.
HEY, DON'T COMPLAIN. YOU'RE THE ONLY ONE I CAN ASK TO DO THIS.
IN THAT CASE, AFTER YOU'VE FINISHED THE RITUAL TO BECOME A DEMON LORD...
...I'LL ASK YOU A QUESTION MEANT TO ASCERTAIN IF YOUR SENSE OF REASON REMAINS.
LIKE A SPECIAL PASS-WORD? WHAT SHOULD IT BE?
HOW ABOUT ...
Heh.

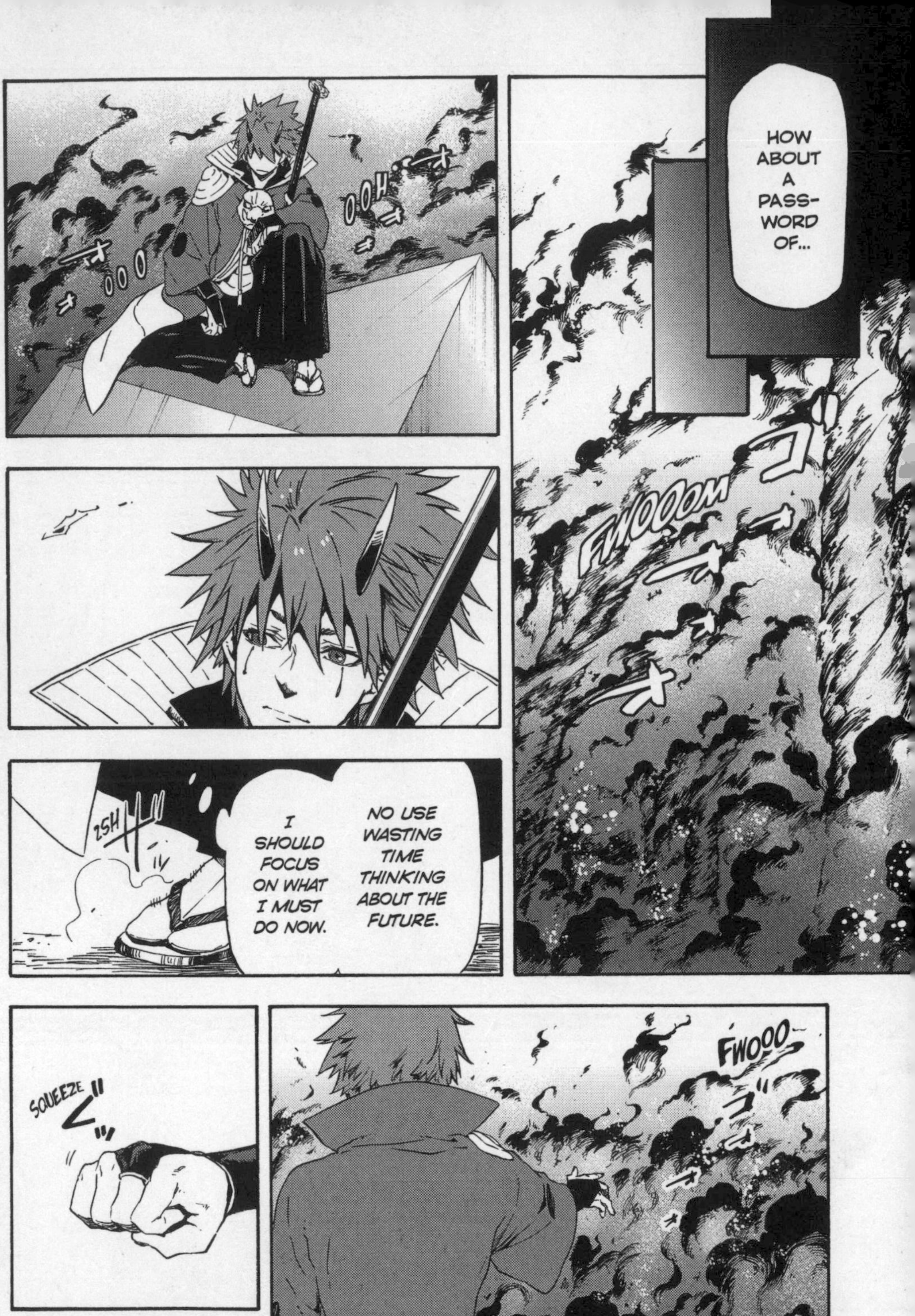
HOW ABOUT A PASS-WORD OF...
FWOOOM
ZSH
NO USE WASTING TIME THINKING ABOUT THE FUTURE.
I SHOULD FOCUS ON WHAT I MUST DO NOW.
FWOOO
SQUEEZE

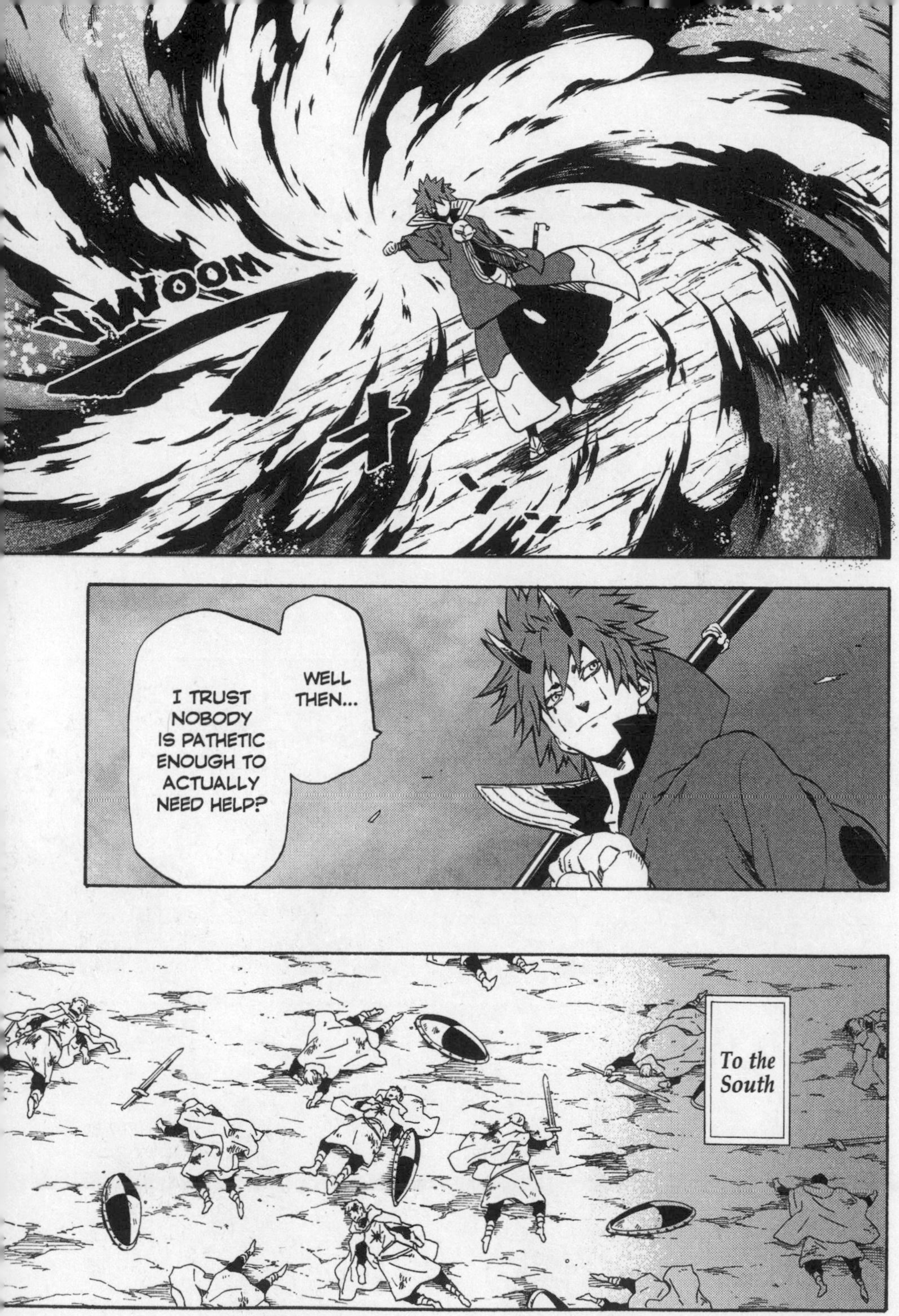
WOOM
WELL THEN...
I TRUST NOBODY IS PATHETIC ENOUGH TO ACTUALLY NEED HELP?
To the South

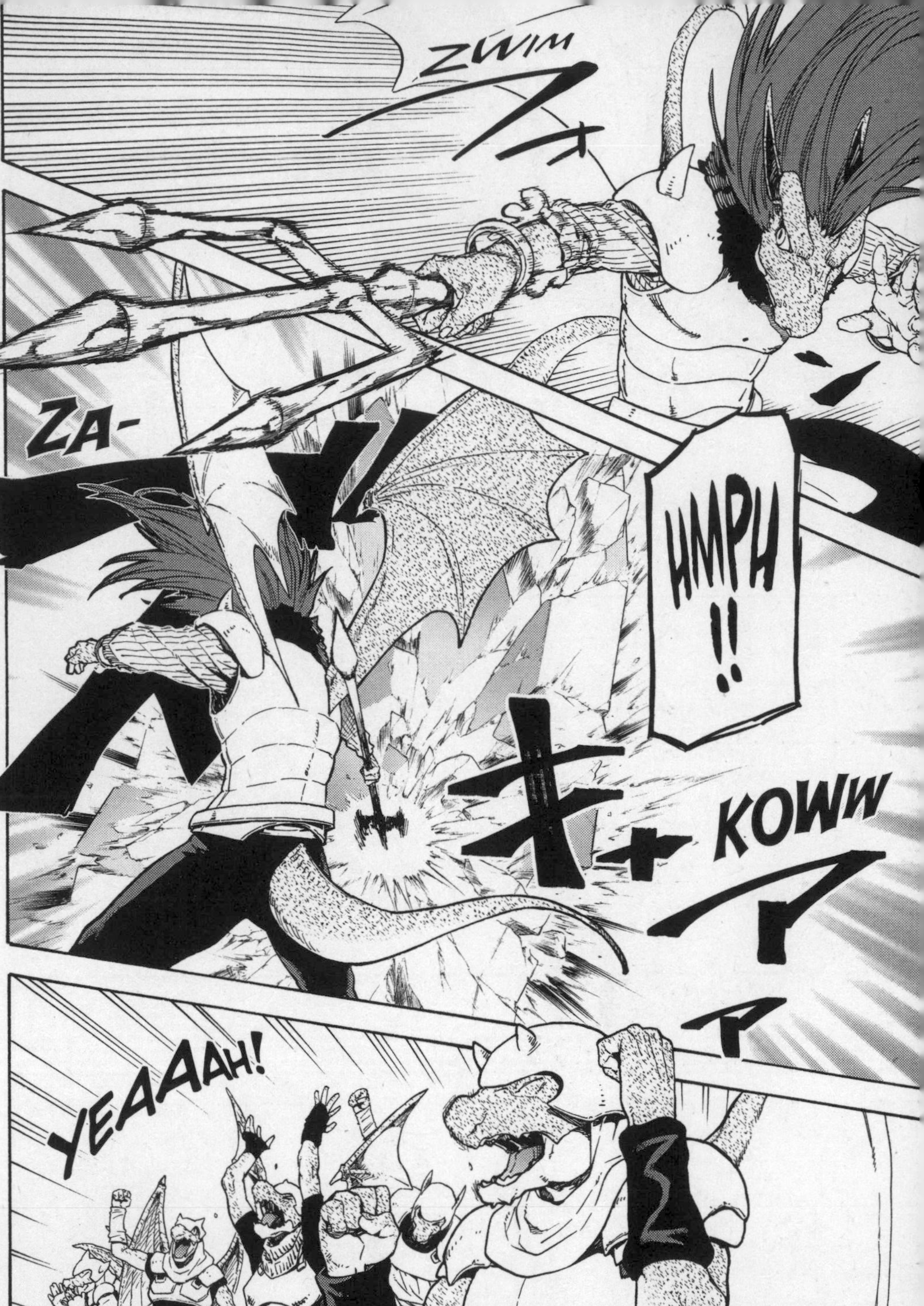

ZWIM
HMPH!!
ZA-
KOWW
YEAAAH!

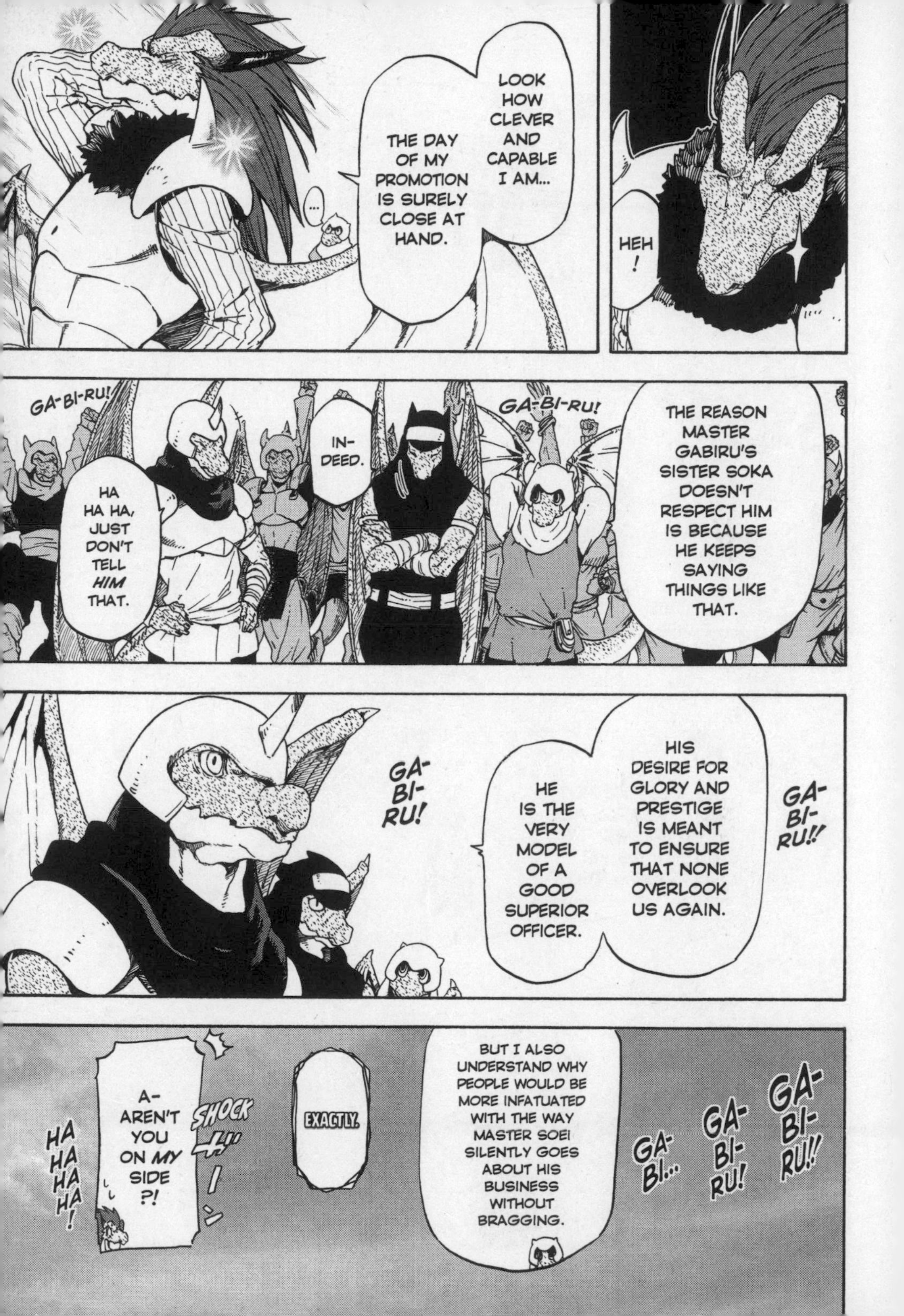
HEH!
LOOK HOW CLEVER AND CAPABLE I AM...
THE DAY OF MY PROMOTION IS SURELY CLOSE AT HAND.
...
THE REASON MASTER GABIRU'S SISTER SOKA DOESN'T RESPECT HIM IS BECAUSE HE KEEPS SAYING THINGS LIKE THAT.
GA-BI-RU!
IN-DEED.
HA HA HA, JUST DON'T TELL *HIM* THAT.
GA-BI-RU!
GA-BI-RU!!
HIS DESIRE FOR GLORY AND PRESTIGE IS MEANT TO ENSURE THAT NONE OVERLOOK US AGAIN.
HE IS THE VERY MODEL OF A GOOD SUPERIOR OFFICER.
GA-BI-RU!
GA-BI-RU!!
GA-BI-RU!
GA-BI...
BUT I ALSO UNDERSTAND WHY PEOPLE WOULD BE MORE INFATUATED WITH THE WAY MASTER SOEI SILENTLY GOES ABOUT HIS BUSINESS WITHOUT BRAGGING.
EXACTLY.
A- AREN'T YOU ON *MY* SIDE?!
SHOCK
HA HA HA HA!

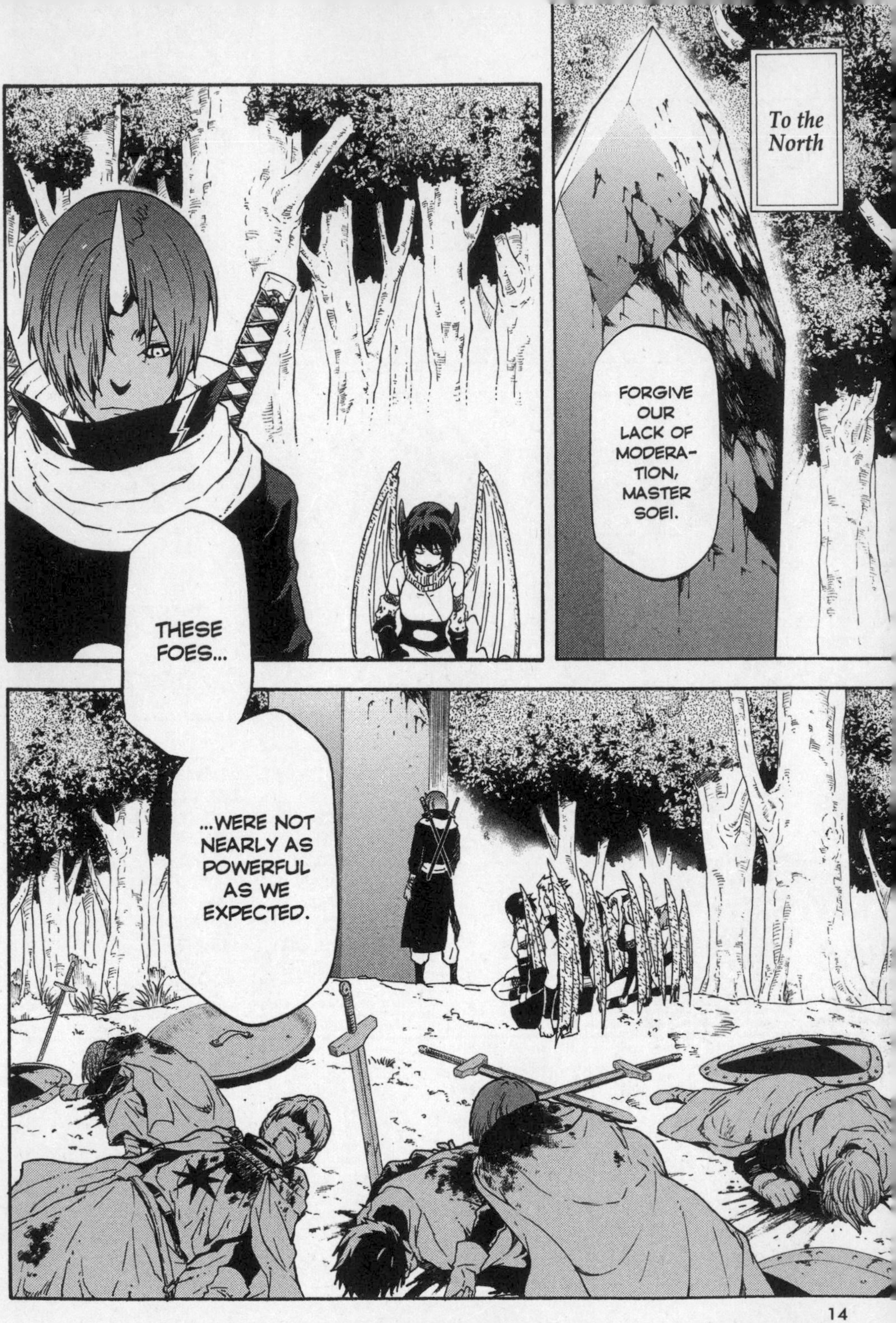
To the North
FORGIVE OUR LACK OF MODERATION, MASTER SOEI.
THESE FOES...
...WERE NOT NEARLY AS POWERFUL AS WE EXPECTED.

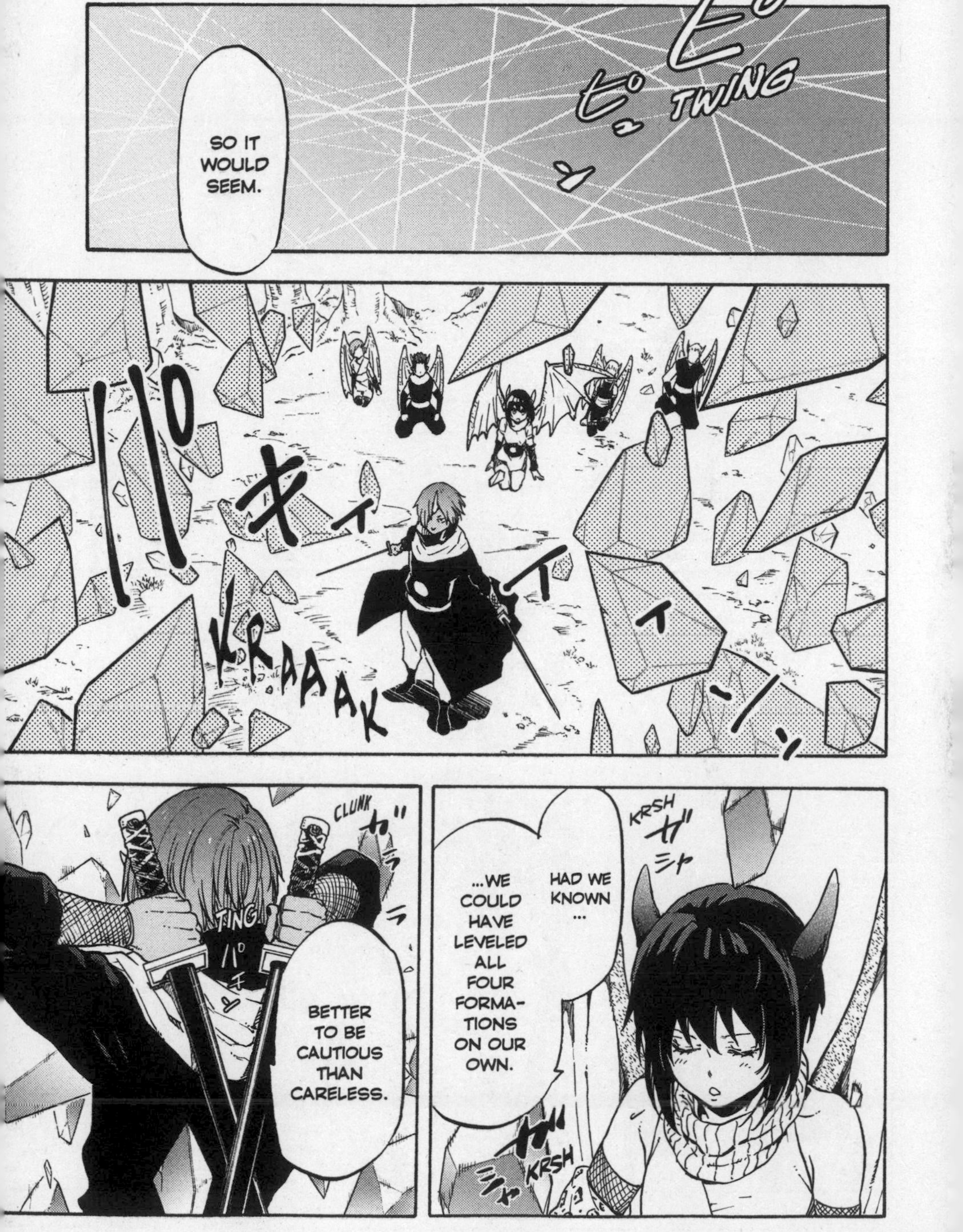
TWING
SO IT WOULD SEEM.
KRAAAK
KRSH
HAD WE KNOWN ...
...WE COULD HAVE LEVELED ALL FOUR FORMATIONS ON OUR OWN.
KRSH
CLUNK
TING
BETTER TO BE CAUTIOUS THAN CARELESS.

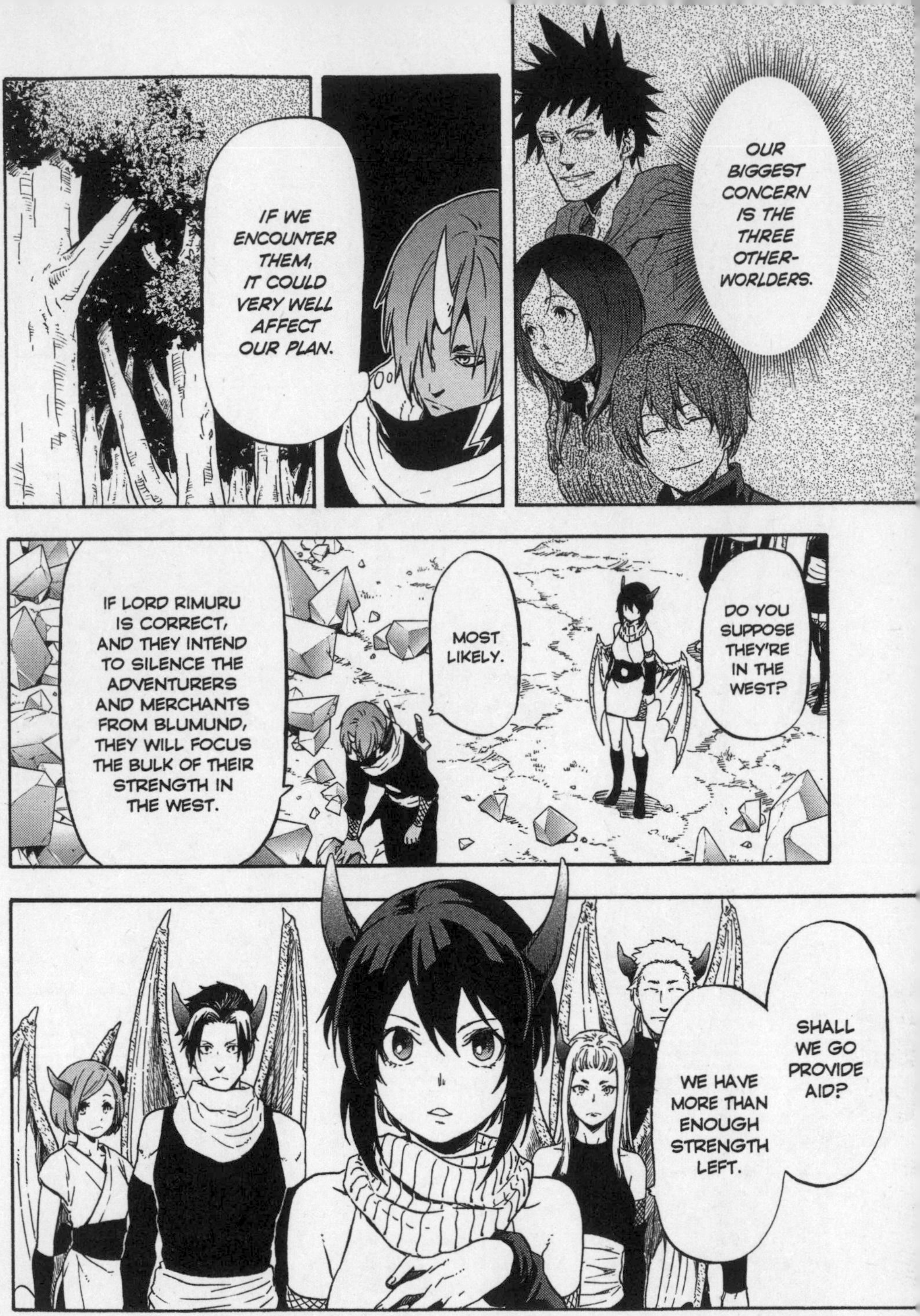
OUR BIGGEST CONCERN IS THE THREE OTHER-WORLDERS.
IF WE ENCOUNTER THEM, IT COULD VERY WELL AFFECT OUR PLAN.
DO YOU SUPPOSE THEY'RE IN THE WEST?
MOST LIKELY.
IF LORD RIMURU IS CORRECT, AND THEY INTEND TO SILENCE THE ADVENTURERS AND MERCHANTS FROM BLUMUND, THEY WILL FOCUS THE BULK OF THEIR STRENGTH IN THE WEST.
SHALL WE GO PROVIDE AID?
WE HAVE MORE THAN ENOUGH STRENGTH LEFT.

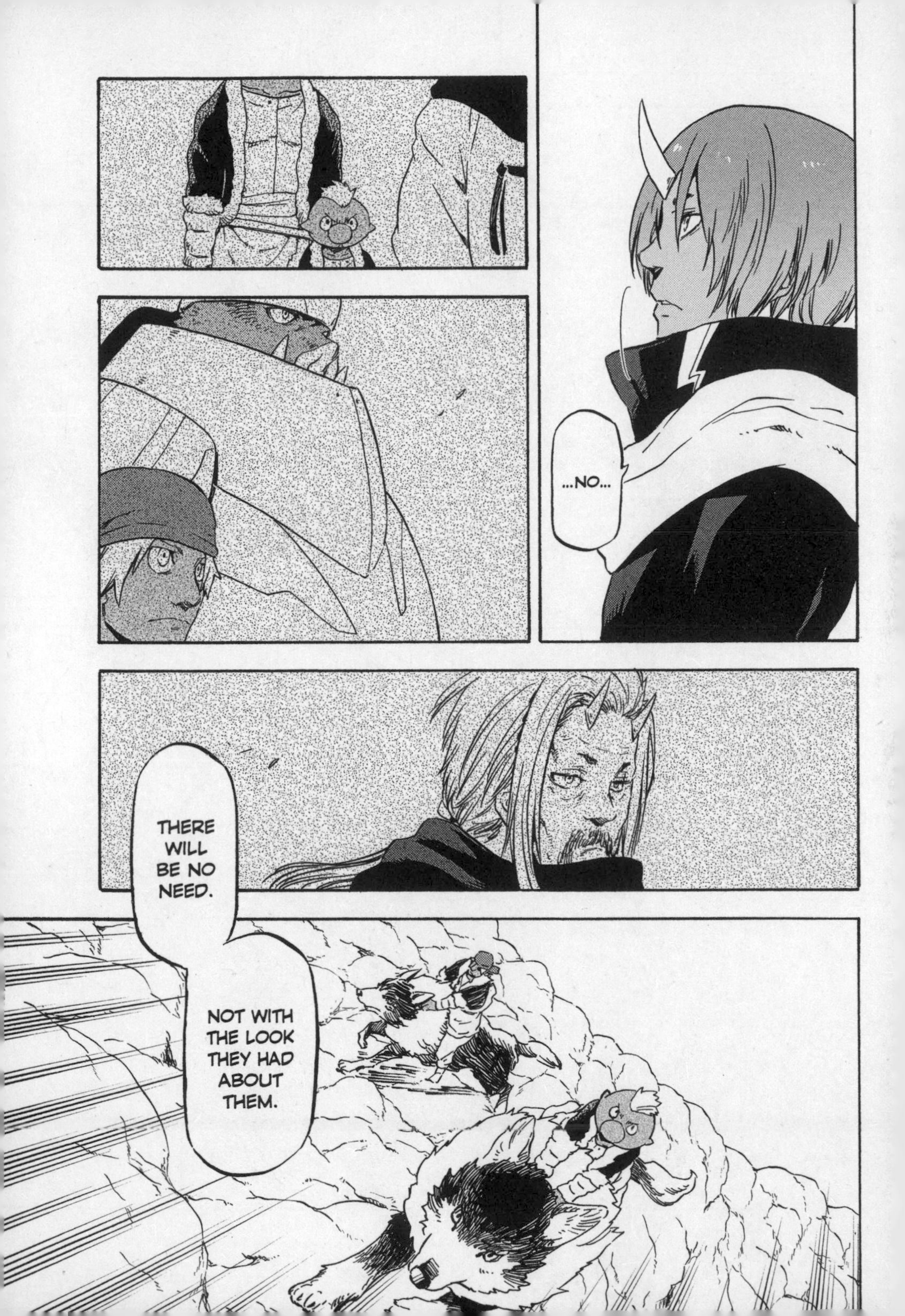
...NO...
THERE WILL BE NO NEED.
NOT WITH THE LOOK THEY HAD ABOUT THEM.

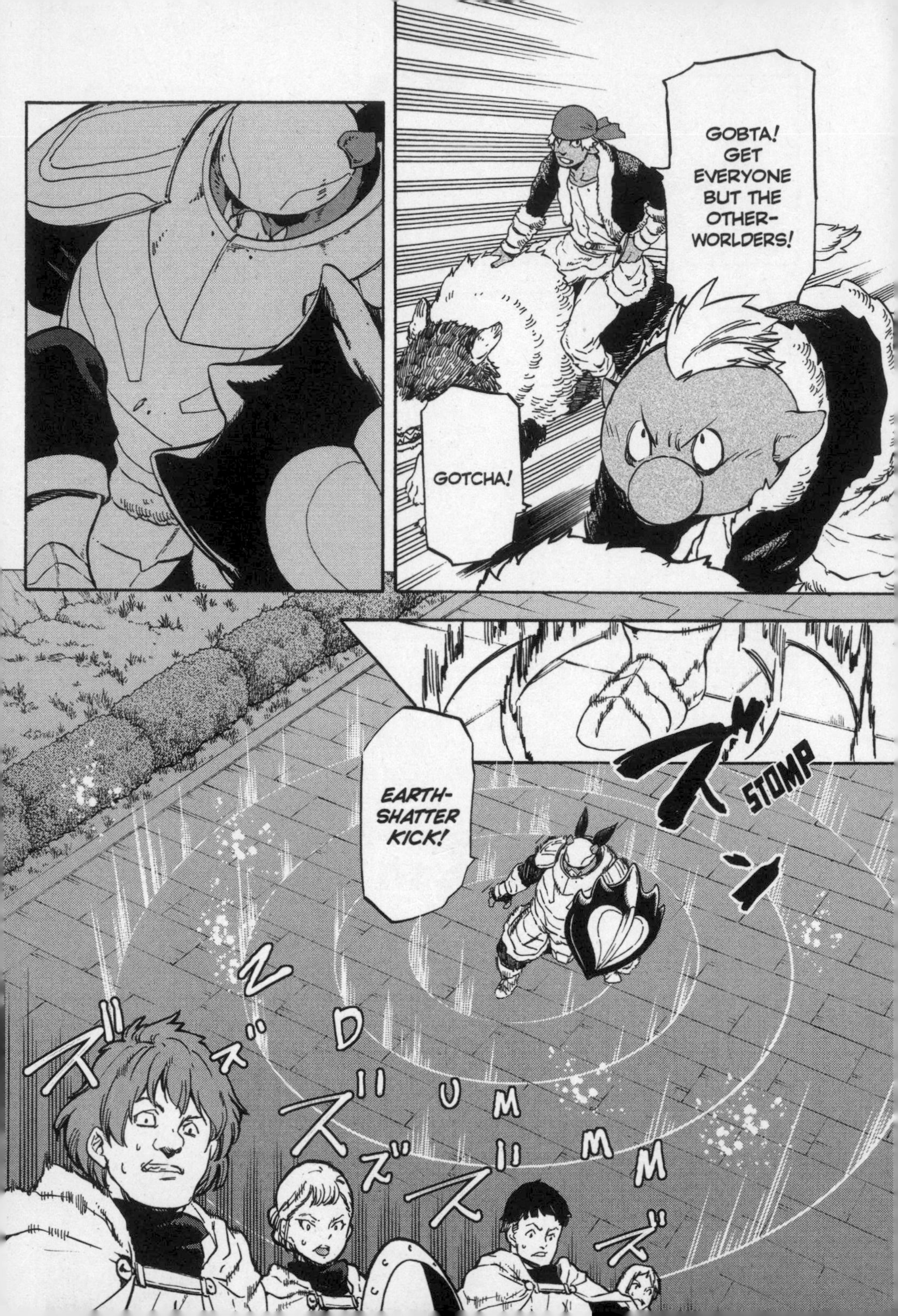
GOBTA! GET EVERYONE BUT THE OTHER-WORLDERS!
GOTCHA!
EARTH-SHATTER KICK!
STOMP
ZUDUMMMM

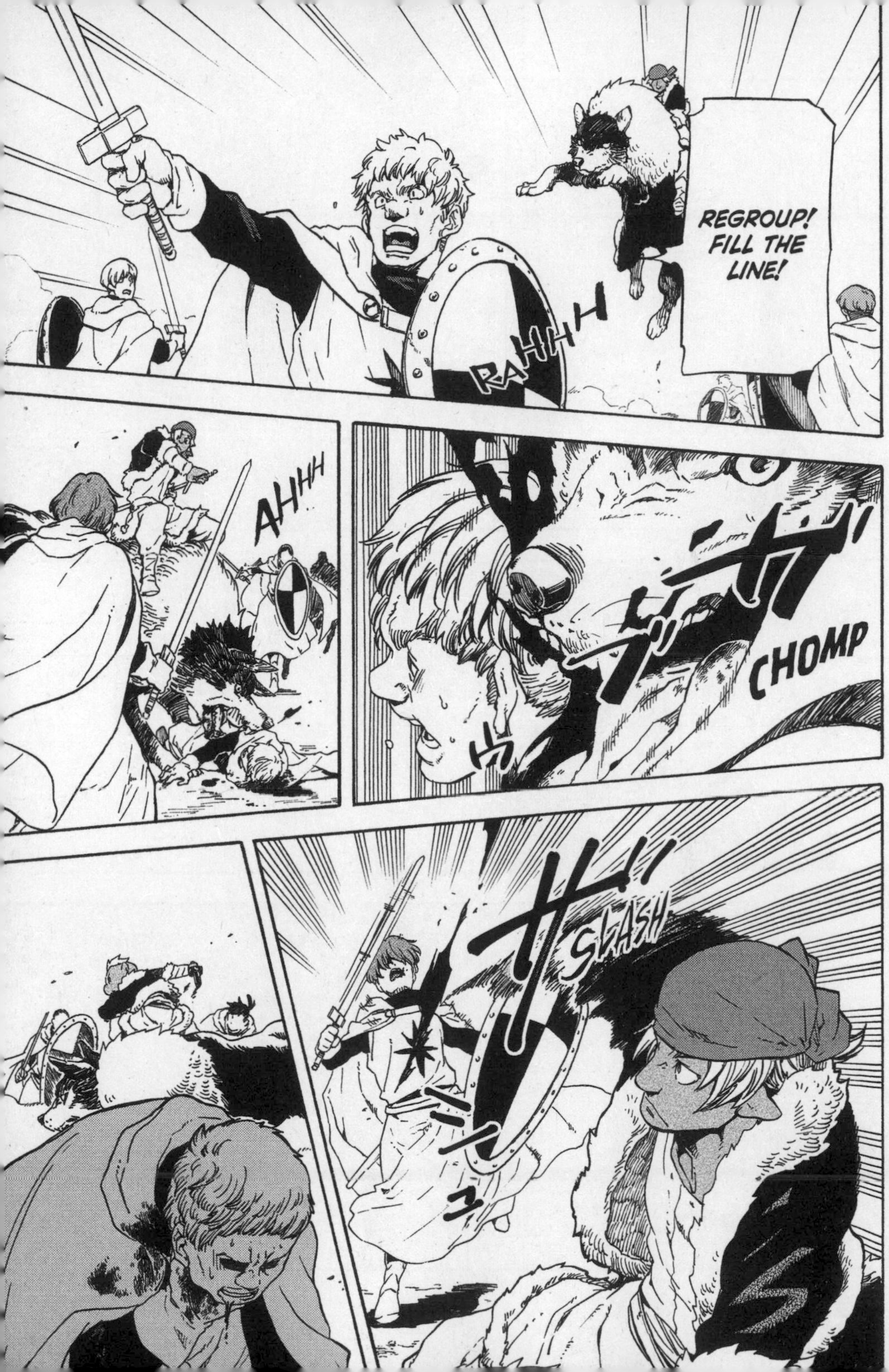
REGROUP! FILL THE LINE!
RAHHHH
CHOMP
AHHH
SLASH

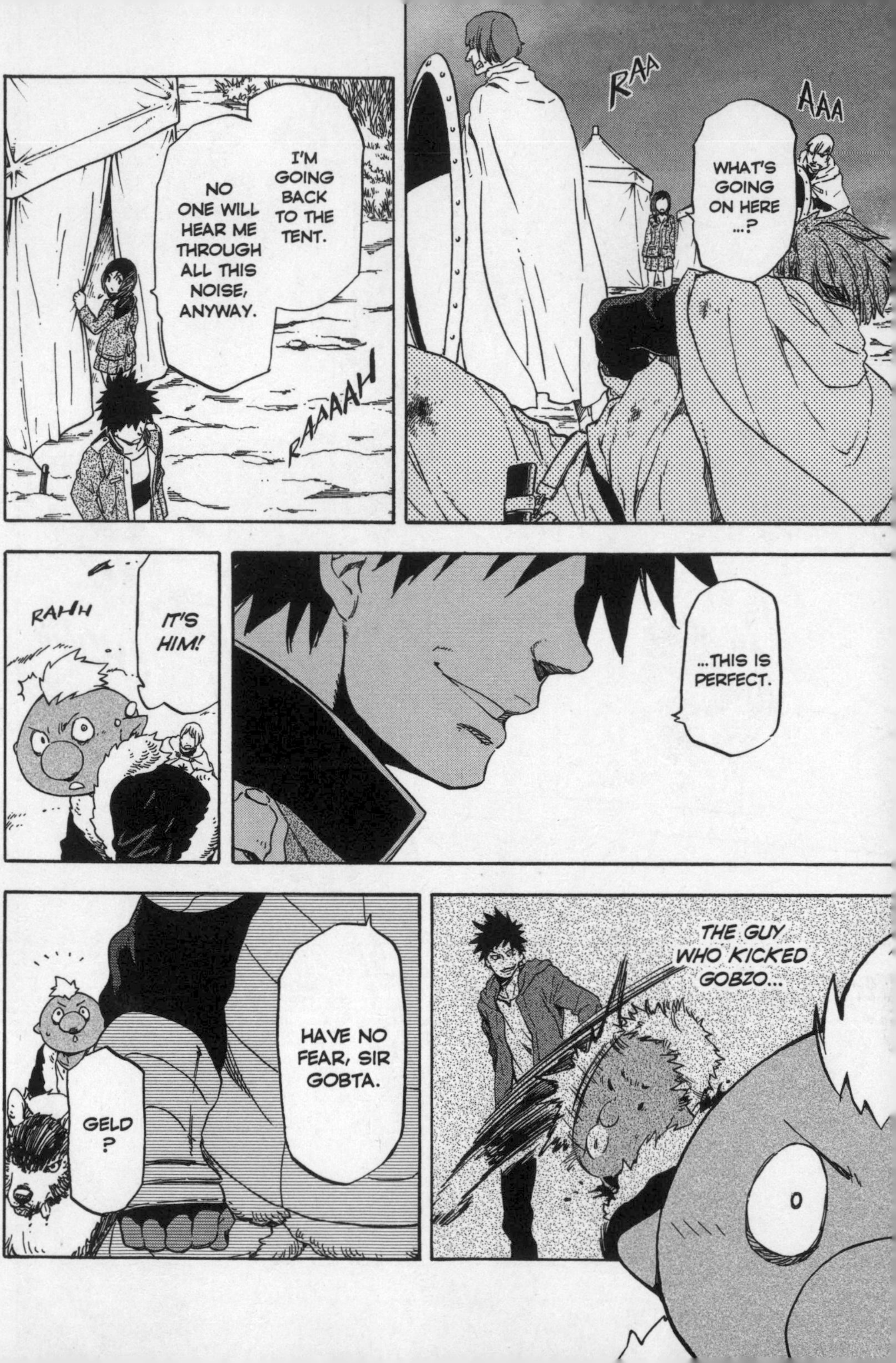
RAA
AAA
WHAT'S GOING ON HERE ...?
I'M GOING BACK TO THE TENT.
NO ONE WILL HEAR ME THROUGH ALL THIS NOISE, ANYWAY.
RAAAAH
...THIS IS PERFECT.
IT'S HIM!
RAHH
THE GUY WHO KICKED GOBZO...
HAVE NO FEAR, SIR GOBTA.
GELD?

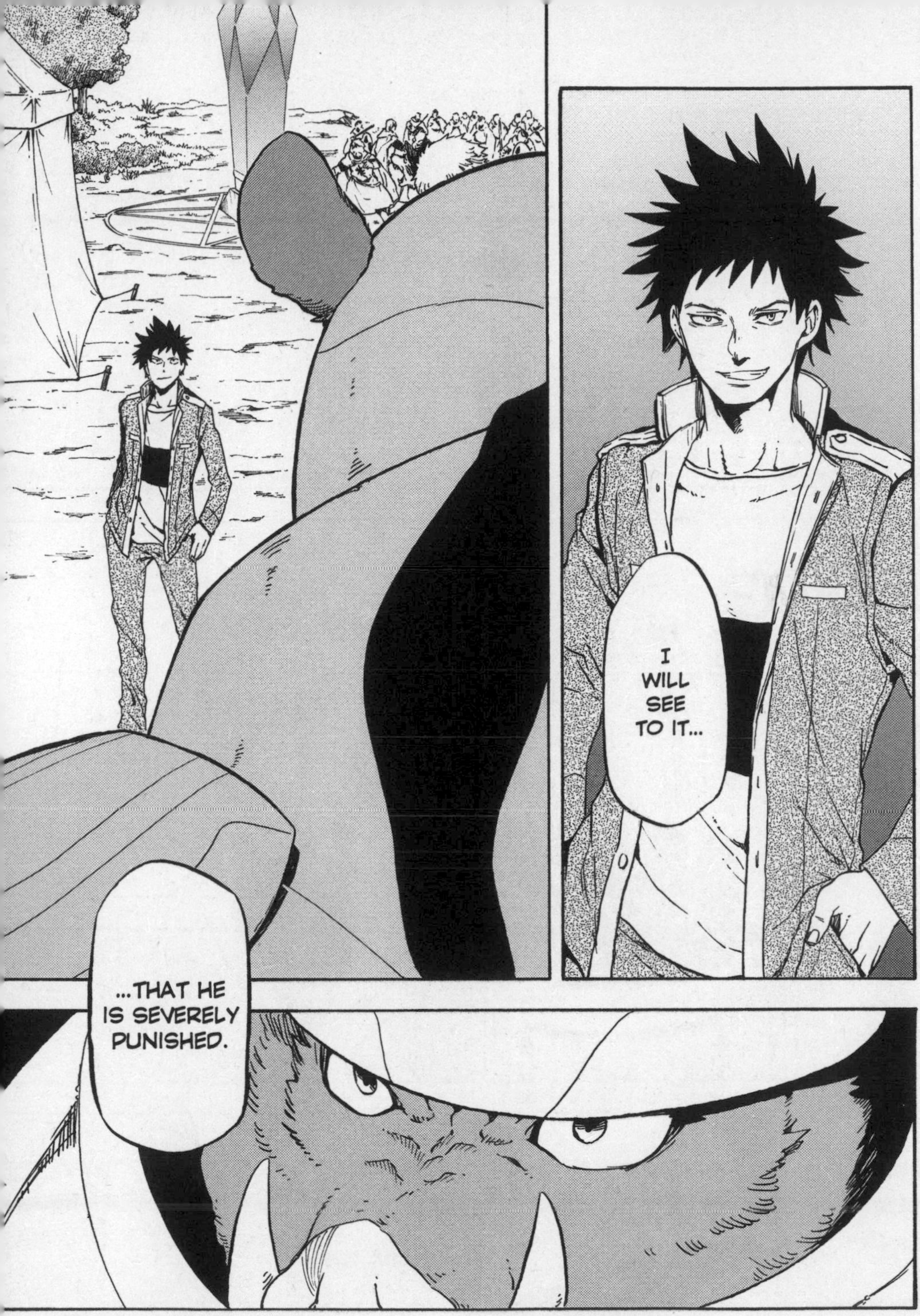
I WILL SEE TO IT...
...THAT HE IS SEVERELY PUNISHED.

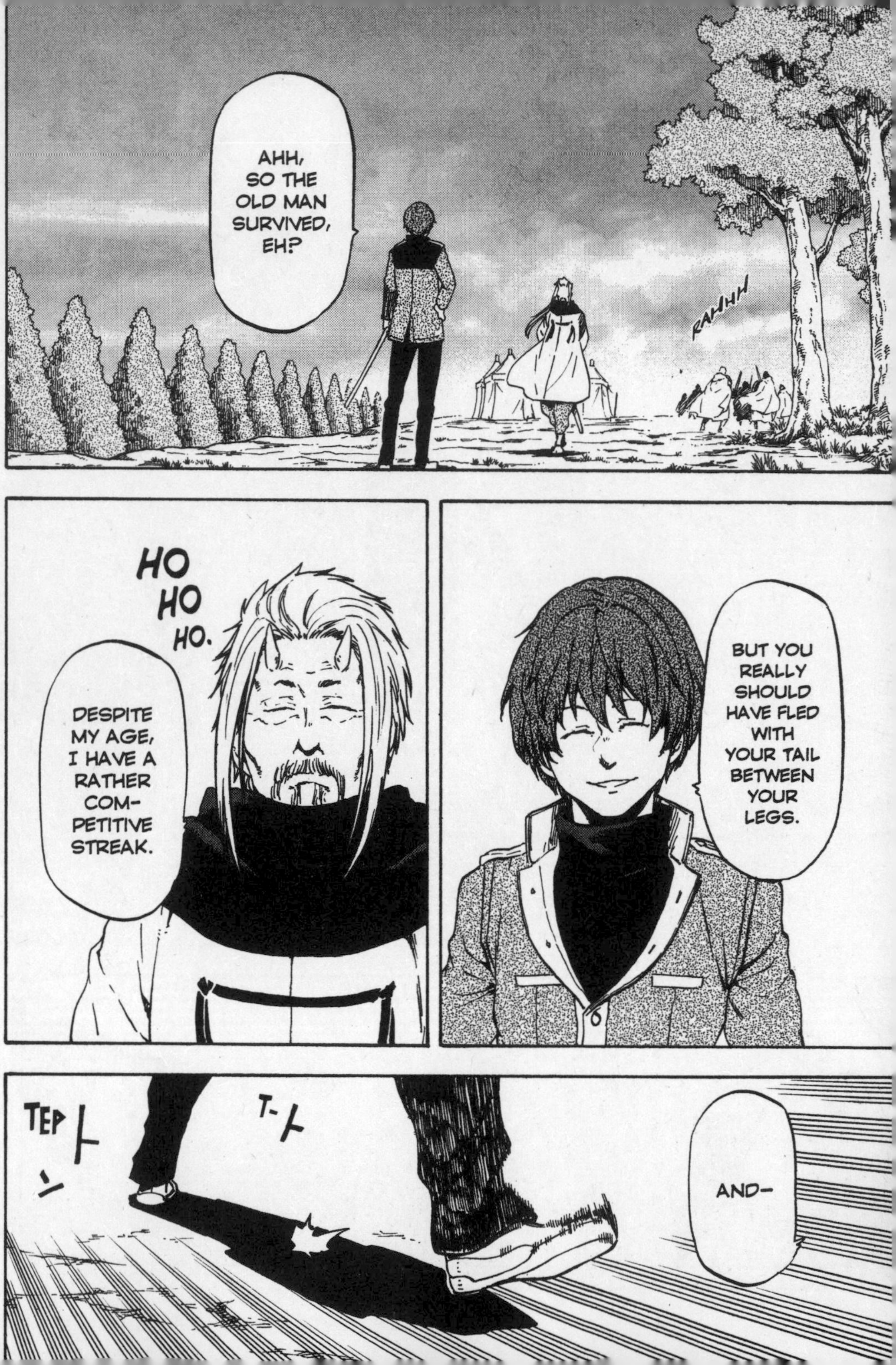
AHH, SO THE OLD MAN SURVIVED, EH?
RAHHH
BUT YOU REALLY SHOULD HAVE FLED WITH YOUR TAIL BETWEEN YOUR LEGS.
HO HO HO.
DESPITE MY AGE, I HAVE A RATHER COM-PETITIVE STREAK.
AND-
T-ト
TEP トン

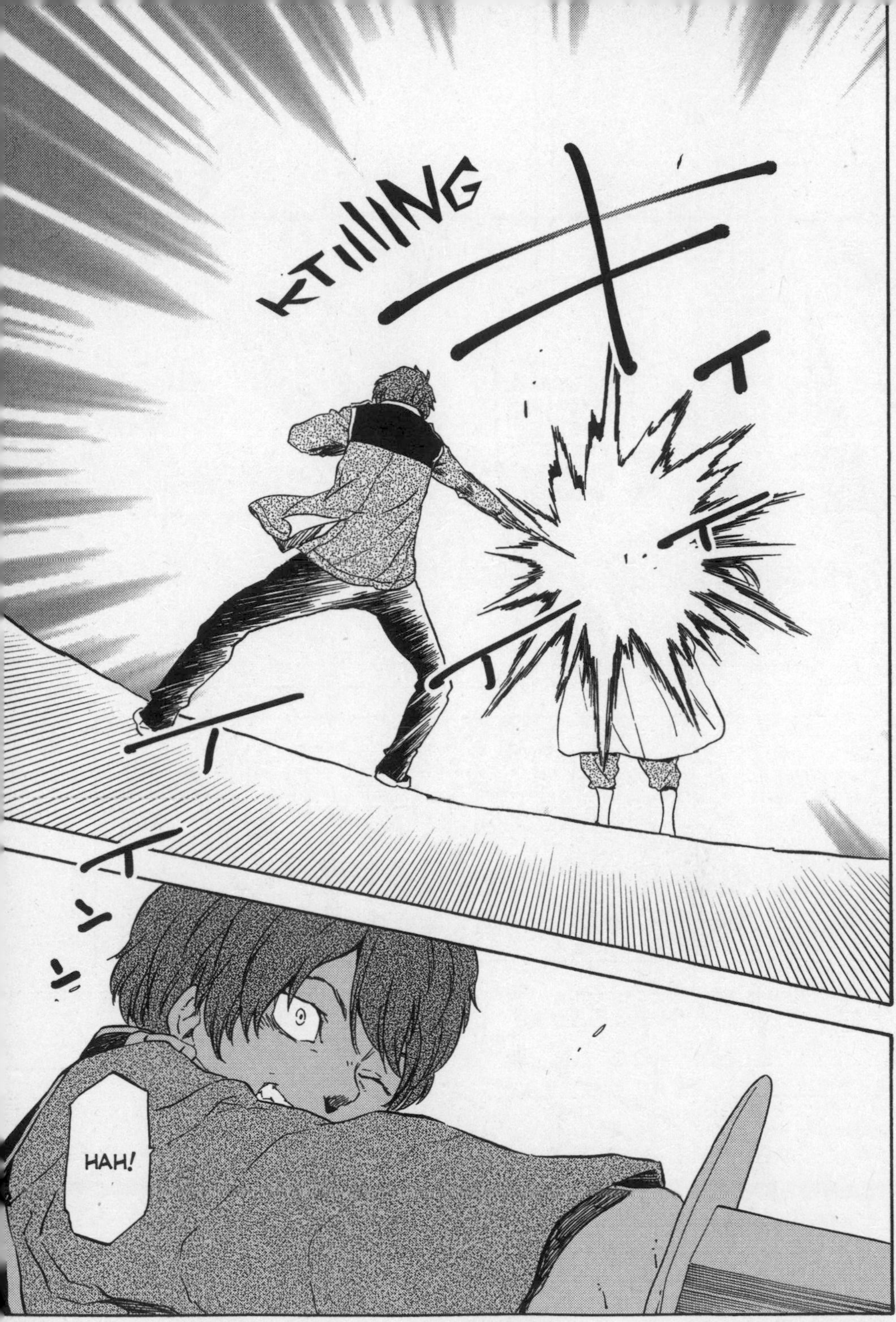
KTIIIING
HAH!

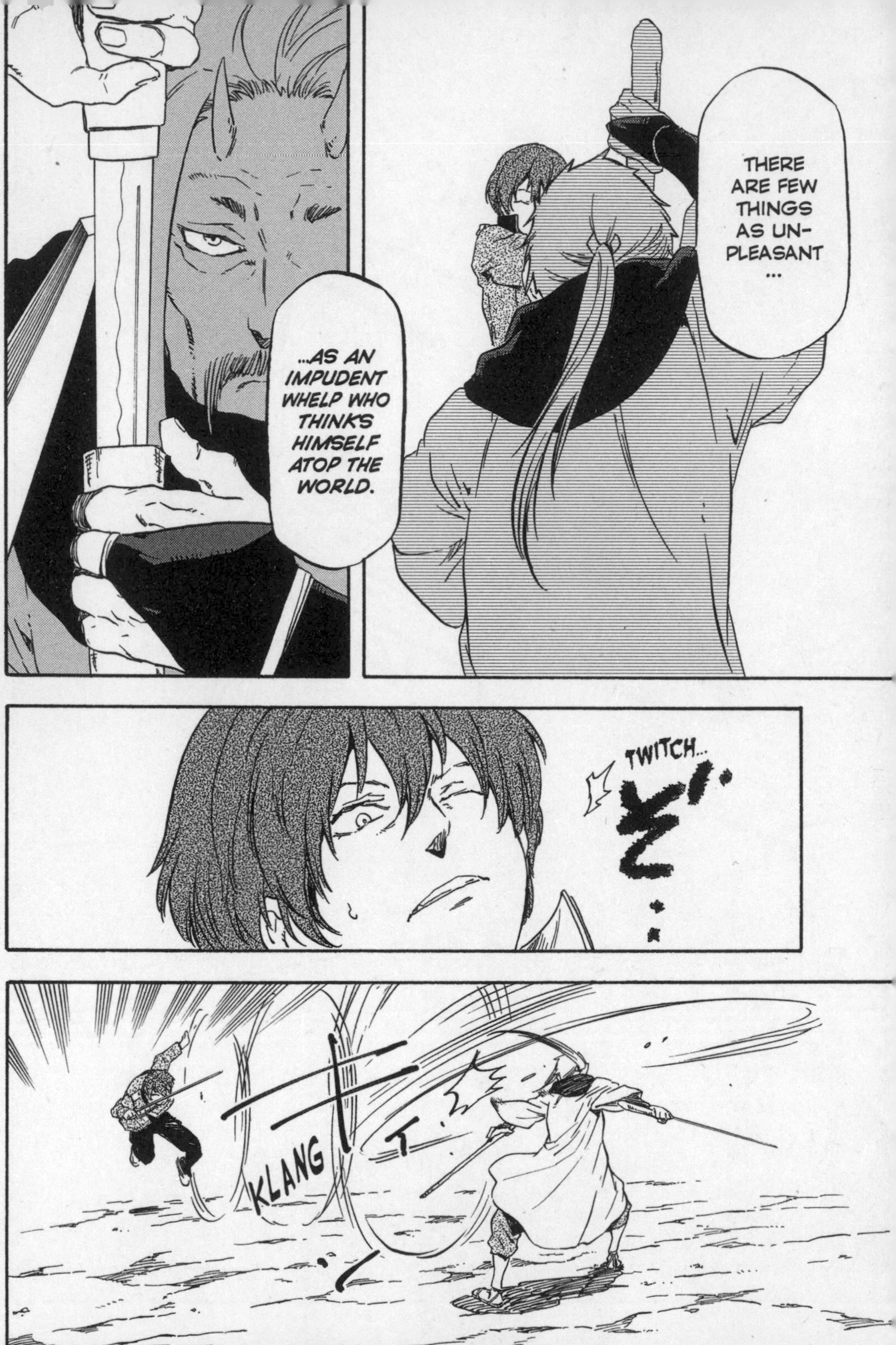
THERE ARE FEW THINGS AS UN-PLEASANT ...
...AS AN IMPUDENT WHELP WHO THINKS HIMSELF ATOP THE WORLD.
TWITCH...
KLANG

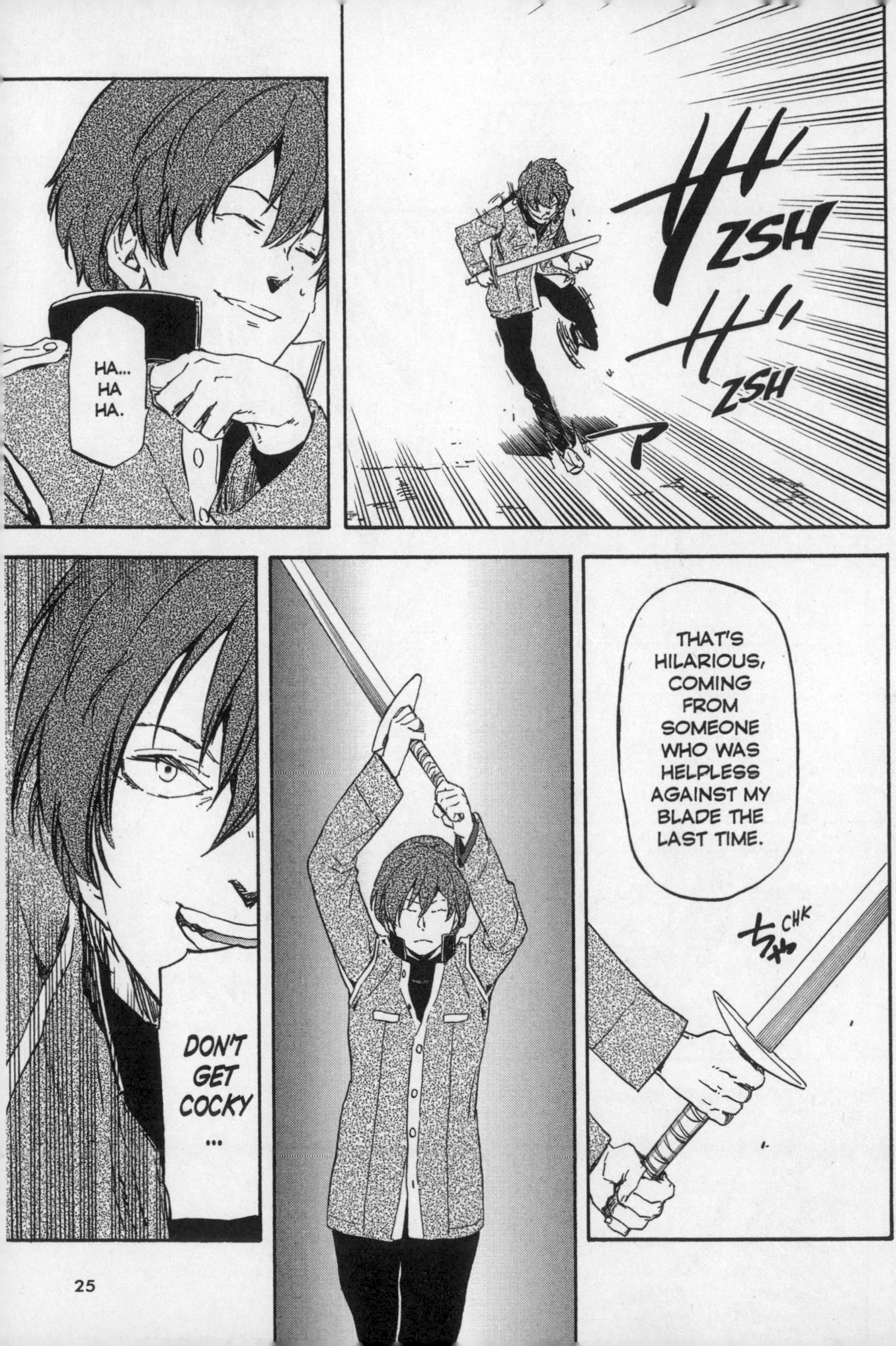
ZSH
ZSH
HA... HA HA.
THAT'S HILARIOUS, COMING FROM SOMEONE WHO WAS HELPLESS AGAINST MY BLADE THE LAST TIME.
CHK
DON'T GET COCKY ...

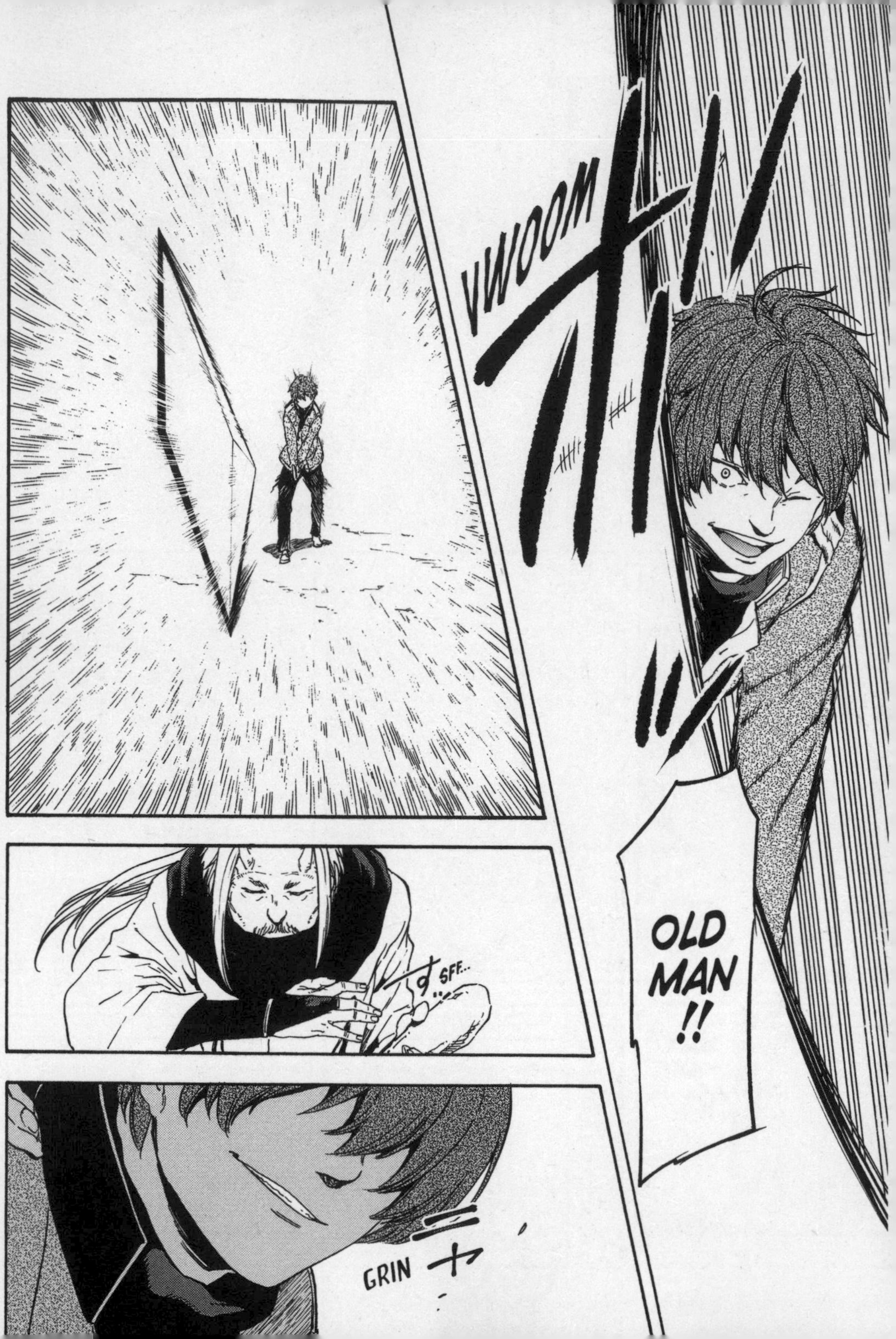
VWOOM
OLD MAN!!
SFF...
GRIN

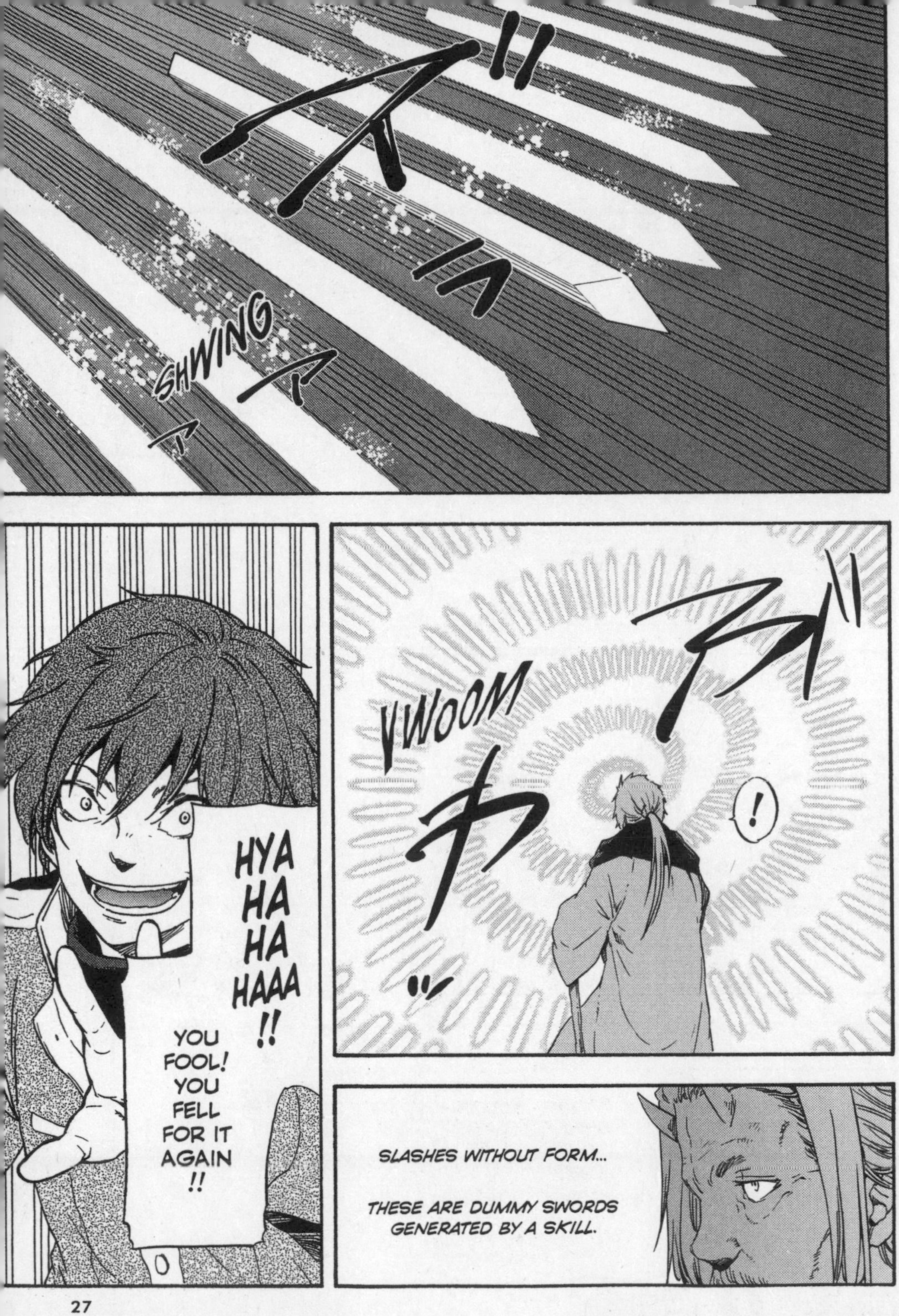
SHWING
VWOOM
!
SLASHES WITHOUT FORM...
THESE ARE DUMMY SWORDS GENERATED BY A SKILL.
HYA HA HA HAAA!!
YOU FOOL! YOU FELL FOR IT AGAIN!!

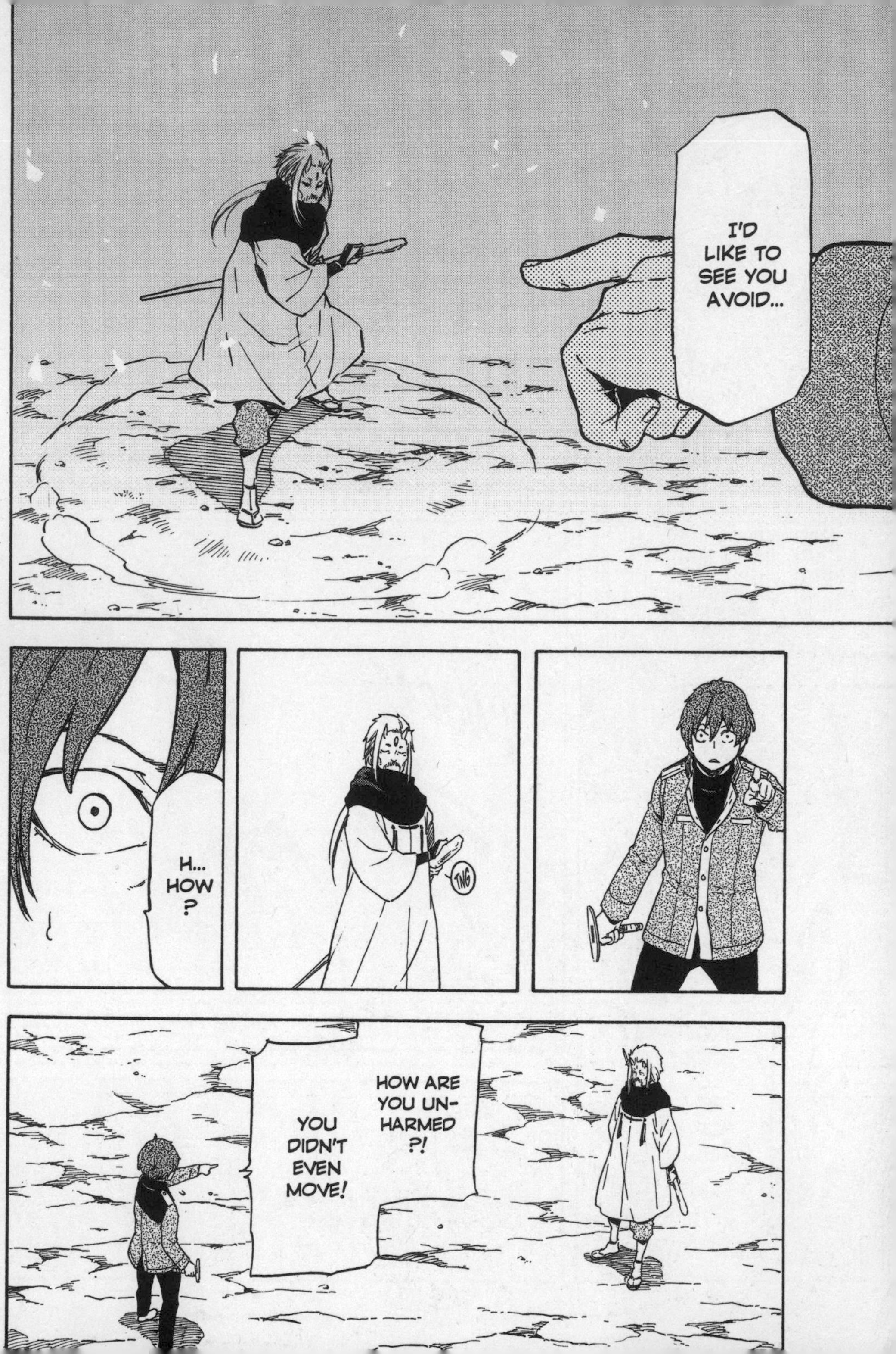
I'D LIKE TO SEE YOU AVOID...
TNG
H... HOW ?
HOW ARE YOU UN-HARMED ?!
YOU DIDN'T EVEN MOVE!

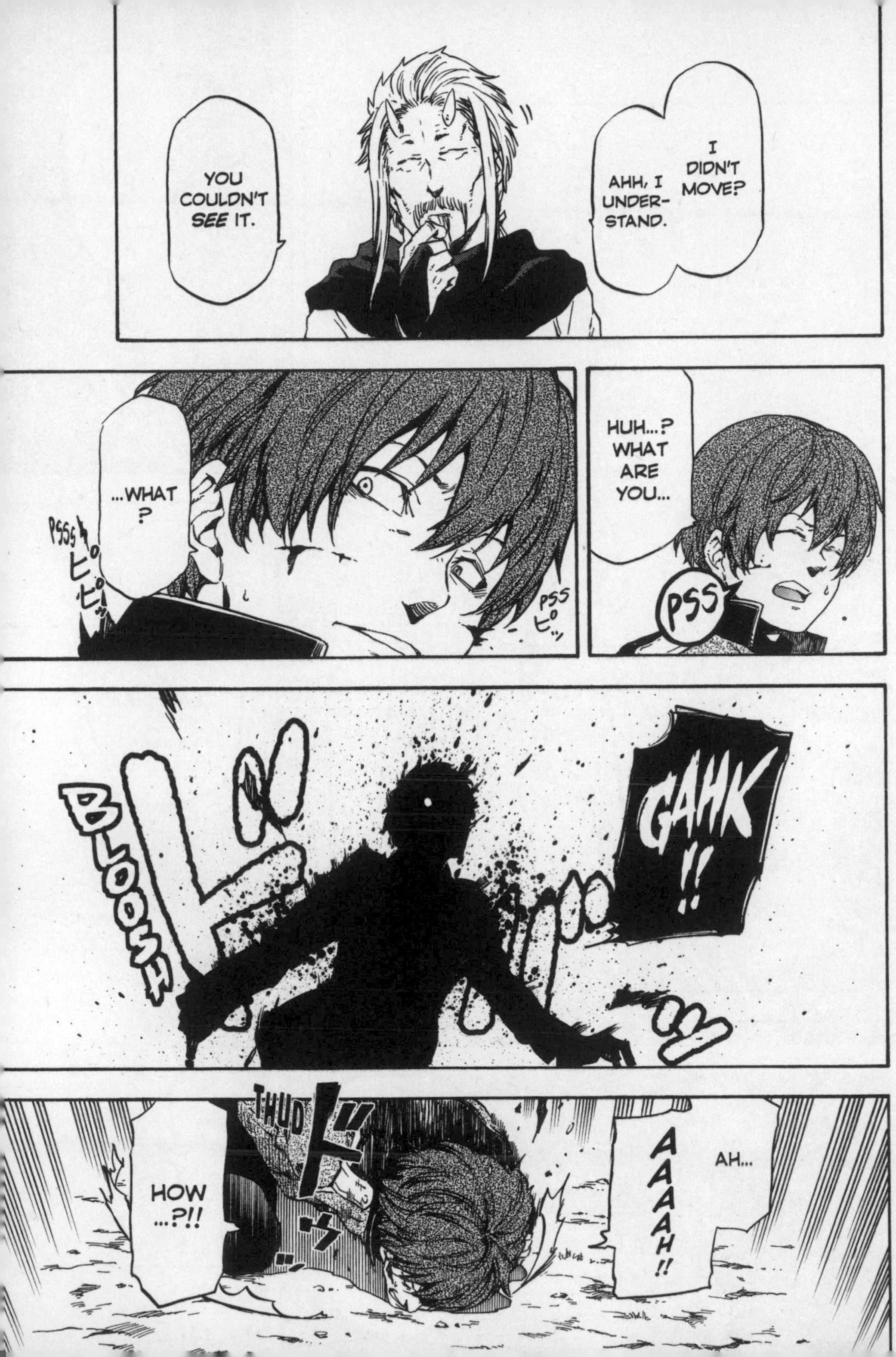
I DIDN'T MOVE?
AHH, I UNDER-STAND.
YOU COULDN'T SEE IT.
HUH...? WHAT ARE YOU...
PSS
...WHAT?
PSSS ピピッ
PSS ピッ
GAHK!!
BLOOSH
AH...
AAAAH!!
THUD ドッ
HOW...?!!

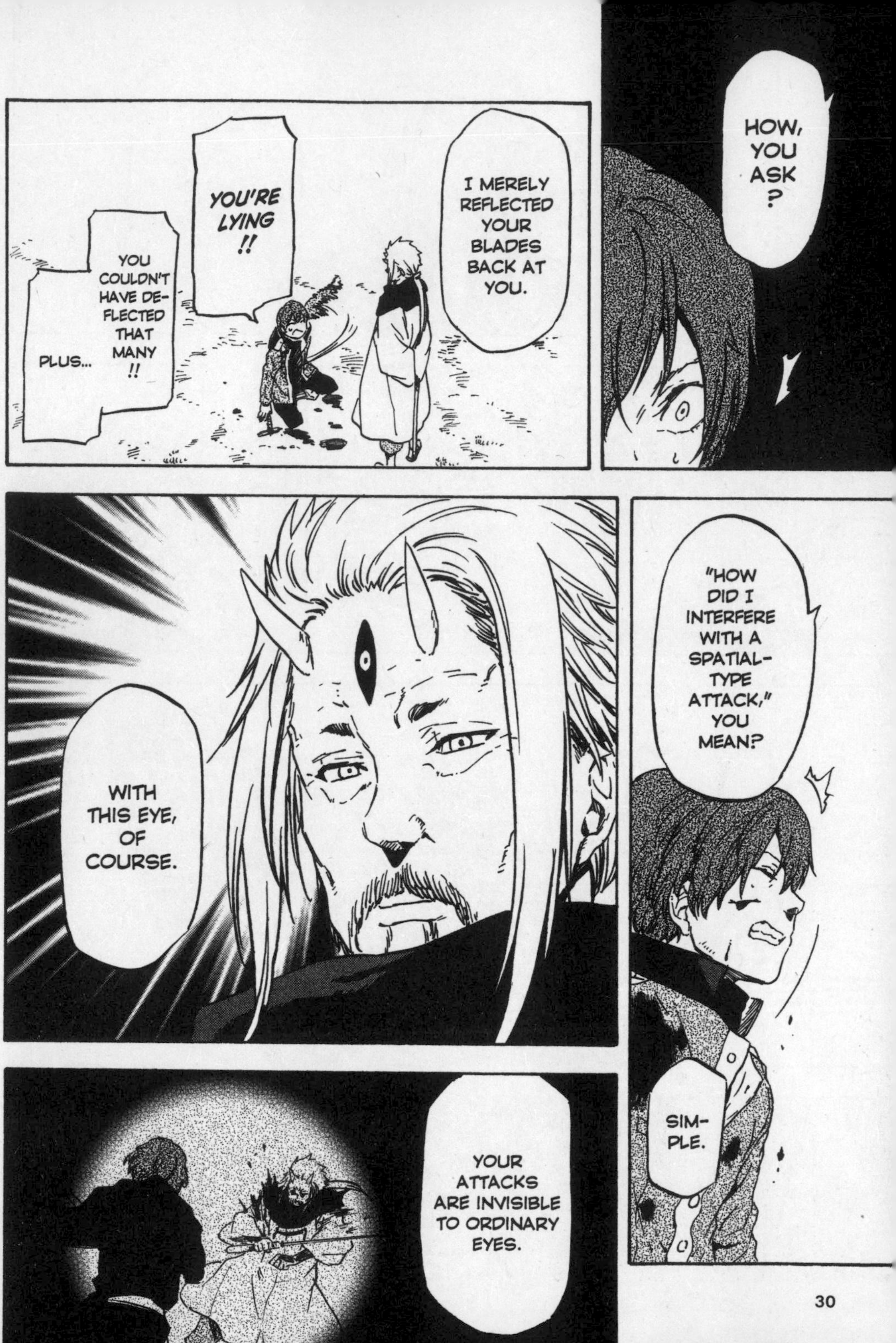
HOW, YOU ASK?
I MERELY REFLECTED YOUR BLADES BACK AT YOU.
YOU'RE LYING!!
YOU COULDN'T HAVE DE-FLECTED THAT MANY!!
PLUS...
"HOW DID I INTERFERE WITH A SPATIAL-TYPE ATTACK," YOU MEAN?
SIM-PLE.
WITH THIS EYE, OF COURSE.
YOUR ATTACKS ARE INVISIBLE TO ORDINARY EYES.

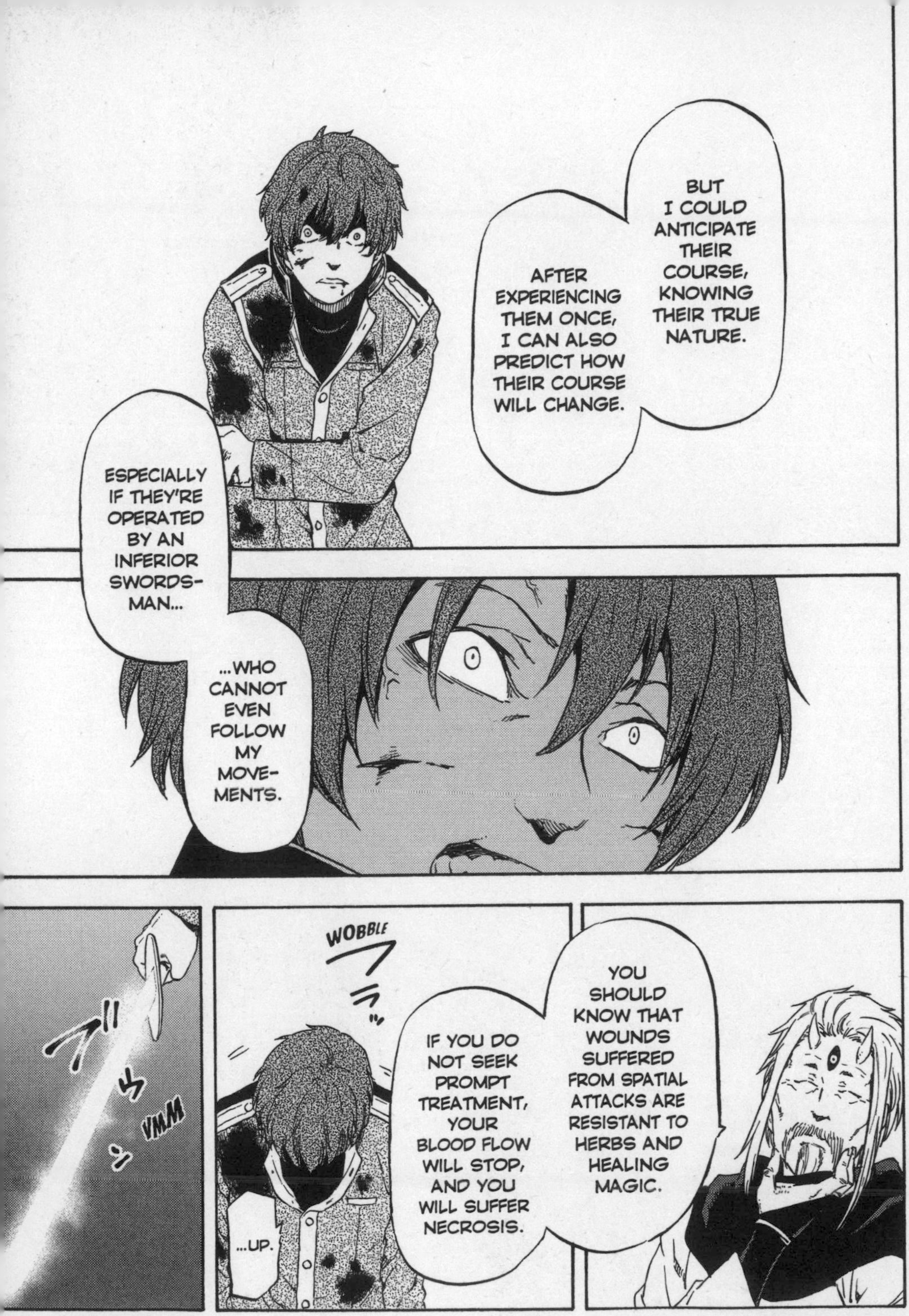
BUT I COULD ANTICIPATE THEIR COURSE, KNOWING THEIR TRUE NATURE.
AFTER EXPERIENCING THEM ONCE, I CAN ALSO PREDICT HOW THEIR COURSE WILL CHANGE.
ESPECIALLY IF THEY'RE OPERATED BY AN INFERIOR SWORDS-MAN...
...WHO CANNOT EVEN FOLLOW MY MOVE-MENTS.
YOU SHOULD KNOW THAT WOUNDS SUFFERED FROM SPATIAL ATTACKS ARE RESISTANT TO HERBS AND HEALING MAGIC.
IF YOU DO NOT SEEK PROMPT TREATMENT, YOUR BLOOD FLOW WILL STOP, AND YOU WILL SUFFER NECROSIS.
WOBBLE
...UP.
VMM

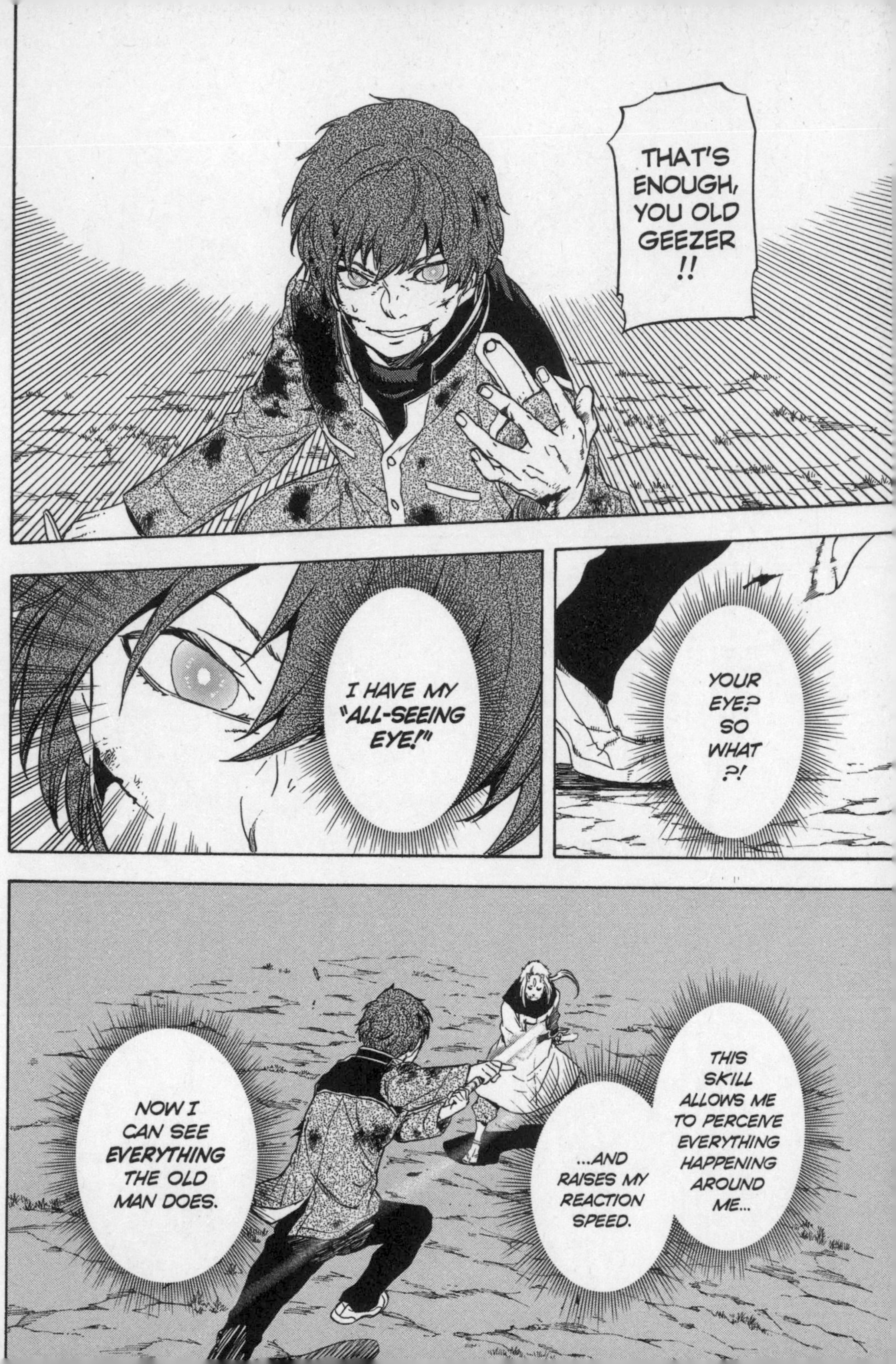
THAT'S ENOUGH, YOU OLD GEEZER!!
YOUR EYE? SO WHAT?!
I HAVE MY "ALL-SEEING EYE!"
THIS SKILL ALLOWS ME TO PERCEIVE EVERYTHING HAPPENING AROUND ME...
...AND RAISES MY REACTION SPEED.
NOW I CAN SEE EVERYTHING THE OLD MAN DOES.

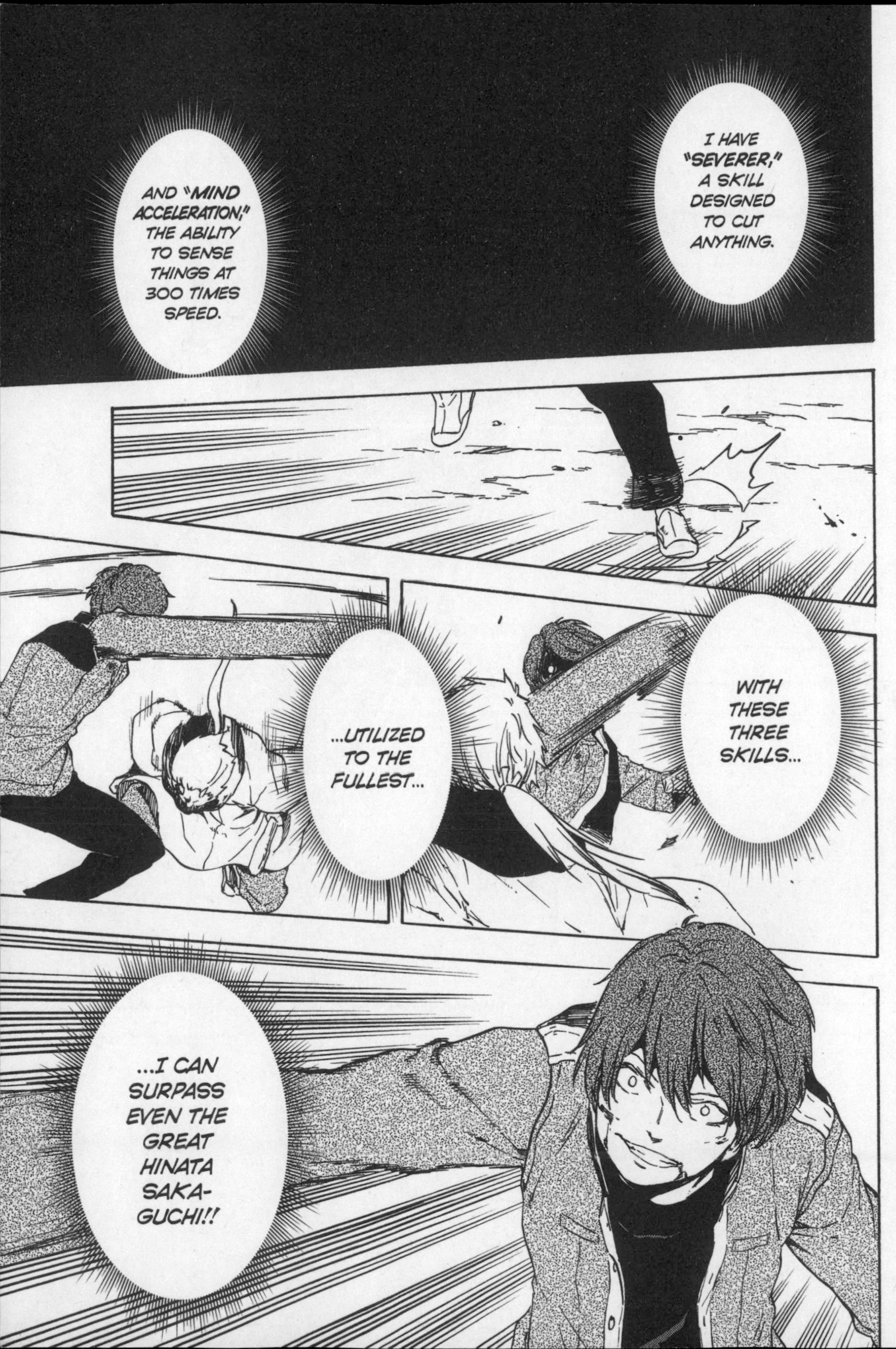
I HAVE "SEVERER," A SKILL DESIGNED TO CUT ANYTHING.
AND "MIND ACCELERATION," THE ABILITY TO SENSE THINGS AT 300 TIMES SPEED.
WITH THESE THREE SKILLS...
...UTILIZED TO THE FULLEST...
...I CAN SURPASS EVEN THE GREAT HINATA SAKA-GUCHI!!

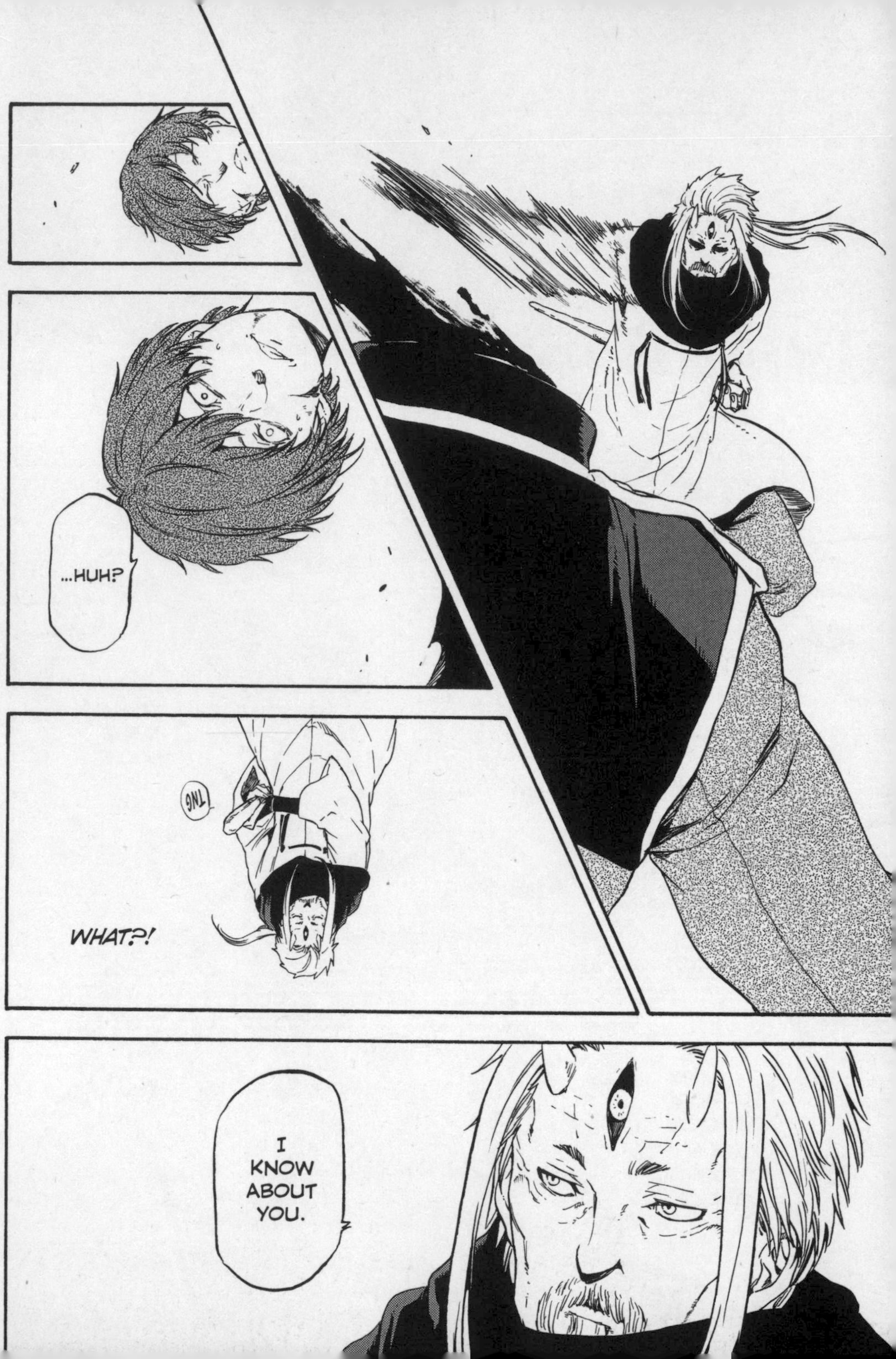
...HUH?
TING
WHAT?!
I KNOW ABOUT YOU.

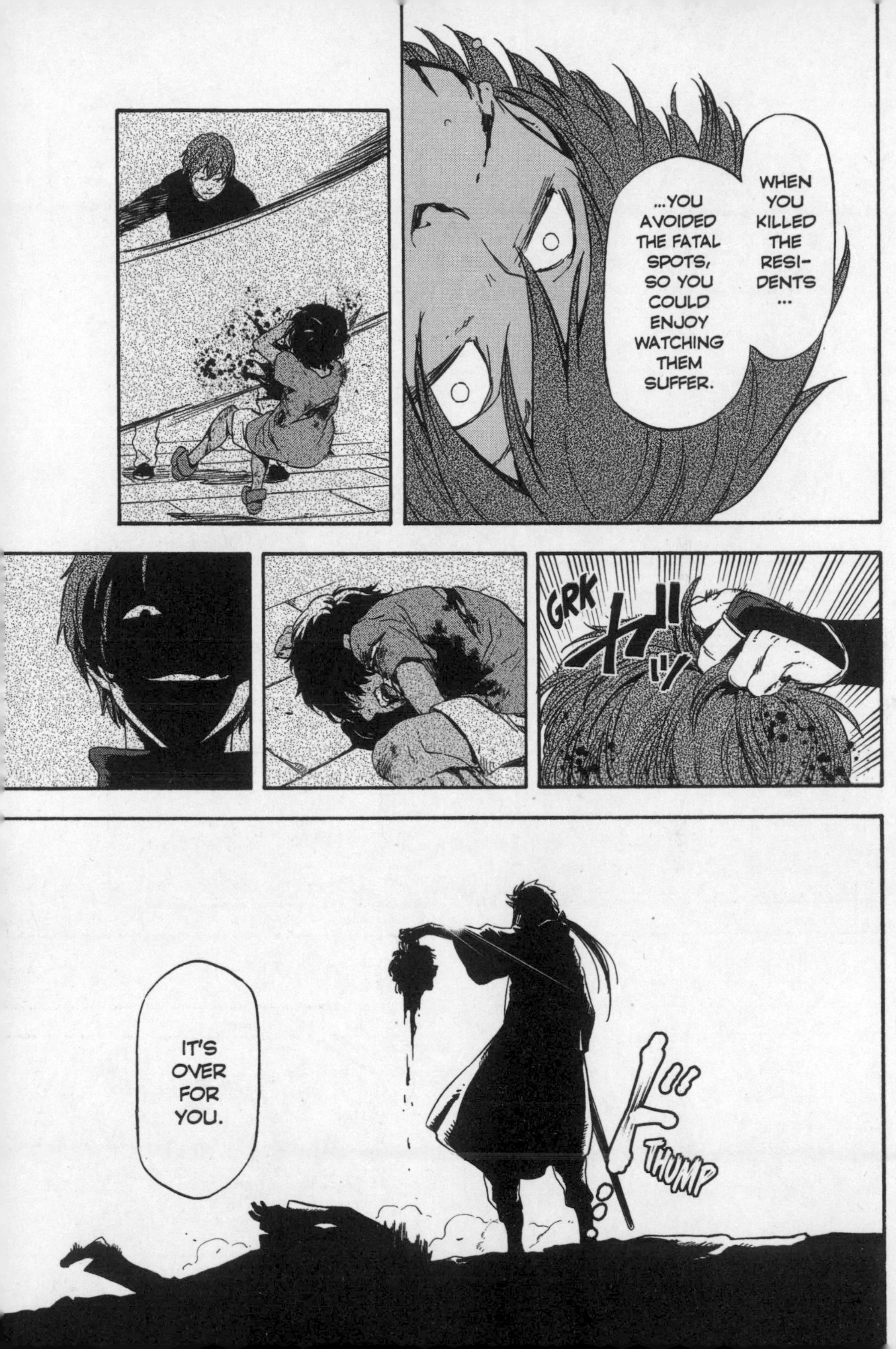
WHEN YOU KILLED THE RESI-DENTS ...
...YOU AVOIDED THE FATAL SPOTS, SO YOU COULD ENJOY WATCHING THEM SUFFER.
GRK
IT'S OVER FOR YOU.
THUMP

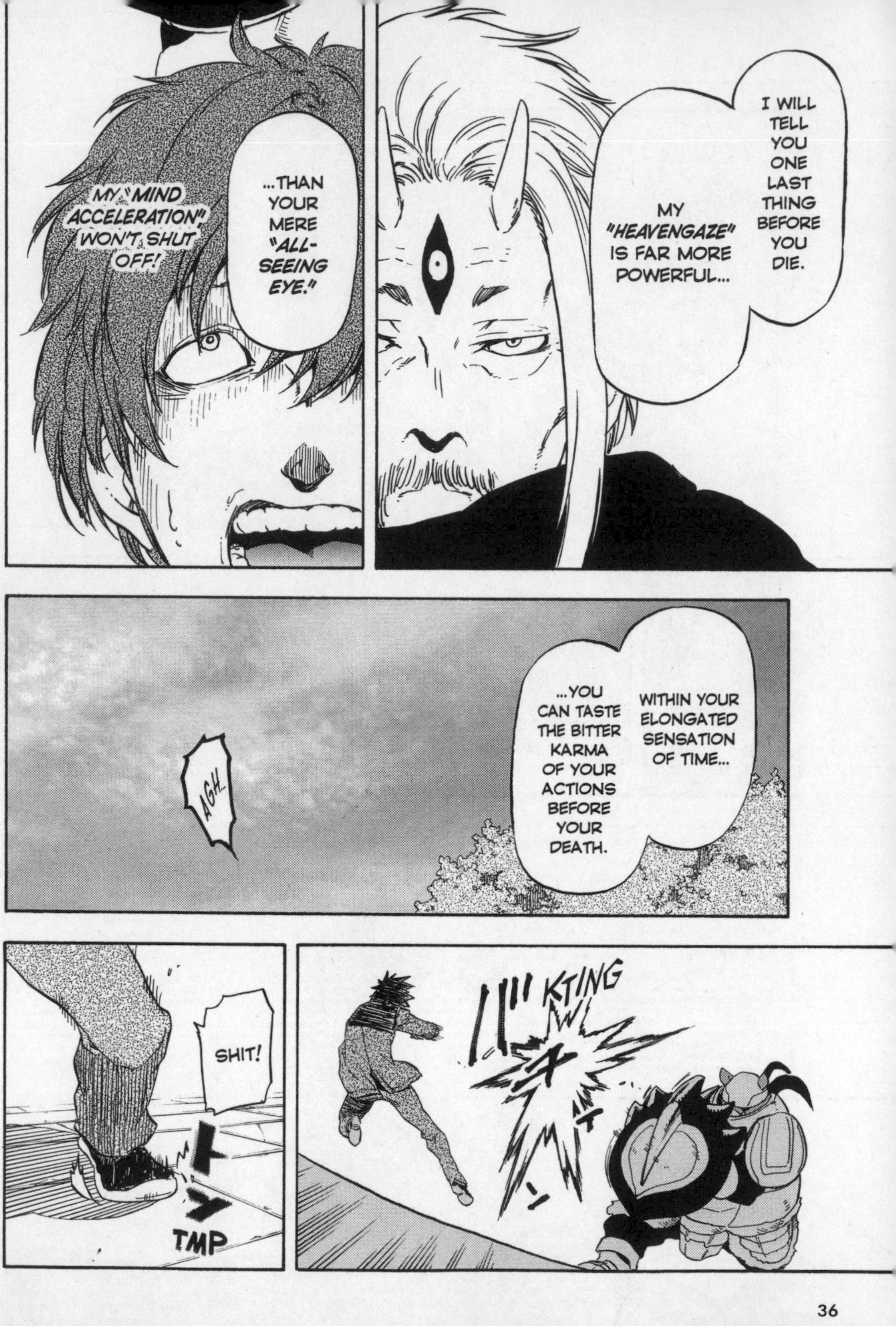
I WILL TELL YOU ONE LAST THING BEFORE YOU DIE.
MY "HEAVENGAZE" IS FAR MORE POWERFUL...
...THAN YOUR MERE "ALL-SEEING EYE."
MY "MIND ACCELERATION" WON'T SHUT OFF!
WITHIN YOUR ELONGATED SENSATION OF TIME...
...YOU CAN TASTE THE BITTER KARMA OF YOUR ACTIONS BEFORE YOUR DEATH.
AGH...
KTING
SHIT!
TMP

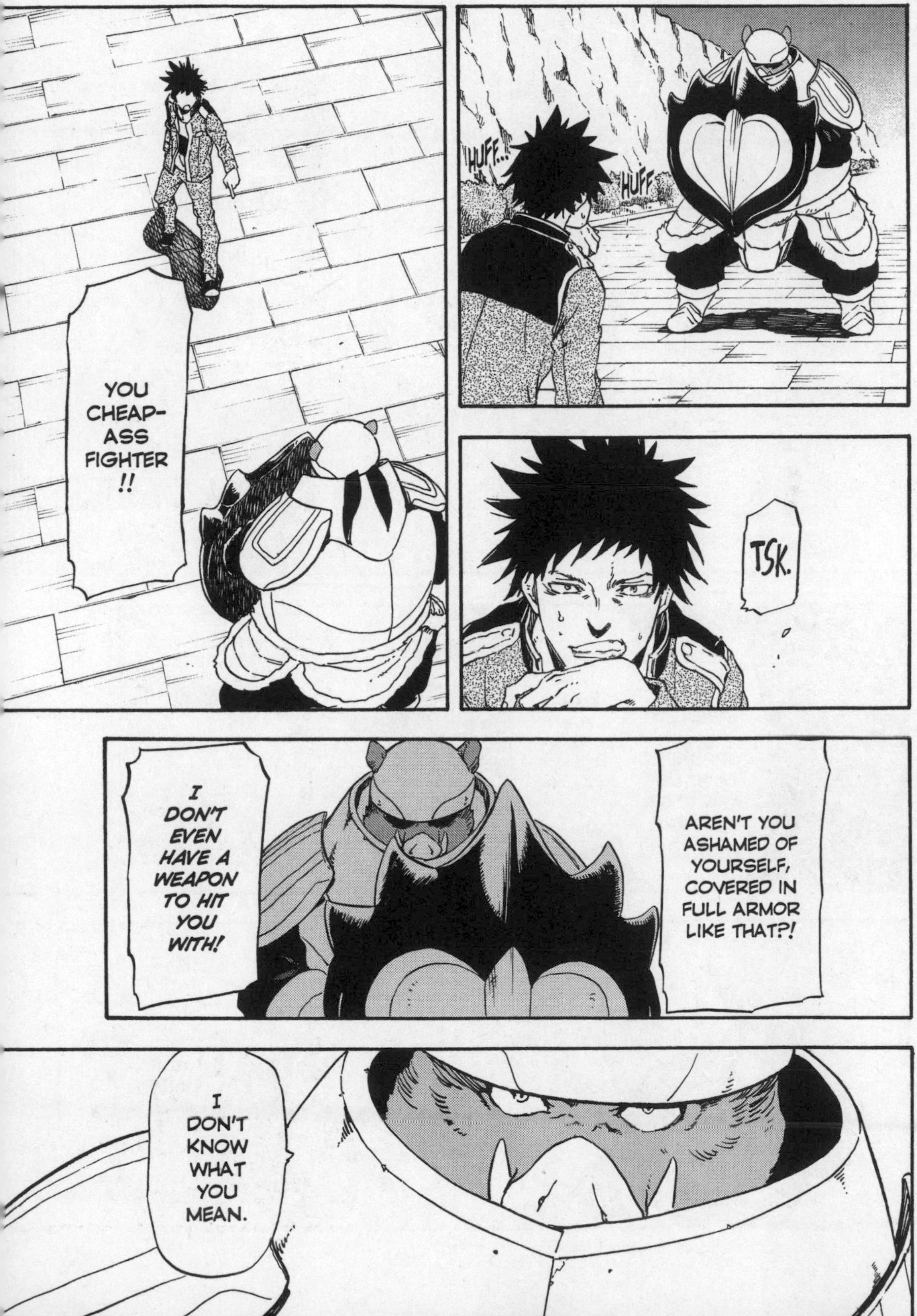
HUFF...
HUFF
TSK.
YOU CHEAP-ASS FIGHTER!!
AREN'T YOU ASHAMED OF YOURSELF, COVERED IN FULL ARMOR LIKE THAT?!
I DON'T EVEN HAVE A WEAPON TO HIT YOU WITH!
I DON'T KNOW WHAT YOU MEAN.

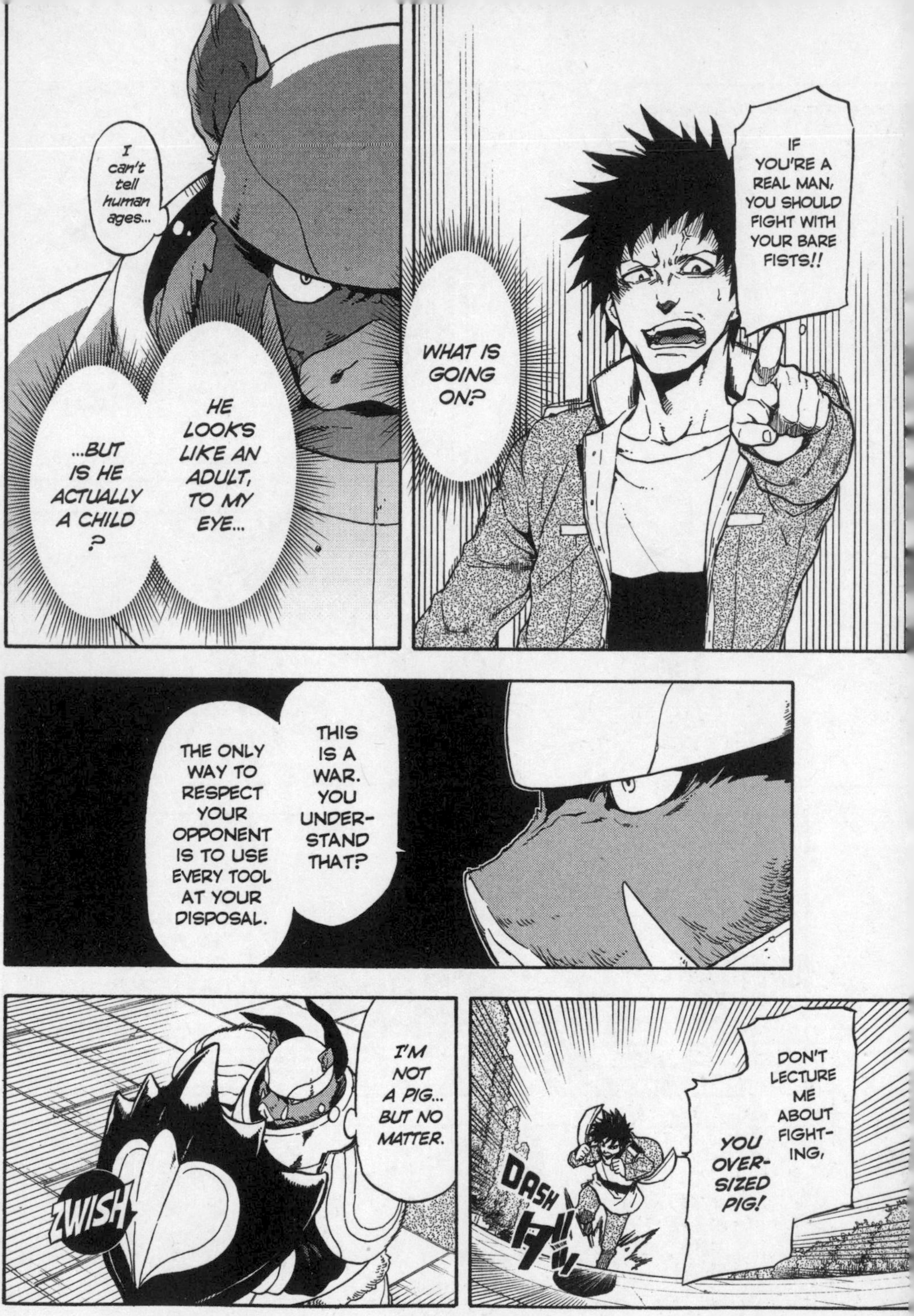

IF YOU'RE A REAL MAN, YOU SHOULD FIGHT WITH YOUR BARE FISTS!!
WHAT IS GOING ON?
I can't tell human ages...
HE LOOKS LIKE AN ADULT, TO MY EYE...
...BUT IS HE ACTUALLY A CHILD?
THIS IS A WAR. YOU UNDER-STAND THAT?
THE ONLY WAY TO RESPECT YOUR OPPONENT IS TO USE EVERY TOOL AT YOUR DISPOSAL.
DON'T LECTURE ME ABOUT FIGHT-ING,
YOU OVER-SIZED PIG!
DASH
I'M NOT A PIG... BUT NO MATTER.
ZWISH

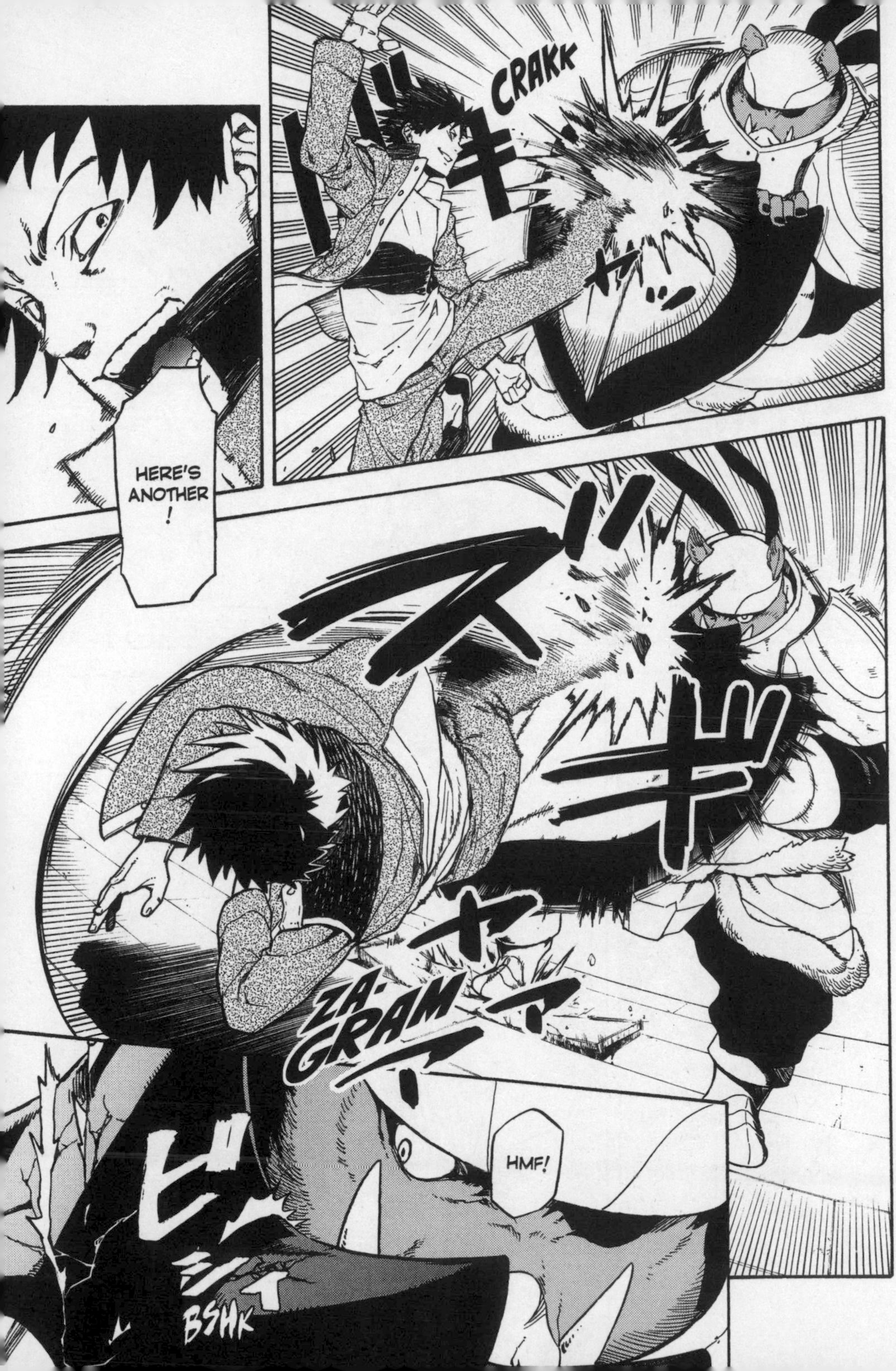
CRAKK
HERE'S ANOTHER!
ZA-GRAM
HMF!
BSHK

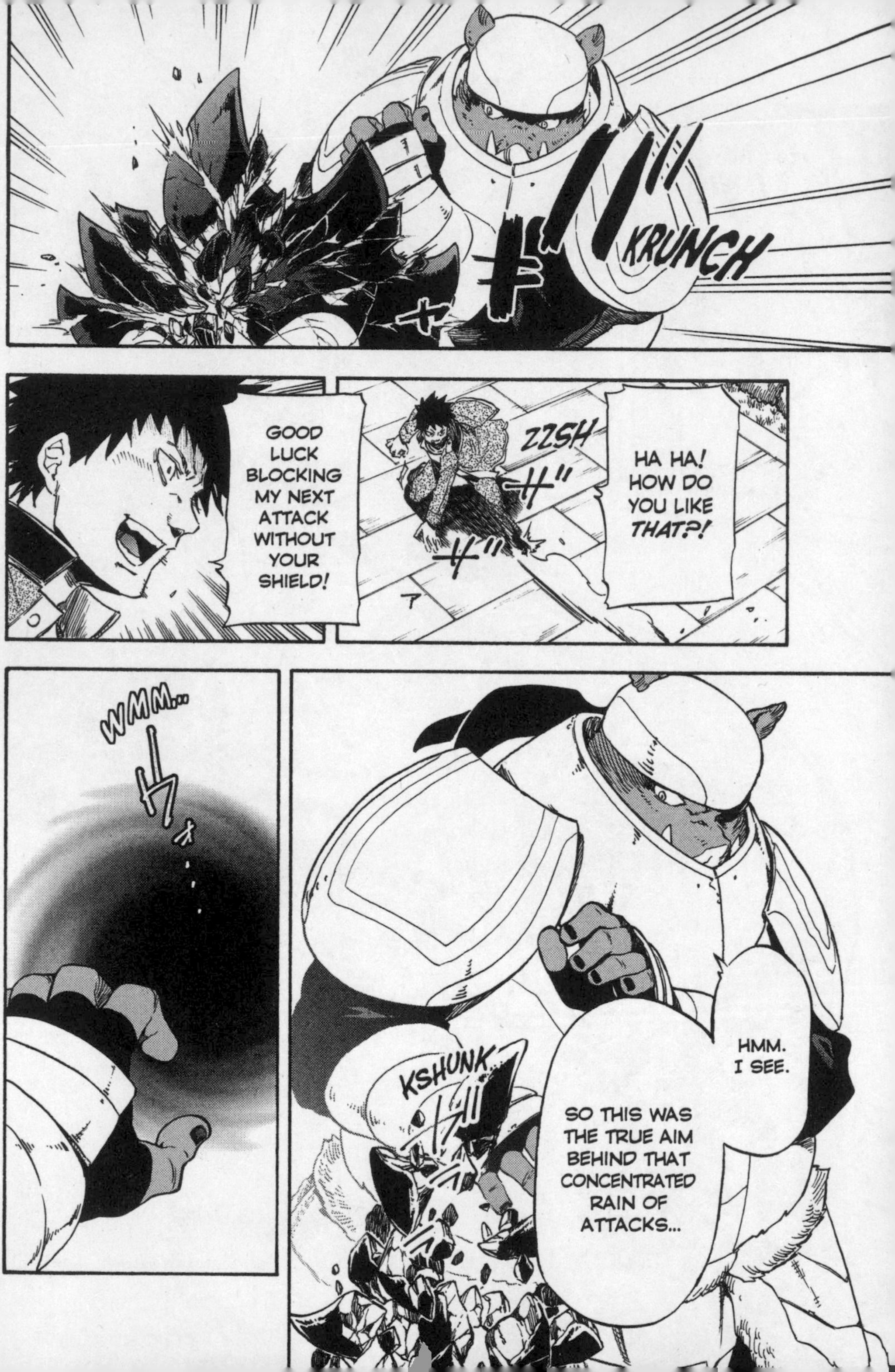
KRUNCH
ZZSH
HA HA! HOW DO YOU LIKE THAT?!
GOOD LUCK BLOCKING MY NEXT ATTACK WITHOUT YOUR SHIELD!
KSHUNK
HMM. I SEE.
SO THIS WAS THE TRUE AIM BEHIND THAT CONCENTRATED RAIN OF ATTACKS...
WMM...

ZRRM...
ズズ
HUH ...?!
WHAT WAS THAT ?!
THAT'S FIGHTING DIRTY !!
WHAT'S FIGHTING DIRTY? DIDN'T I JUST TELL YOU?
THIS IS WAR.

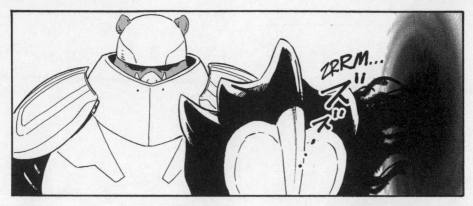

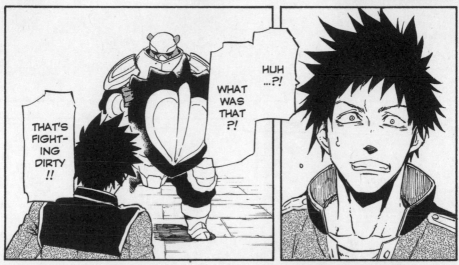

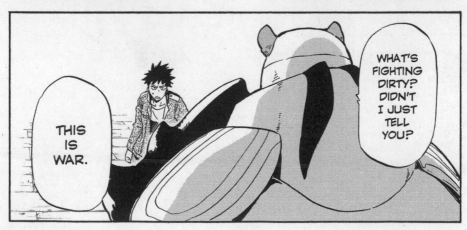

ALL'S FAIR IN WAR. I WILL NOT COMPLAIN, NO MATTER HOW MANY DIRTY, UNDER-HANDED TRICKS YOU ATTEMPT ON ME.

THINK THIS IS SOME KINDA JOKE?

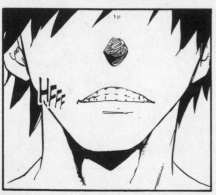

HFFF

HAHH

FWAP

FINE. YOU WANT MY BEST? YOU GOT IT.

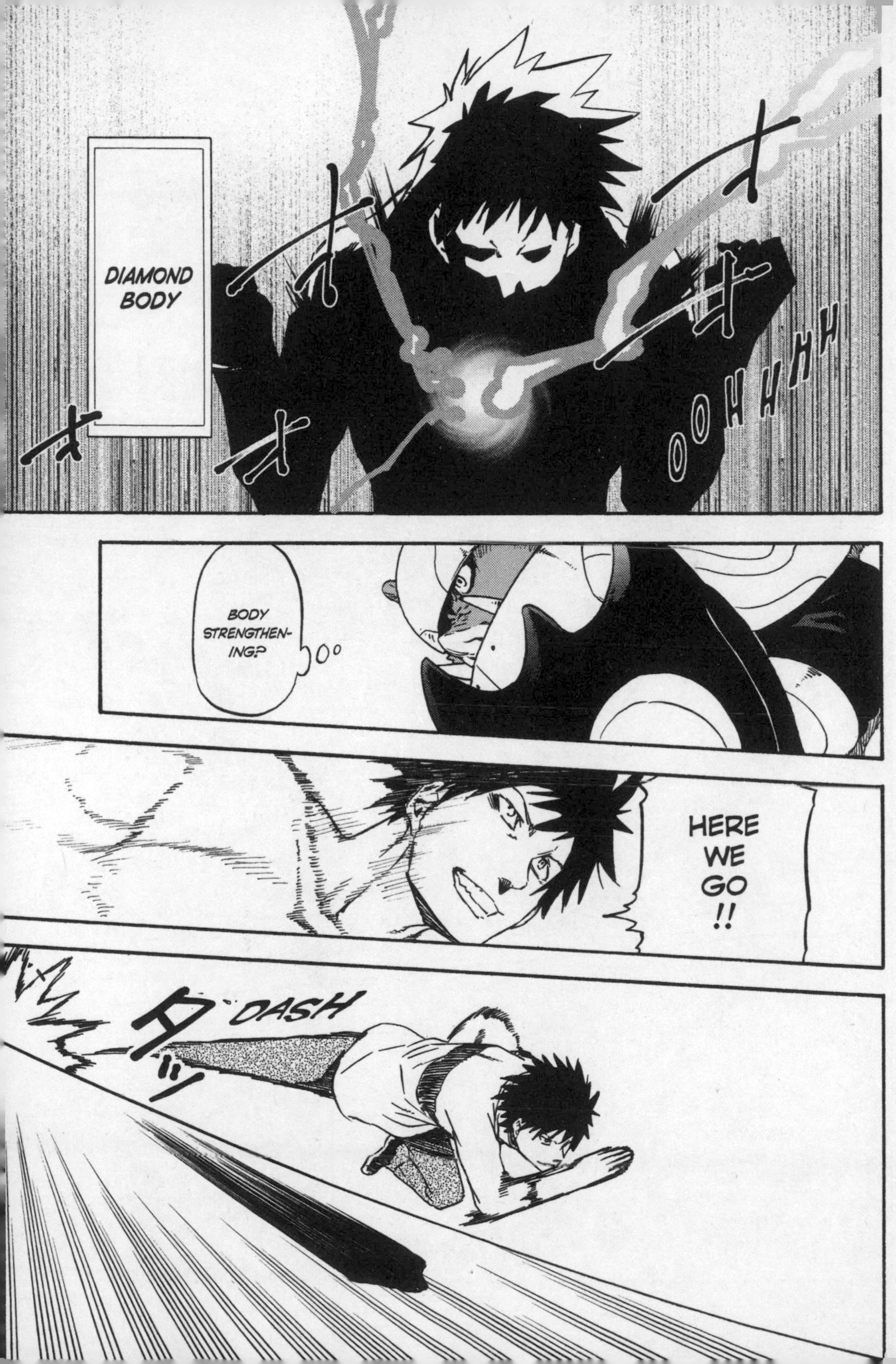
DIAMOND BODY
OOHHHH
BODY STRENGTHEN-ING?
HERE WE GO!!
DASH

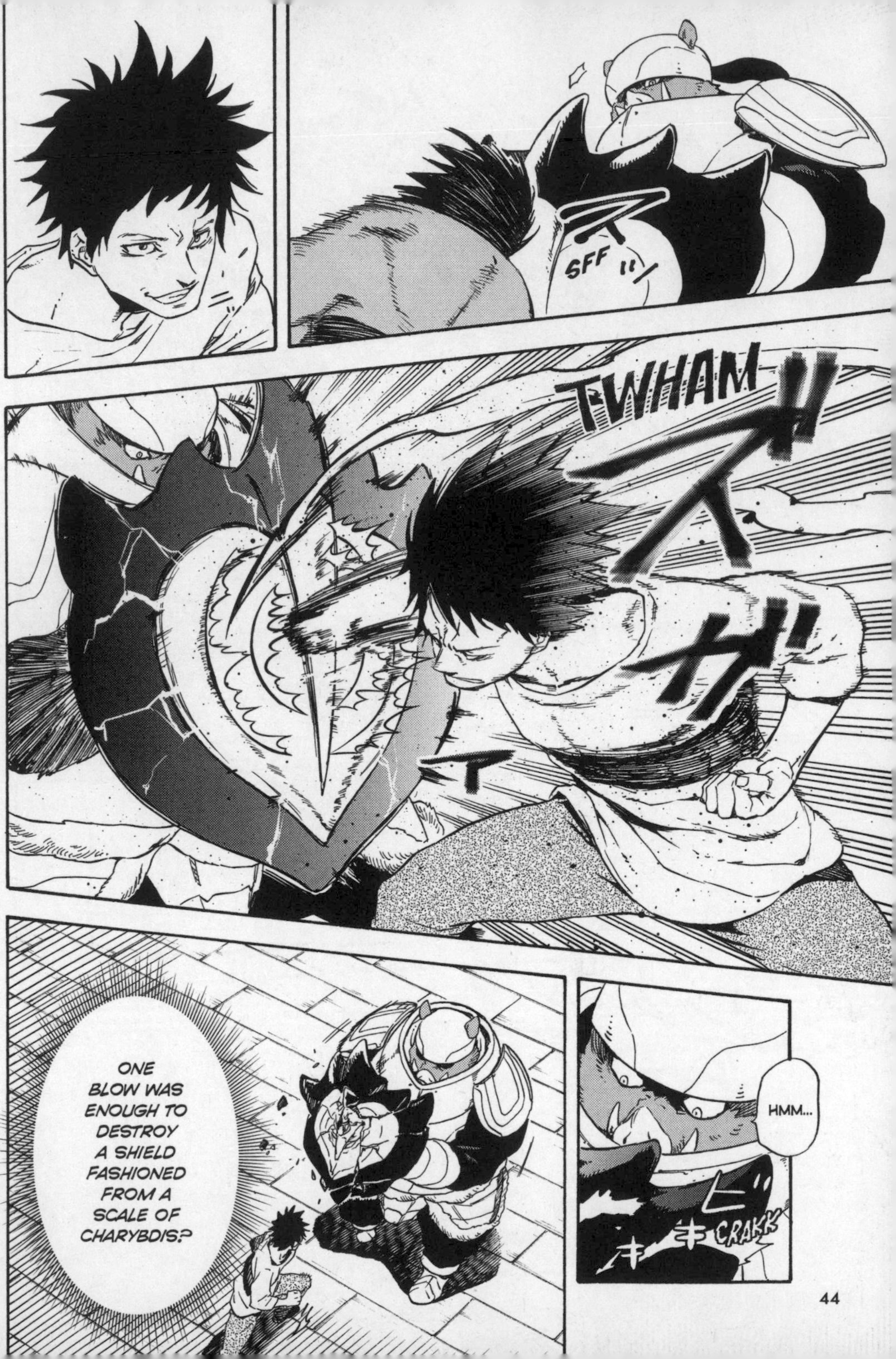
SFF
TWHAM
HMM...
CRAKK
ONE BLOW WAS ENOUGH TO DESTROY A SHIELD FASHIONED FROM A SCALE OF CHARYBDIS?

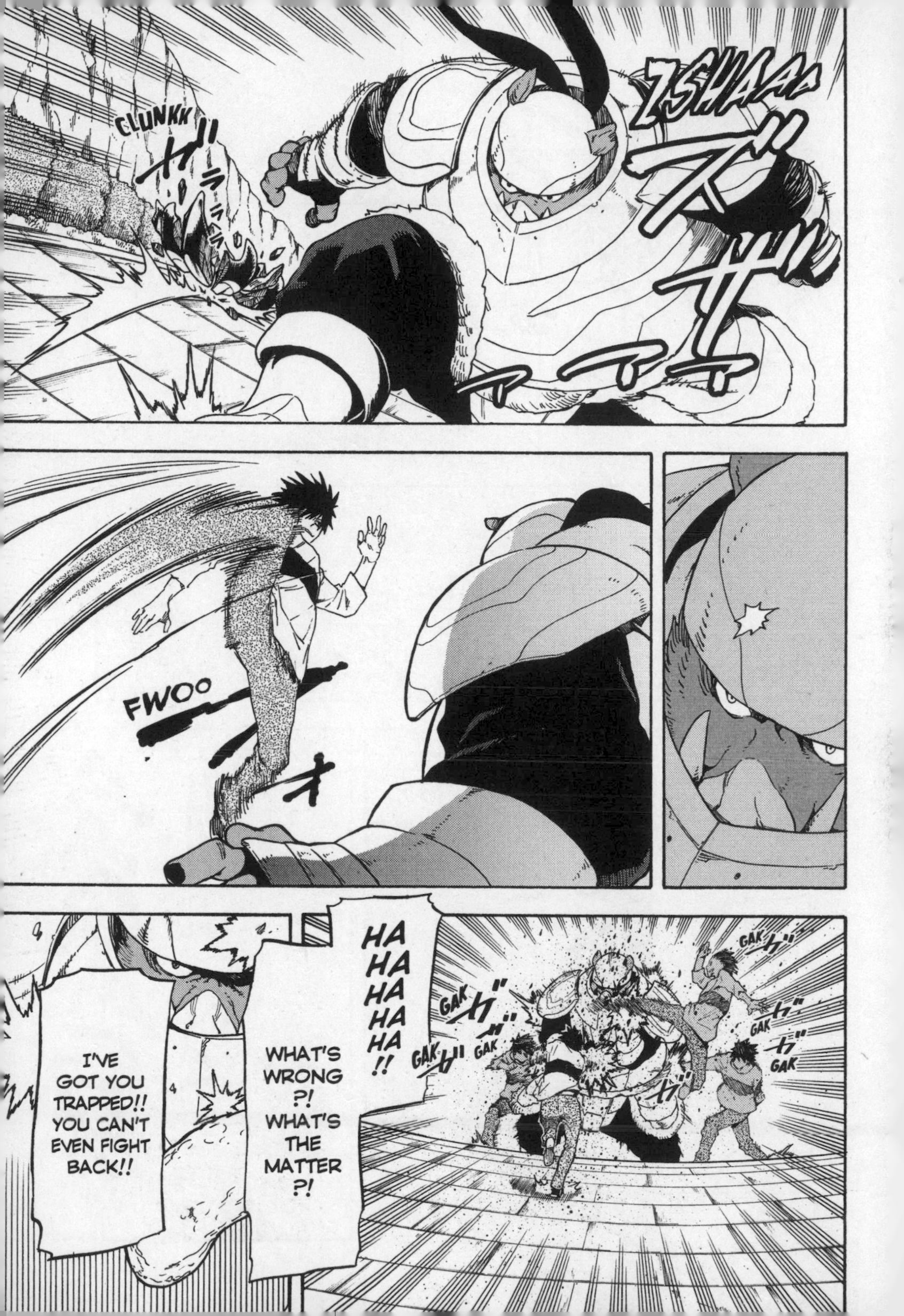
ZSHAAA
CLUNKK
FWOO
GAK
GAK
GAK
GAK
GAK
HA HA HA HA HA HA!!
WHAT'S WRONG?! WHAT'S THE MATTER?!
I'VE GOT YOU TRAPPED!! YOU CAN'T EVEN FIGHT BACK!!

ZRRK

W-WHAT WAS THAT ?!

HA HA HA HA !!

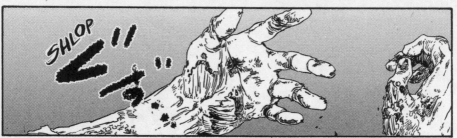

SHLOP

MY... MY HANDS!

MY LEGS !!

AAAAGH!!

46

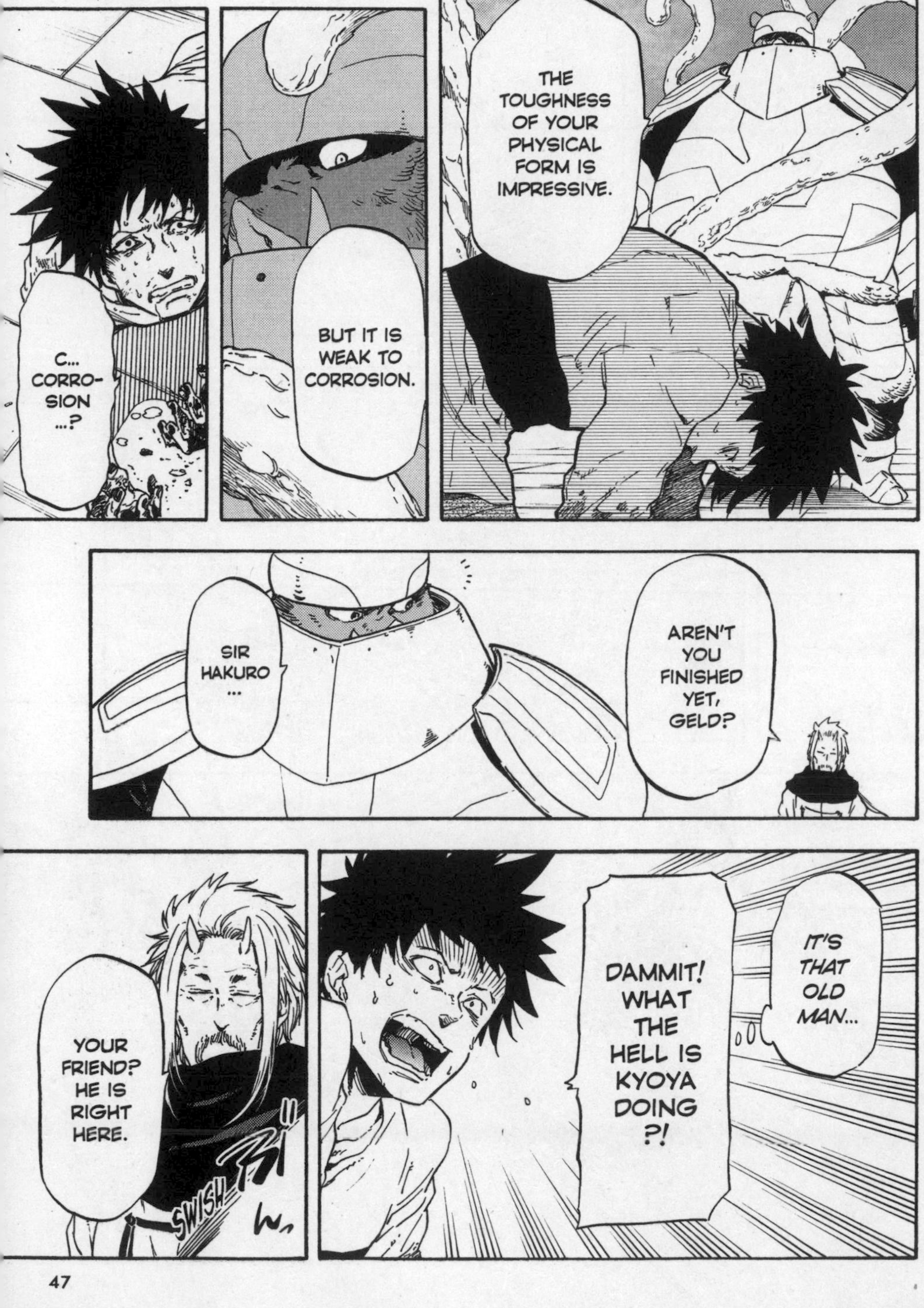
THE TOUGHNESS OF YOUR PHYSICAL FORM IS IMPRESSIVE.
BUT IT IS WEAK TO CORROSION.
C... CORRO-SION ...?
AREN'T YOU FINISHED YET, GELD?
SIR HAKURO ...
IT'S THAT OLD MAN...
DAMMIT! WHAT THE HELL IS KYOYA DOING ?!
YOUR FRIEND? HE IS RIGHT HERE.
SWISH

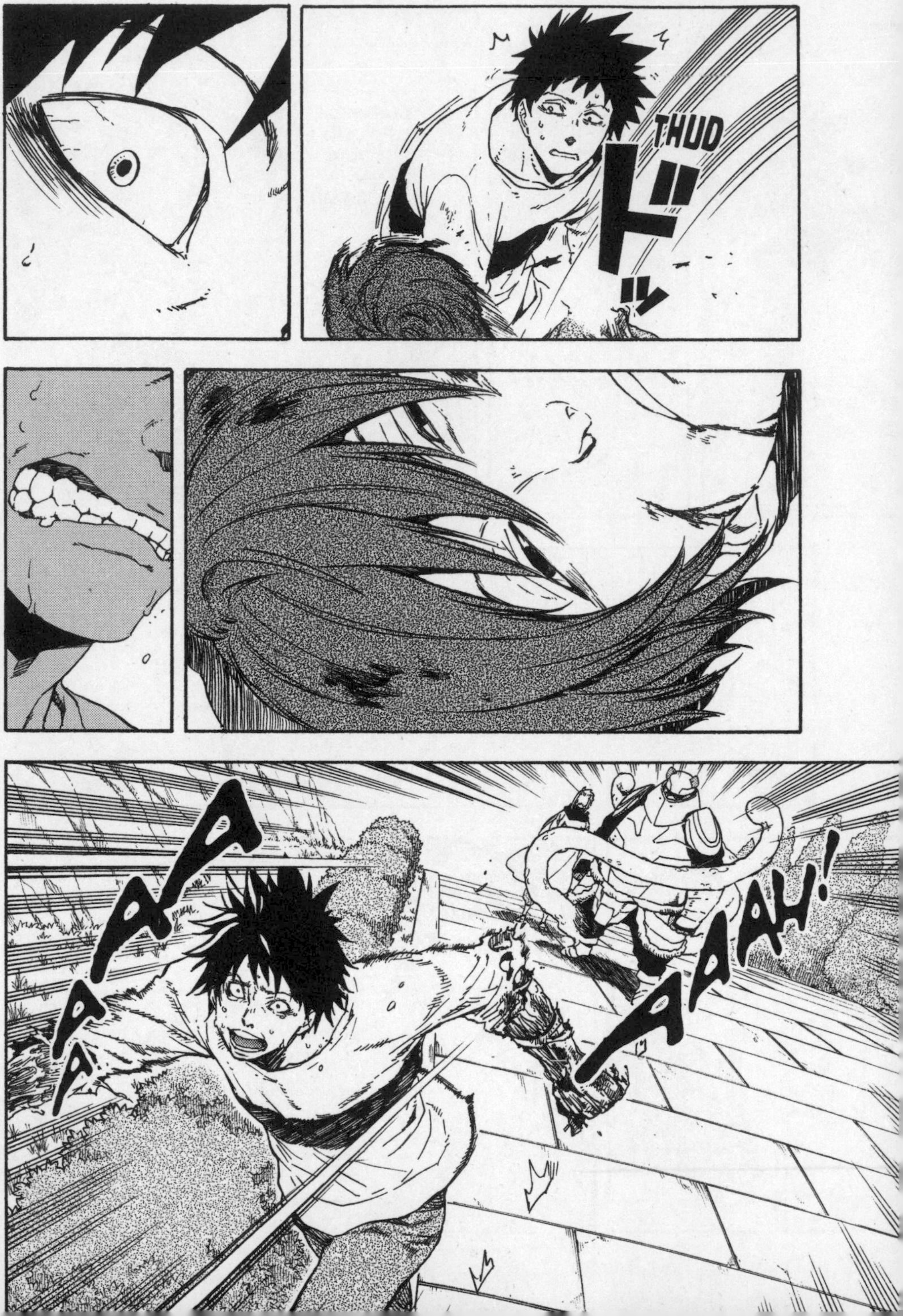
THUD
ドッ
AAAAA
AAAH!

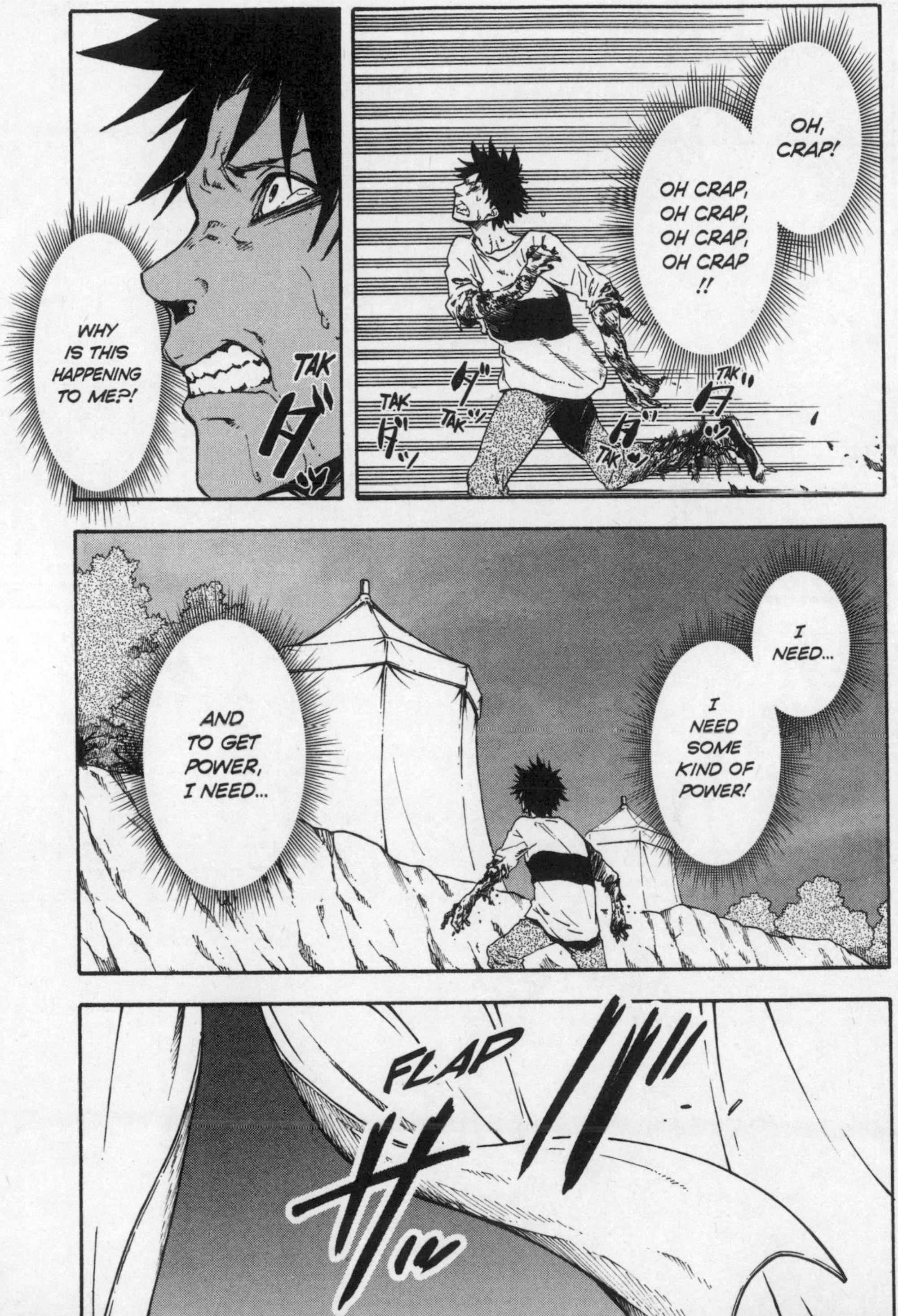
OH, CRAP!
OH CRAP, OH CRAP, OH CRAP, OH CRAP !!
TAK
TAK
TAK
TAK
WHY IS THIS HAPPENING TO ME?!
TAK
I NEED...
I NEED SOME KIND OF POWER!
AND TO GET POWER, I NEED...
FLAP

HUFF

HUFF...

YOU DONE?

TOOK YOU GUYS A LOT LONGER THAN USUAL.

WHAT?

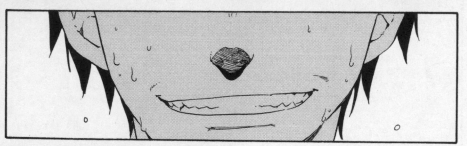

LISTEN, KIRARA, I'M SORRY ABOUT THIS.

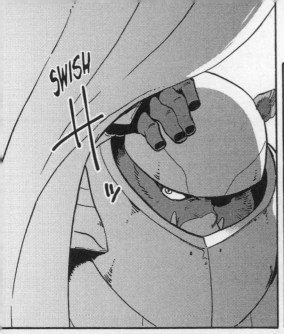

SWISH
SO YOU'D SINK THIS LOW...
SKILL ACQUISITION CONFIRMED.
UNIQUE SKILL "SURVIVOR" ACQUIRED.

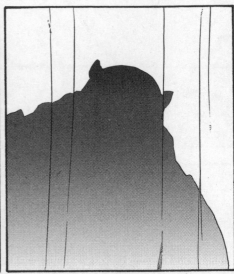

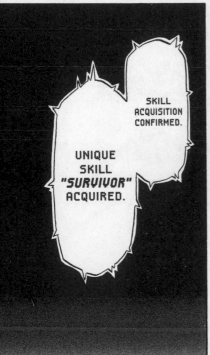

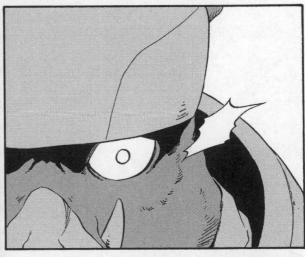

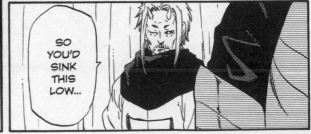

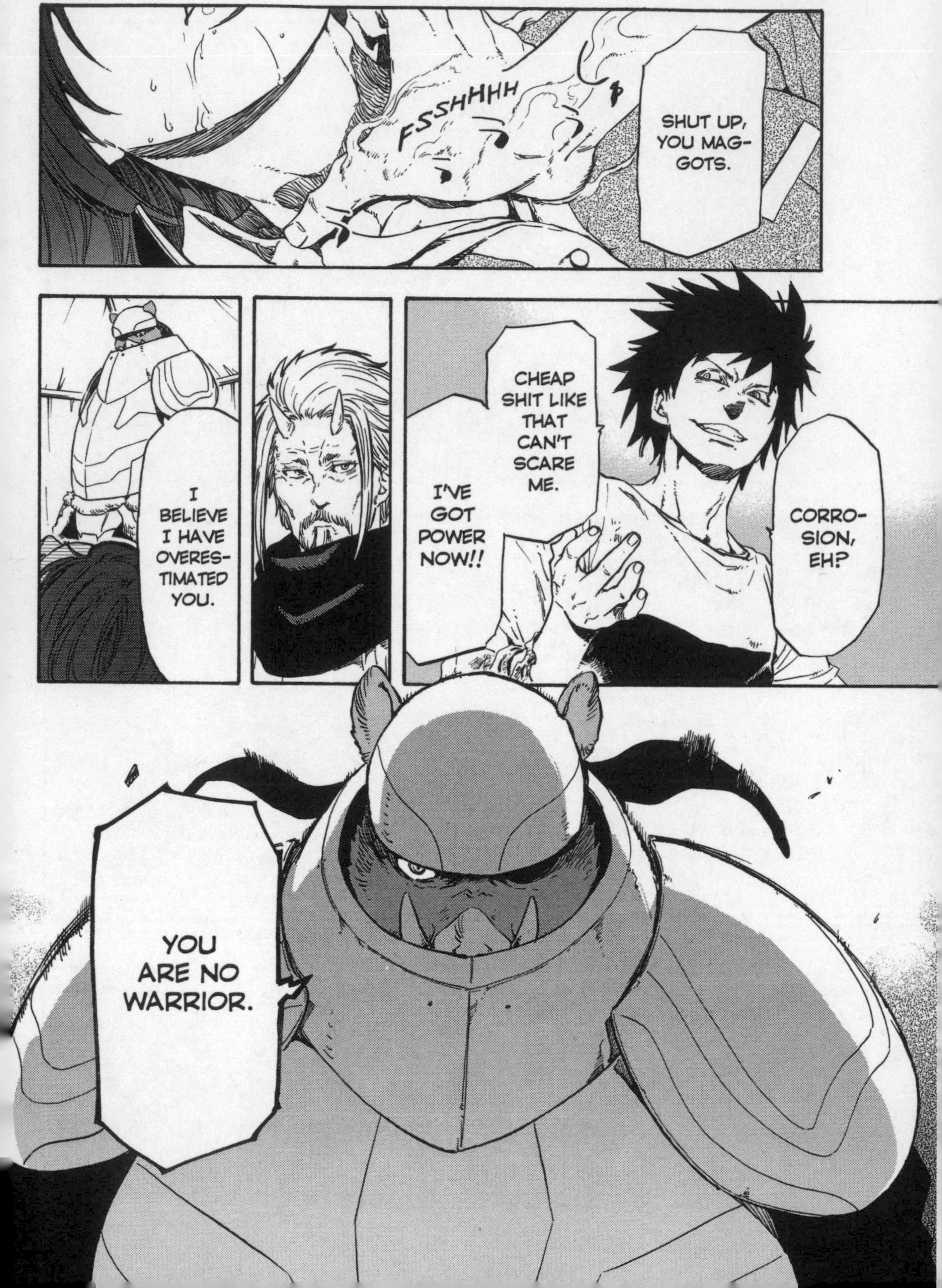
FSSHHHH
SHUT UP, YOU MAG-GOTS.
CORRO-SION, EH?
CHEAP SHIT LIKE THAT CAN'T SCARE ME.
I'VE GOT POWER NOW!!
I BELIEVE I HAVE OVERES-TIMATED YOU.
YOU ARE NO WARRIOR.

Gobta's Short Sword

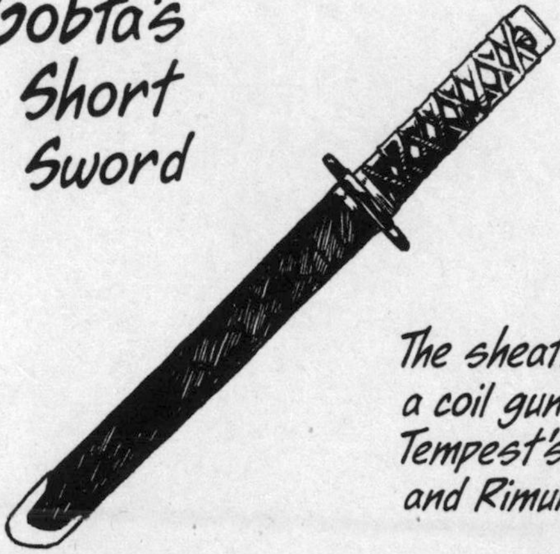

The sheath is actually a coil gun made with Tempest's technology and Rimuru's skills.

It's called the "Case Cannon."

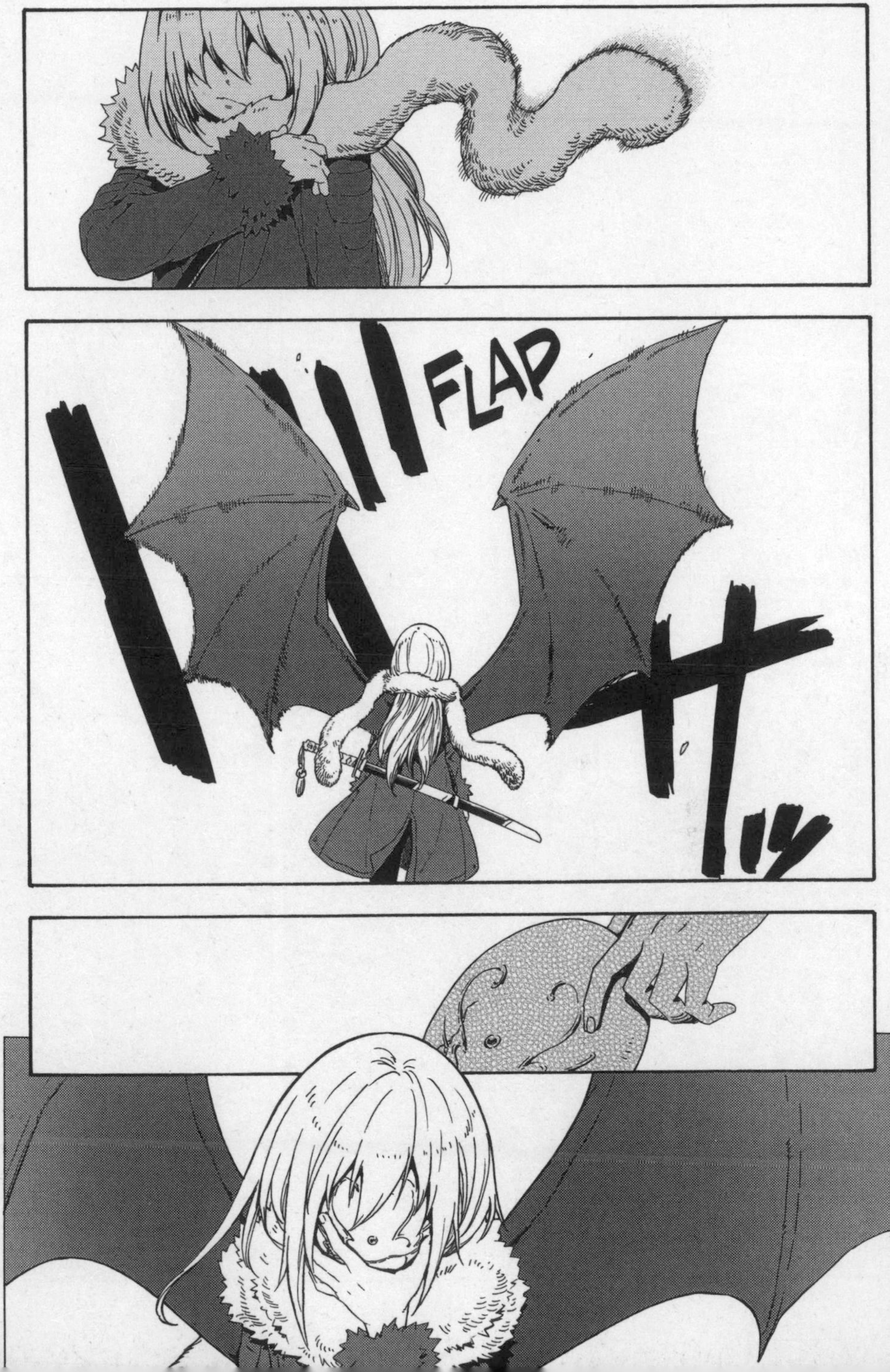
FLAP

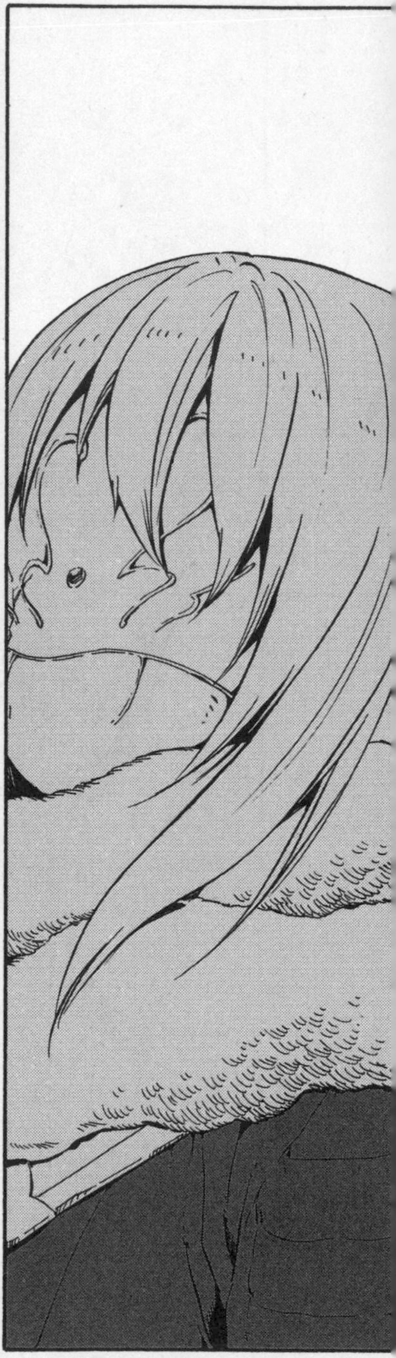

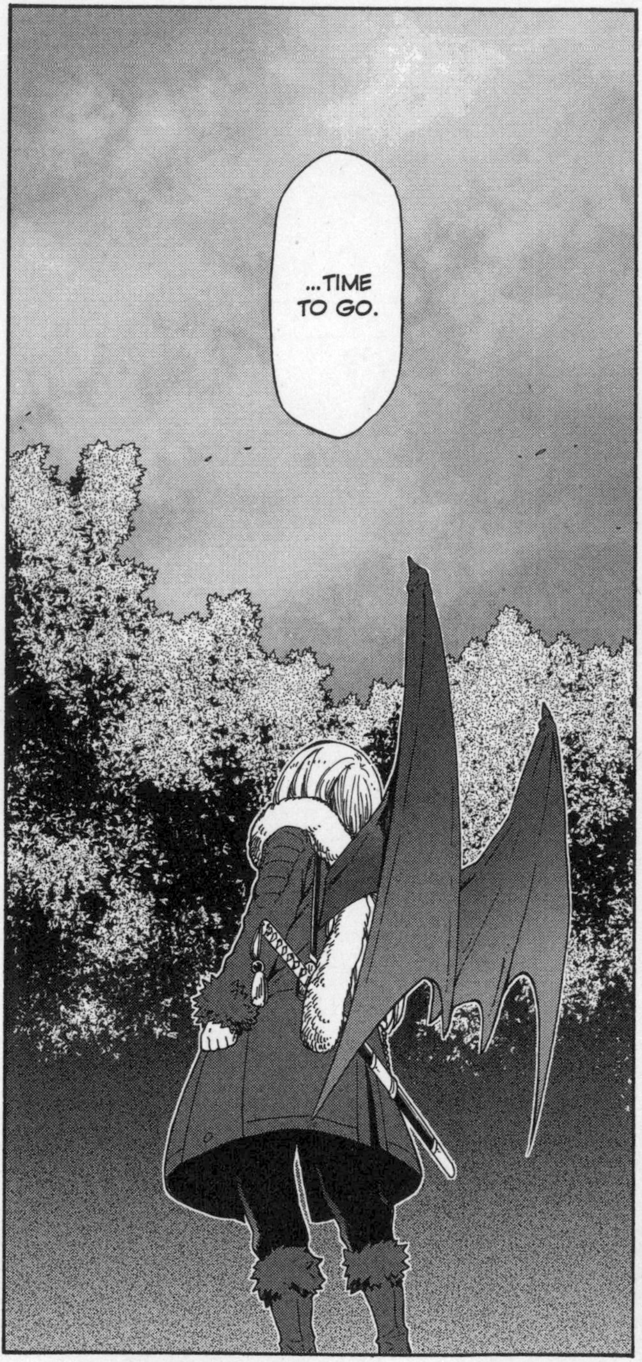
...TIME TO GO.

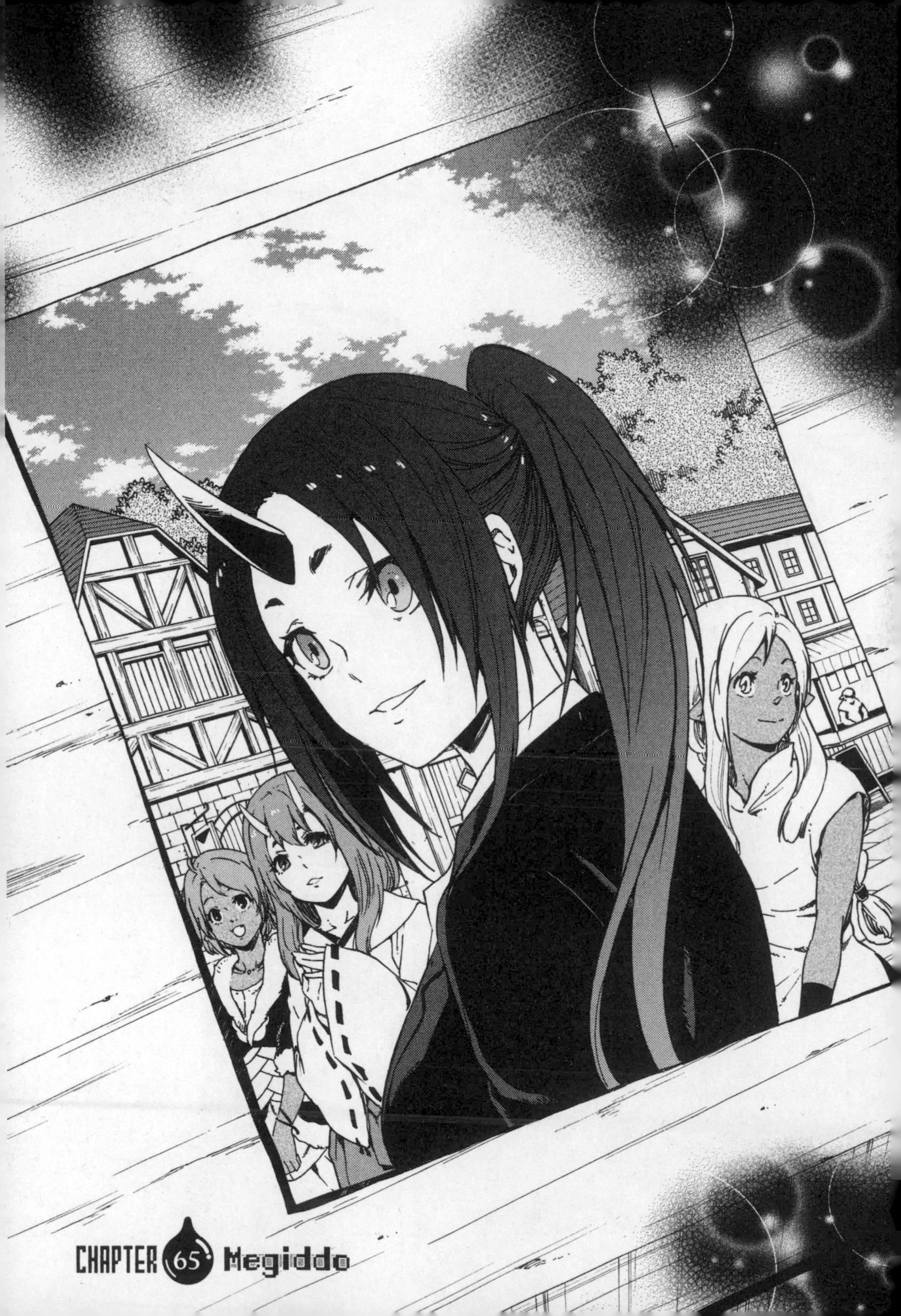

CHAPTER 65 Megiddo

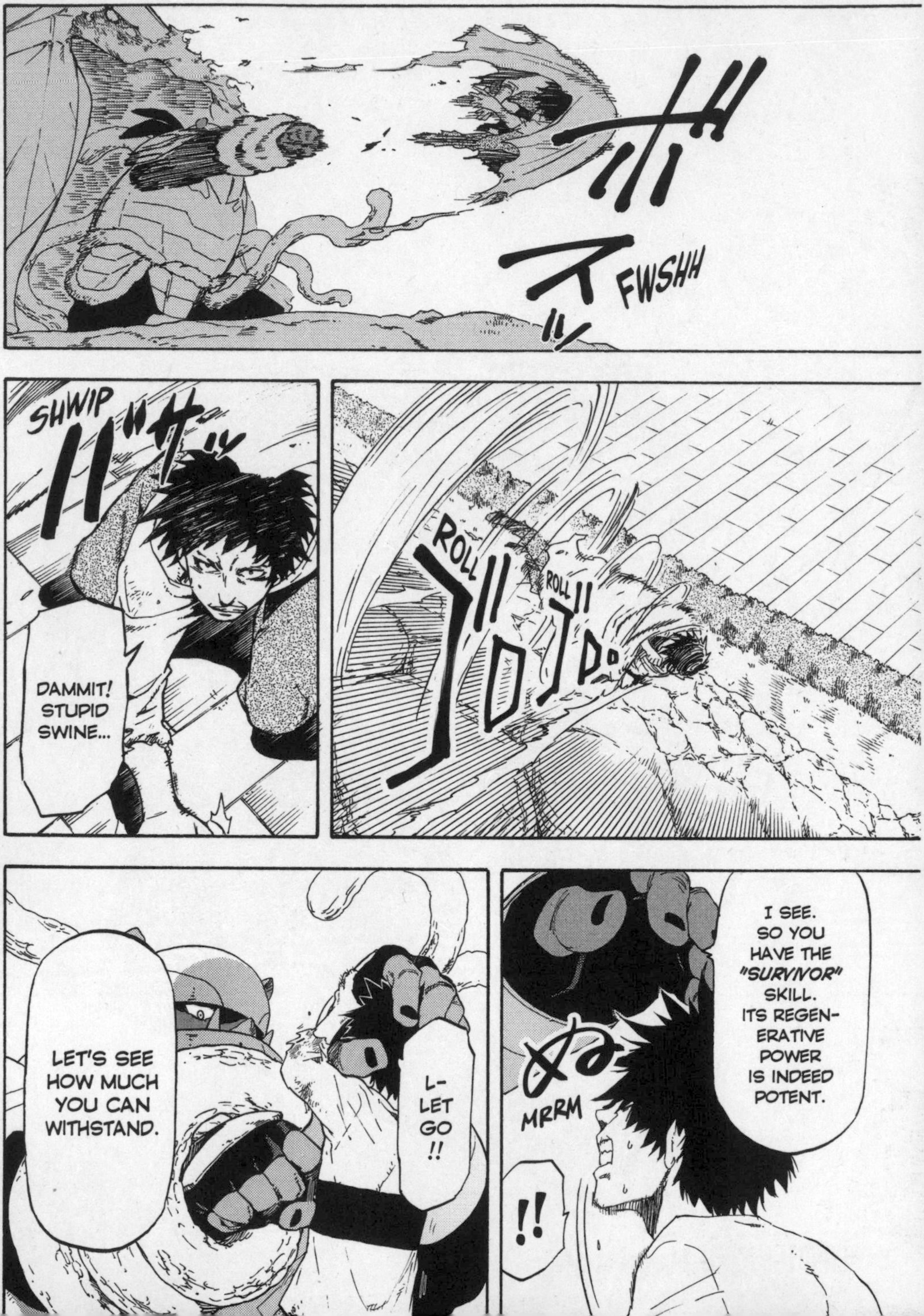
FWSHH
ROLL
ROLL!!
SHWIP
DAMMIT! STUPID SWINE...
I SEE. SO YOU HAVE THE "SURVIVOR" SKILL. ITS REGENERATIVE POWER IS INDEED POTENT.
MRRM
!!
L-LET GO!!
LET'S SEE HOW MUCH YOU CAN WITHSTAND.

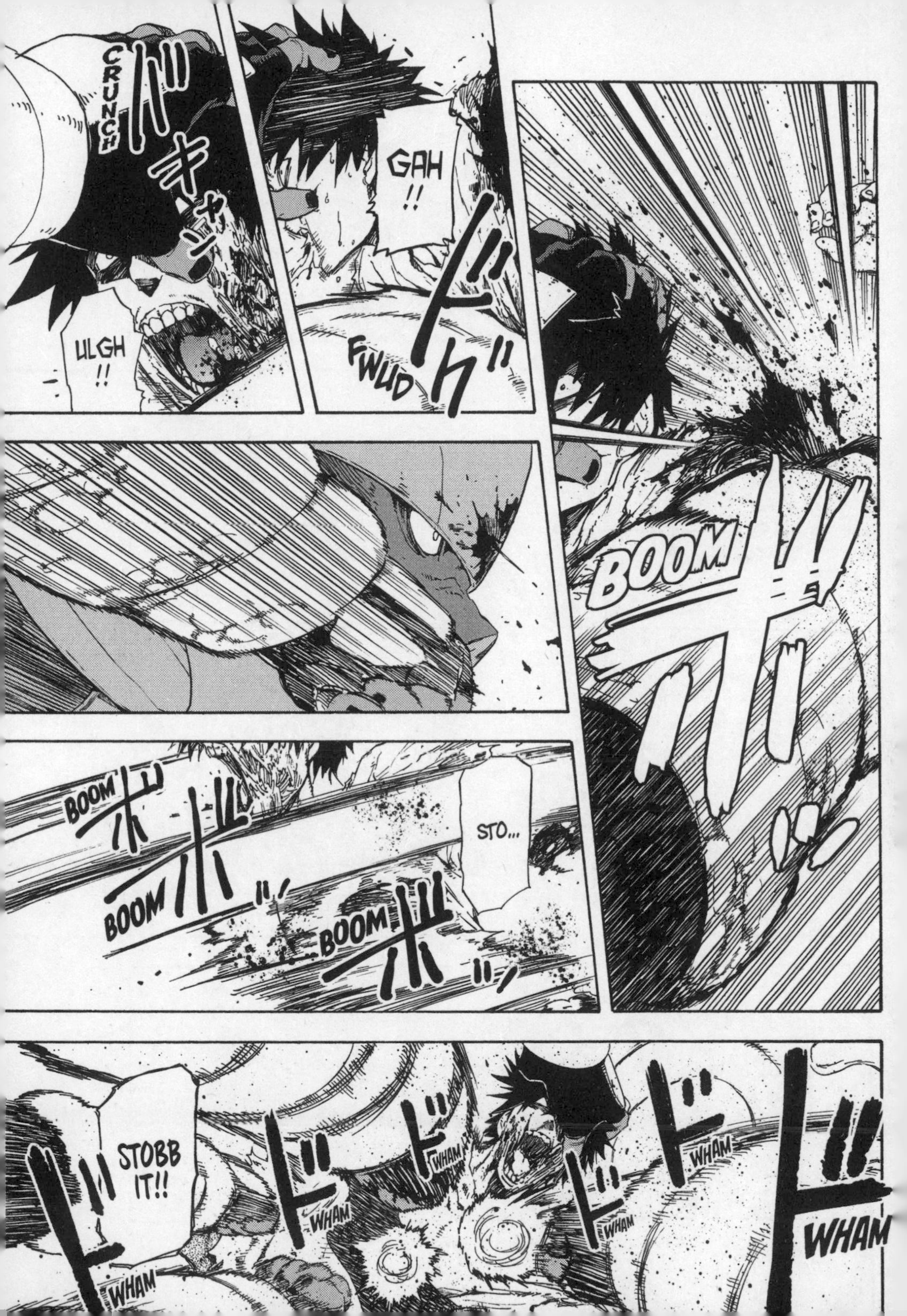
BOOM
GAH!!
FWUD
CRUNCH
ULGH!!
STO...
BOOM
BOOM
BOOM
WHAM
WHAM
WHAM
WHAM
WHAM
STOBB IT!!
WHAM

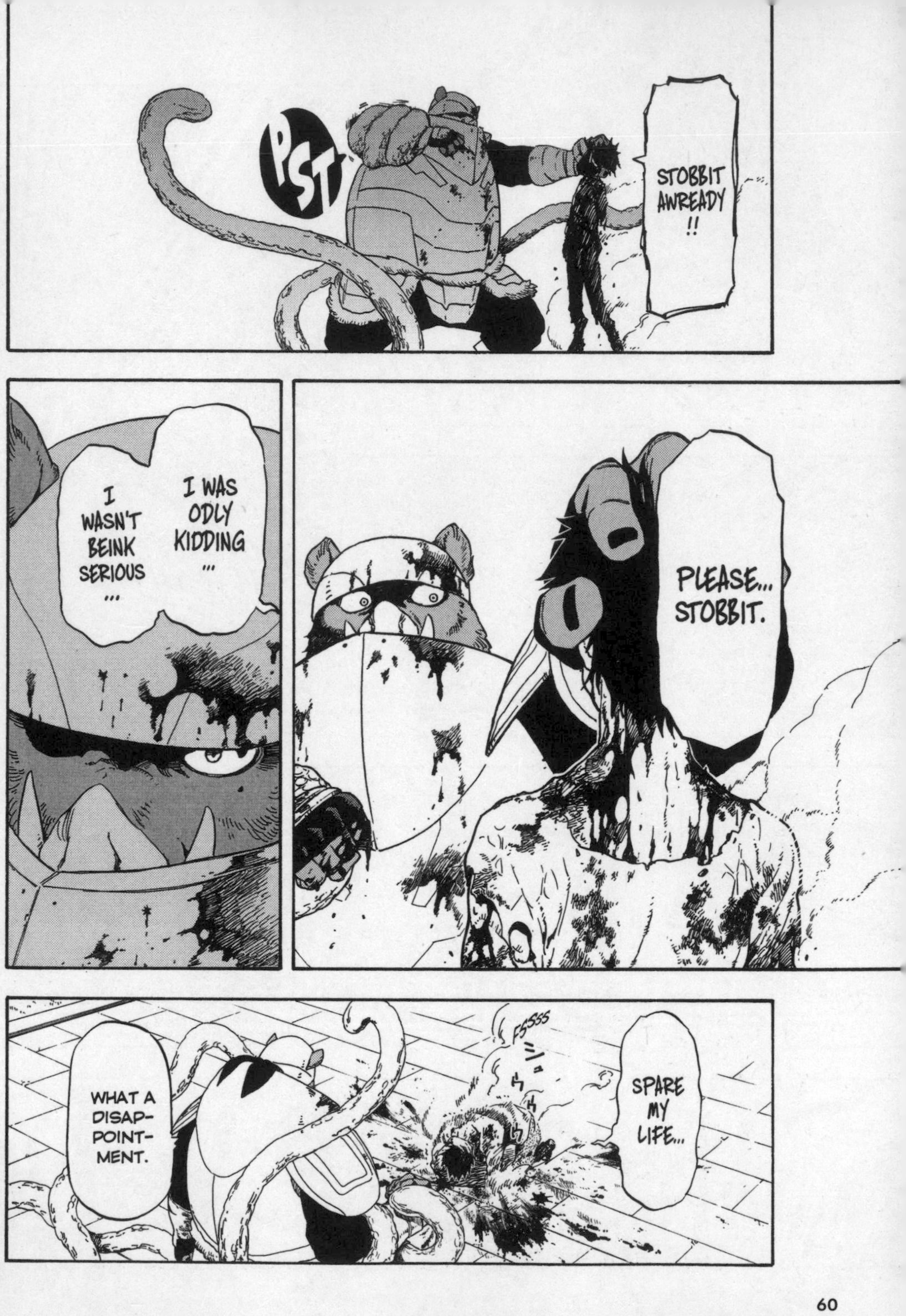
STOBBIT AWREADY !!
PST
PLEASE... STOBBIT.
I WAS ODLY KIDDING ...
I WASN'T BEINK SERIOUS ...
FSSSS
SPARE MY LIFE...
WHAT A DISAP-POINT-MENT.

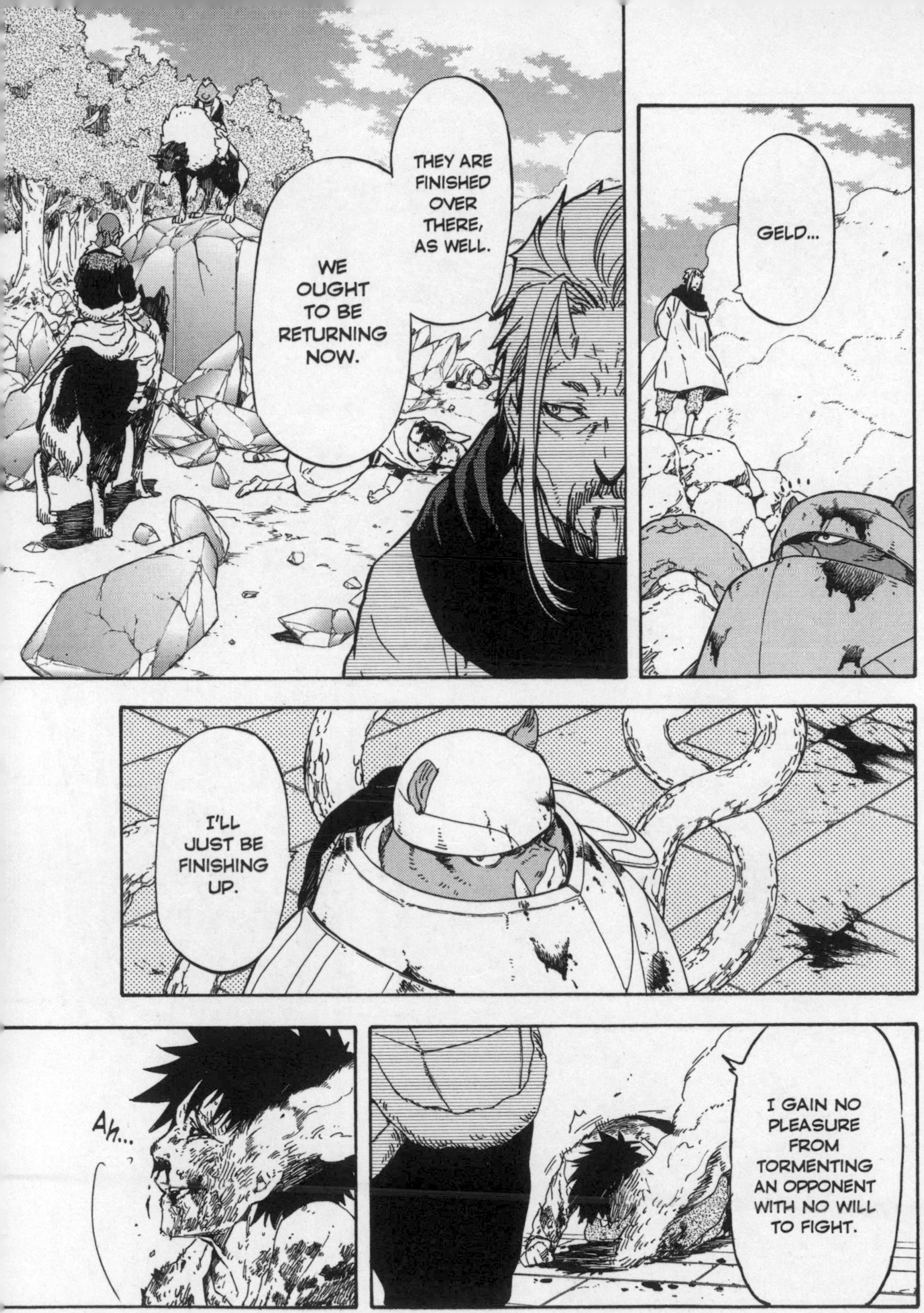
GELD...
THEY ARE FINISHED OVER THERE, AS WELL.
WE OUGHT TO BE RETURNING NOW.
I'LL JUST BE FINISHING UP.
I GAIN NO PLEASURE FROM TORMENTING AN OPPONENT WITH NO WILL TO FIGHT.
Ah...

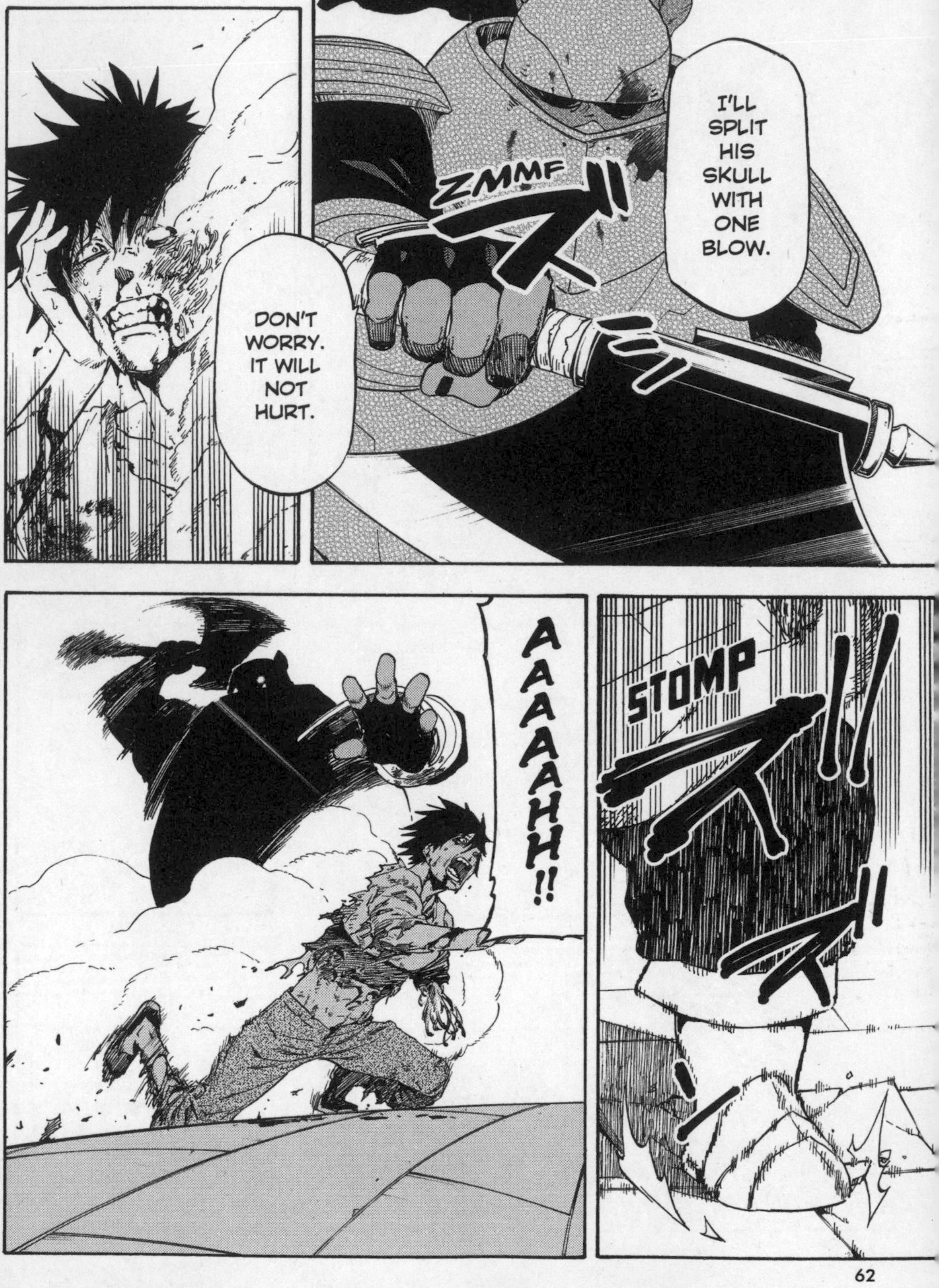
I'LL SPLIT HIS SKULL WITH ONE BLOW.
ZMMF
DON'T WORRY. IT WILL NOT HURT.
STOMP
AAAAAHH!!

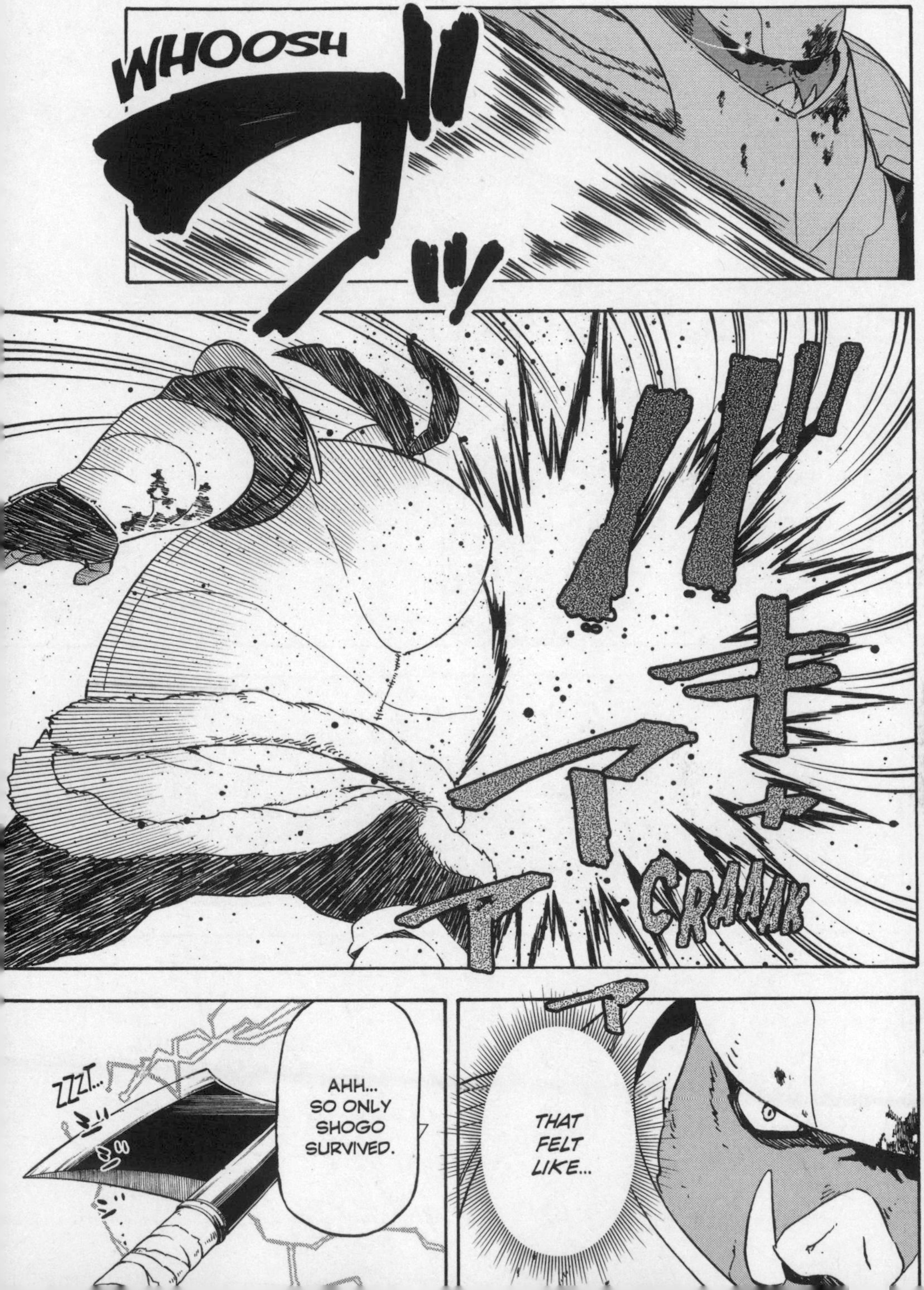
WHOOSH
CRAAAK
THAT FELT LIKE...
ZZZT...
AHH... SO ONLY SHOGO SURVIVED.

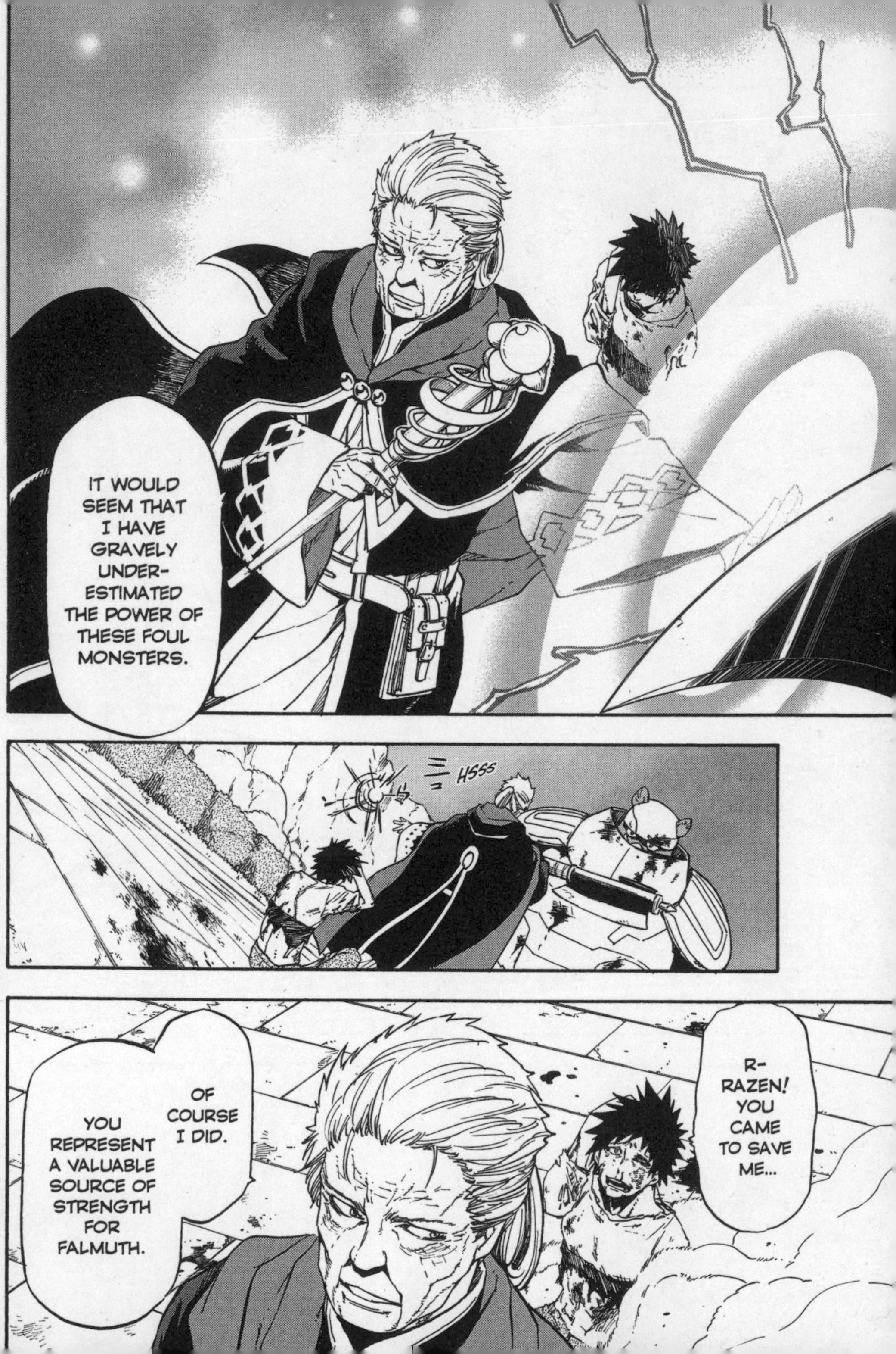
IT WOULD SEEM THAT I HAVE GRAVELY UNDER-ESTIMATED THE POWER OF THESE FOUL MONSTERS.
HSSS
R-RAZEN! YOU CAME TO SAVE ME...
OF COURSE I DID.
YOU REPRESENT A VALUABLE SOURCE OF STRENGTH FOR FALMUTH.

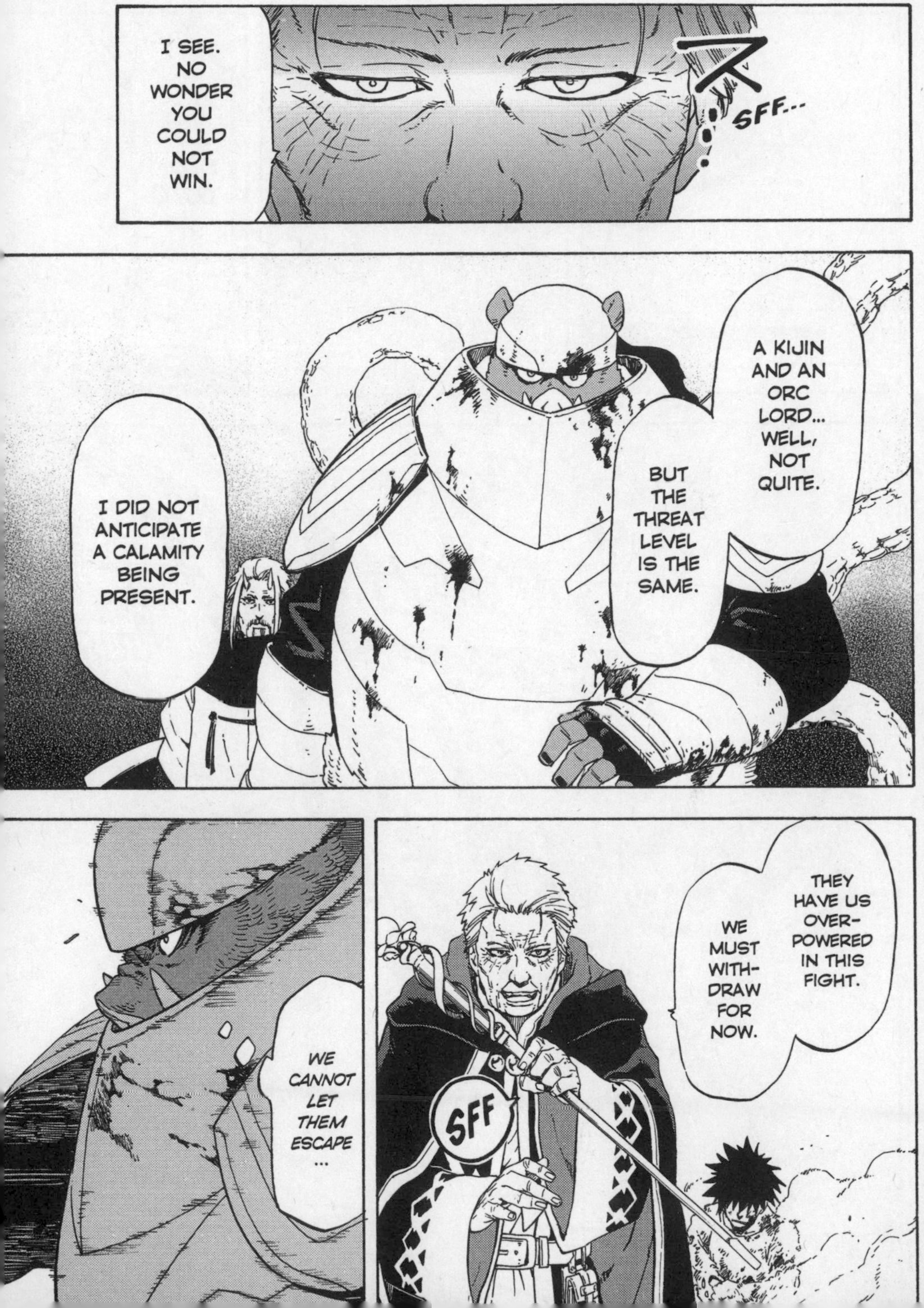
ス
SFF...
I SEE. NO WONDER YOU COULD NOT WIN.
A KIJIN AND AN ORC LORD... WELL, NOT QUITE.
BUT THE THREAT LEVEL IS THE SAME.
I DID NOT ANTICIPATE A CALAMITY BEING PRESENT.
THEY HAVE US OVER-POWERED IN THIS FIGHT.
WE MUST WITH-DRAW FOR NOW.
SFF
WE CANNOT LET THEM ESCAPE...

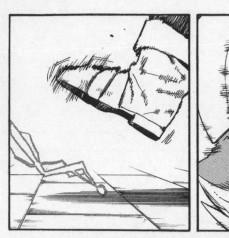

STOP, GELD !!

KABOOM

NWAH!!

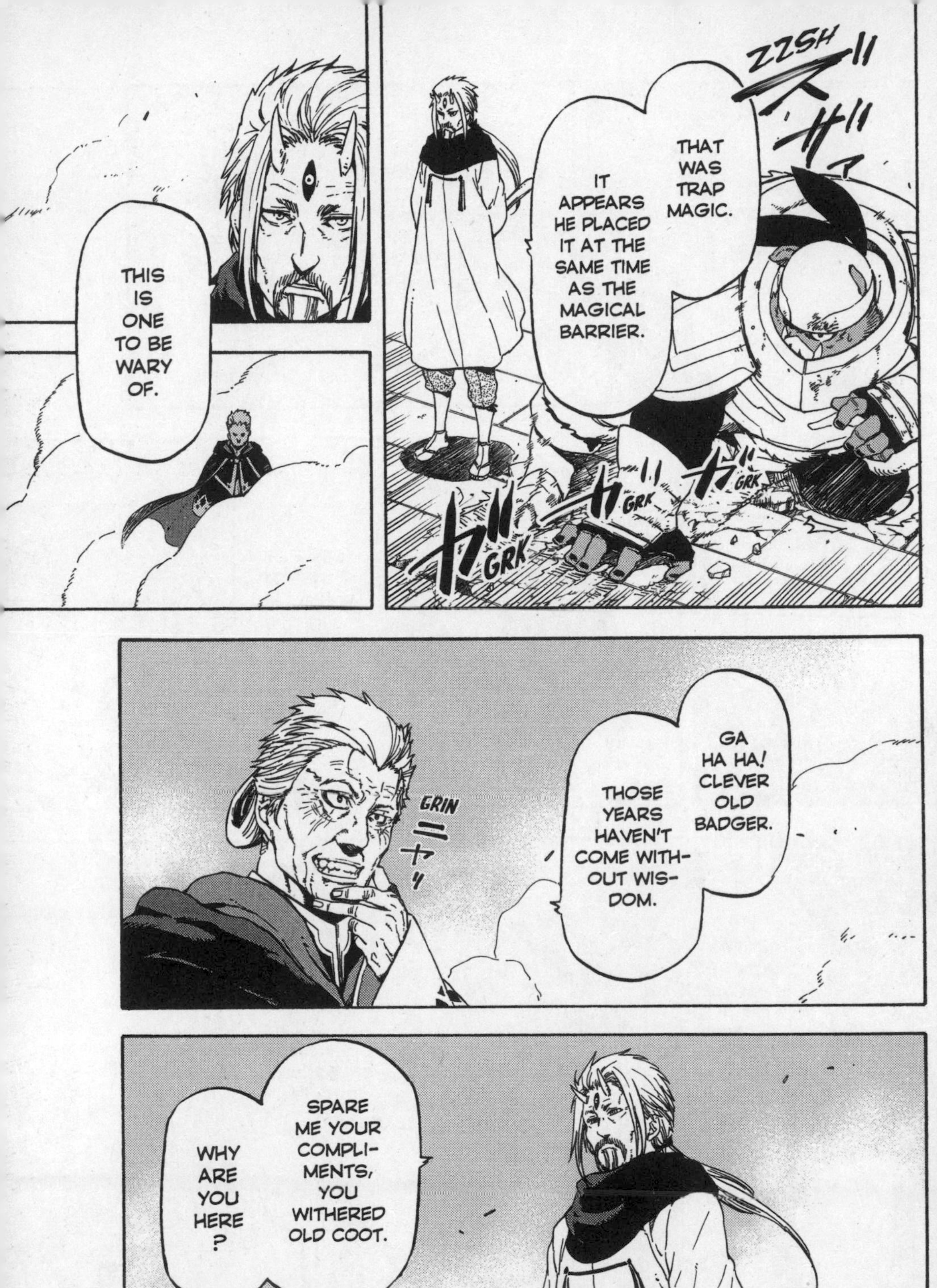
ZZSH
THAT WAS TRAP MAGIC.
IT APPEARS HE PLACED IT AT THE SAME TIME AS THE MAGICAL BARRIER.
GRK
GRK
GRK
THIS IS ONE TO BE WARY OF.
GA HA HA! CLEVER OLD BADGER.
THOSE YEARS HAVEN'T COME WITH-OUT WIS-DOM.
GRIN
SPARE ME YOUR COMPLI-MENTS, YOU WITHERED OLD COOT.
WHY ARE YOU HERE?

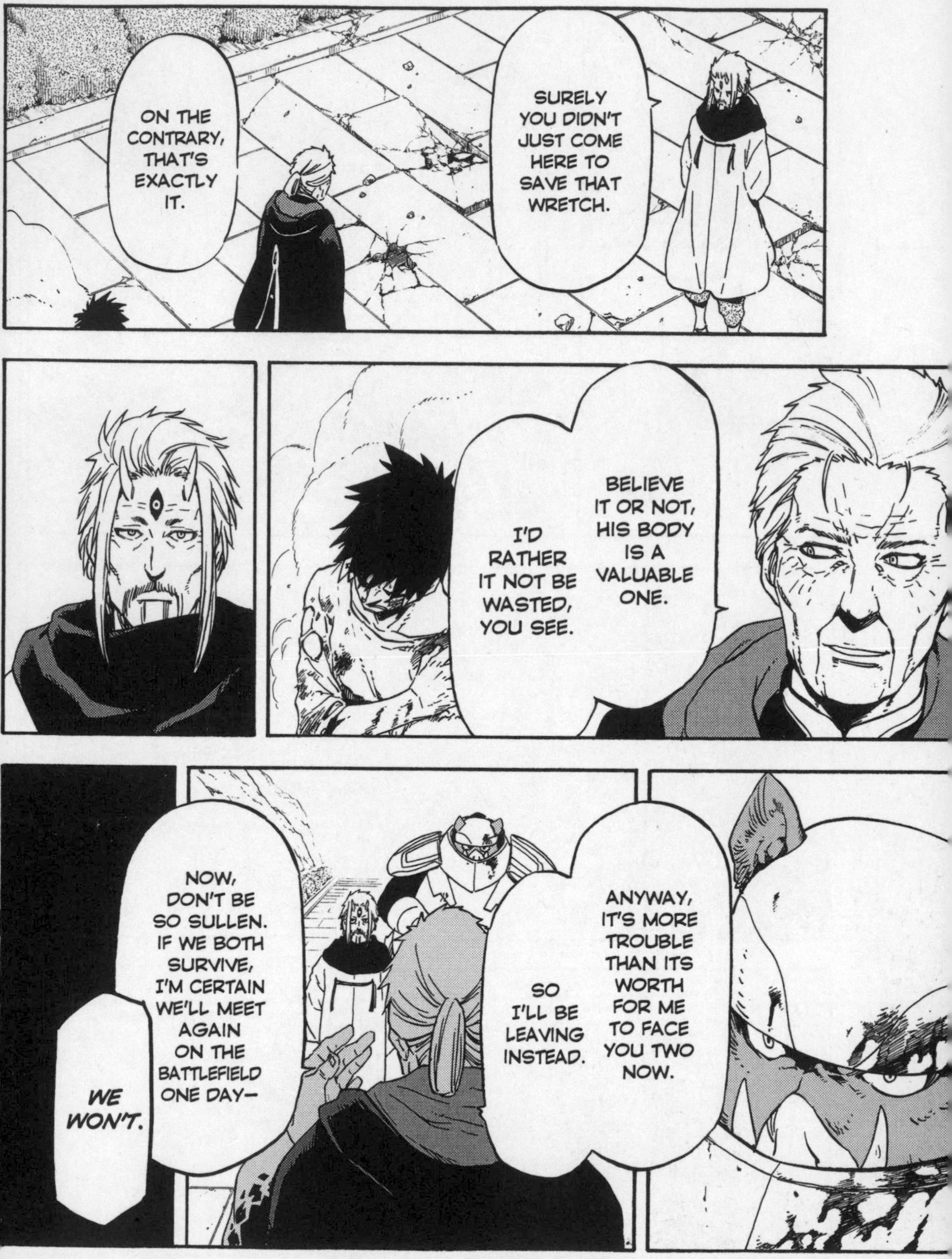
SURELY YOU DIDN'T JUST COME HERE TO SAVE THAT WRETCH.
ON THE CONTRARY, THAT'S EXACTLY IT.
BELIEVE IT OR NOT, HIS BODY IS A VALUABLE ONE.
I'D RATHER IT NOT BE WASTED, YOU SEE.
ANYWAY, IT'S MORE TROUBLE THAN ITS WORTH FOR ME TO FACE YOU TWO NOW.
SO I'LL BE LEAVING INSTEAD.
NOW, DON'T BE SO SULLEN. IF WE BOTH SURVIVE, I'M CERTAIN WE'LL MEET AGAIN ON THE BATTLEFIELD ONE DAY—
WE WON'T.

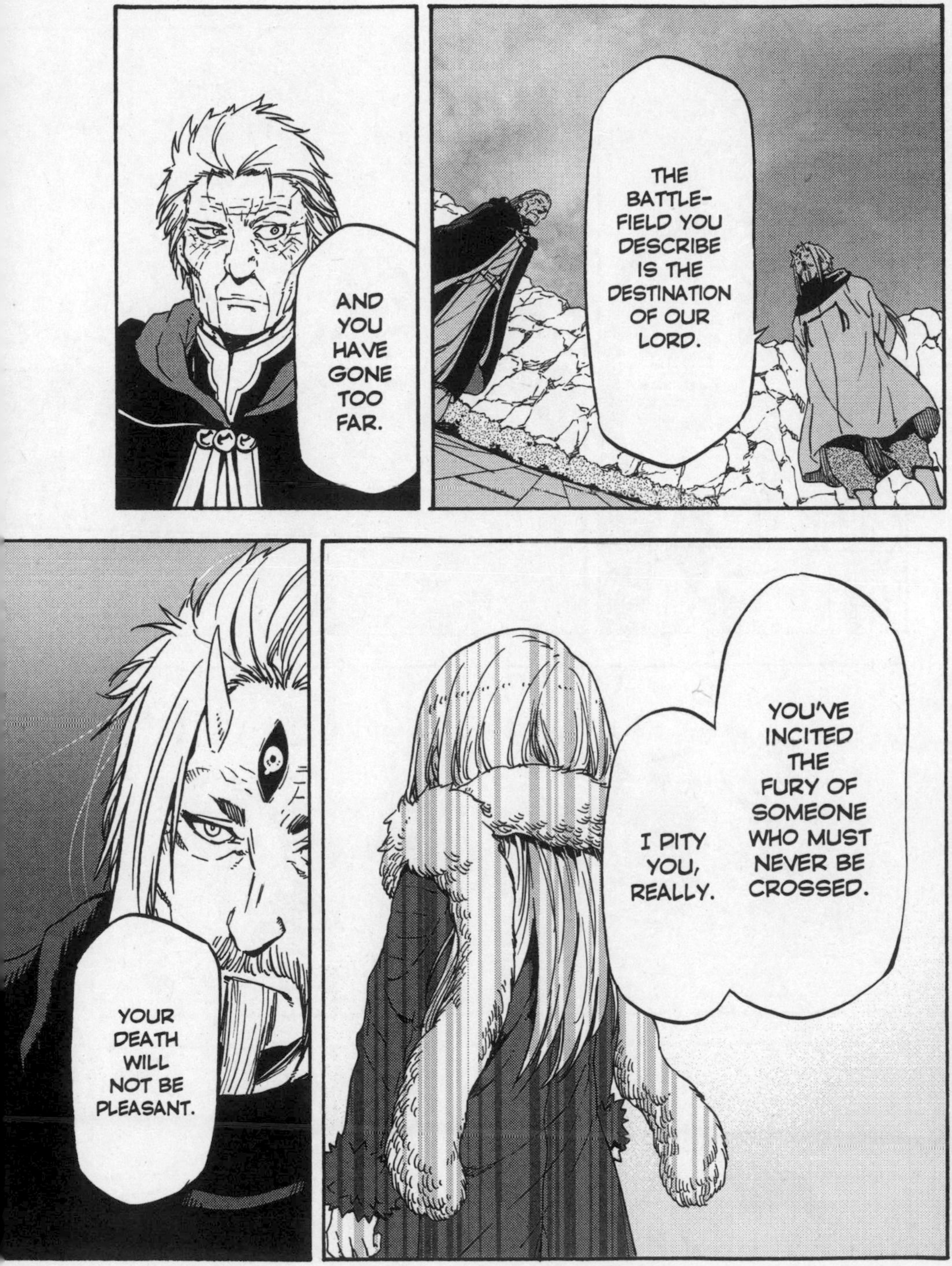
THE BATTLE-FIELD YOU DESCRIBE IS THE DESTINATION OF OUR LORD.
AND YOU HAVE GONE TOO FAR.
YOU'VE INCITED THE FURY OF SOMEONE WHO MUST NEVER BE CROSSED.
I PITY YOU, REALLY.
YOUR DEATH WILL NOT BE PLEASANT.

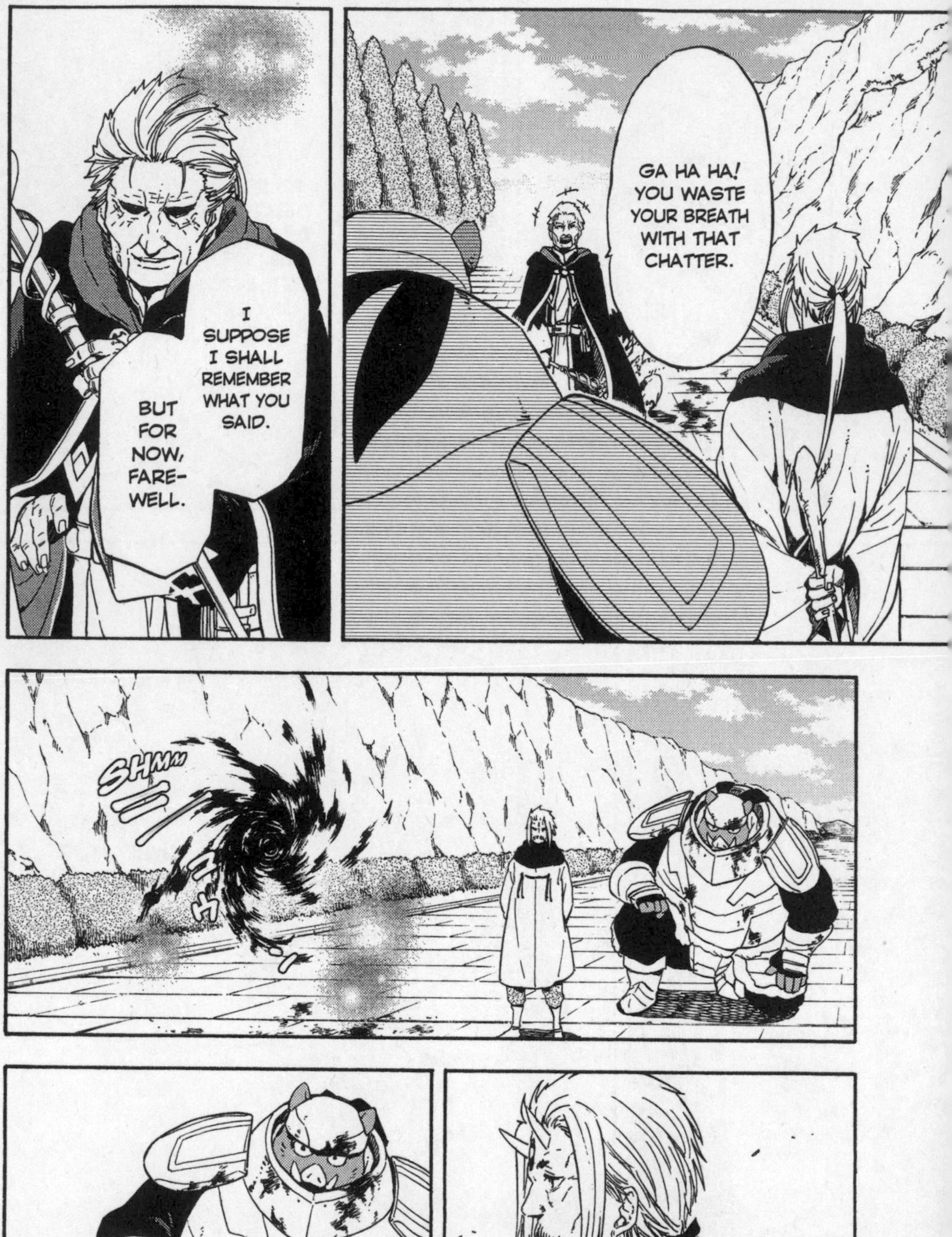
GA HA HA! YOU WASTE YOUR BREATH WITH THAT CHATTER.
I SUPPOSE I SHALL REMEMBER WHAT YOU SAID.
BUT FOR NOW, FARE-WELL.
SHMM

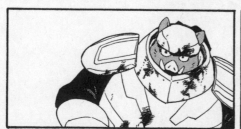

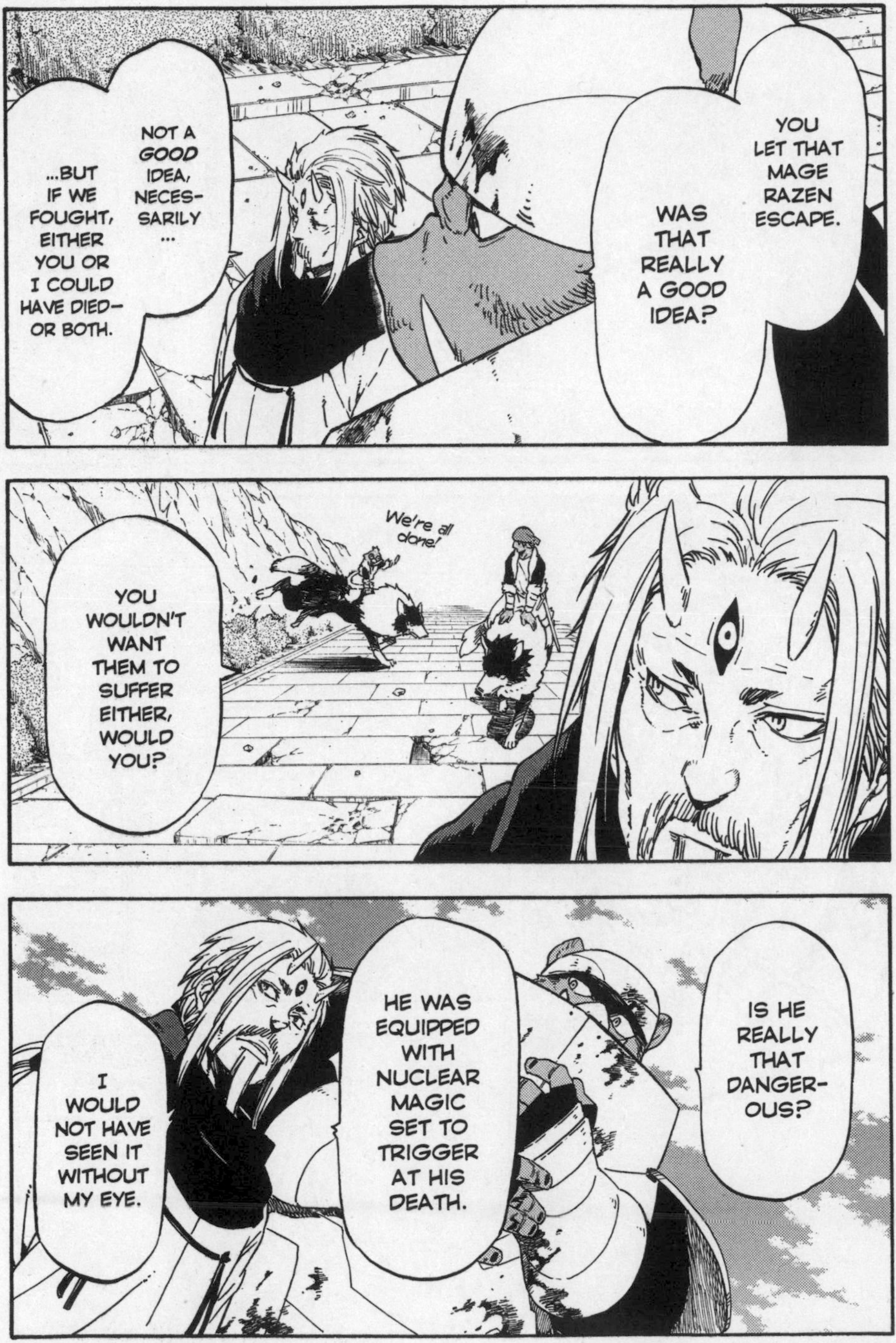
YOU LET THAT MAGE RAZEN ESCAPE.
WAS THAT REALLY A GOOD IDEA?
NOT A GOOD IDEA, NECES-SARILY...
...BUT IF WE FOUGHT, EITHER YOU OR I COULD HAVE DIED— OR BOTH.
We're all done!
YOU WOULDN'T WANT THEM TO SUFFER EITHER, WOULD YOU?
IS HE REALLY THAT DANGER-OUS?
HE WAS EQUIPPED WITH NUCLEAR MAGIC SET TO TRIGGER AT HIS DEATH.
I WOULD NOT HAVE SEEN IT WITHOUT MY EYE.

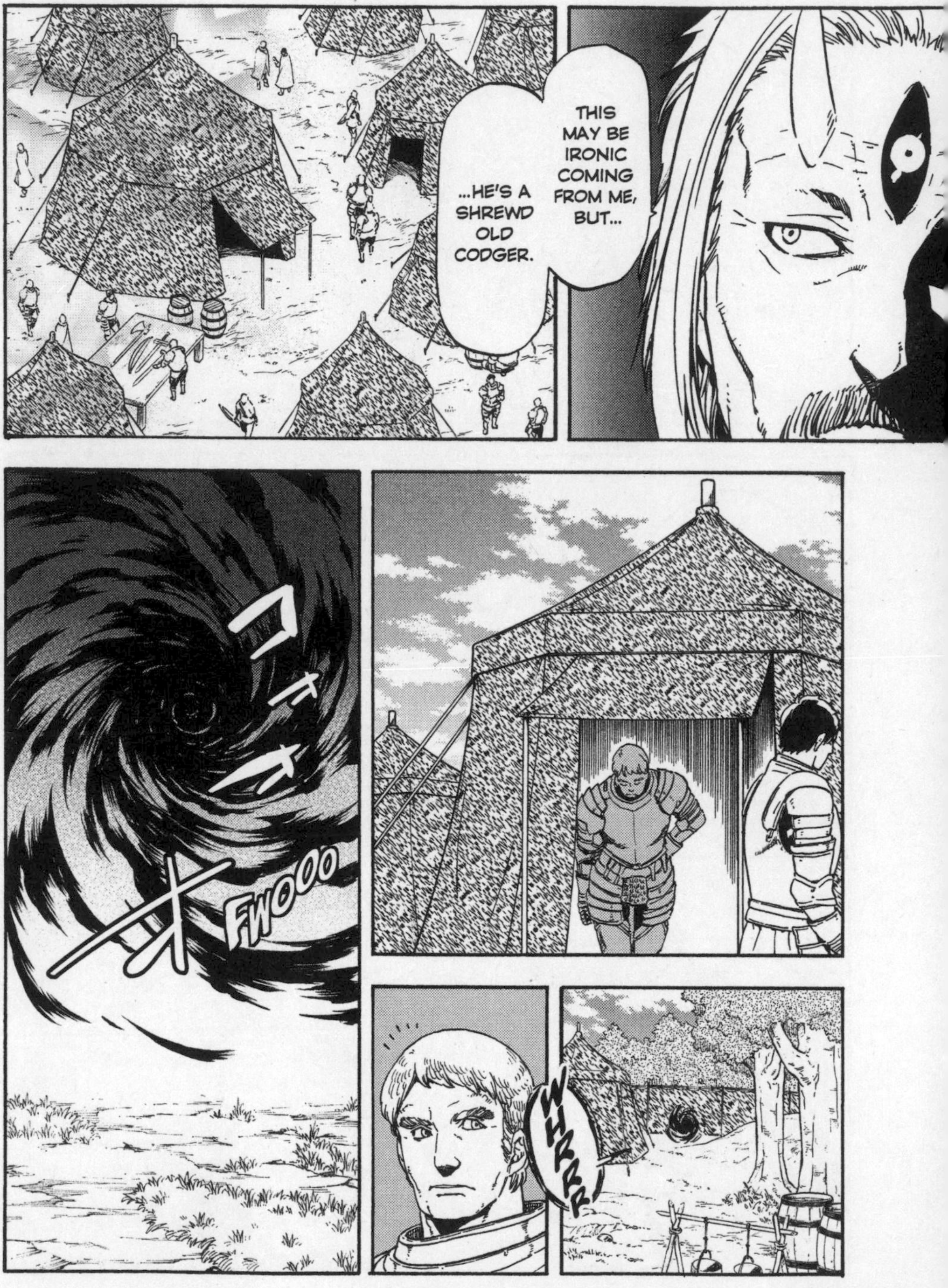
THIS MAY BE IRONIC COMING FROM ME, BUT...
...HE'S A SHREWD OLD CODGER.
WHRRR
FWOOO

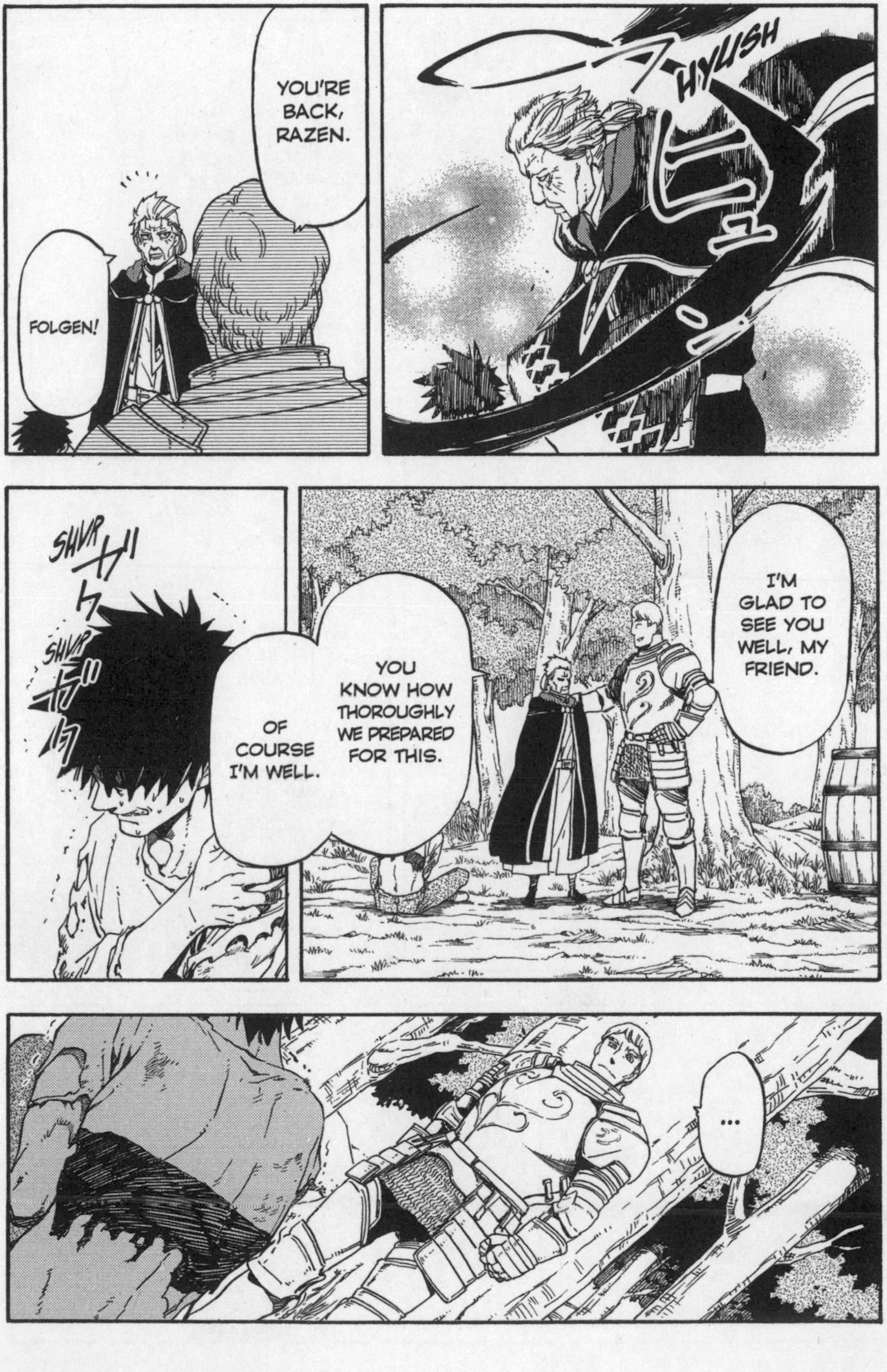
HYUSH
YOU'RE BACK, RAZEN.
FOLGEN!
I'M GLAD TO SEE YOU WELL, MY FRIEND.
YOU KNOW HOW THOROUGHLY WE PREPARED FOR THIS.
OF COURSE I'M WELL.
SHVR
SHVR
...

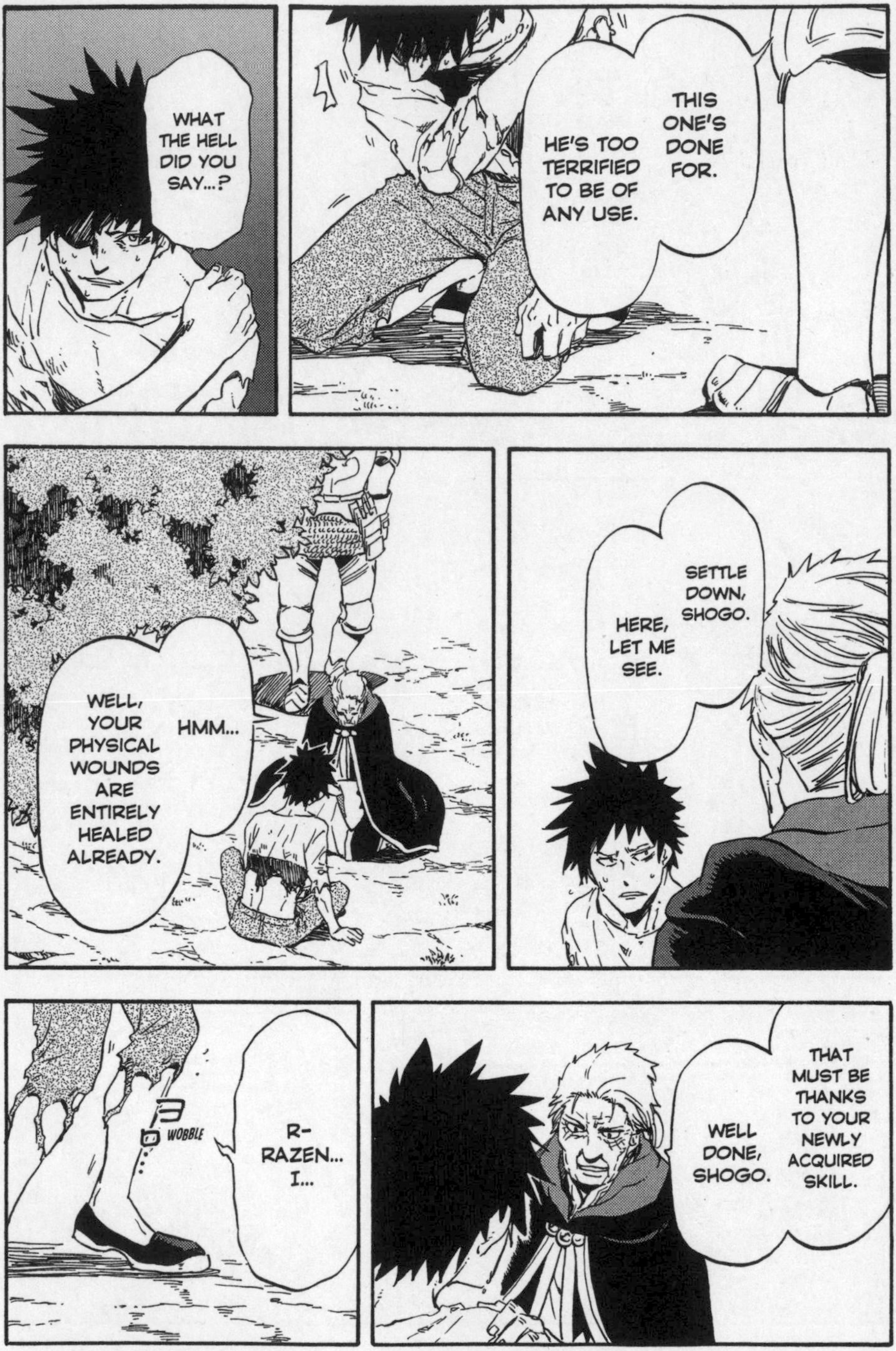
THIS ONE'S DONE FOR.
HE'S TOO TERRIFIED TO BE OF ANY USE.
WHAT THE HELL DID YOU SAY...?
SETTLE DOWN, SHOGO.
HERE, LET ME SEE.
HMM...
WELL, YOUR PHYSICAL WOUNDS ARE ENTIRELY HEALED ALREADY.
THAT MUST BE THANKS TO YOUR NEWLY ACQUIRED SKILL.
WELL DONE, SHOGO.
R-RAZEN... I...
WOBBLE

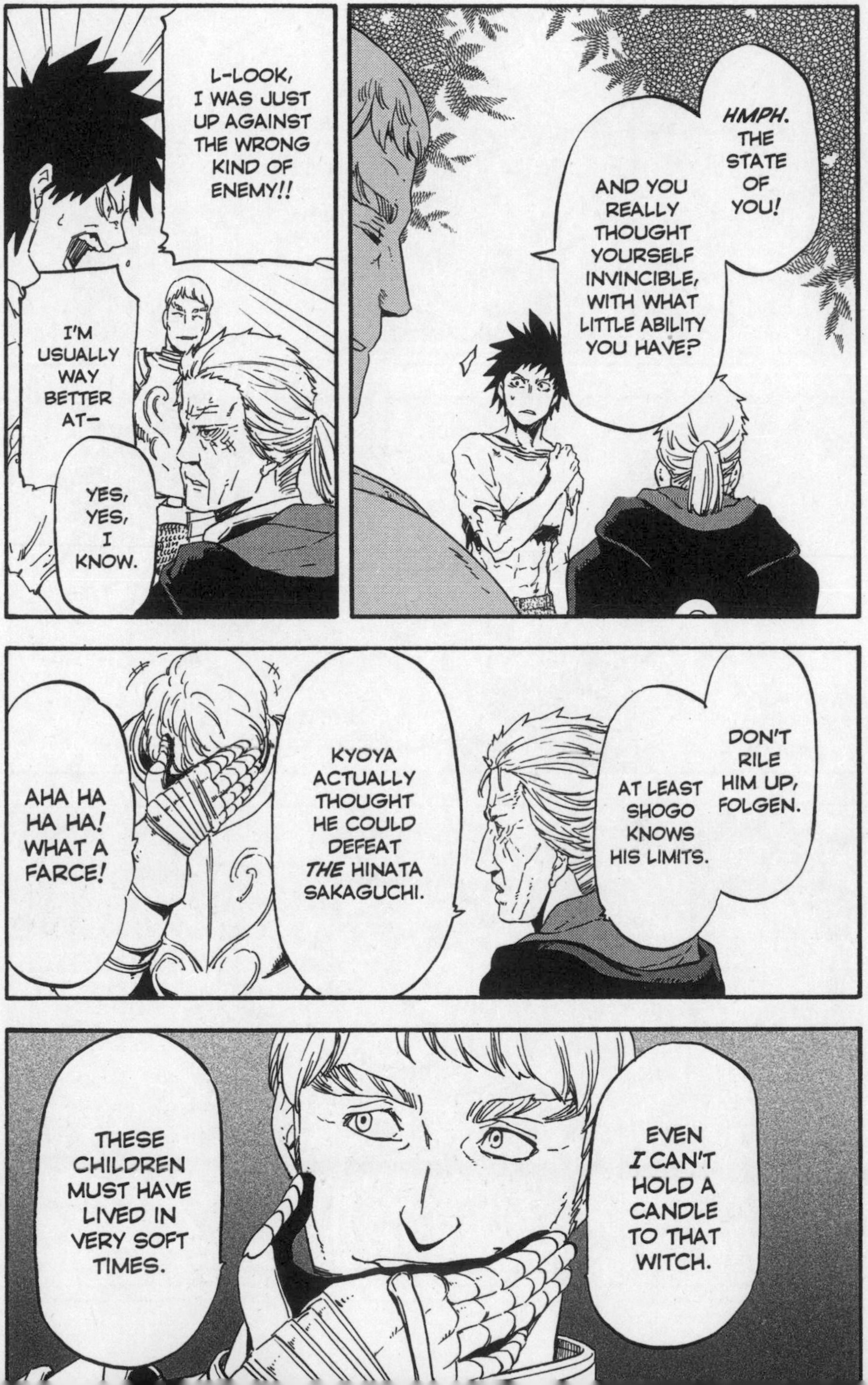
HMPH. THE STATE OF YOU!
AND YOU REALLY THOUGHT YOURSELF INVINCIBLE, WITH WHAT LITTLE ABILITY YOU HAVE?
L-LOOK, I WAS JUST UP AGAINST THE WRONG KIND OF ENEMY!!
I'M USUALLY WAY BETTER AT—
YES, YES, I KNOW.
DON'T RILE HIM UP, FOLGEN.
AT LEAST SHOGO KNOWS HIS LIMITS.
KYOYA ACTUALLY THOUGHT HE COULD DEFEAT THE HINATA SAKAGUCHI.
AHA HA HA HA! WHAT A FARCE!
EVEN I CAN'T HOLD A CANDLE TO THAT WITCH.
THESE CHILDREN MUST HAVE LIVED IN VERY SOFT TIMES.

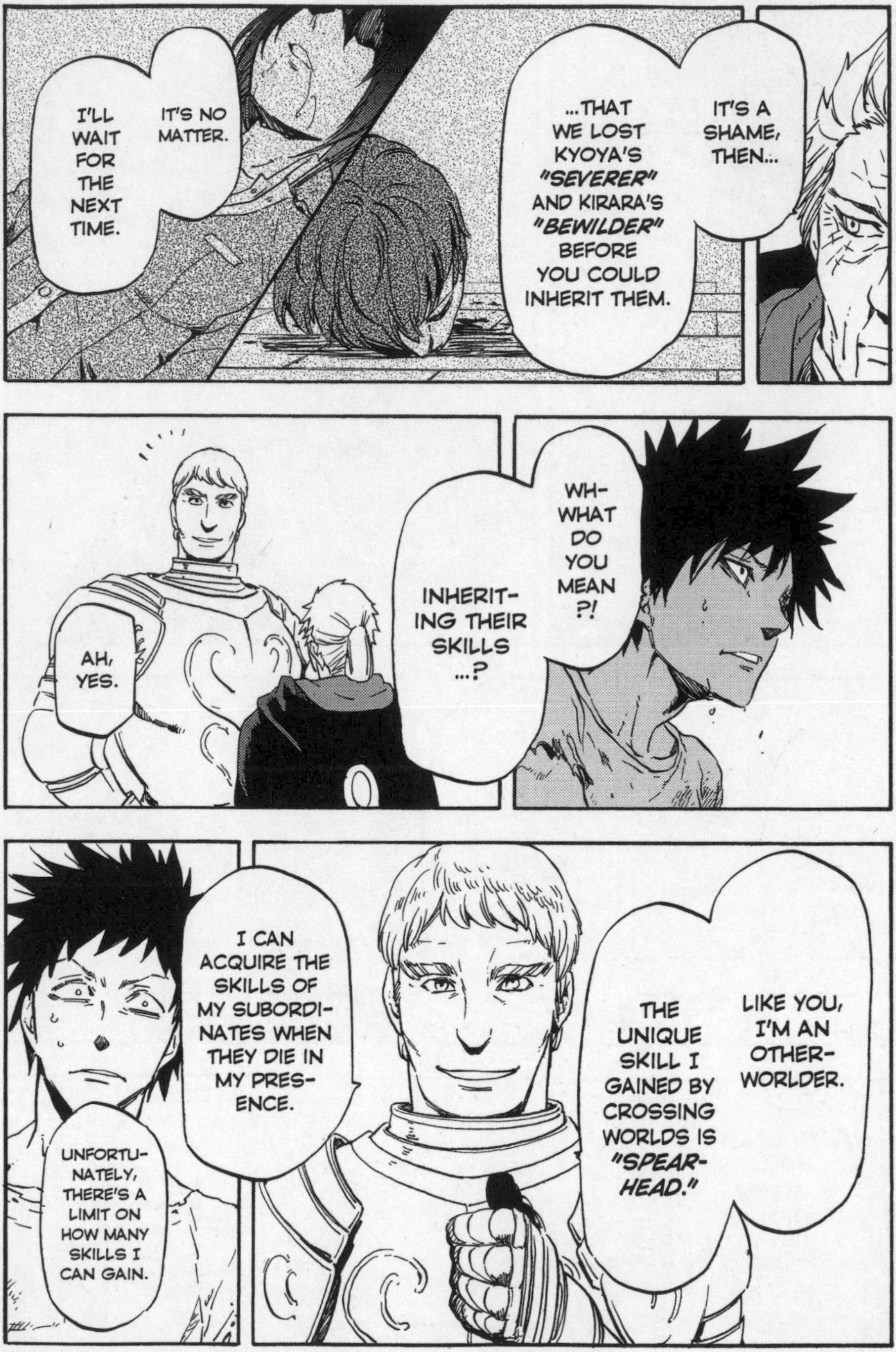
IT'S A SHAME, THEN...
...THAT WE LOST KYOYA'S "SEVERER" AND KIRARA'S "BEWILDER" BEFORE YOU COULD INHERIT THEM.
IT'S NO MATTER.
I'LL WAIT FOR THE NEXT TIME.
WH-WHAT DO YOU MEAN?!
INHERITING THEIR SKILLS...?
AH, YES.
LIKE YOU, I'M AN OTHERWORLDER.
THE UNIQUE SKILL I GAINED BY CROSSING WORLDS IS "SPEARHEAD."
I CAN ACQUIRE THE SKILLS OF MY SUBORDINATES WHEN THEY DIE IN MY PRESENCE.
UNFORTUNATELY, THERE'S A LIMIT ON HOW MANY SKILLS I CAN GAIN.

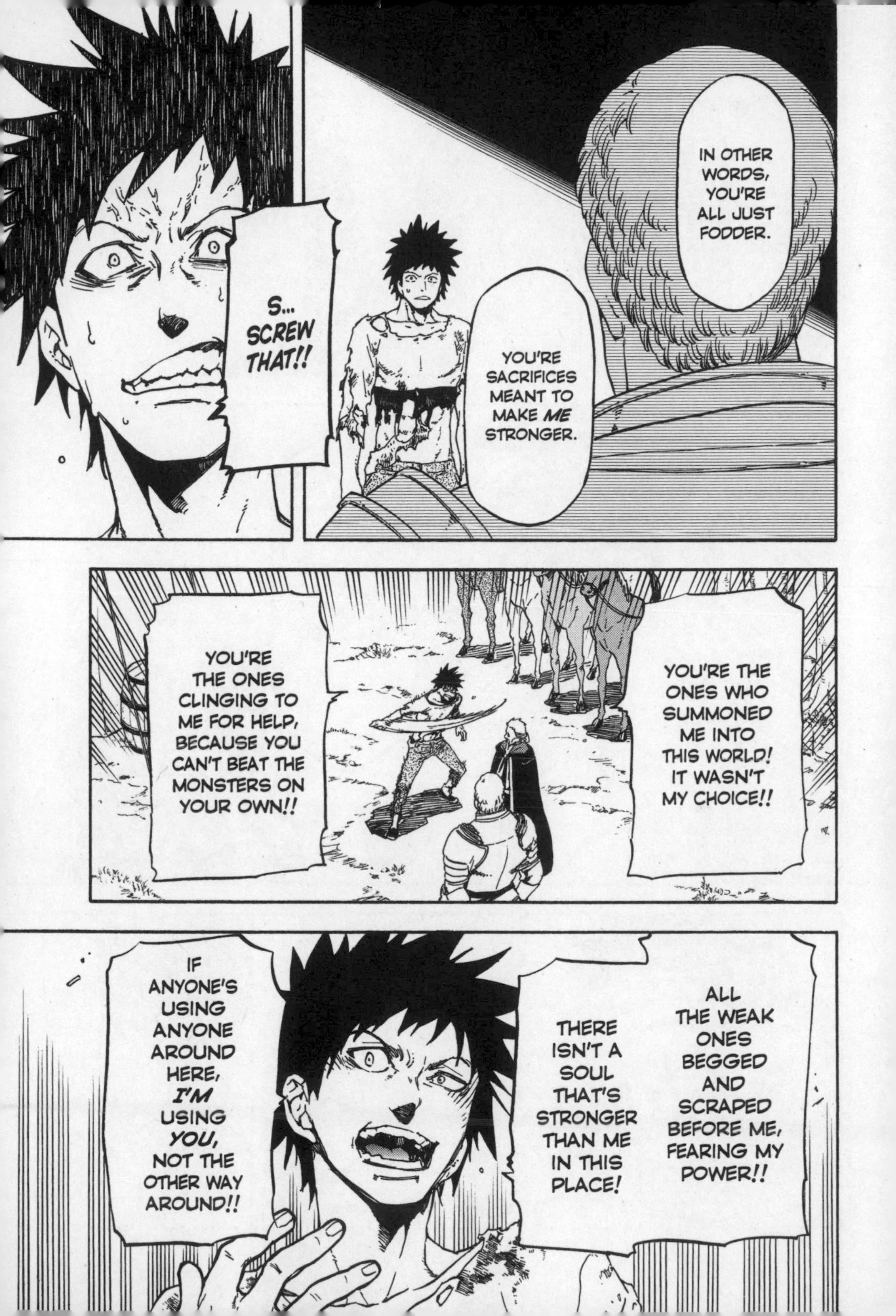
IN OTHER WORDS, YOU'RE ALL JUST FODDER.
YOU'RE SACRIFICES MEANT TO MAKE *ME* STRONGER.
S... SCREW THAT!!
YOU'RE THE ONES WHO SUMMONED ME INTO THIS WORLD! IT WASN'T MY CHOICE!!
YOU'RE THE ONES CLINGING TO ME FOR HELP, BECAUSE YOU CAN'T BEAT THE MONSTERS ON YOUR OWN!!
ALL THE WEAK ONES BEGGED AND SCRAPED BEFORE ME, FEARING MY POWER!!
THERE ISN'T A SOUL THAT'S STRONGER THAN ME IN THIS PLACE!
IF ANYONE'S USING ANYONE AROUND HERE, *I'M* USING *YOU*, NOT THE OTHER WAY AROUND!!

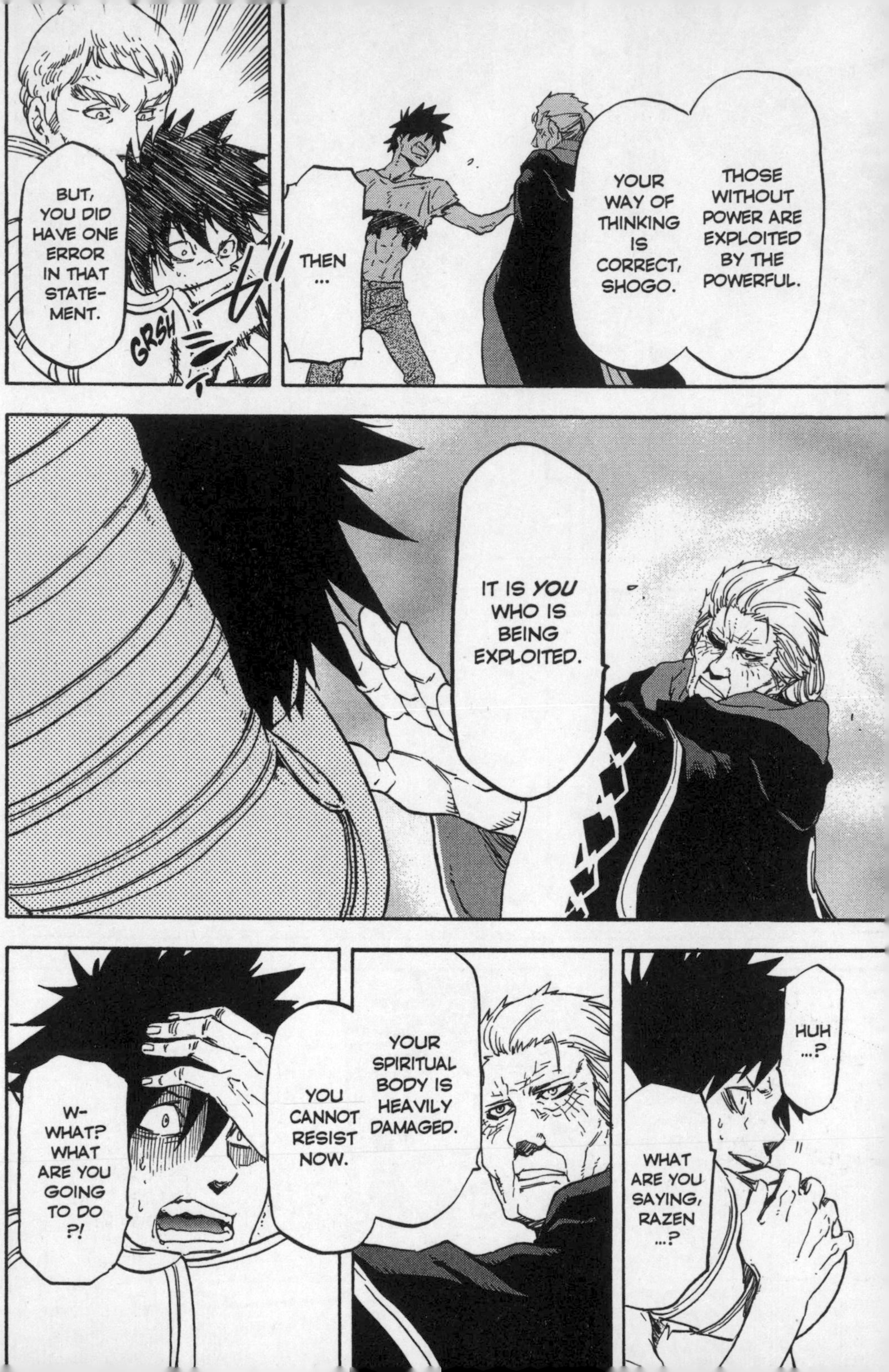
THOSE WITHOUT POWER ARE EXPLOITED BY THE POWERFUL.
YOUR WAY OF THINKING IS CORRECT, SHOGO.
THEN ...
BUT, YOU DID HAVE ONE ERROR IN THAT STATEMENT.
GRSH
IT IS *YOU* WHO IS BEING EXPLOITED.
HUH ...?
WHAT ARE YOU SAYING, RAZEN ...?
YOUR SPIRITUAL BODY IS HEAVILY DAMAGED.
YOU CANNOT RESIST NOW.
W-WHAT? WHAT ARE YOU GOING TO DO ?!

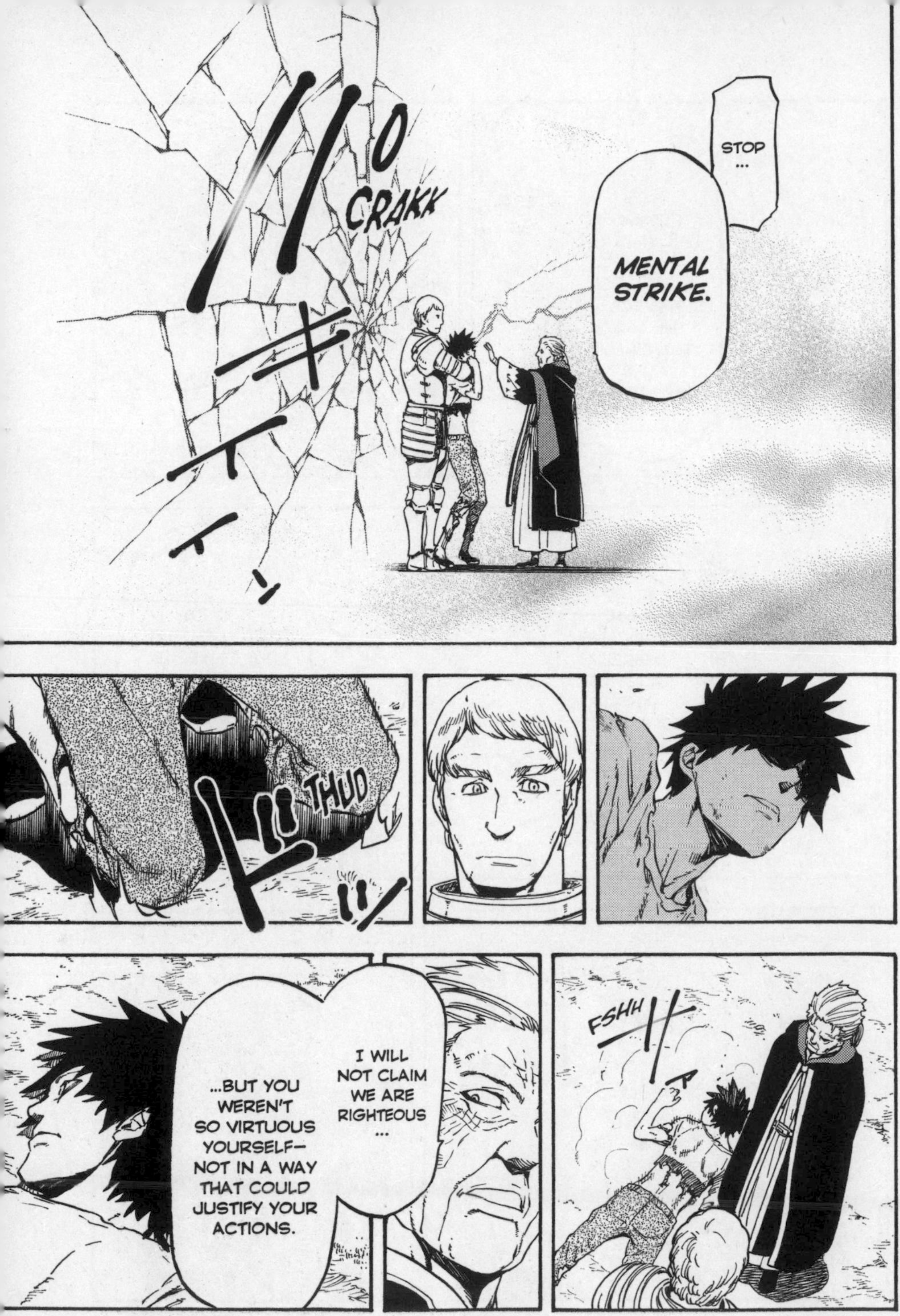
STOP ...
MENTAL STRIKE.
CRAKK
THUD
FSHH
I WILL NOT CLAIM WE ARE RIGHTEOUS ...
...BUT YOU WEREN'T SO VIRTUOUS YOURSELF— NOT IN A WAY THAT COULD JUSTIFY YOUR ACTIONS.

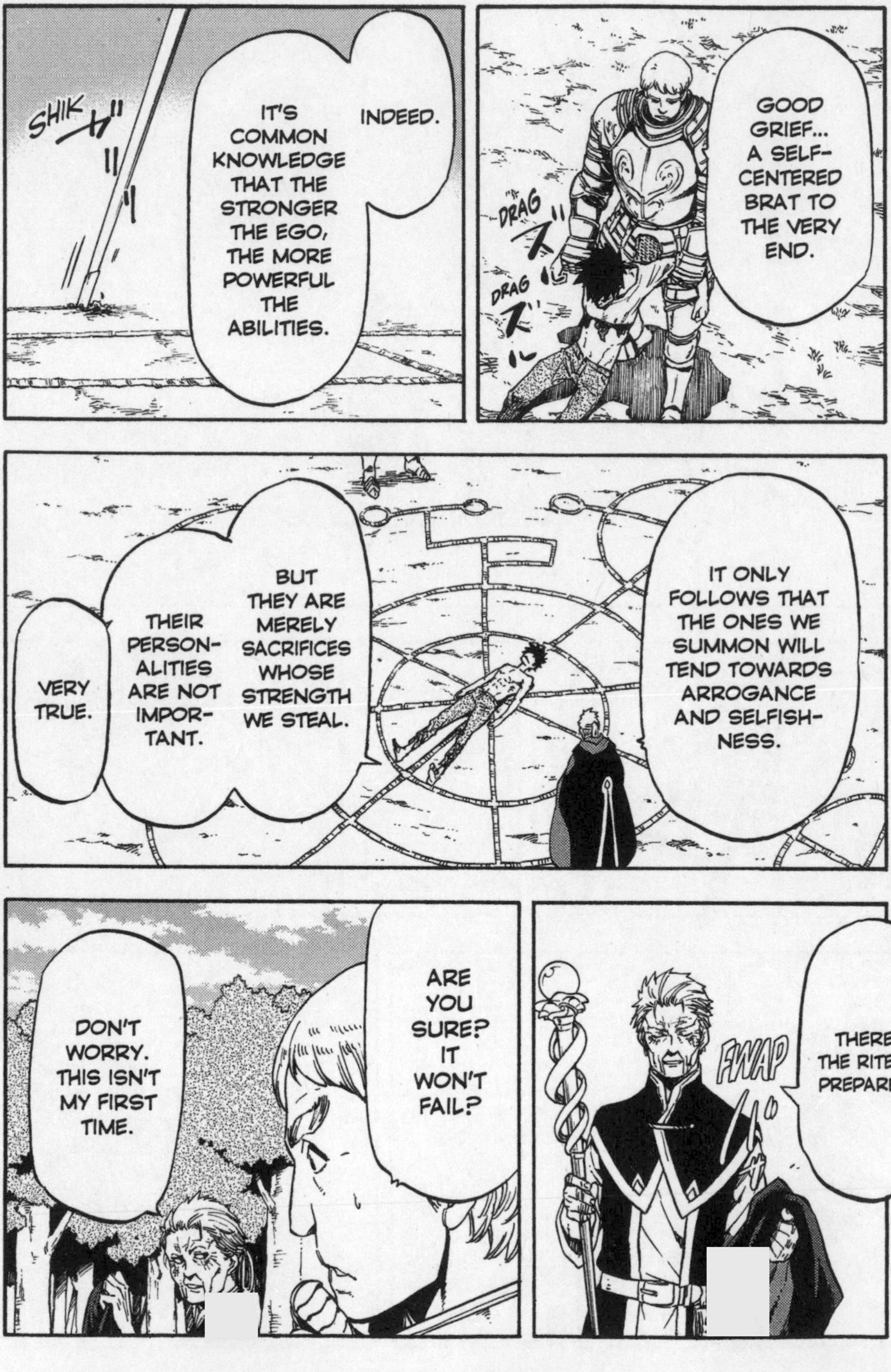
DRAG
DRAG
GOOD GRIEF... A SELF-CENTERED BRAT TO THE VERY END.
INDEED.
IT'S COMMON KNOWLEDGE THAT THE STRONGER THE EGO, THE MORE POWERFUL THE ABILITIES.
SHIK
IT ONLY FOLLOWS THAT THE ONES WE SUMMON WILL TEND TOWARDS ARROGANCE AND SELFISHNESS.
BUT THEY ARE MERELY SACRIFICES WHOSE STRENGTH WE STEAL.
THEIR PERSONALITIES ARE NOT IMPORTANT.
VERY TRUE.
THERE... THE RITE IS PREPARED.
FWAP
ARE YOU SURE? IT WON'T FAIL?
DON'T WORRY. THIS ISN'T MY FIRST TIME.

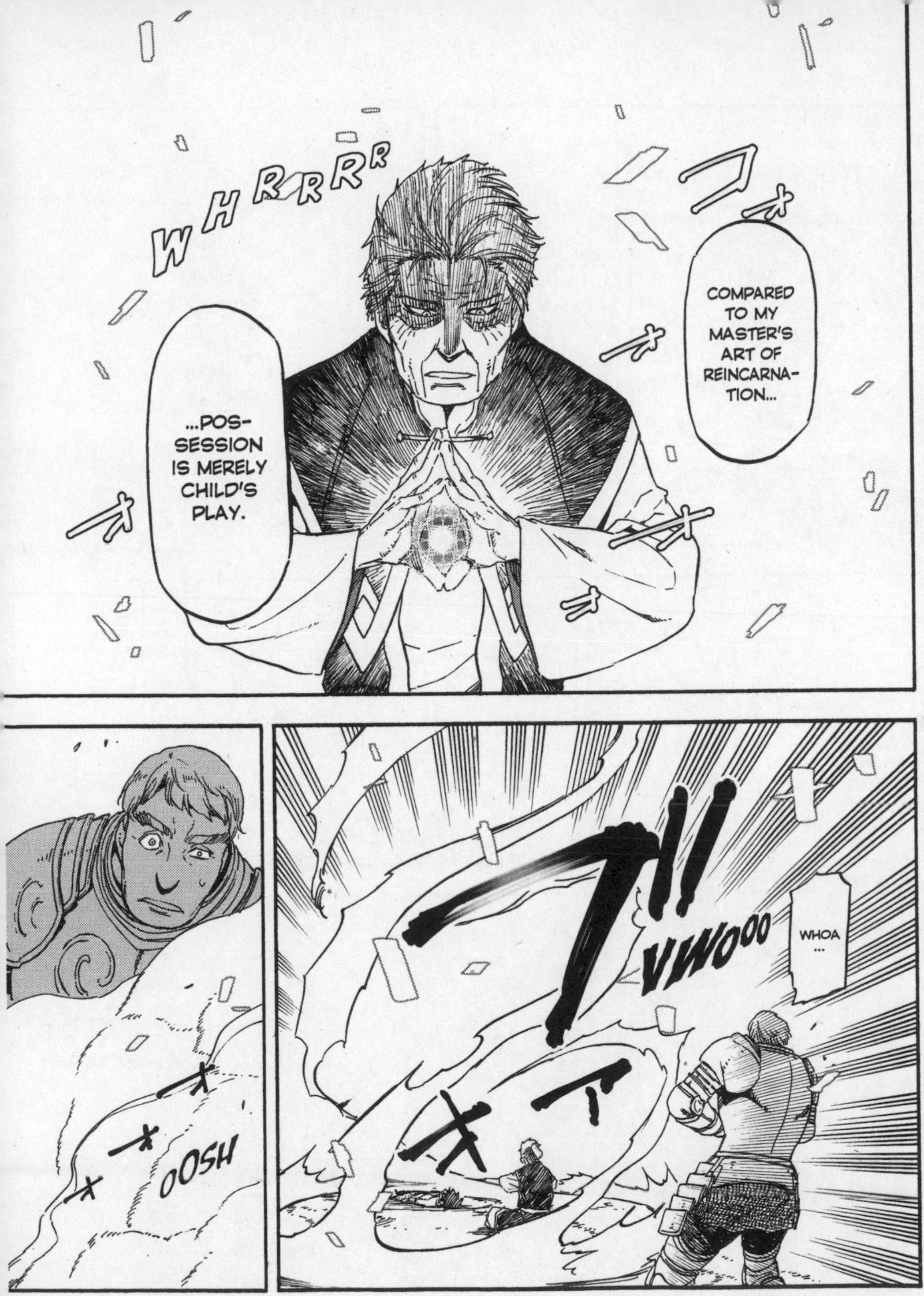
WHRRRR
COMPARED TO MY MASTER'S ART OF REINCARNATION...
...POSSESSION IS MERELY CHILD'S PLAY.
VWOOO
WHOA ...
OOSH

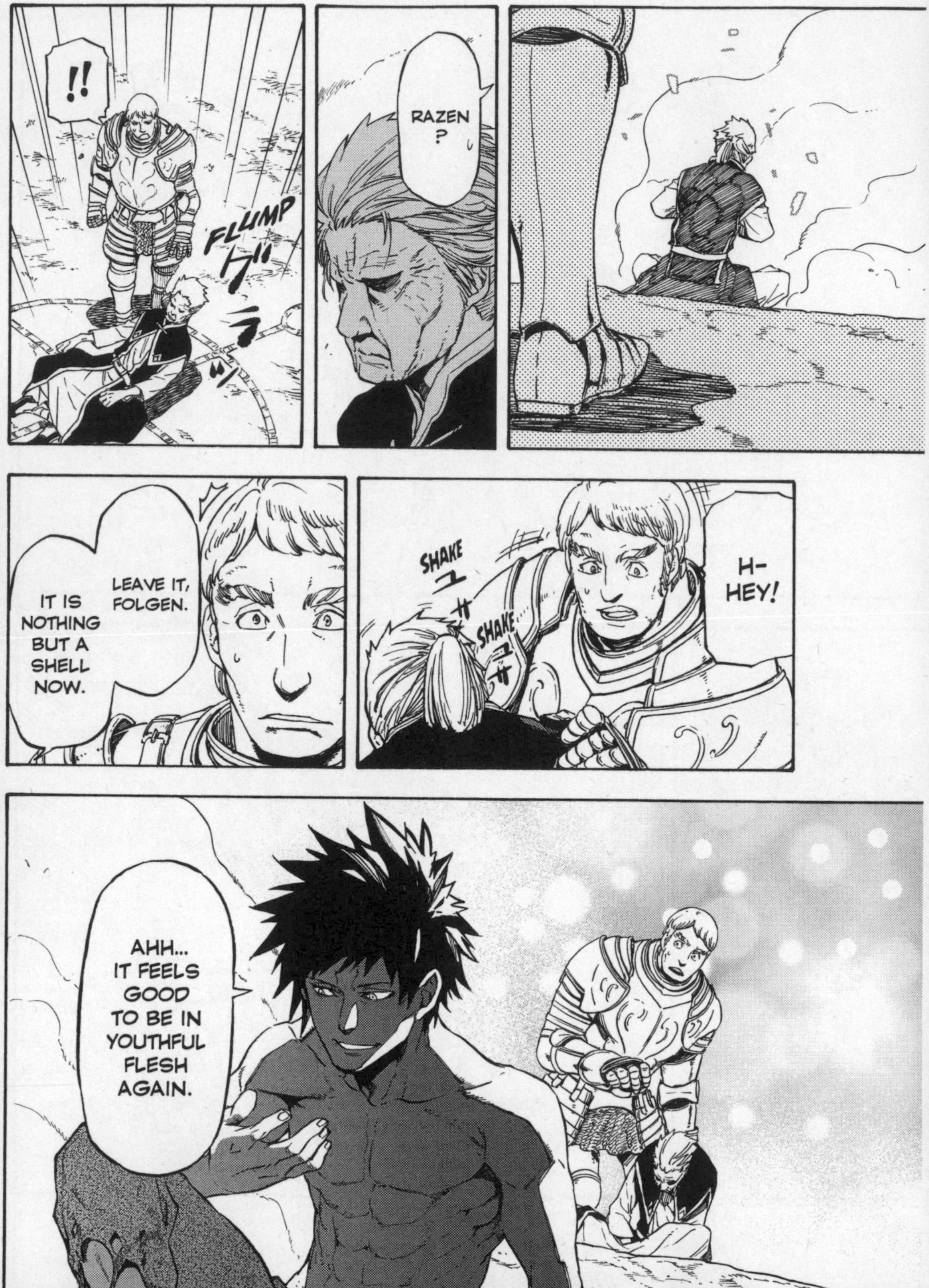
RAZEN ?
!!
FLUMP
H- HEY!
SHAKE
SHAKE
LEAVE IT, FOLGEN.
IT IS NOTHING BUT A SHELL NOW.
AHH... IT FEELS GOOD TO BE IN YOUTHFUL FLESH AGAIN.

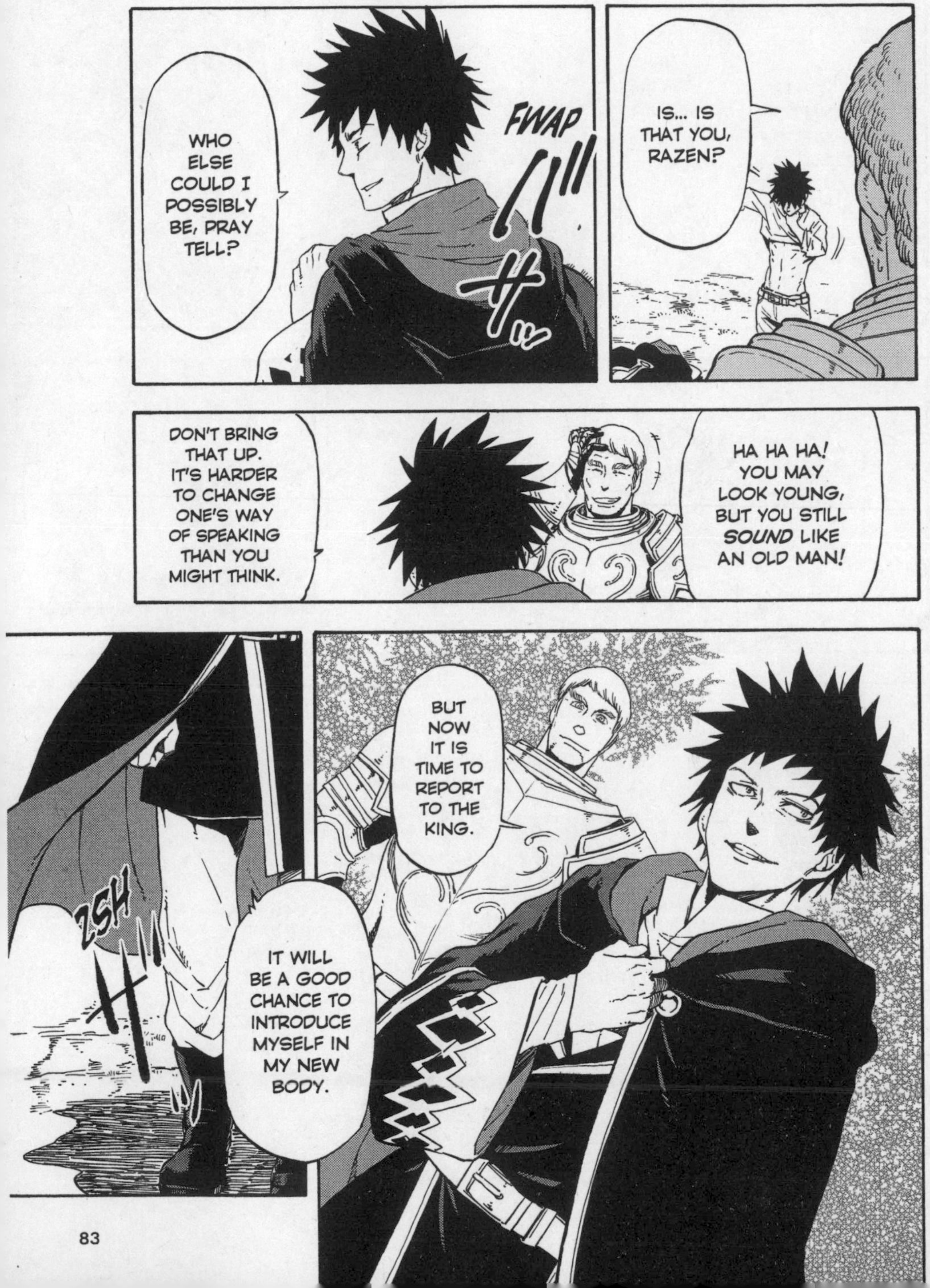
IS... IS THAT YOU, RAZEN?
FWAP
WHO ELSE COULD I POSSIBLY BE, PRAY TELL?
HA HA HA! YOU MAY LOOK YOUNG, BUT YOU STILL *SOUND* LIKE AN OLD MAN!
DON'T BRING THAT UP. IT'S HARDER TO CHANGE ONE'S WAY OF SPEAKING THAN YOU MIGHT THINK.
BUT NOW IT IS TIME TO REPORT TO THE KING.
IT WILL BE A GOOD CHANCE TO INTRODUCE MYSELF IN MY NEW BODY.
ZSH

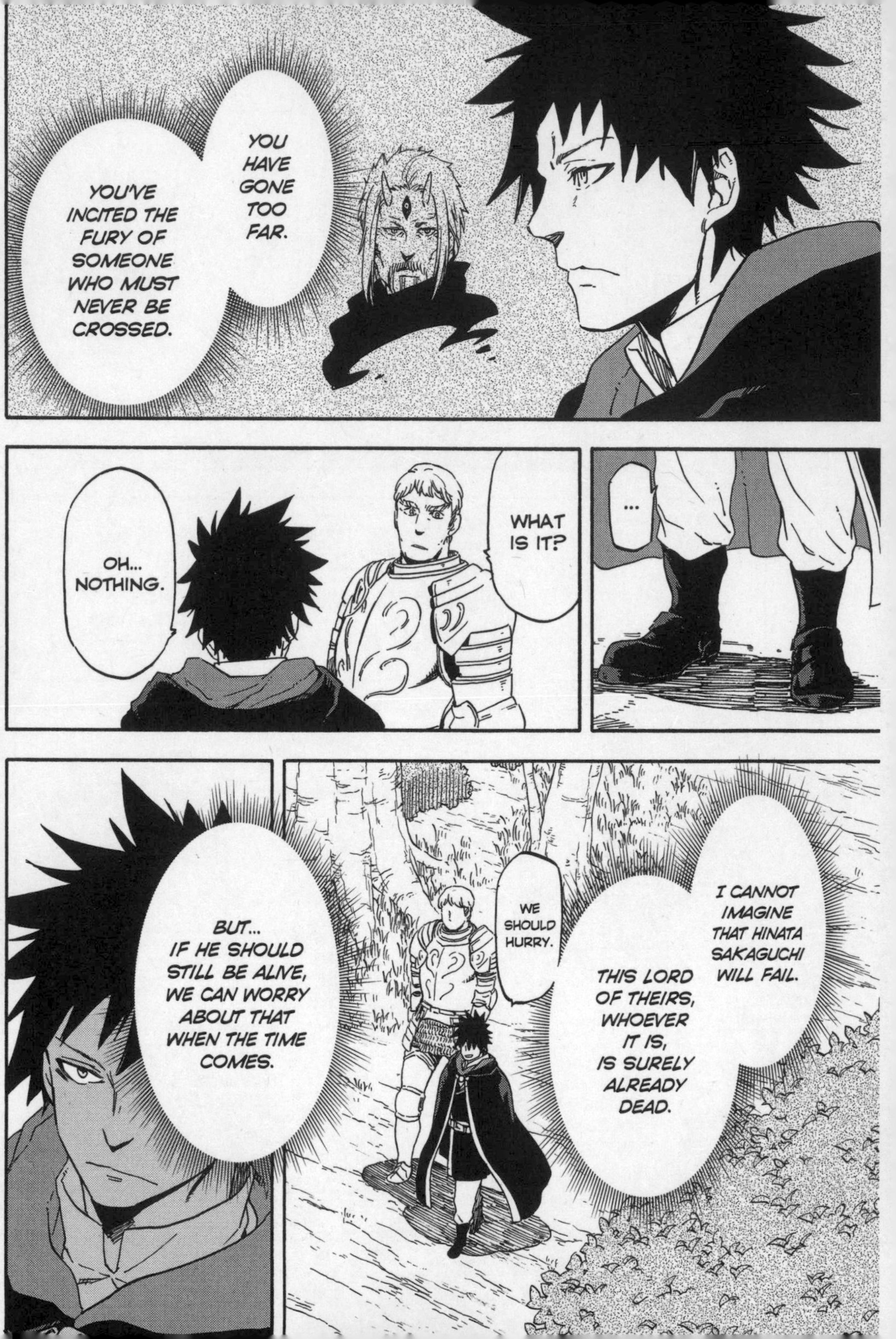
YOU HAVE GONE TOO FAR.
YOU'VE INCITED THE FURY OF SOMEONE WHO MUST NEVER BE CROSSED.
...
WHAT IS IT?
OH... NOTHING.
I CANNOT IMAGINE THAT HINATA SAKAGUCHI WILL FAIL.
THIS LORD OF THEIRS, WHOEVER IT IS, IS SURELY ALREADY DEAD.
WE SHOULD HURRY.
BUT... IF HE SHOULD STILL BE ALIVE, WE CAN WORRY ABOUT THAT WHEN THE TIME COMES.

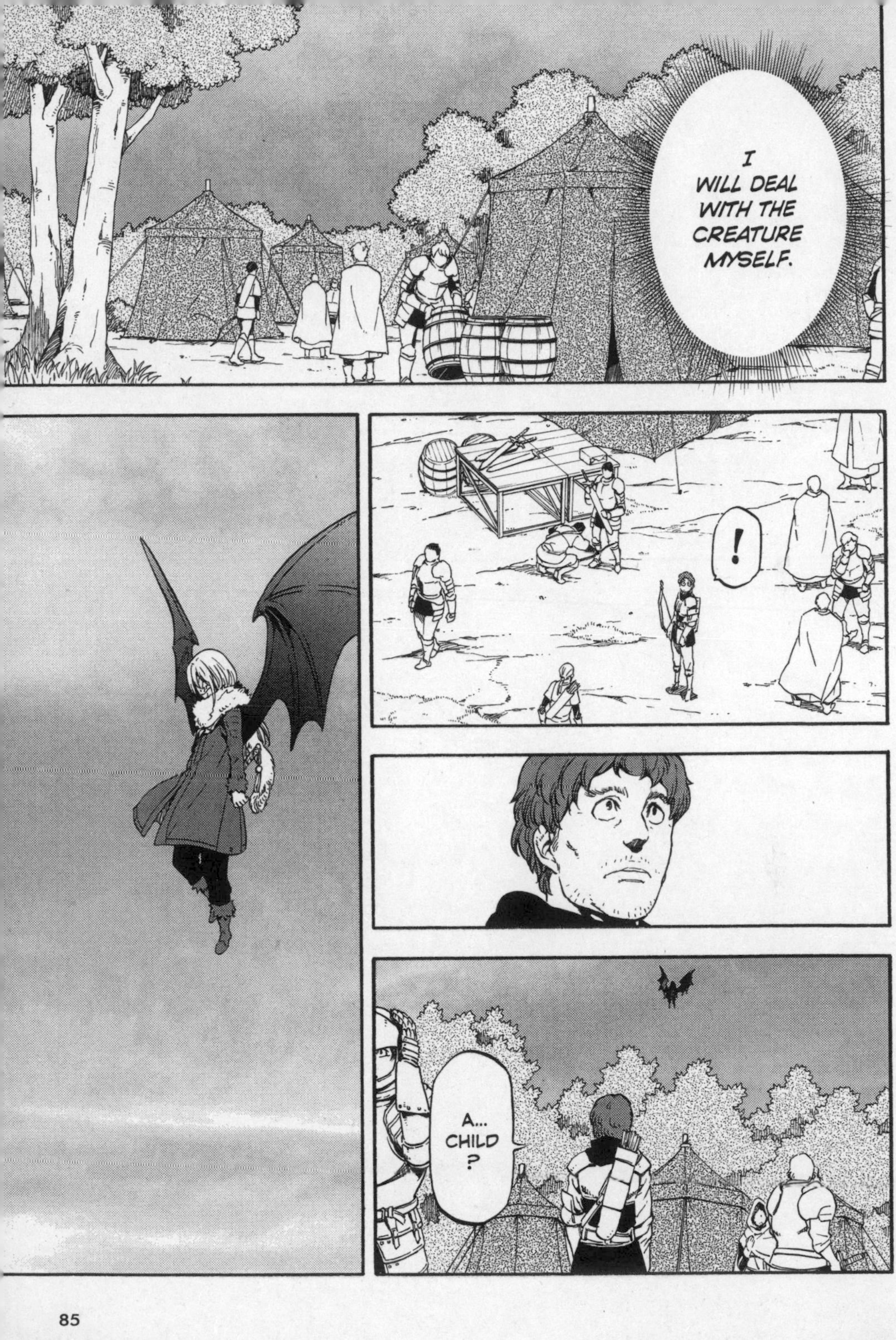
I WILL DEAL WITH THE CREATURE MYSELF.
!
A... CHILD?

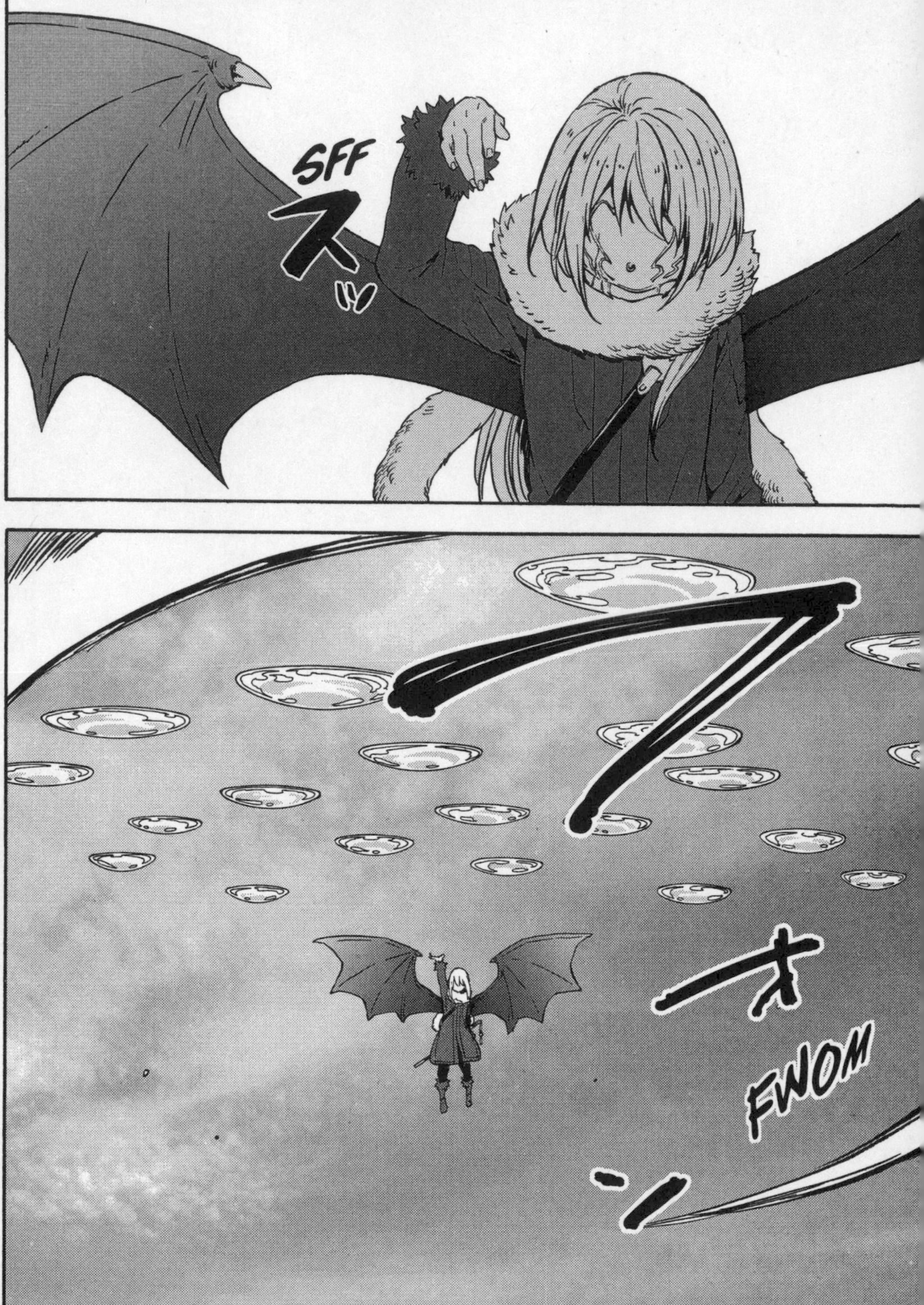
SFF
スッ
FWOM
オ
ー

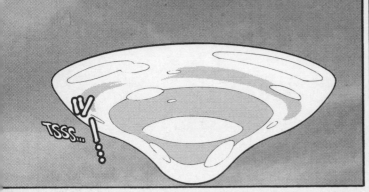

TSSS...

PLIP

MURMUR

MURMUR

HEY, WHAT'S THAT?

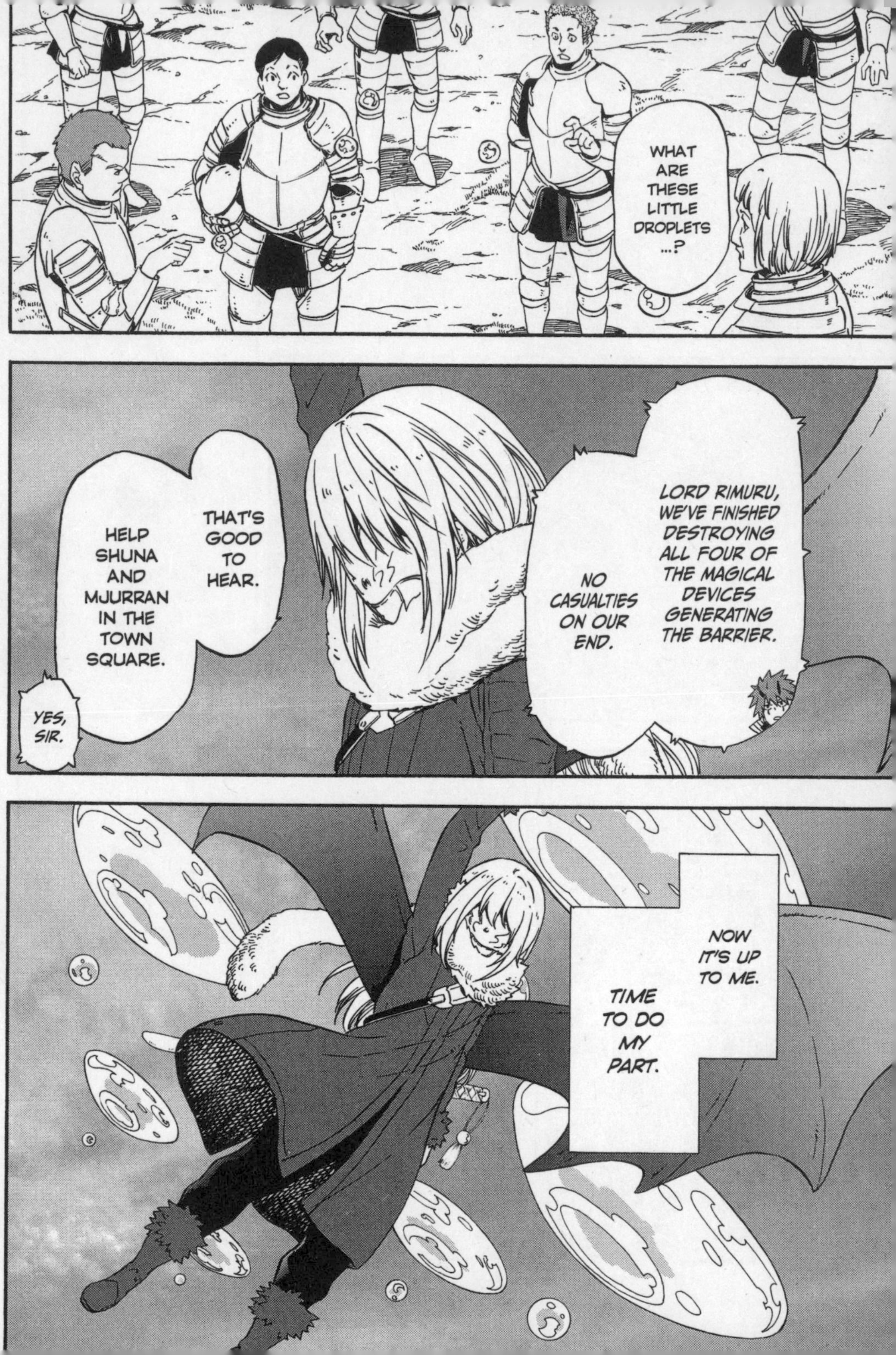
WHAT ARE THESE LITTLE DROPLETS ...?
LORD RIMURU, WE'VE FINISHED DESTROYING ALL FOUR OF THE MAGICAL DEVICES GENERATING THE BARRIER.
NO CASUALTIES ON OUR END.
THAT'S GOOD TO HEAR.
HELP SHUNA AND MJURRAN IN THE TOWN SQUARE.
YES, SIR.
NOW IT'S UP TO ME.
TIME TO DO MY PART.

YOU HUMANS HAVE RAN-SACKED MY TERRITORY...
MURMUR
MURMUR
...AND YOU MUST PAY FOR THIS CRIME WITH YOUR LIVES.
MURMUR

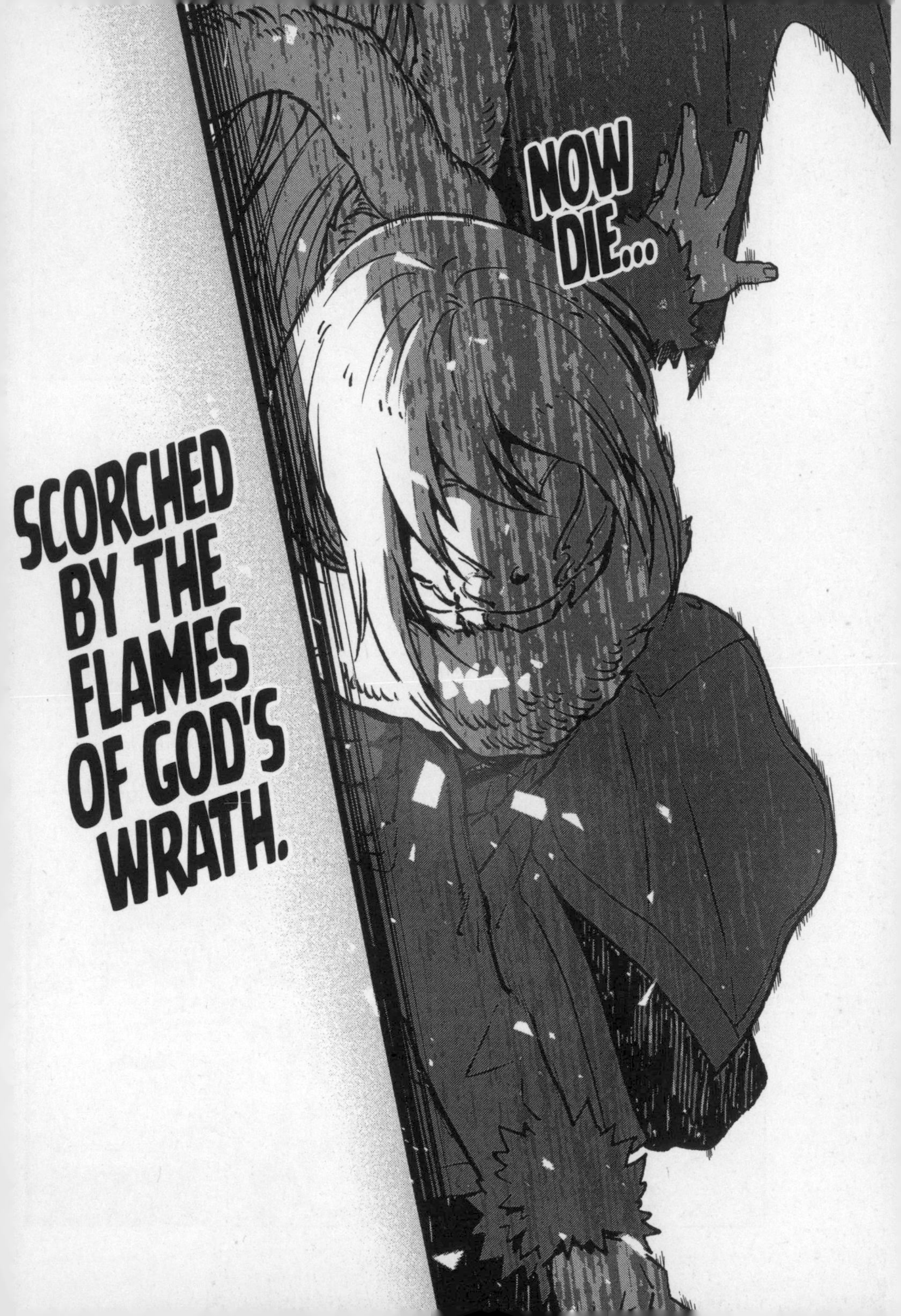
NOW DIE...
SCORCHED BY THE FLAMES OF GOD'S WRATH.

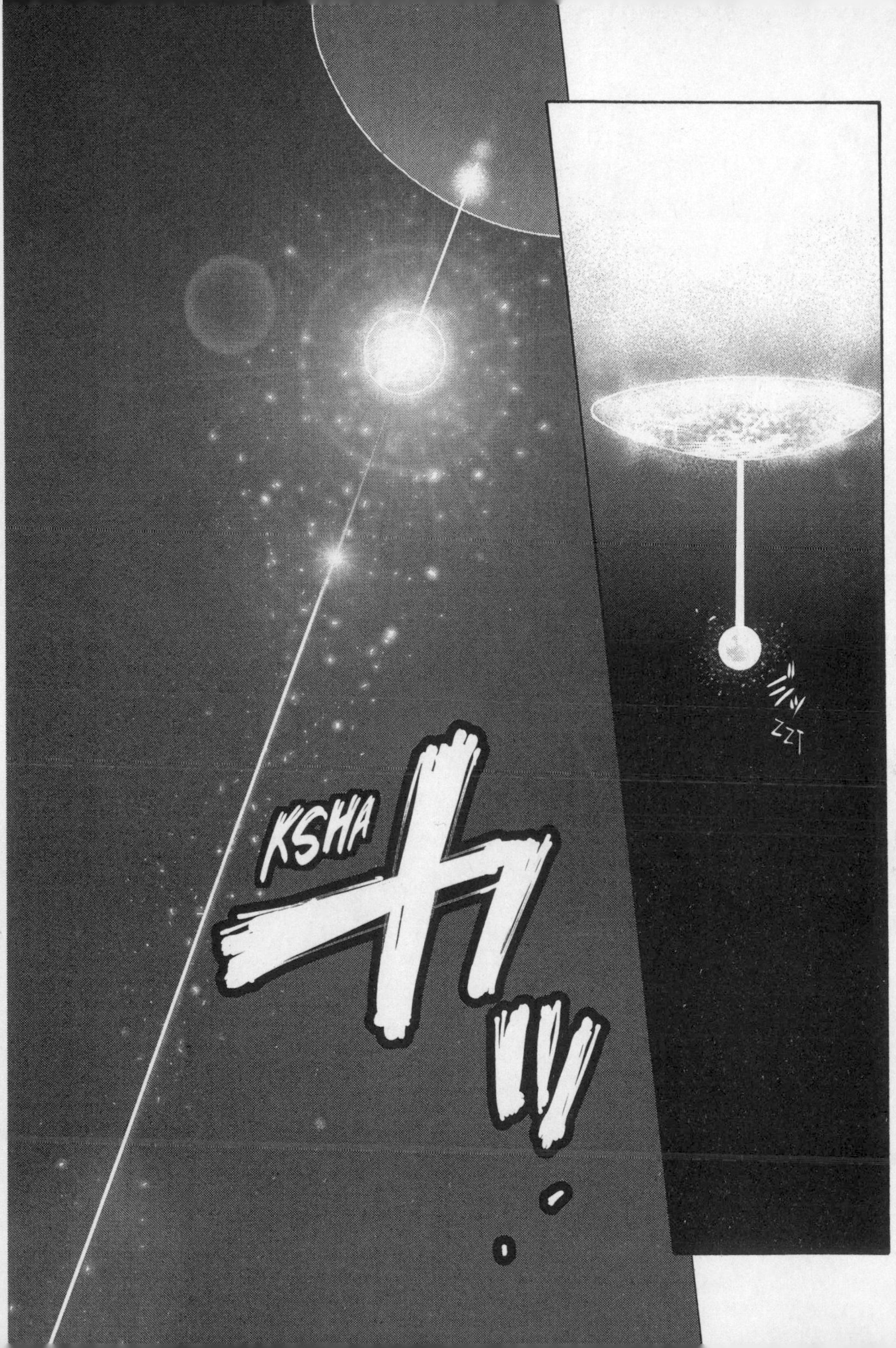
ZZT
KSHA

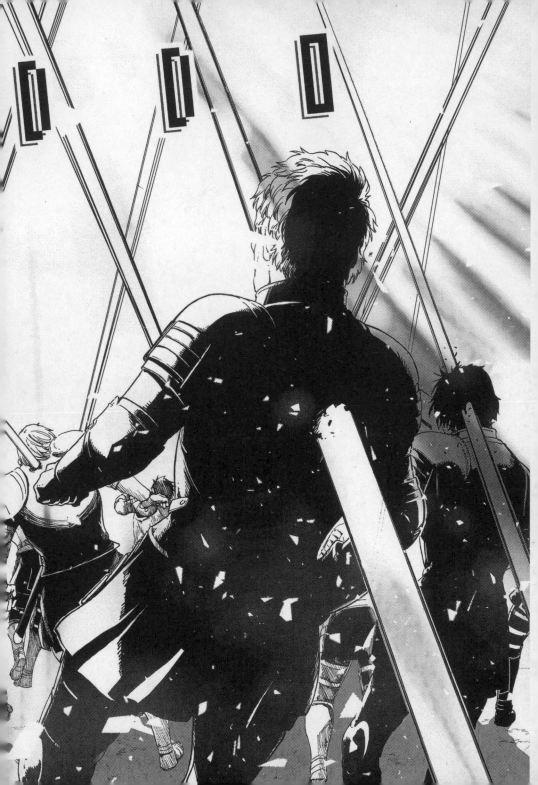

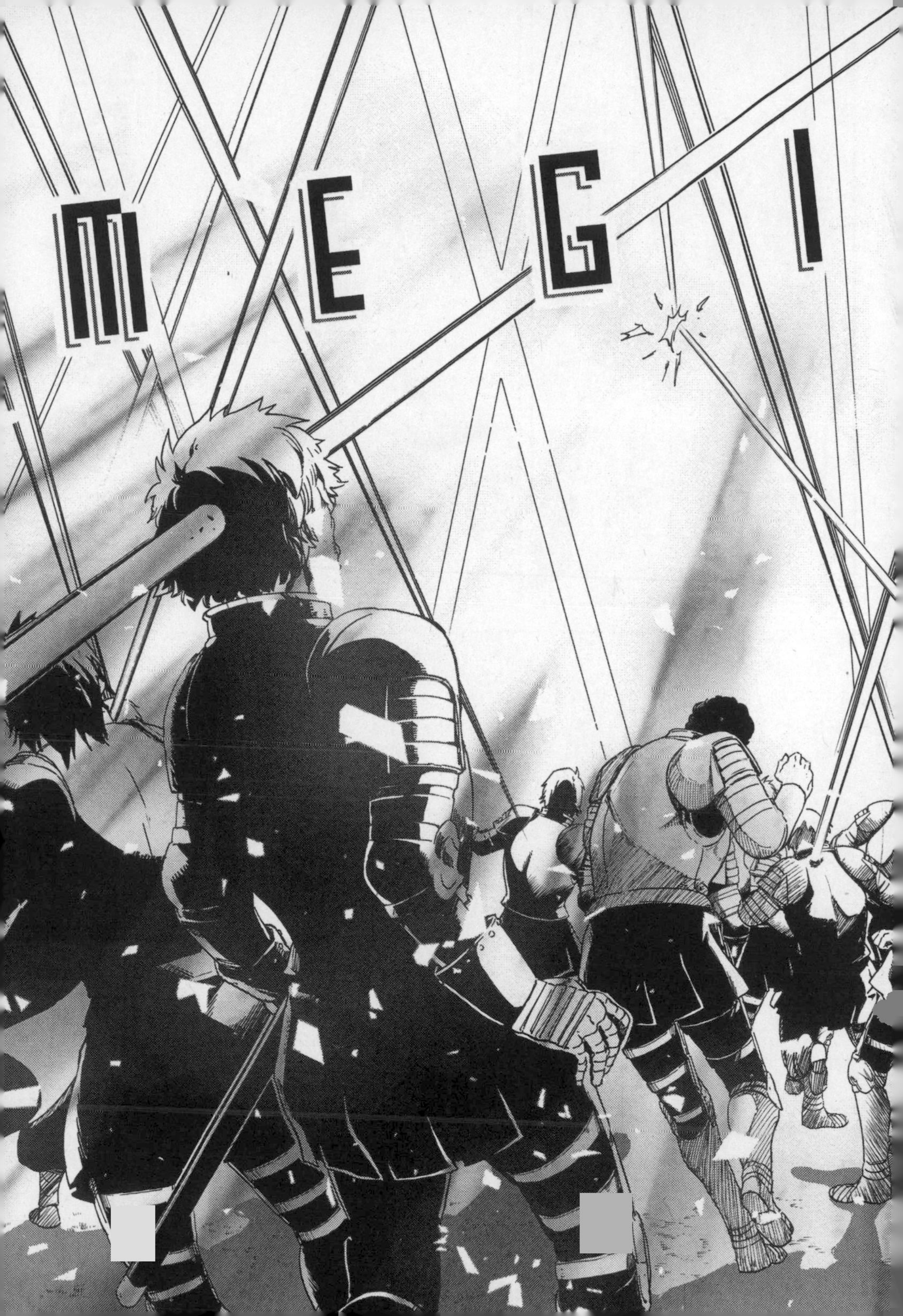
MEGI

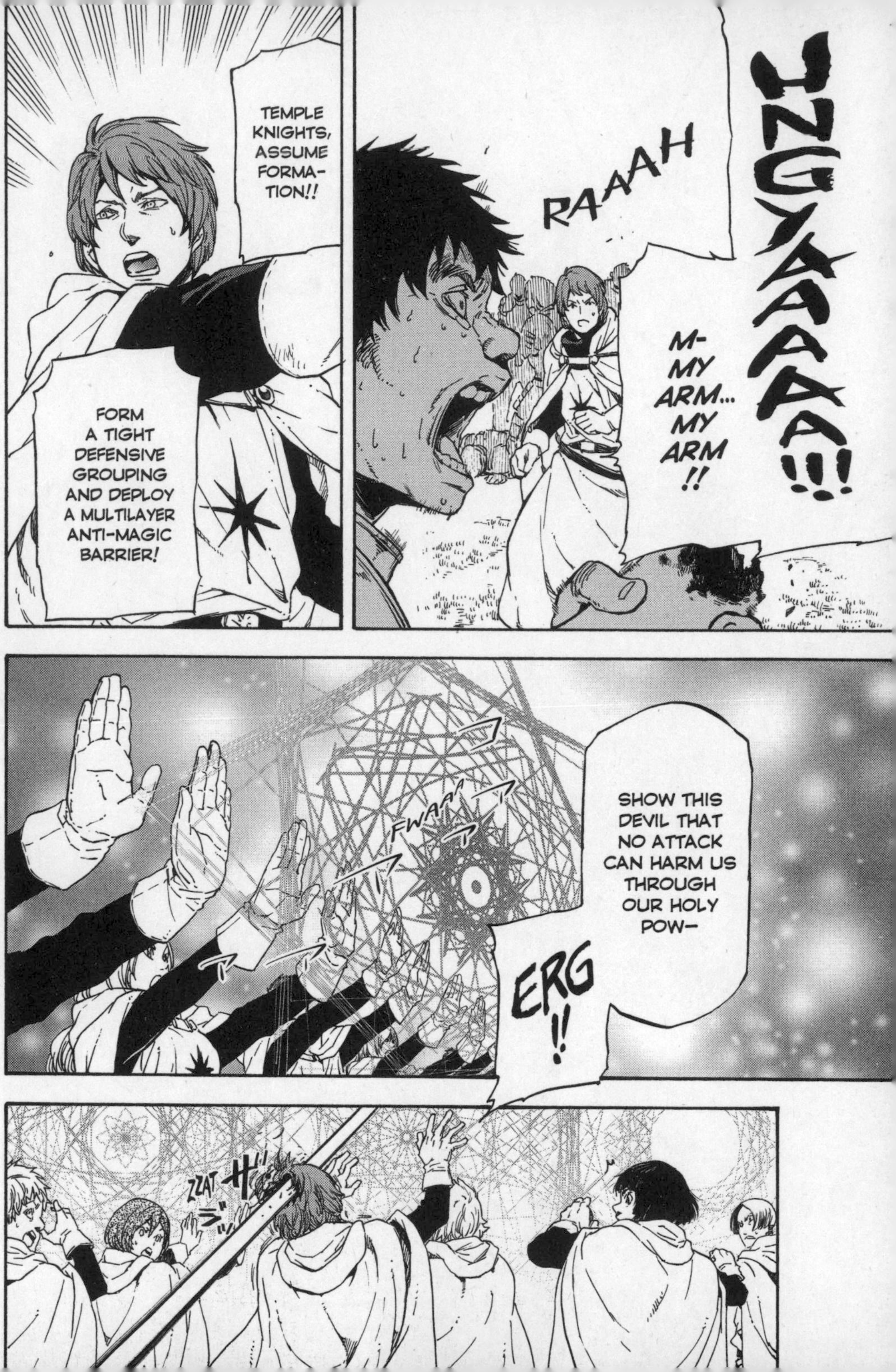
HNGYAAAAA!!!
RAAAH
M-MY ARM... MY ARM!!
TEMPLE KNIGHTS, ASSUME FORMA-TION!!
FORM A TIGHT DEFENSIVE GROUPING AND DEPLOY A MULTILAYER ANTI-MAGIC BARRIER!
SHOW THIS DEVIL THAT NO ATTACK CAN HARM US THROUGH OUR HOLY POW–
FWAAA
ERG!!
ZZAT

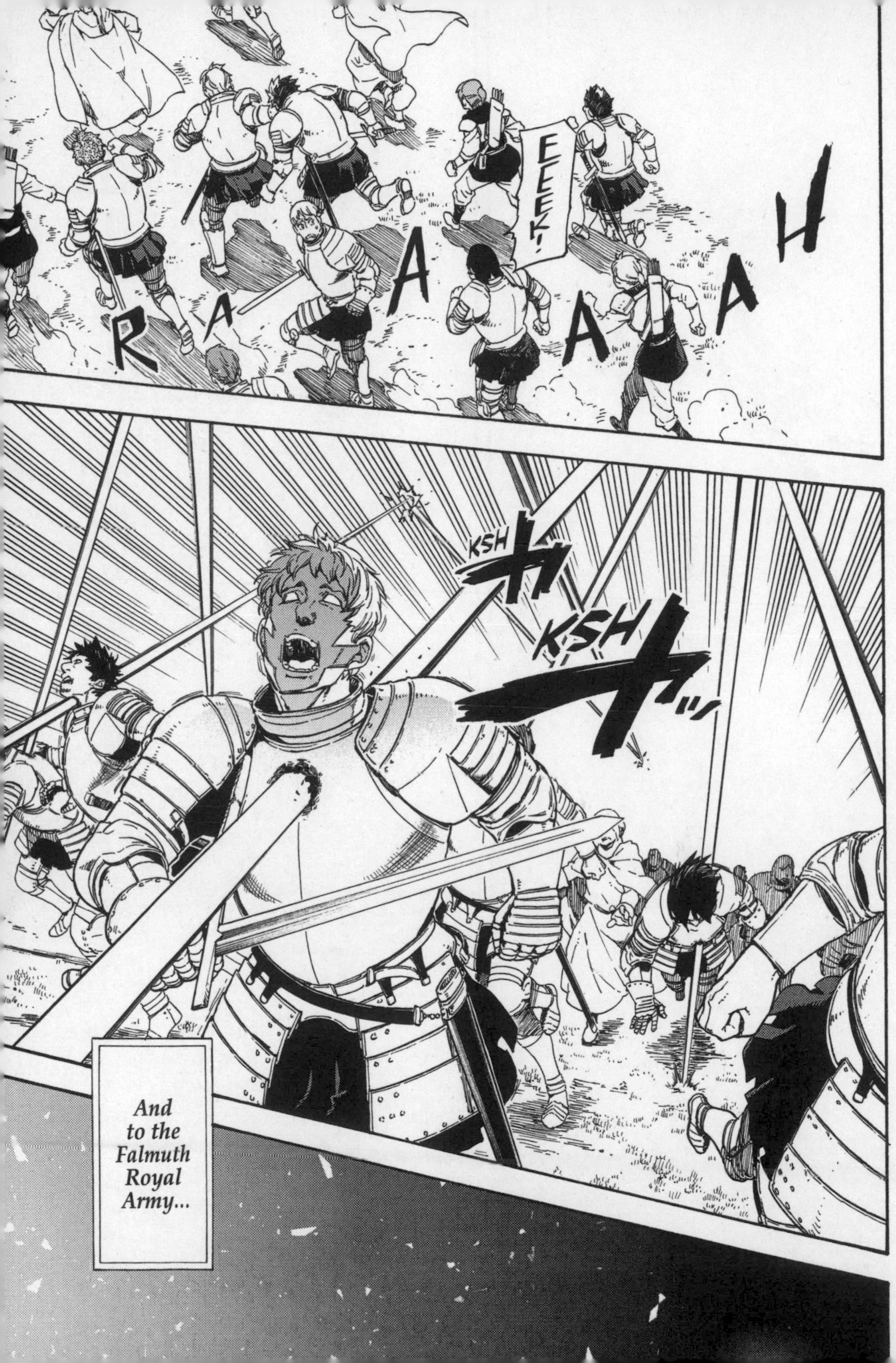
RAAAAH
EEEK!
KSH
KSH
And to the Falmuth Royal Army...

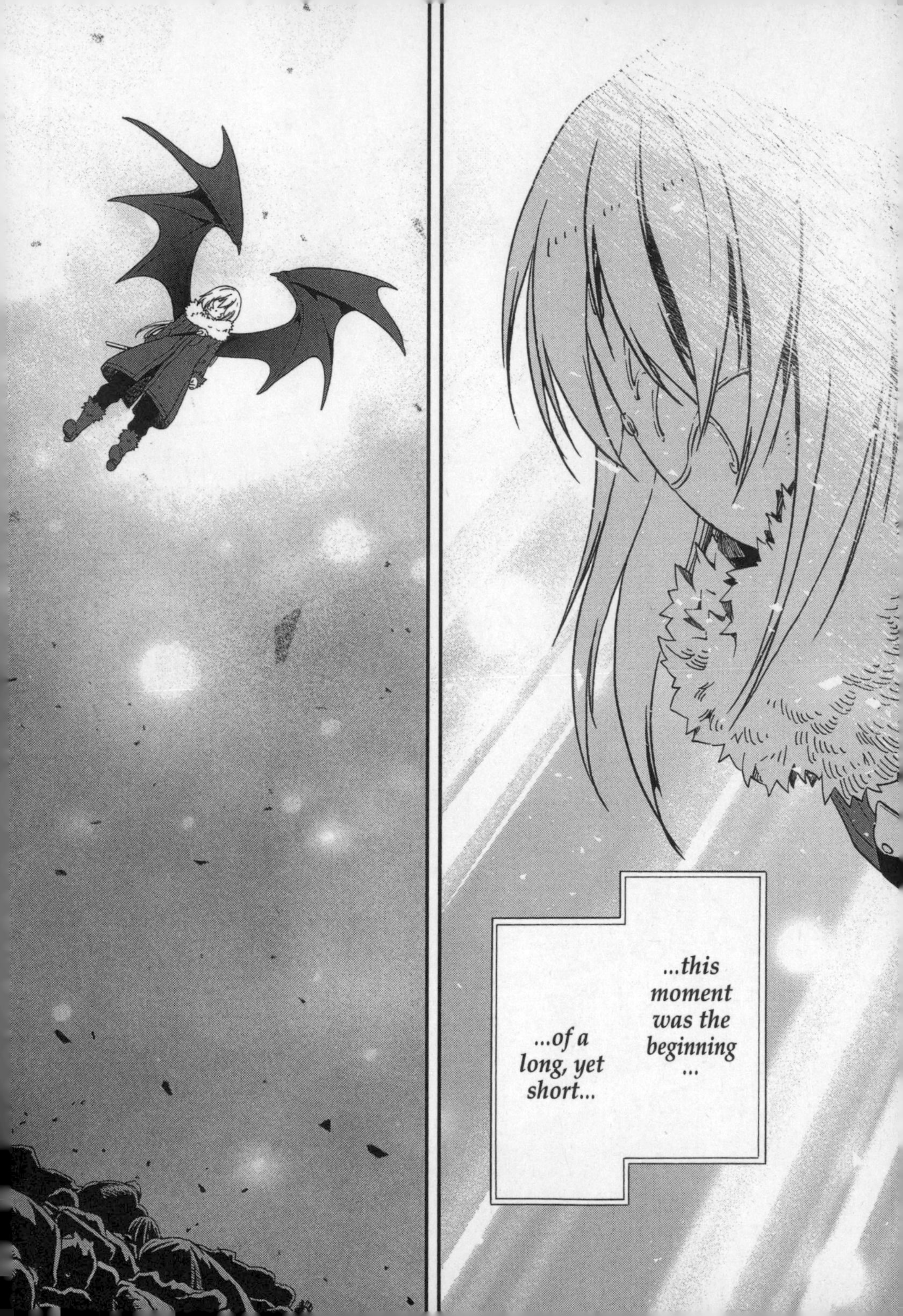
...this moment was the beginning...
...of a long, yet short...

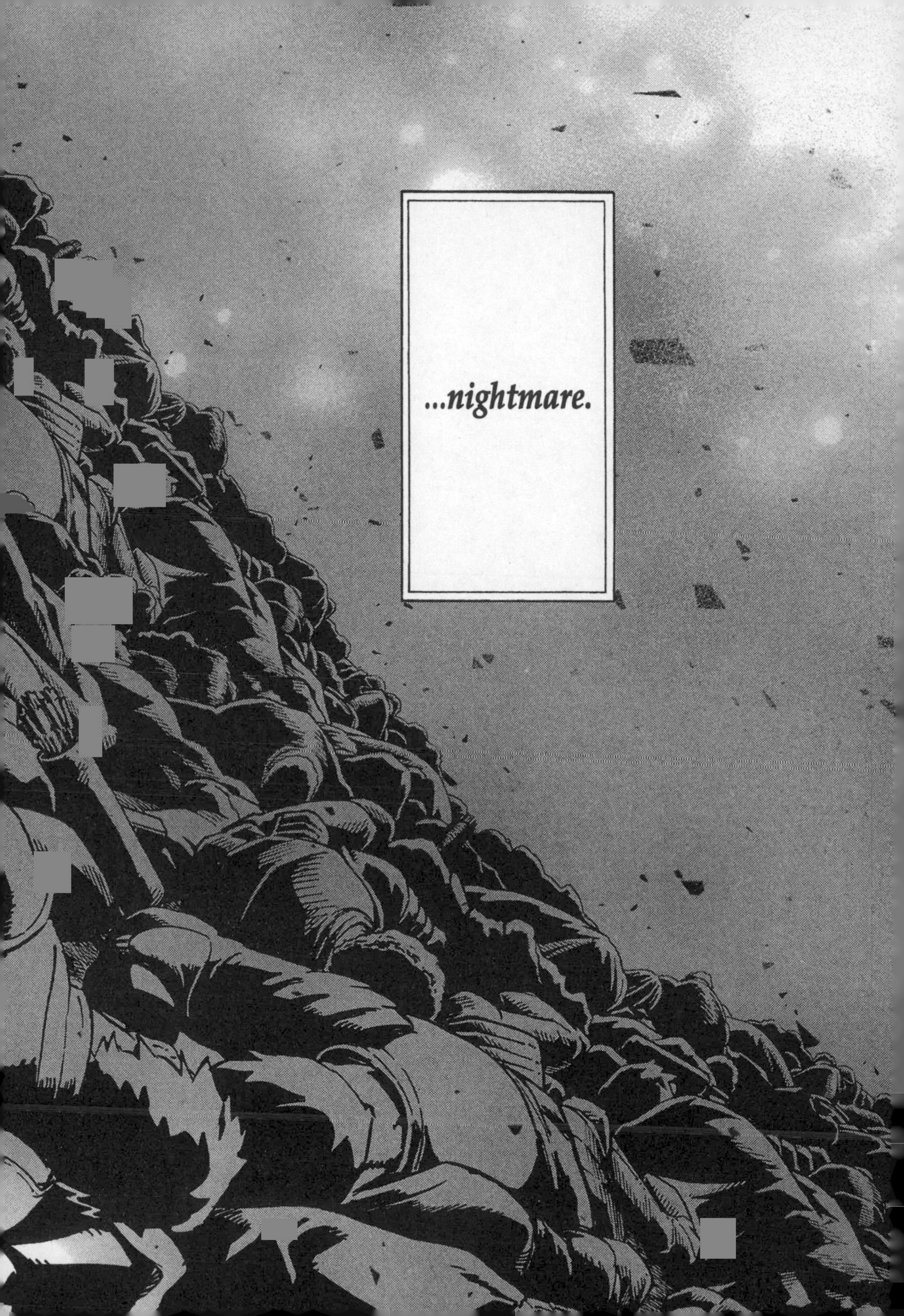
...nightmare.

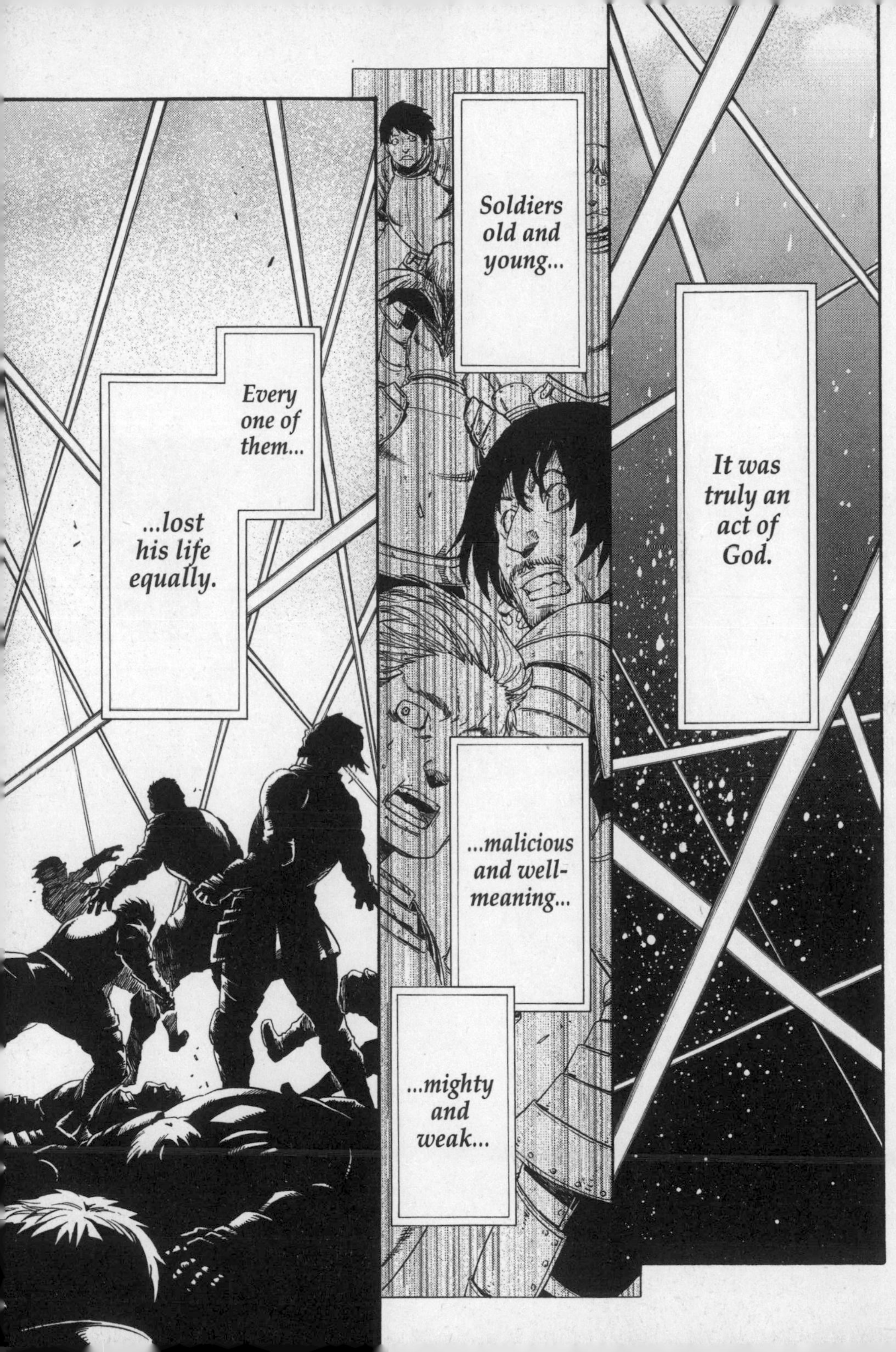
It was truly an act of God.
Soldiers old and young...
...malicious and well-meaning...
...mighty and weak...
Every one of them...
...lost his life equally.

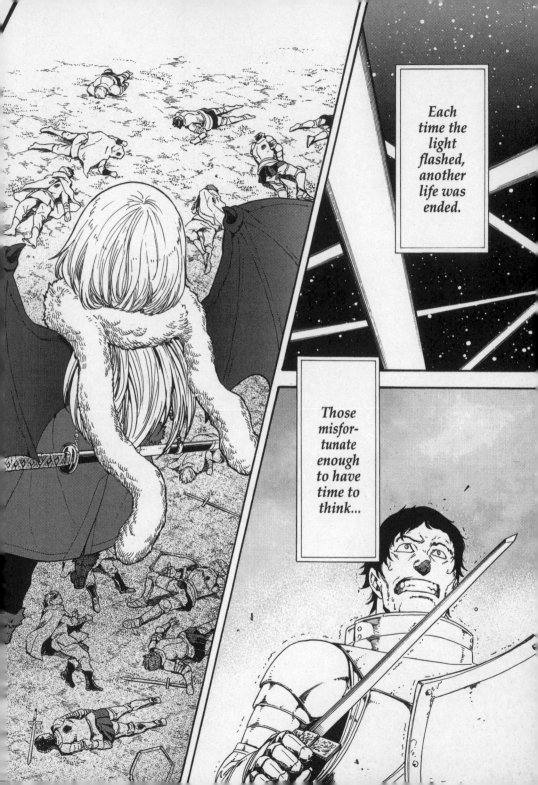

Each time the light flashed, another life was ended.

Those misfortunate enough to have time to think...

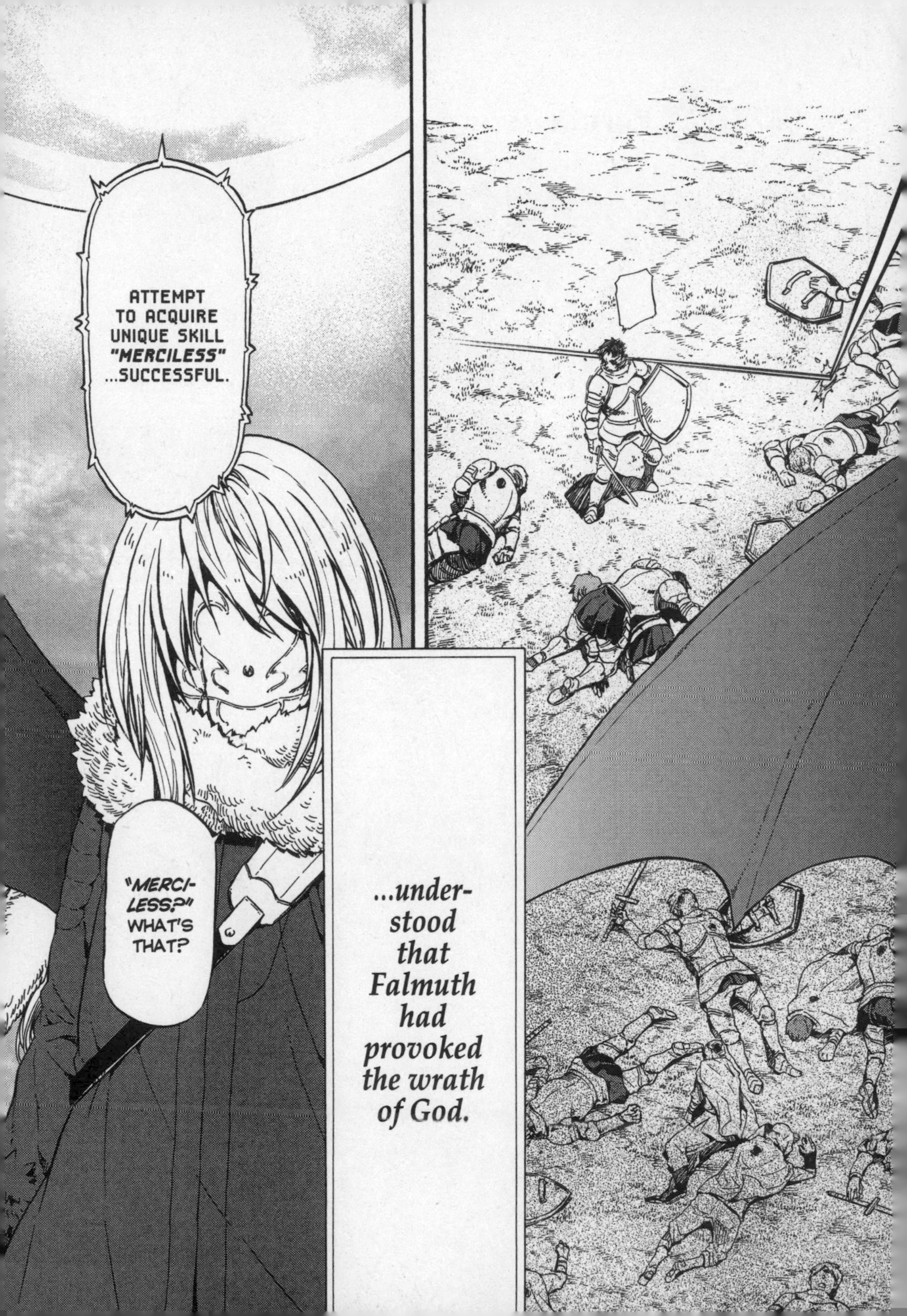
...understood that Falmuth had provoked the wrath of God.
ATTEMPT TO ACQUIRE UNIQUE SKILL "MERCILESS" ...SUCCESSFUL.
"MERCILESS?" WHAT'S THAT?

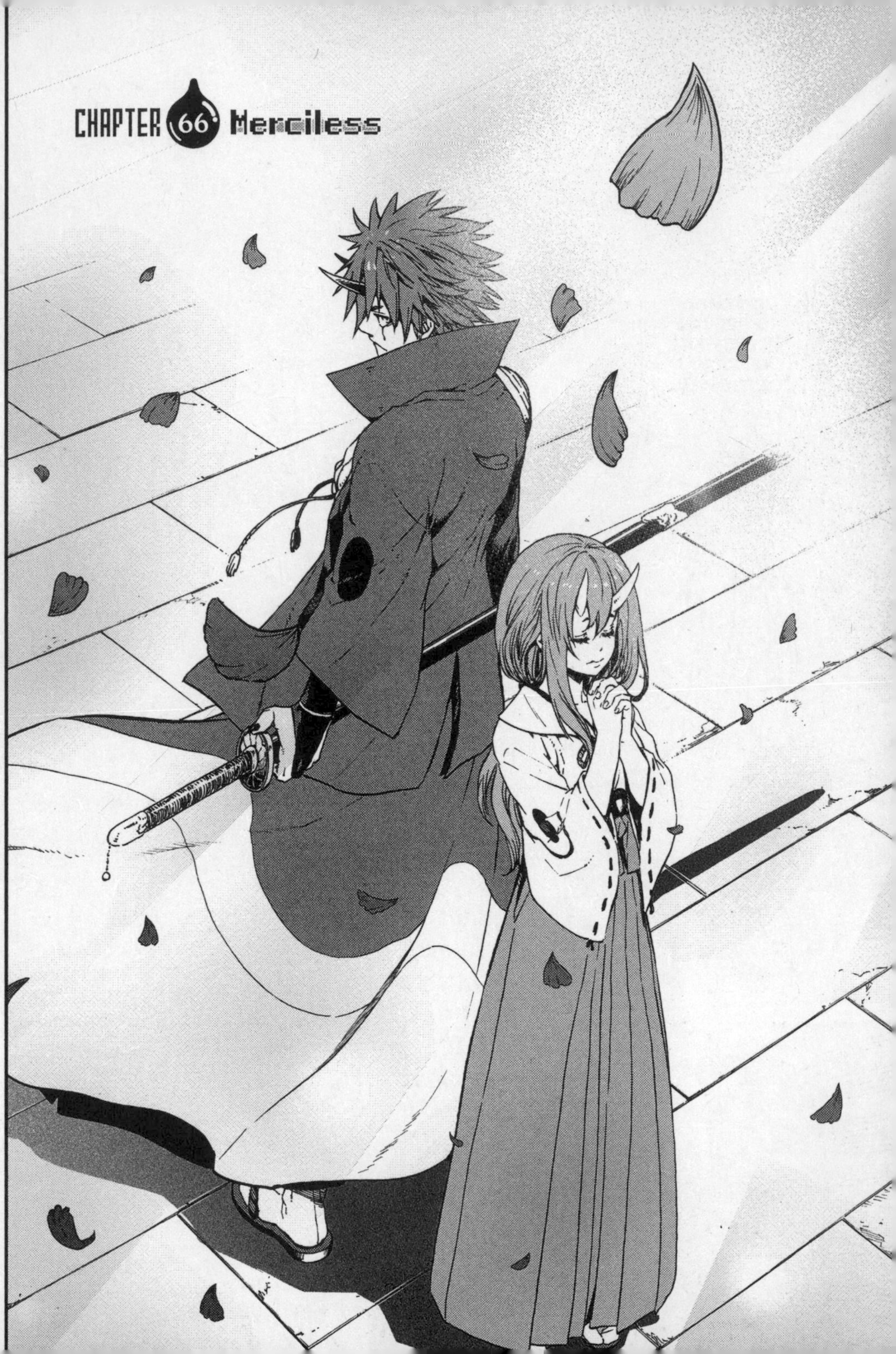
CHAPTER 66 Merciless

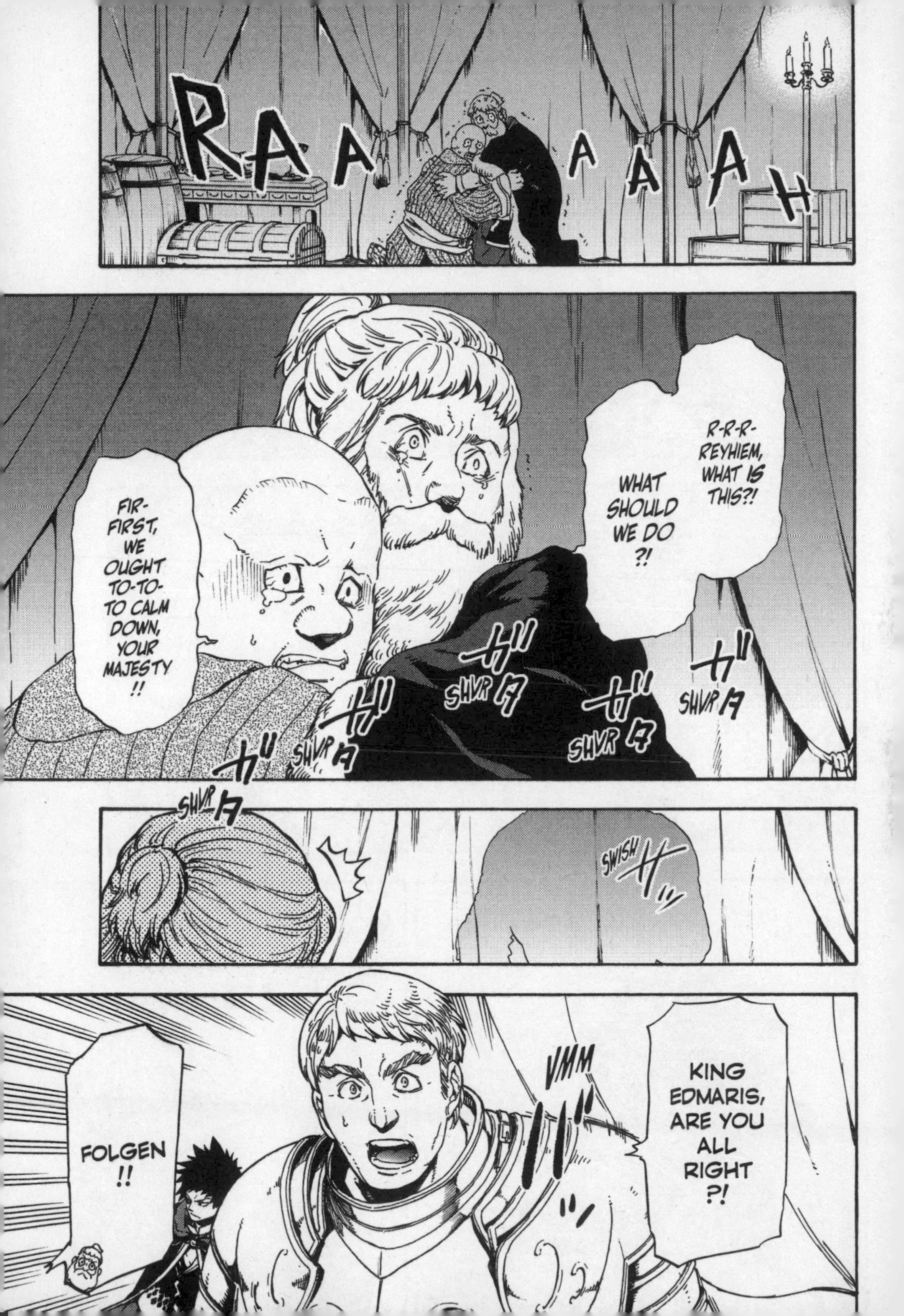
RAAAAAAH
R-R-R-REYHIEM, WHAT IS THIS?!
WHAT SHOULD WE DO?!
FIR-FIRST, WE OUGHT TO-TO-TO CALM DOWN, YOUR MAJESTY!!
SHVR
SHVR
SHVR
SHVR
SWISH
SHVR
KING EDMARIS, ARE YOU ALL RIGHT?!
VMM
FOLGEN!!

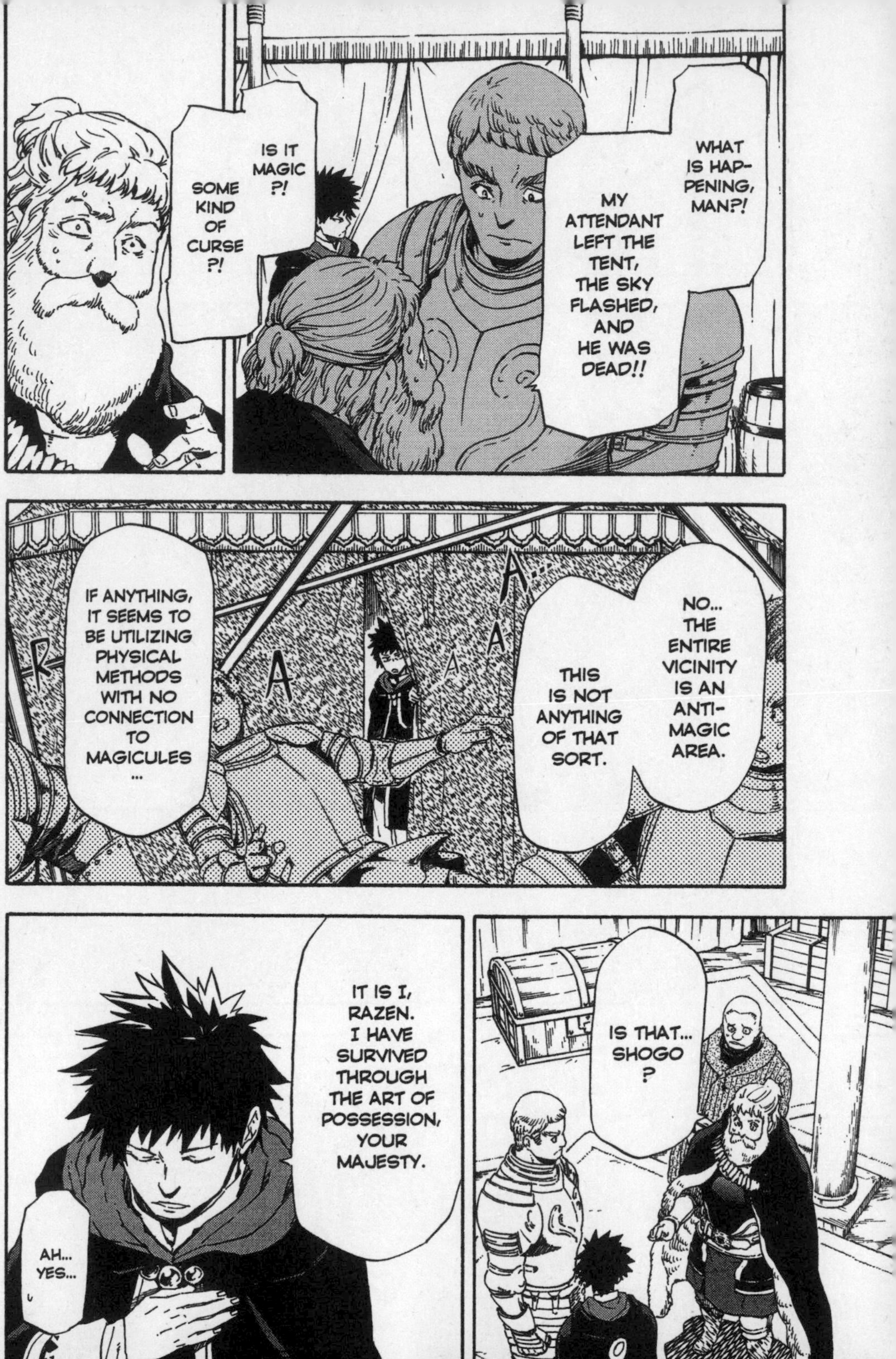
WHAT IS HAPPENING, MAN?!
MY ATTENDANT LEFT THE TENT, THE SKY FLASHED, AND HE WAS DEAD!!
IS IT MAGIC ?!
SOME KIND OF CURSE ?!
NO... THE ENTIRE VICINITY IS AN ANTI-MAGIC AREA.
THIS IS NOT ANYTHING OF THAT SORT.
IF ANYTHING, IT SEEMS TO BE UTILIZING PHYSICAL METHODS WITH NO CONNECTION TO MAGICULES ...
IS THAT... SHOGO ?
IT IS I, RAZEN. I HAVE SURVIVED THROUGH THE ART OF POSSESSION, YOUR MAJESTY.
AH... YES...

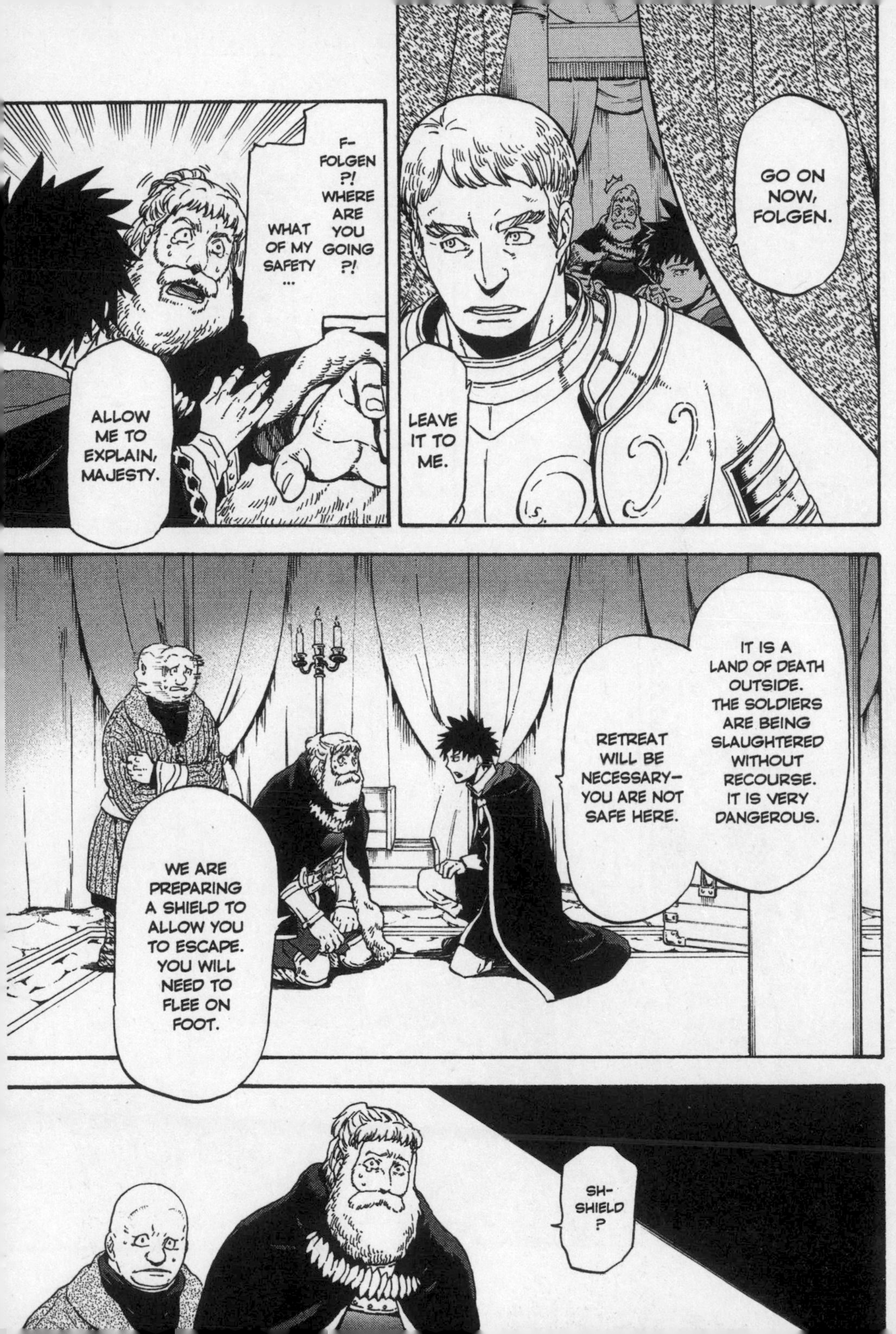
GO ON NOW, FOLGEN.
LEAVE IT TO ME.
F-FOLGEN?! WHERE ARE YOU GOING?!
WHAT OF MY SAFETY...
ALLOW ME TO EXPLAIN, MAJESTY.
IT IS A LAND OF DEATH OUTSIDE. THE SOLDIERS ARE BEING SLAUGHTERED WITHOUT RECOURSE. IT IS VERY DANGEROUS.
RETREAT WILL BE NECESSARY—YOU ARE NOT SAFE HERE.
WE ARE PREPARING A SHIELD TO ALLOW YOU TO ESCAPE. YOU WILL NEED TO FLEE ON FOOT.
SH-SHIELD?

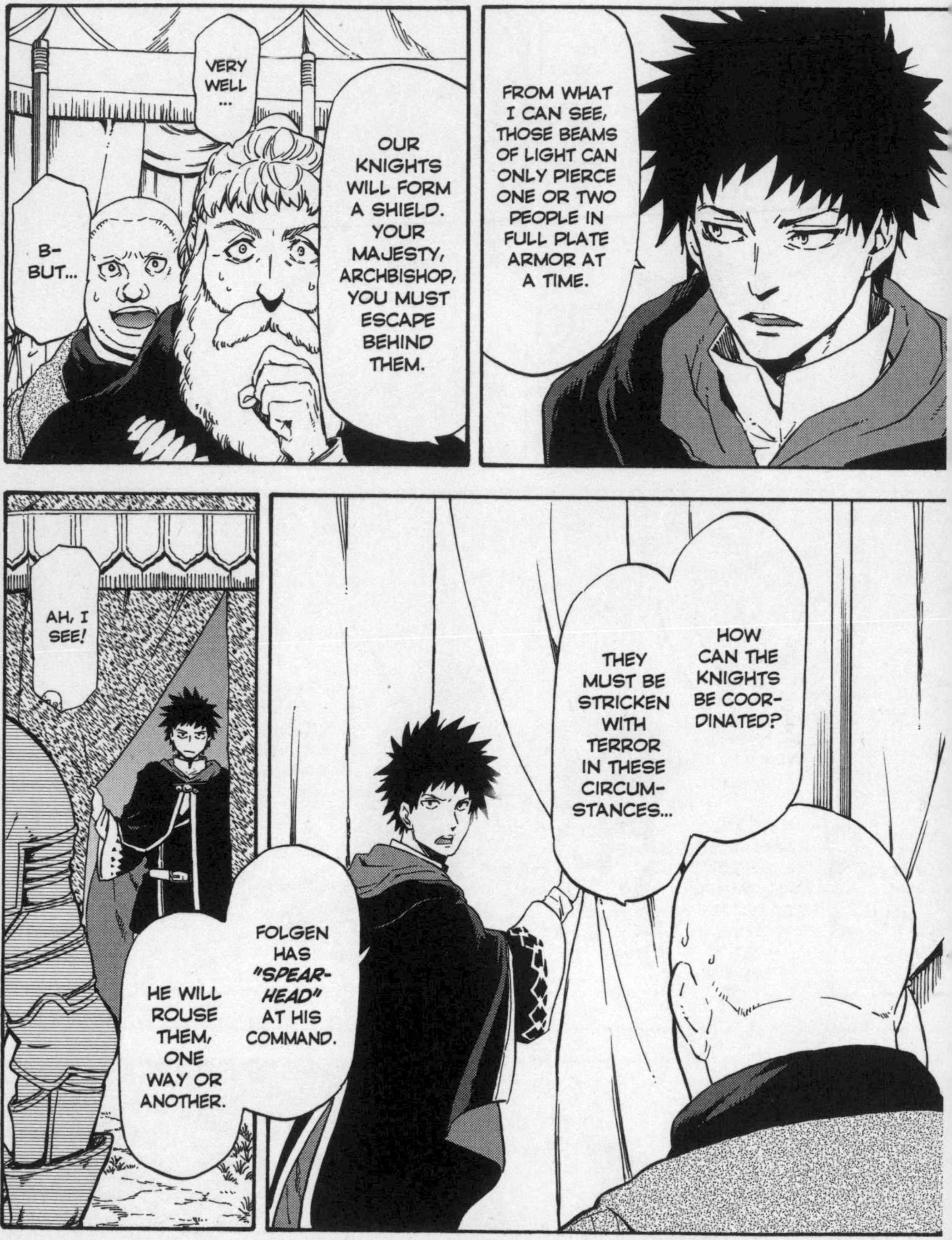
FROM WHAT I CAN SEE, THOSE BEAMS OF LIGHT CAN ONLY PIERCE ONE OR TWO PEOPLE IN FULL PLATE ARMOR AT A TIME.
OUR KNIGHTS WILL FORM A SHIELD. YOUR MAJESTY, ARCHBISHOP, YOU MUST ESCAPE BEHIND THEM.
VERY WELL ...
B-BUT...
HOW CAN THE KNIGHTS BE COORDINATED?
THEY MUST BE STRICKEN WITH TERROR IN THESE CIRCUMSTANCES...
FOLGEN HAS "SPEARHEAD" AT HIS COMMAND.
HE WILL ROUSE THEM, ONE WAY OR ANOTHER.
AH, I SEE!

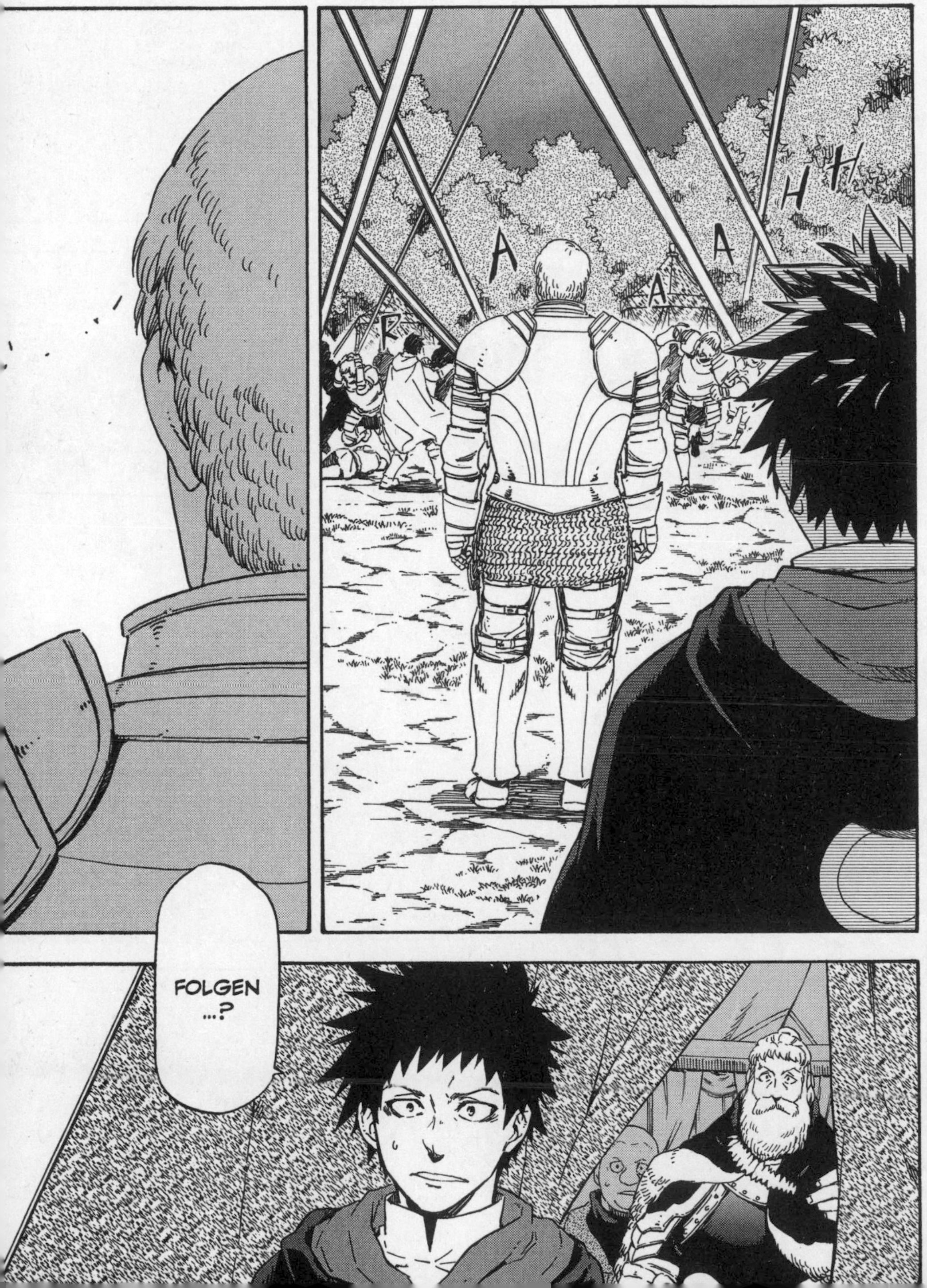
RAAAHH
...
FOLGEN ...?

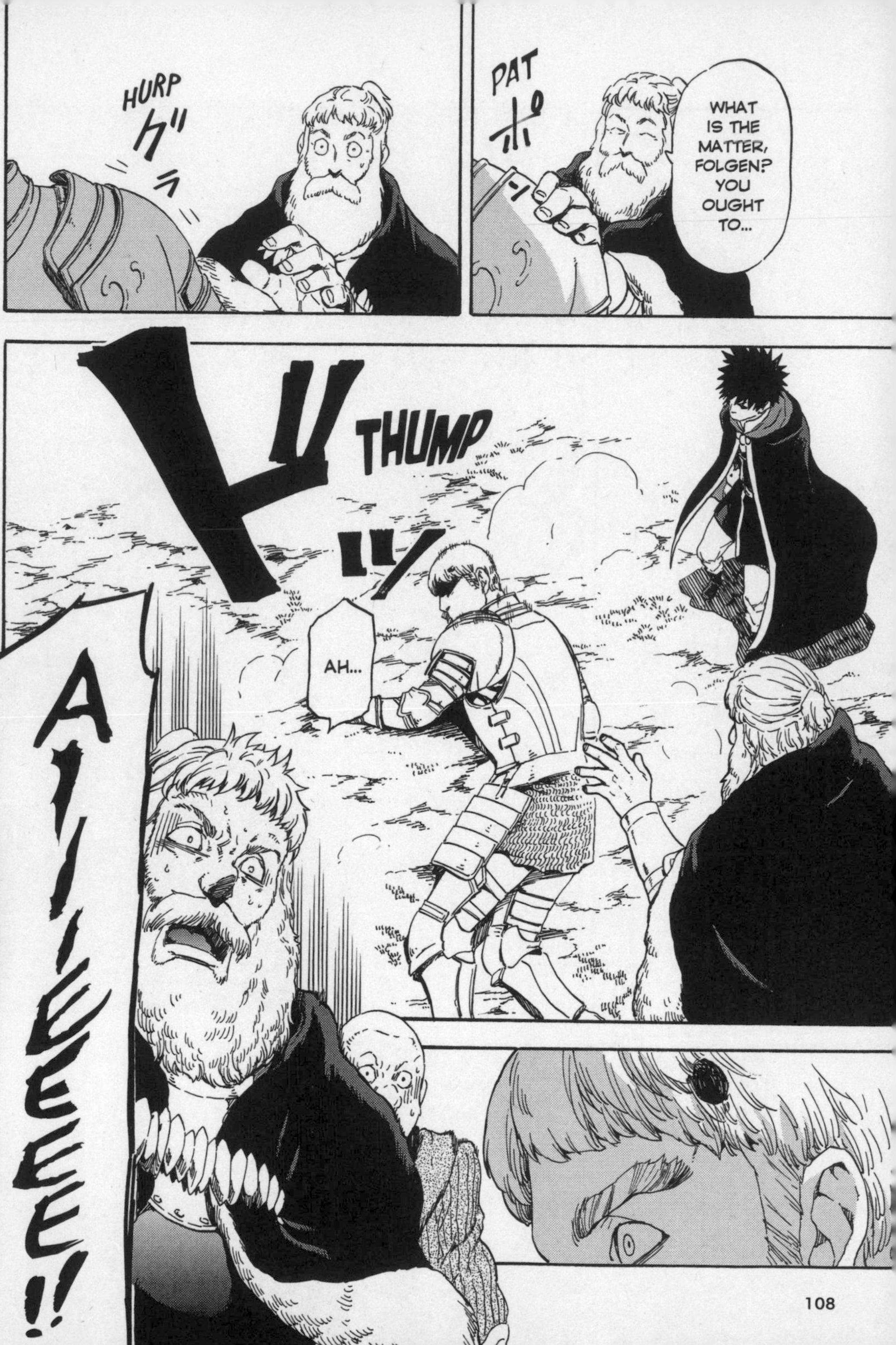
PAT
WHAT IS THE MATTER, FOLGEN? YOU OUGHT TO...
HURP
THUMP
AH...
AIIIEEEE!!

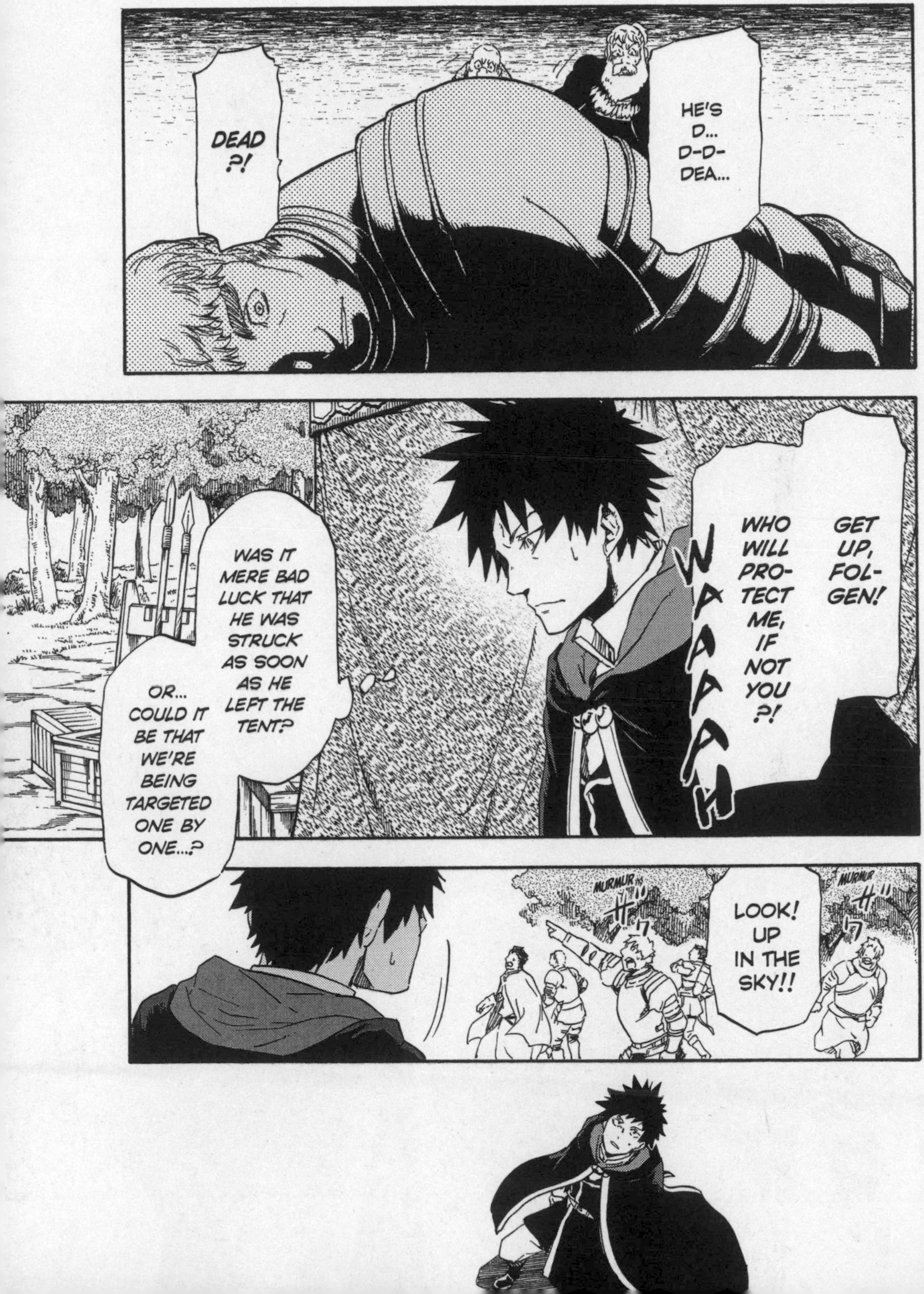
HE'S D... D-D-DEA...
DEAD ?!
GET UP, FOLGEN!
WHO WILL PROTECT ME, IF NOT YOU ?!
WAAAAH
WAS IT MERE BAD LUCK THAT HE WAS STRUCK AS SOON AS HE LEFT THE TENT?
OR... COULD IT BE THAT WE'RE BEING TARGETED ONE BY ONE...?
MURMUR
LOOK! UP IN THE SKY!!
MURMUR

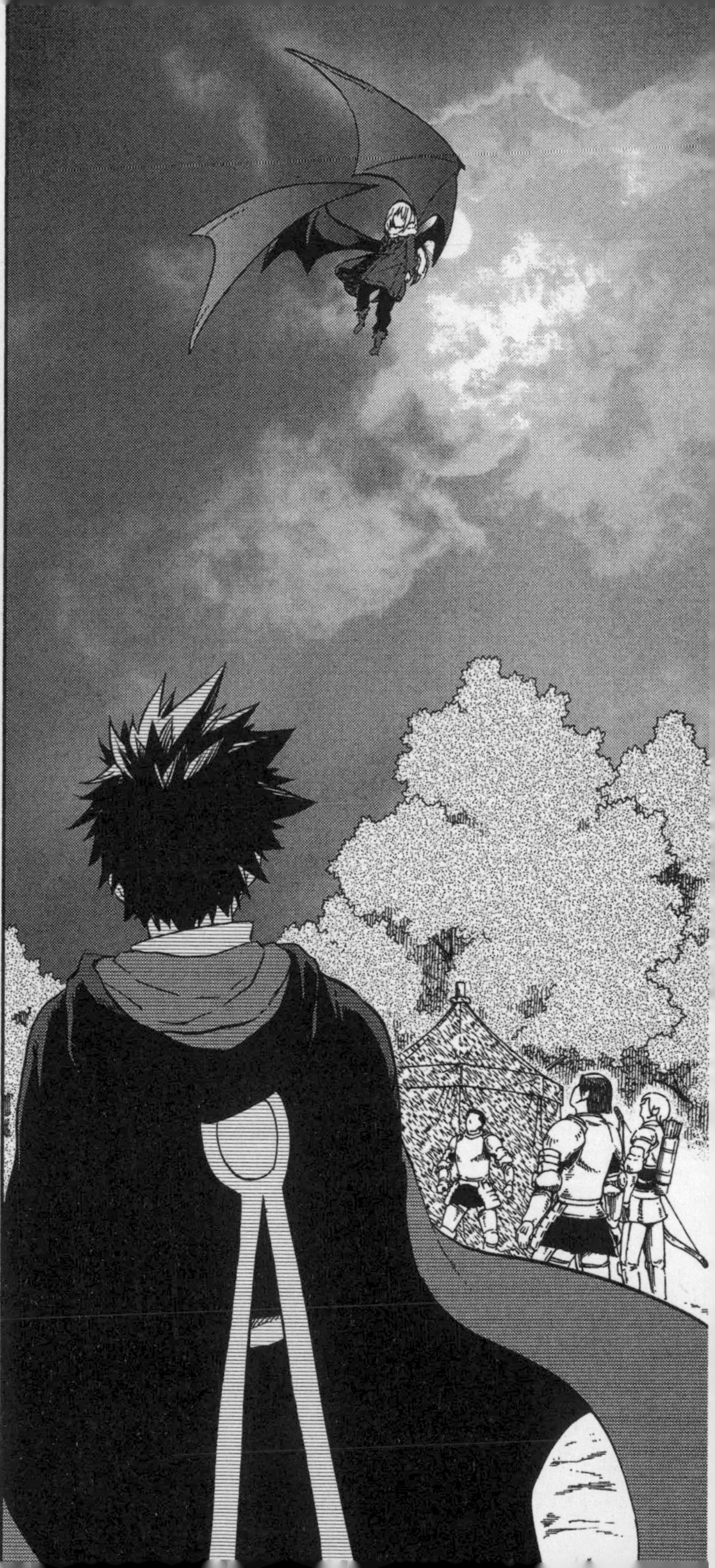
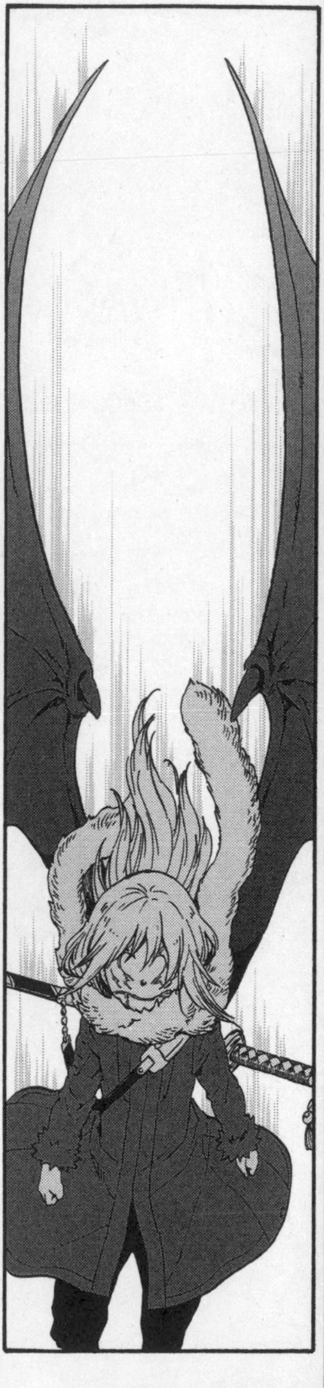

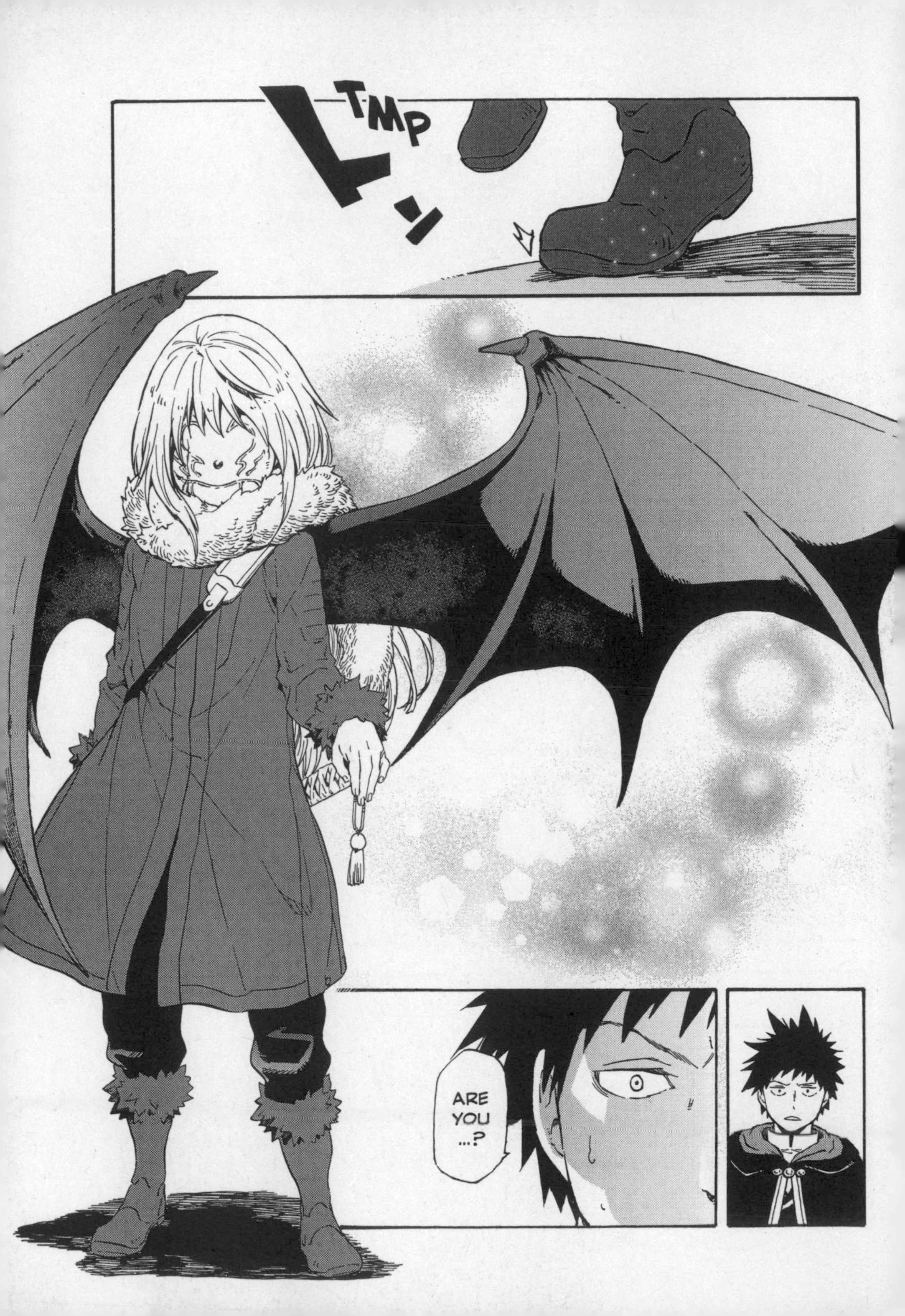
TMP
ARE YOU ...?

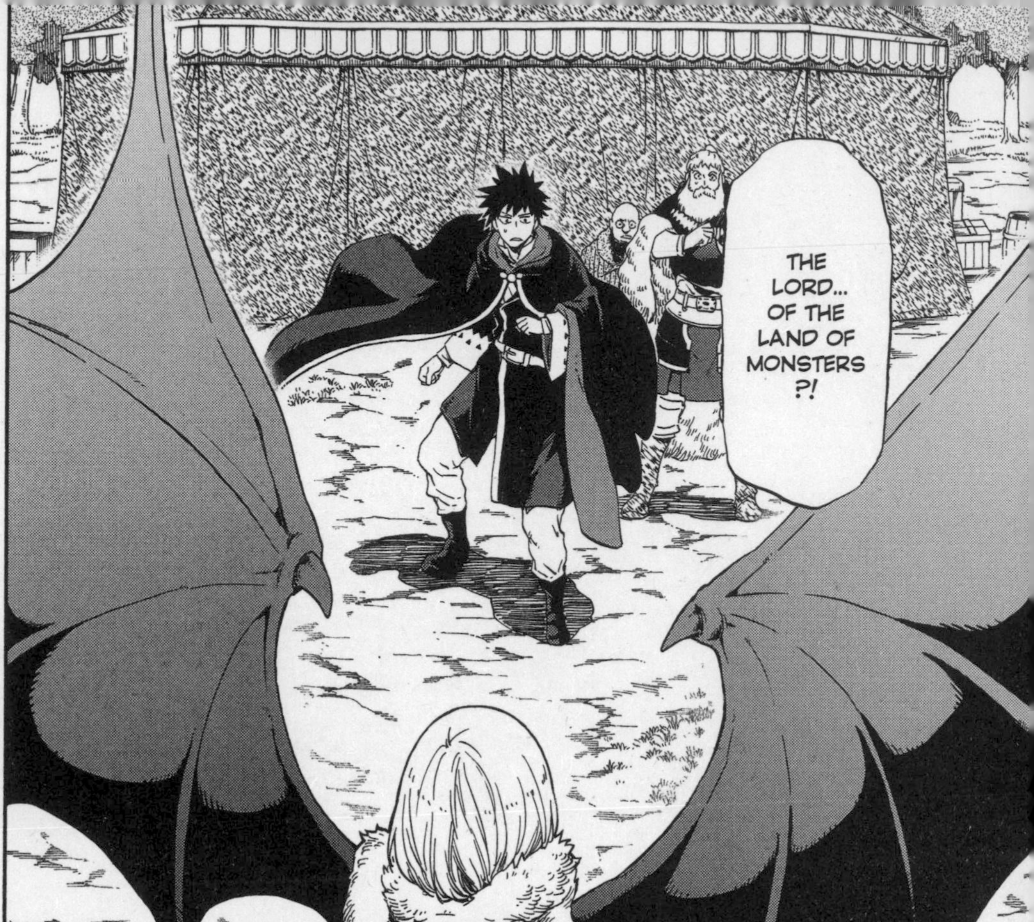
THE LORD... OF THE LAND OF MONSTERS ?!
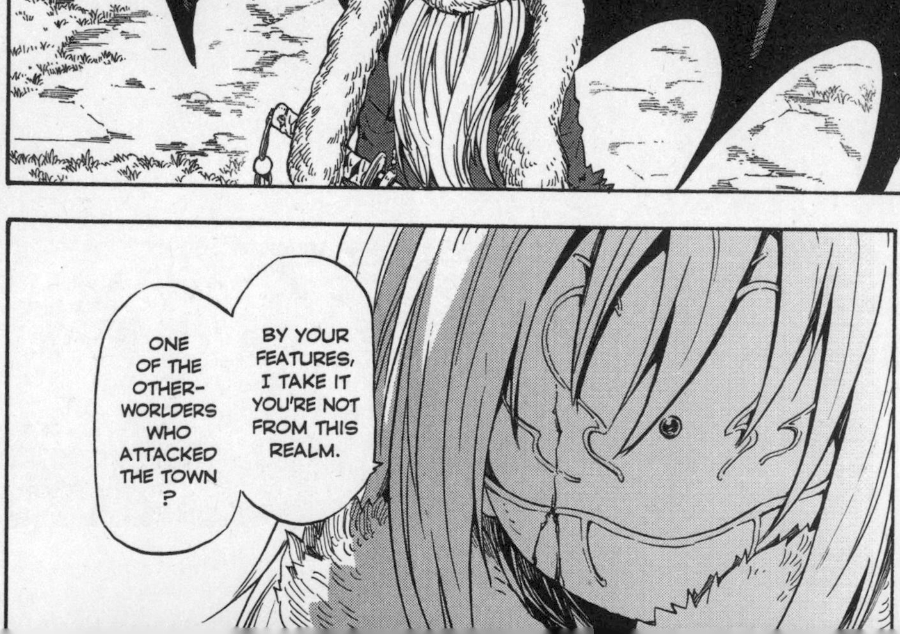
BY YOUR FEATURES, I TAKE IT YOU'RE NOT FROM THIS REALM.
ONE OF THE OTHER-WORLDERS WHO ATTACKED THE TOWN ?

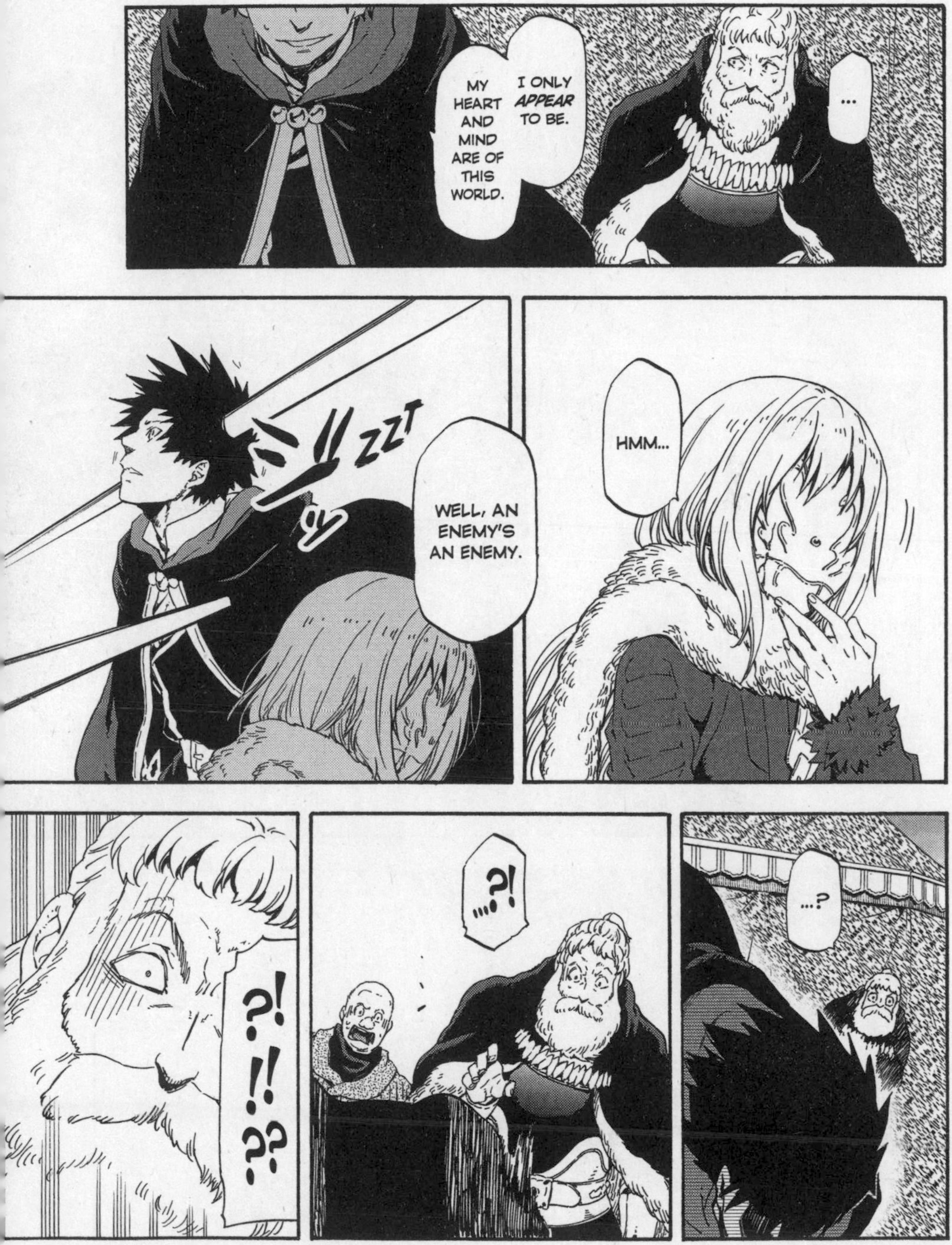
...
I ONLY *APPEAR* TO BE.
MY HEART AND MIND ARE OF THIS WORLD.
HMM...
WELL, AN ENEMY'S AN ENEMY.
ZZT
...?
...?!
?! !? ??

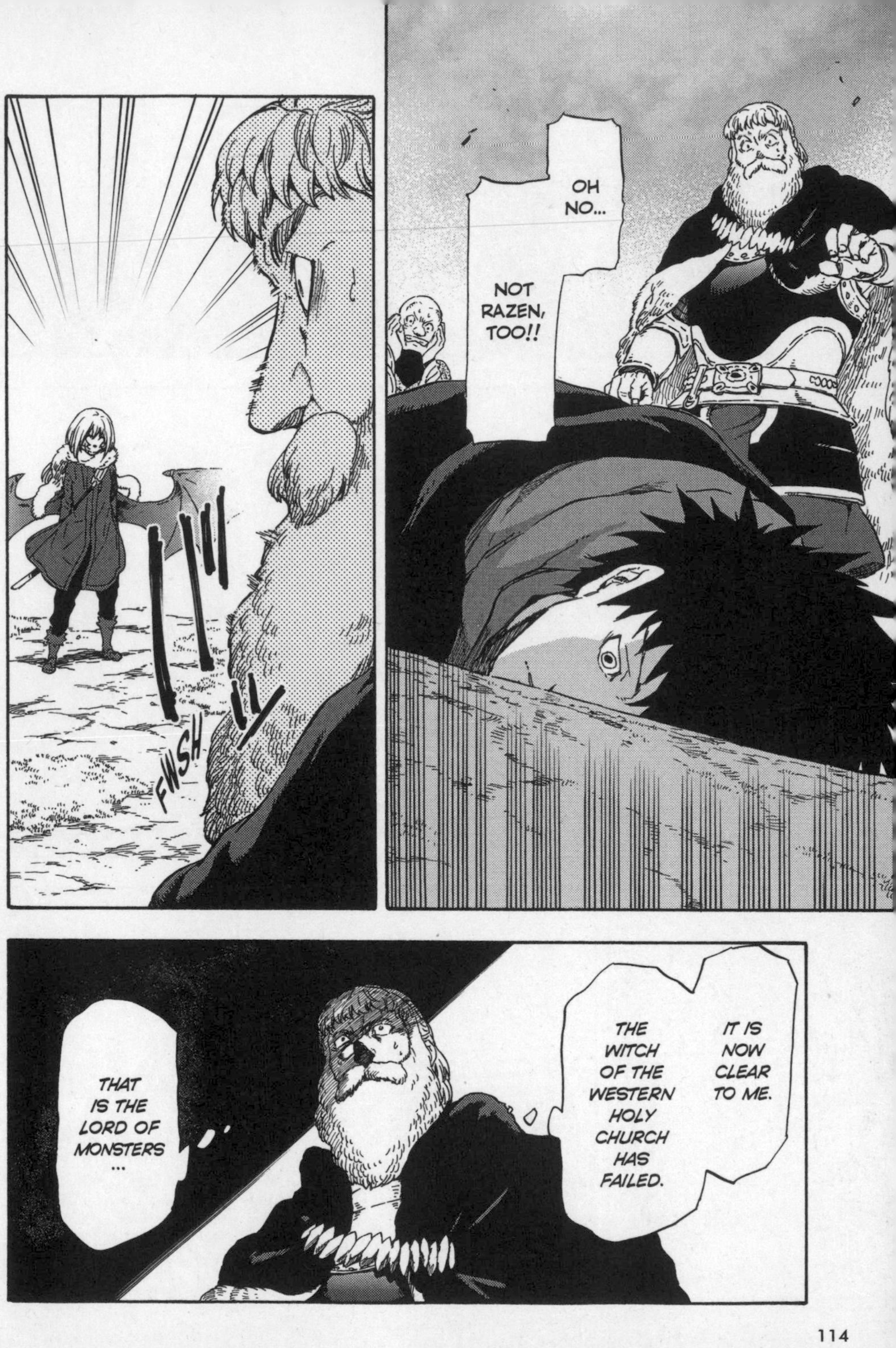
OH NO...
NOT RAZEN, TOO!!
FWSH
IT IS NOW CLEAR TO ME.
THE WITCH OF THE WESTERN HOLY CHURCH HAS FAILED.
THAT IS THE LORD OF MONSTERS...

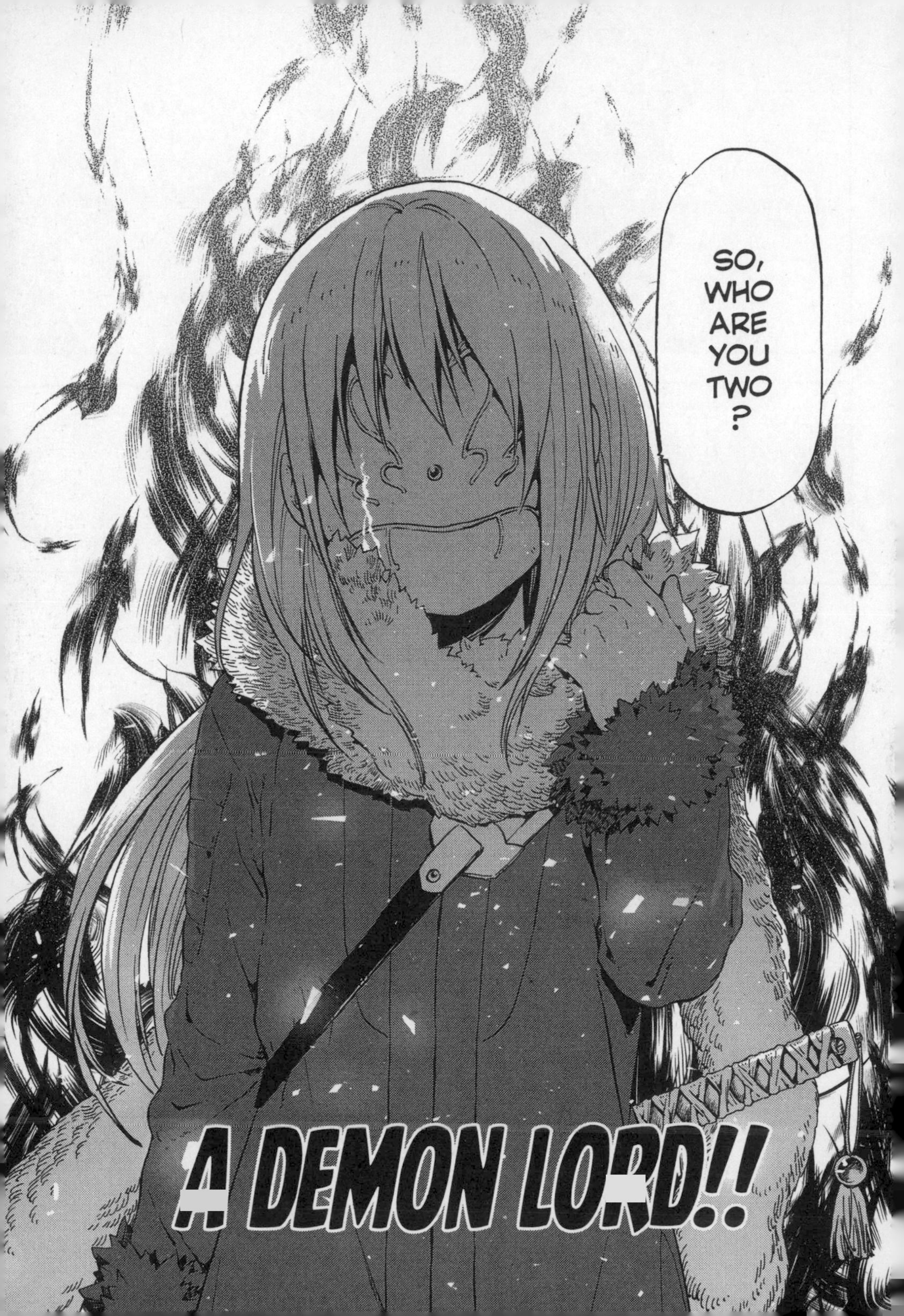
SO, WHO ARE YOU TWO?
A DEMON LORD!!

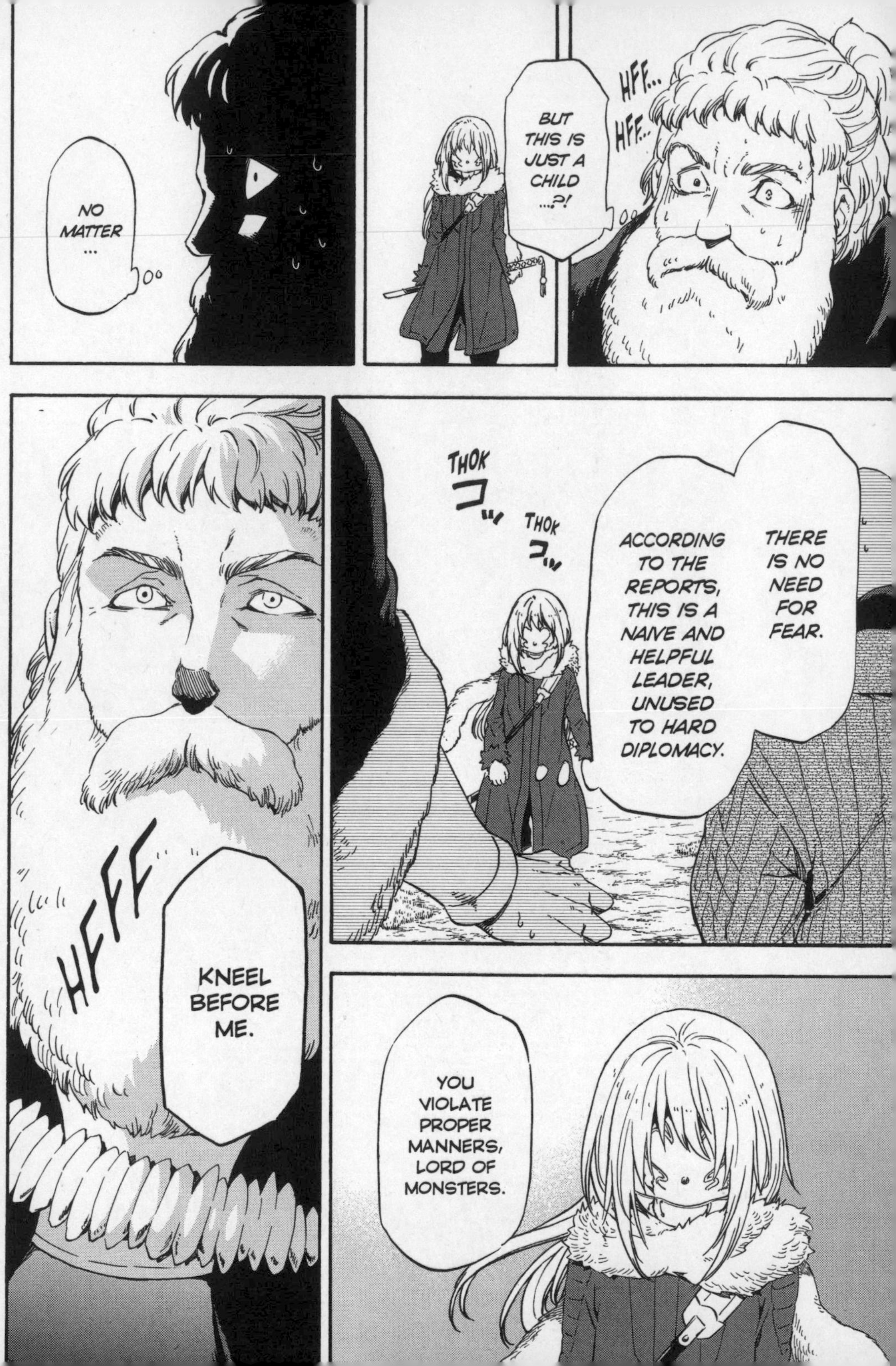
HFF...
HFF...
BUT THIS IS JUST A CHILD ...?!
NO MATTER ...
THOK
コッ
THOK
コッ
THERE IS NO NEED FOR FEAR.
ACCORDING TO THE REPORTS, THIS IS A NAIVE AND HELPFUL LEADER, UNUSED TO HARD DIPLOMACY.
YOU VIOLATE PROPER MANNERS, LORD OF MONSTERS.
HFFF
KNEEL BEFORE ME.

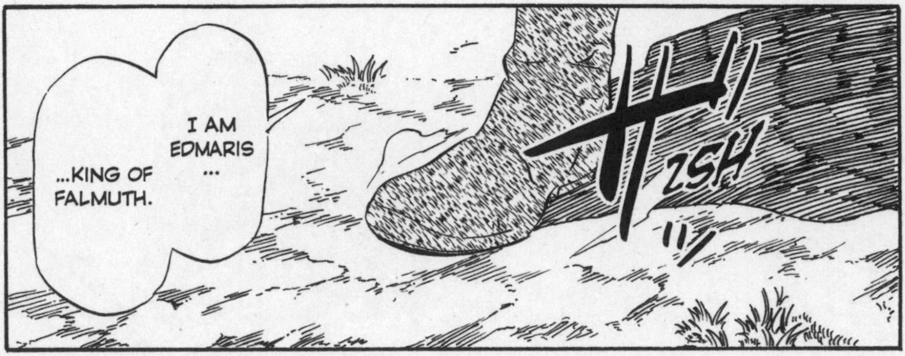
ZSH
I AM EDMARIS ...
...KING OF FALMUTH.

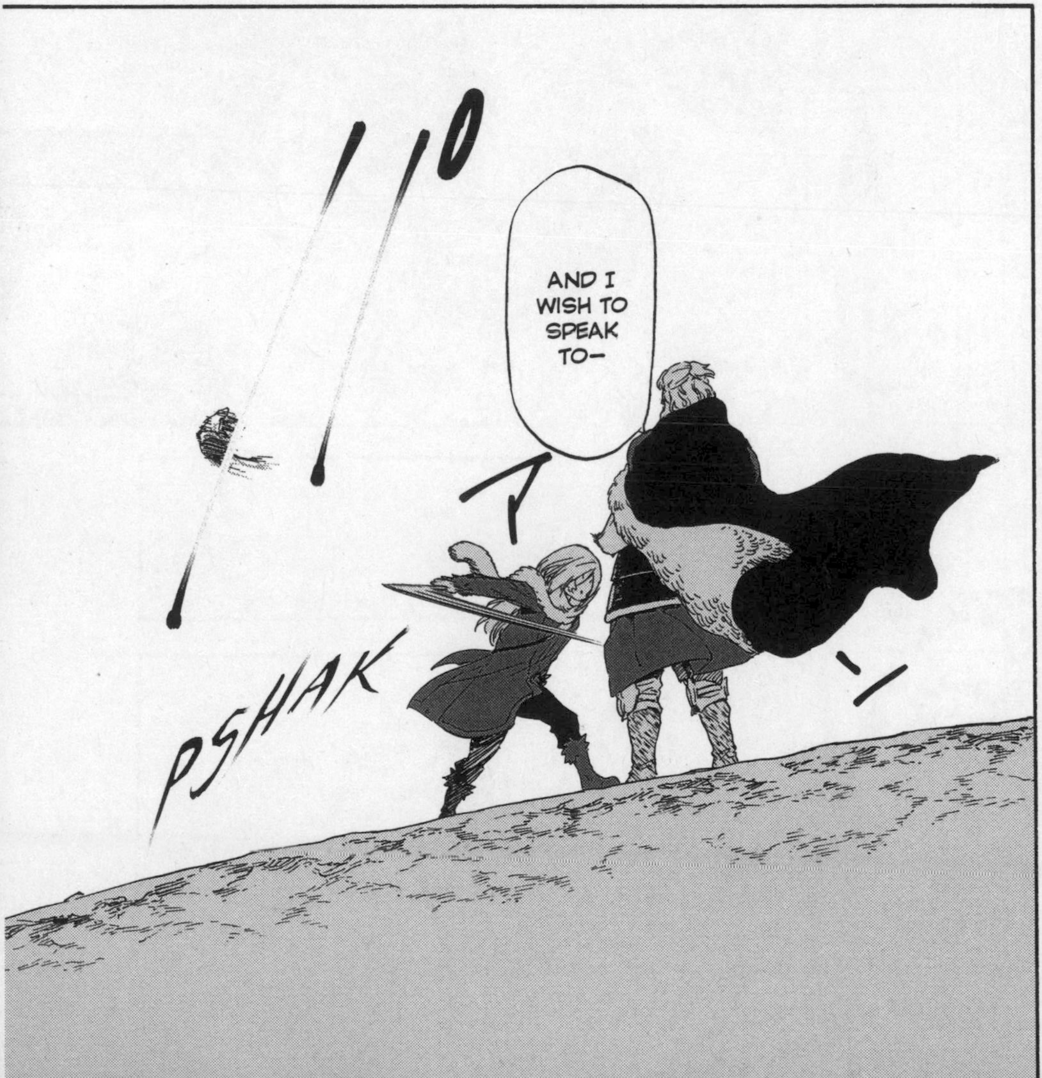
AND I WISH TO SPEAK TO—
PSHAK

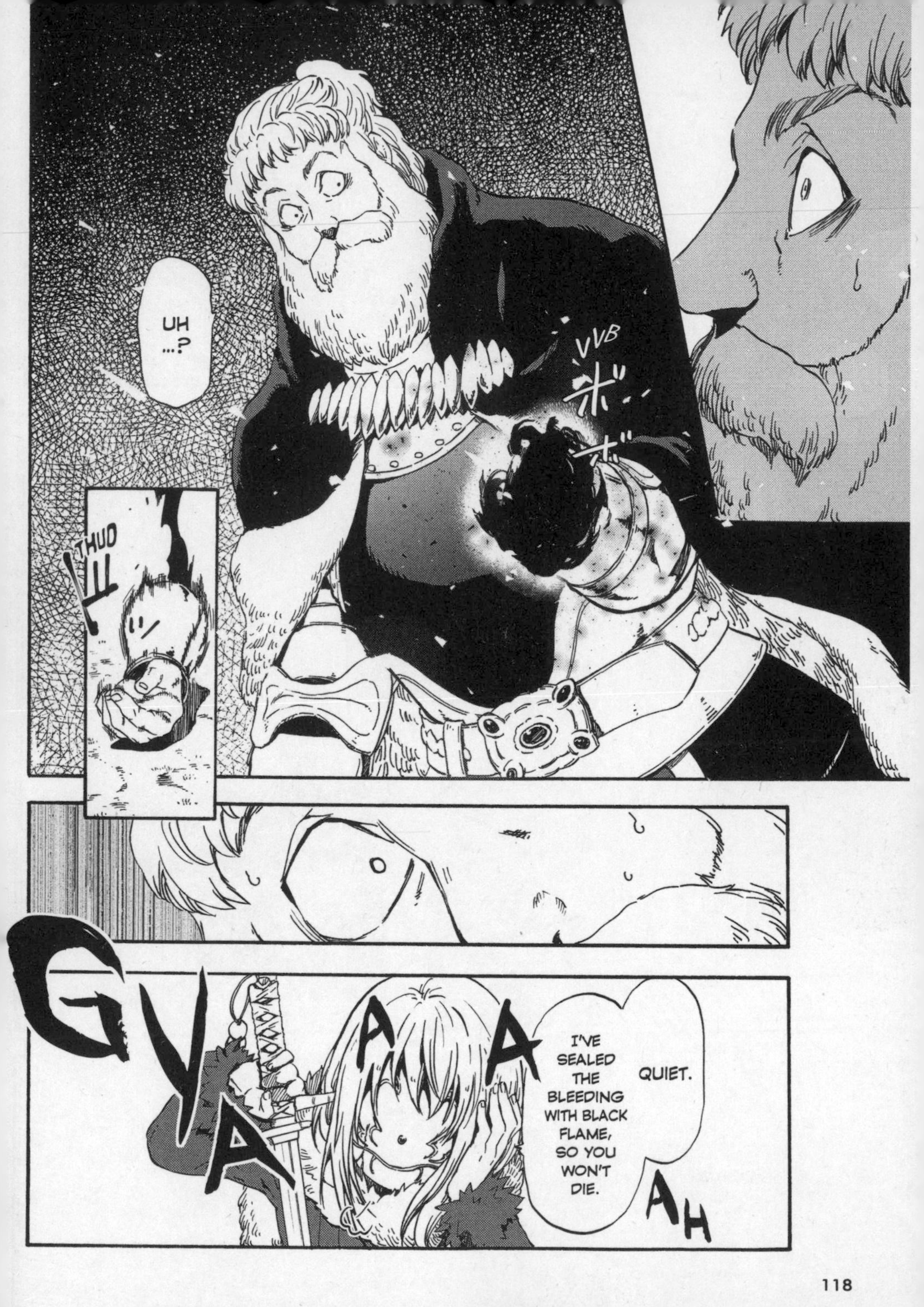
VVB
ボボ
UH ...?
THUD
GYAAAAH
QUIET.
I'VE SEALED THE BLEEDING WITH BLACK FLAME, SO YOU WON'T DIE.

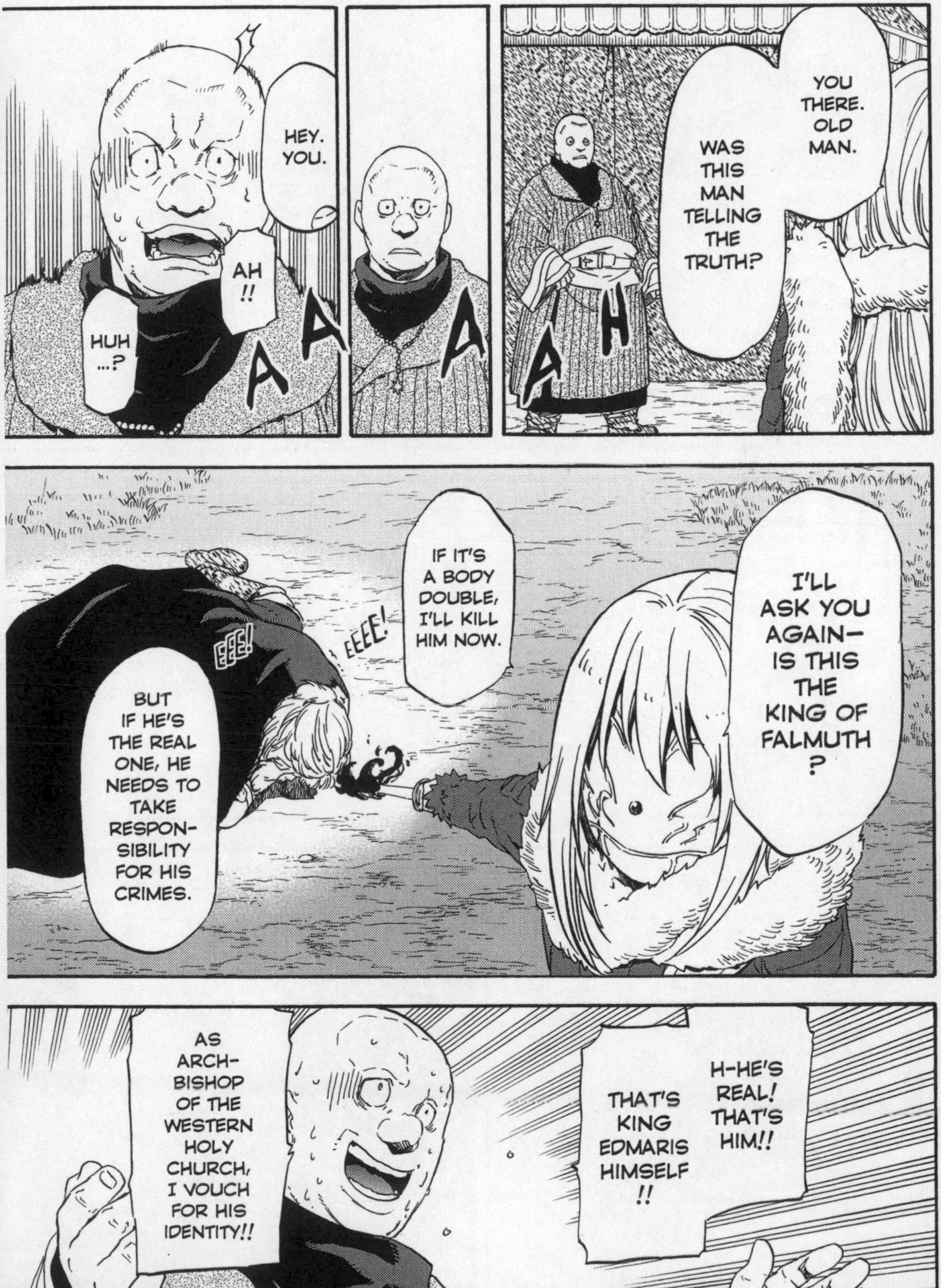
YOU THERE. OLD MAN.
WAS THIS MAN TELLING THE TRUTH?
AAAAH
HEY. YOU.
AH!!
HUH...?
I'LL ASK YOU AGAIN— IS THIS THE KING OF FALMUTH?
IF IT'S A BODY DOUBLE, I'LL KILL HIM NOW.
EEEE!
EEE!
BUT IF HE'S THE REAL ONE, HE NEEDS TO TAKE RESPON- SIBILITY FOR HIS CRIMES.
H-HE'S REAL! THAT'S HIM!!
THAT'S KING EDMARIS HIMSELF!!
AS ARCH- BISHOP OF THE WESTERN HOLY CHURCH, I VOUCH FOR HIS IDENTITY!!

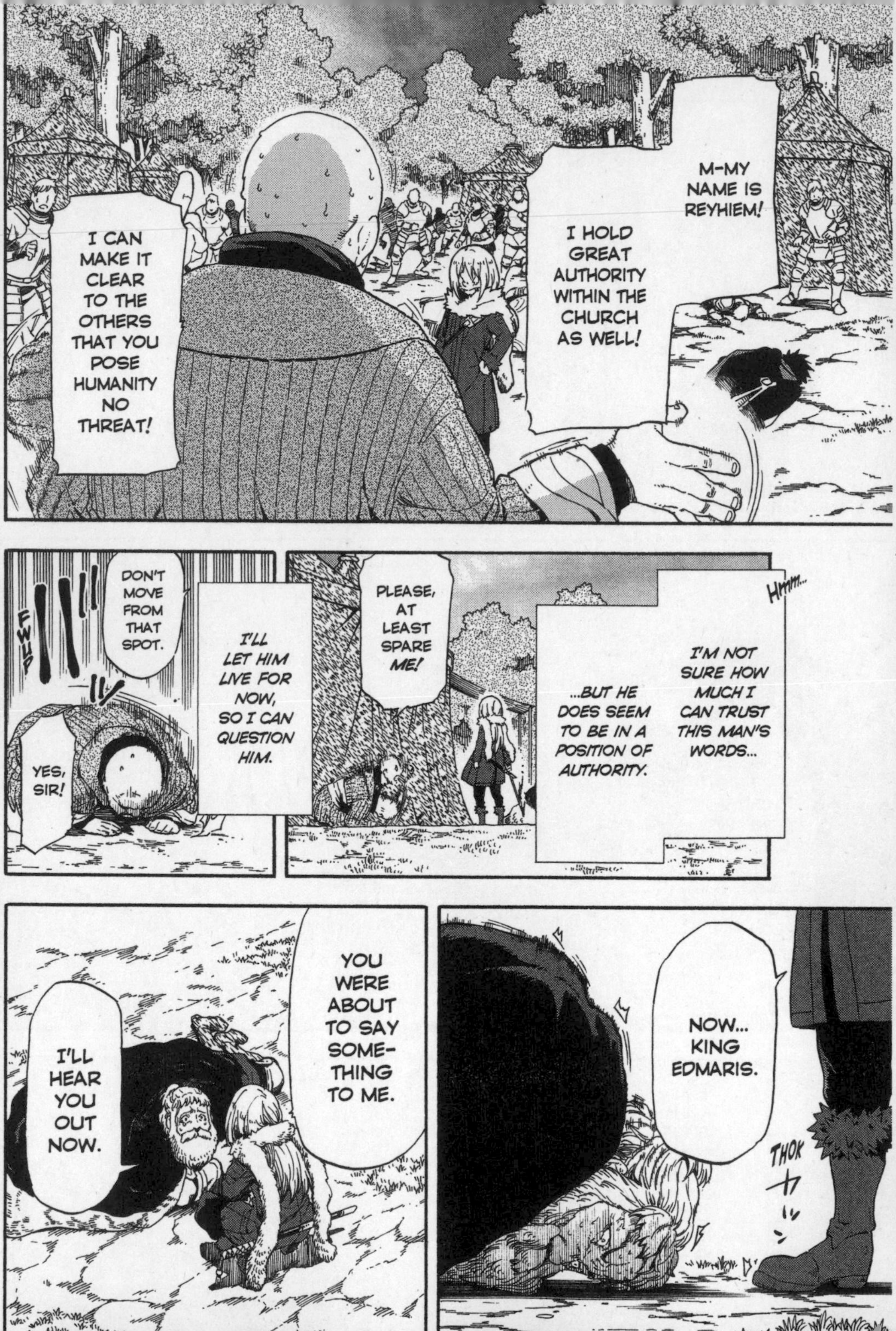
M-MY NAME IS REYHIEM!
I HOLD GREAT AUTHORITY WITHIN THE CHURCH AS WELL!
I CAN MAKE IT CLEAR TO THE OTHERS THAT YOU POSE HUMANITY NO THREAT!
Hmm...
I'M NOT SURE HOW MUCH I CAN TRUST THIS MAN'S WORDS...
...BUT HE DOES SEEM TO BE IN A POSITION OF AUTHORITY.
PLEASE, AT LEAST SPARE ME!
I'LL LET HIM LIVE FOR NOW, SO I CAN QUESTION HIM.
DON'T MOVE FROM THAT SPOT.
FWUP
YES, SIR!
NOW... KING EDMARIS.
THOK
YOU WERE ABOUT TO SAY SOMETHING TO ME.
I'LL HEAR YOU OUT NOW.

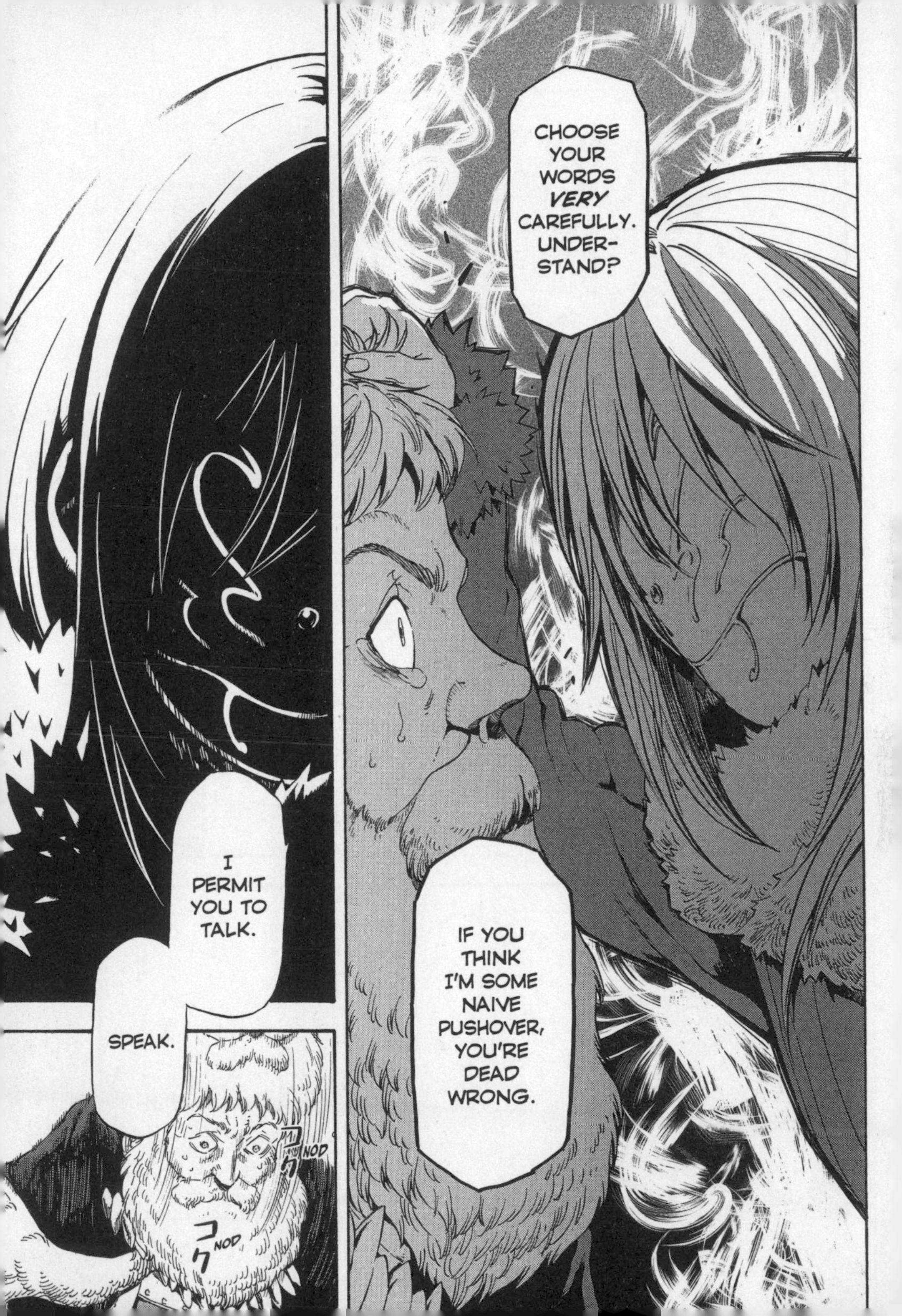
CHOOSE YOUR WORDS *VERY* CAREFULLY. UNDER-STAND?
IF YOU THINK I'M SOME NAIVE PUSHOVER, YOU'RE DEAD WRONG.
I PERMIT YOU TO TALK.
SPEAK.
コク NOD
コク NOD

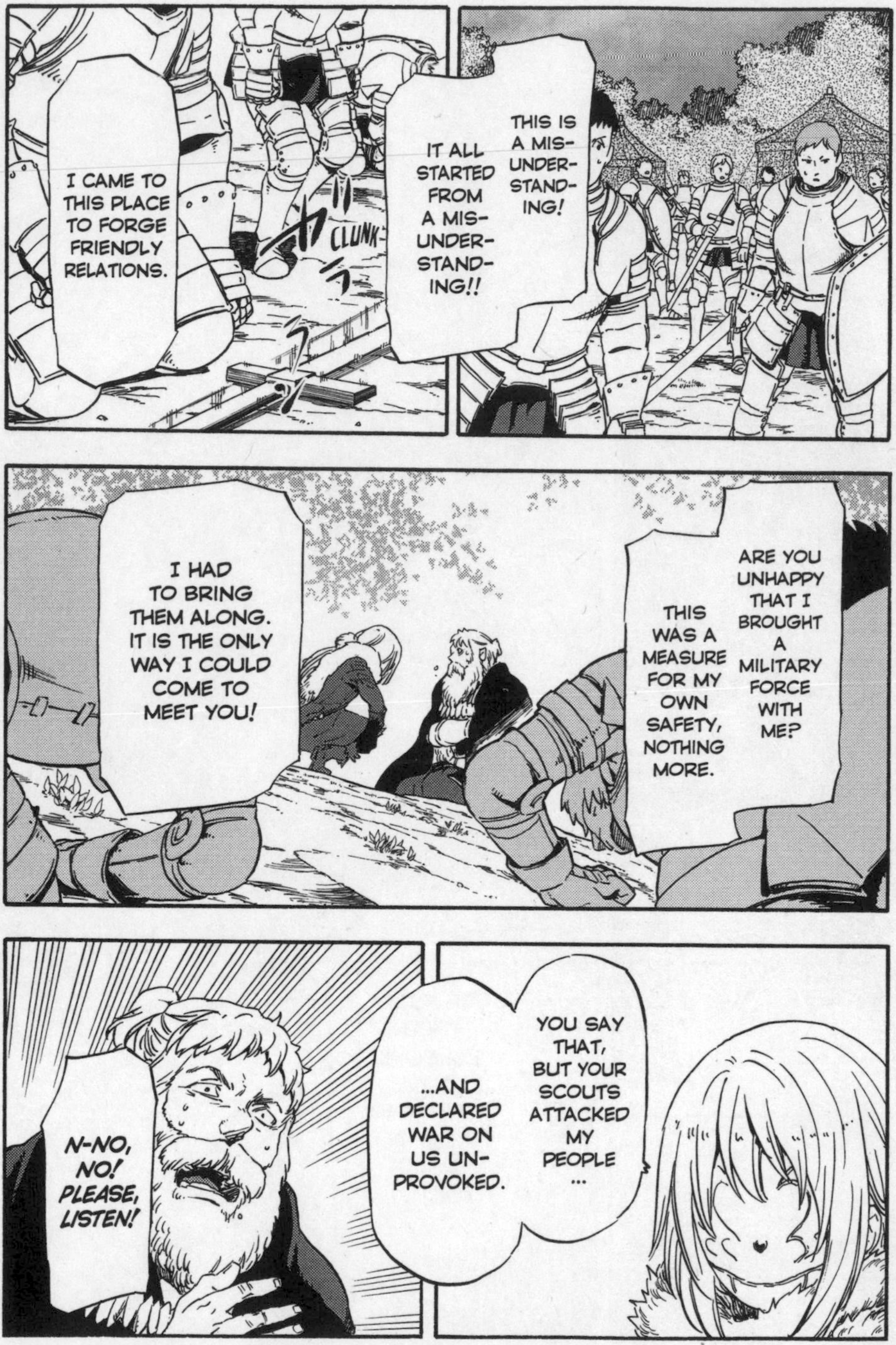
THIS IS A MIS-UNDER-STAND-ING!
IT ALL STARTED FROM A MIS-UNDER-STAND-ING!!
CLUNK
I CAME TO THIS PLACE TO FORGE FRIENDLY RELATIONS.
ARE YOU UNHAPPY THAT I BROUGHT A MILITARY FORCE WITH ME?
THIS WAS A MEASURE FOR MY OWN SAFETY, NOTHING MORE.
I HAD TO BRING THEM ALONG. IT IS THE ONLY WAY I COULD COME TO MEET YOU!
YOU SAY THAT, BUT YOUR SCOUTS ATTACKED MY PEOPLE ...
...AND DECLARED WAR ON US UN-PROVOKED.
N-NO, NO! PLEASE, LISTEN!

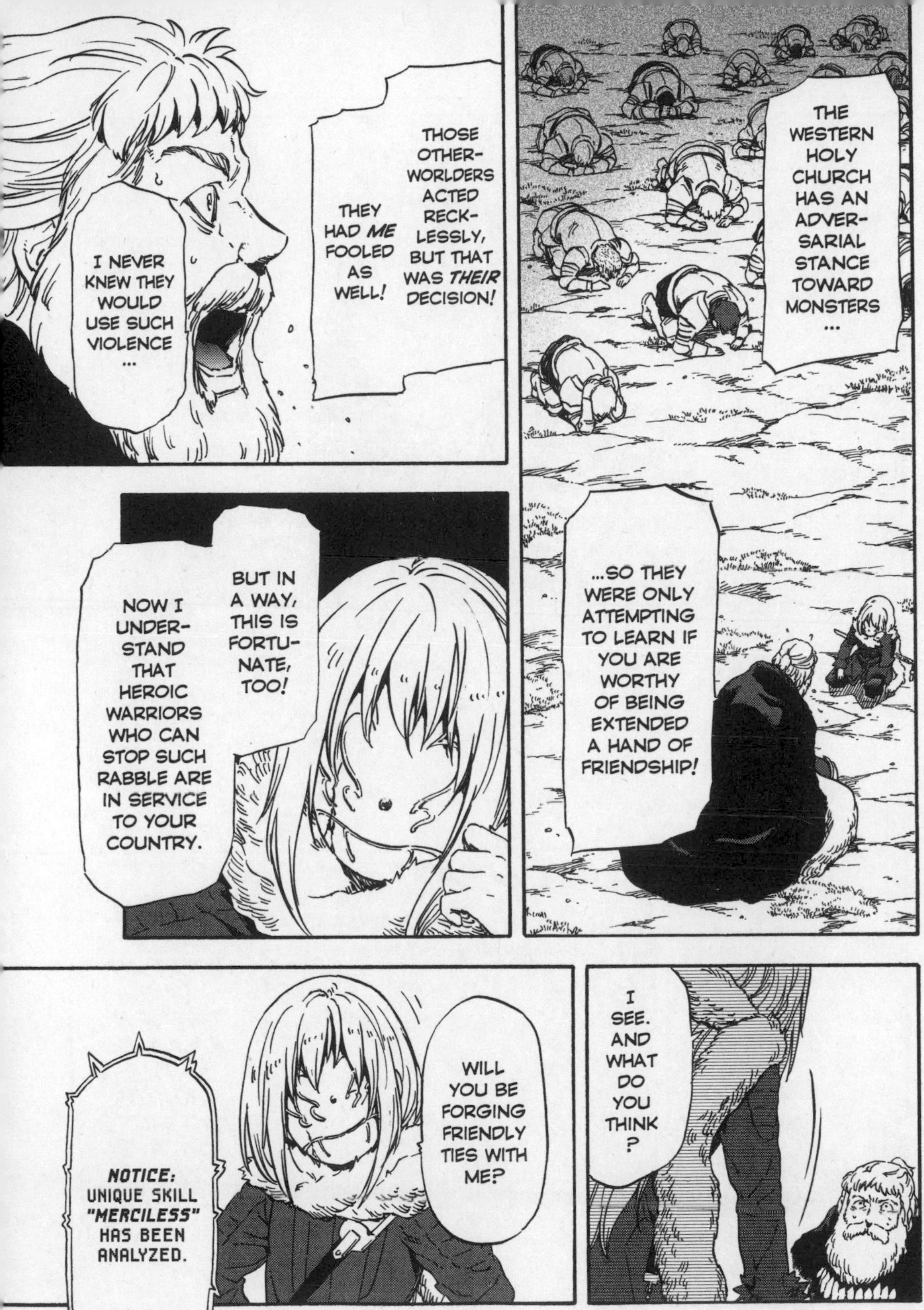
THE WESTERN HOLY CHURCH HAS AN ADVER-SARIAL STANCE TOWARD MONSTERS...
...SO THEY WERE ONLY ATTEMPTING TO LEARN IF YOU ARE WORTHY OF BEING EXTENDED A HAND OF FRIENDSHIP!
THOSE OTHER-WORLDERS ACTED RECK-LESSLY, BUT THAT WAS *THEIR* DECISION!
THEY HAD *ME* FOOLED AS WELL!
I NEVER KNEW THEY WOULD USE SUCH VIOLENCE...
BUT IN A WAY, THIS IS FORTU-NATE, TOO!
NOW I UNDER-STAND THAT HEROIC WARRIORS WHO CAN STOP SUCH RABBLE ARE IN SERVICE TO YOUR COUNTRY.
I SEE. AND WHAT DO YOU THINK?
WILL YOU BE FORGING FRIENDLY TIES WITH ME?
NOTICE: UNIQUE SKILL ***"MERCILESS"*** HAS BEEN ANALYZED.

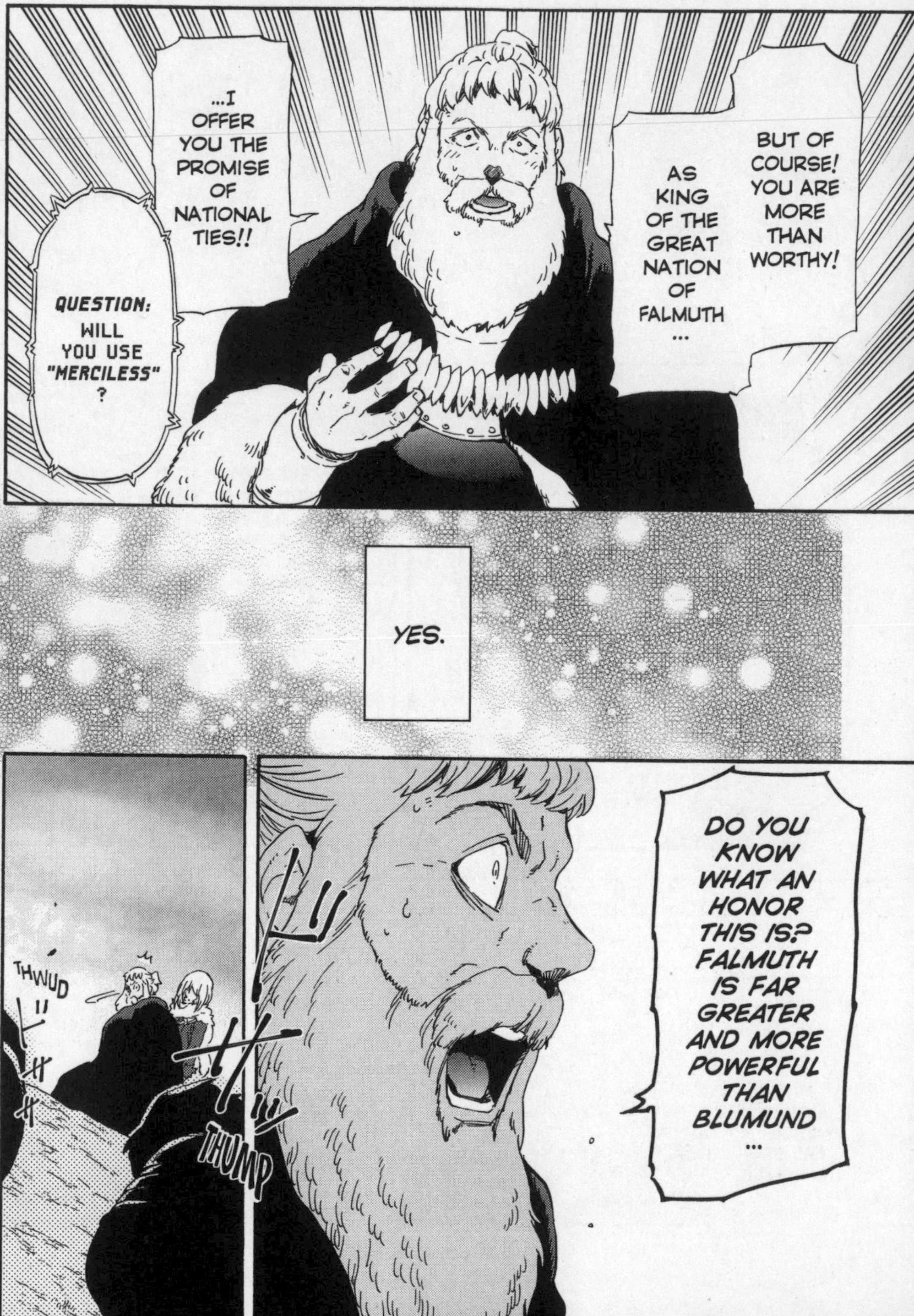
BUT OF COURSE! YOU ARE MORE THAN WORTHY!
AS KING OF THE GREAT NATION OF FALMUTH...
...I OFFER YOU THE PROMISE OF NATIONAL TIES!!
QUESTION: WILL YOU USE "MERCILESS"?
YES.
DO YOU KNOW WHAT AN HONOR THIS IS? FALMUTH IS FAR GREATER AND MORE POWERFUL THAN BLUMUND...
THUMP
THWUD

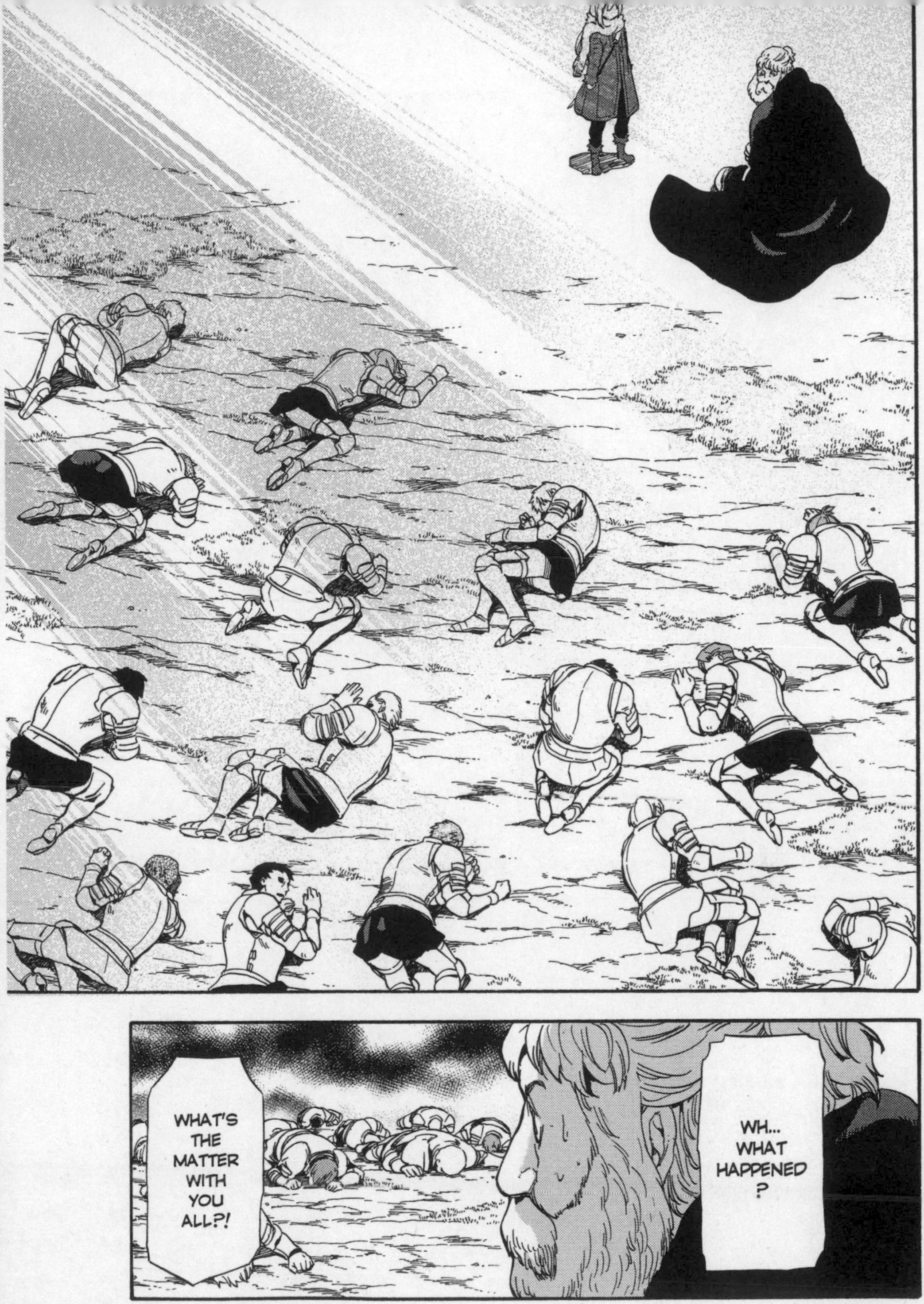
WH... WHAT HAPPENED?
WHAT'S THE MATTER WITH YOU ALL?!

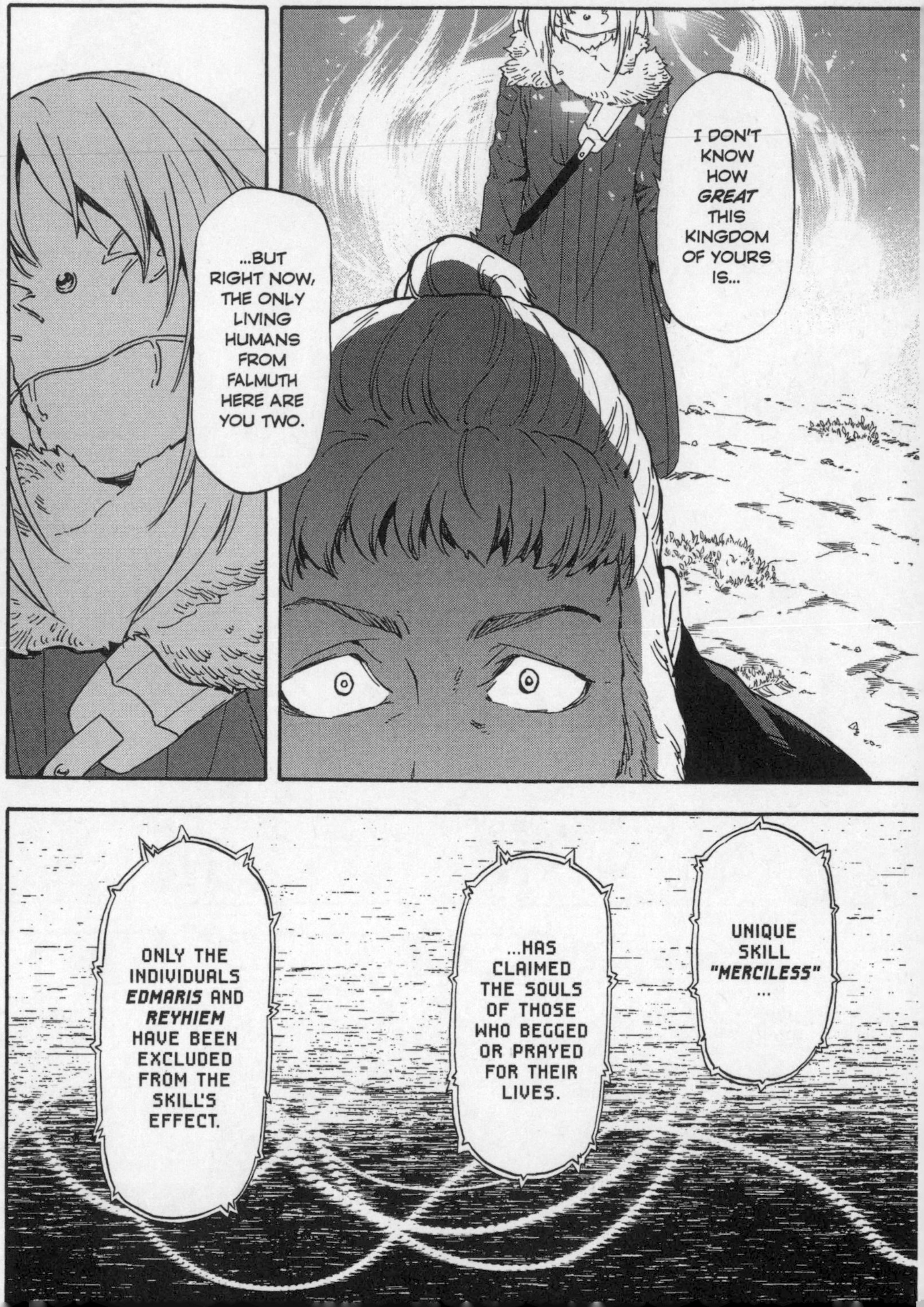
I DON'T KNOW HOW GREAT THIS KINGDOM OF YOURS IS...
...BUT RIGHT NOW, THE ONLY LIVING HUMANS FROM FALMUTH HERE ARE YOU TWO.
UNIQUE SKILL "MERCILESS" ...
...HAS CLAIMED THE SOULS OF THOSE WHO BEGGED OR PRAYED FOR THEIR LIVES.
ONLY THE INDIVIDUALS EDMARIS AND REYHIEM HAVE BEEN EXCLUDED FROM THE SKILL'S EFFECT.

WITH OUR OPINIONS CLASHING THIS MUCH...

...IT MAKES YOU VERY HARD TO TRUST.

IF YOU WERE NOT THE KING...

"...I WOULD HAVE HURLED THE BRUNT OF MY ANGER AT YOU.

IT'S TOO BAD.

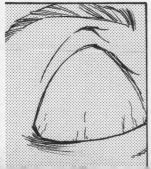

BUT I CAN LEAVE THAT TO SHION, I SUPPOSE.

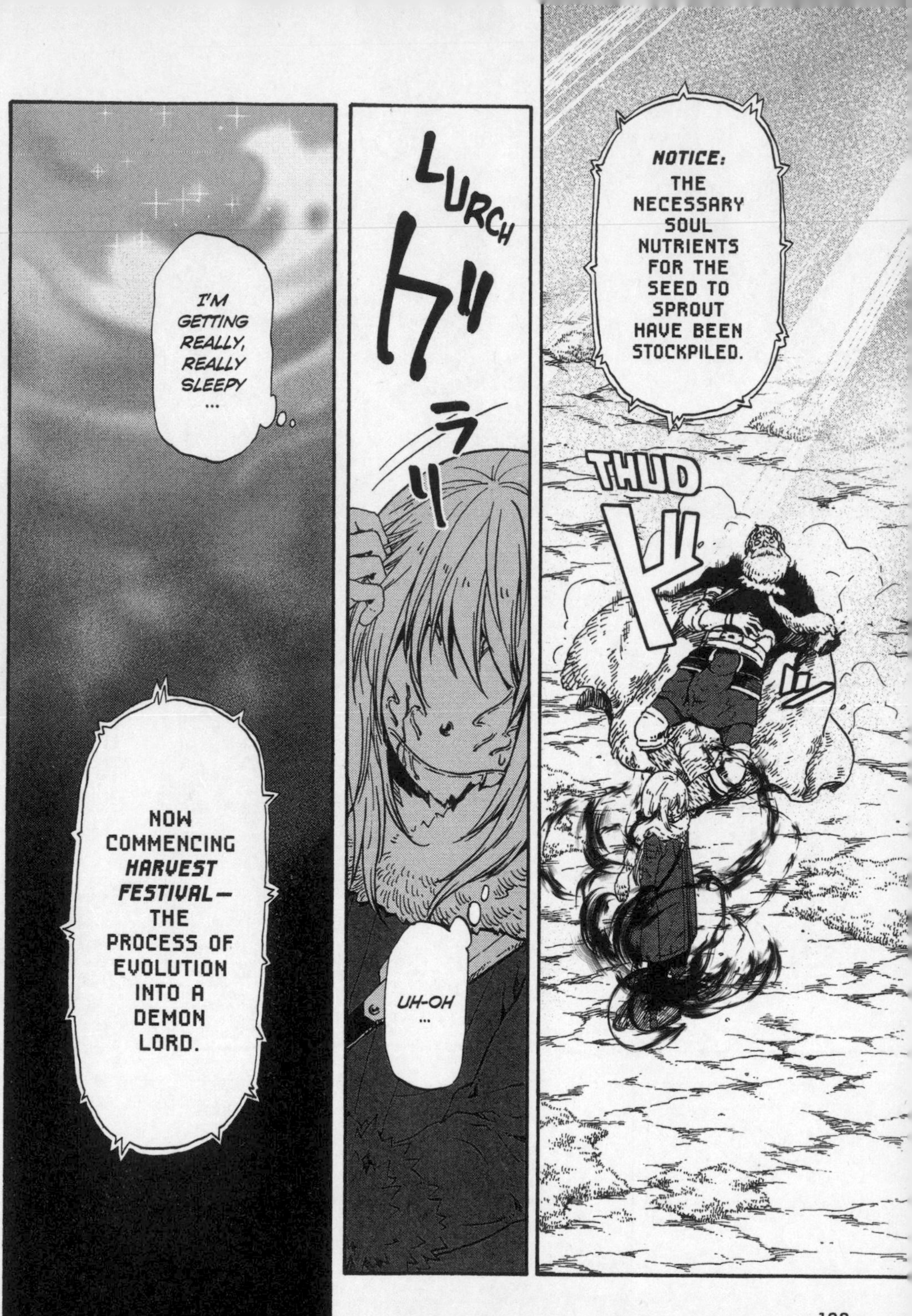
NOTICE: THE NECESSARY SOUL NUTRIENTS FOR THE SEED TO SPROUT HAVE BEEN STOCKPILED.
THUD
LURCH
UH-OH ...
I'M GETTING REALLY, REALLY SLEEPY ...
NOW COMMENCING HARVEST FESTIVAL—THE PROCESS OF EVOLUTION INTO A DEMON LORD.

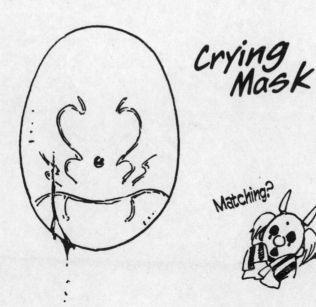

Crying
Mask

Matching?

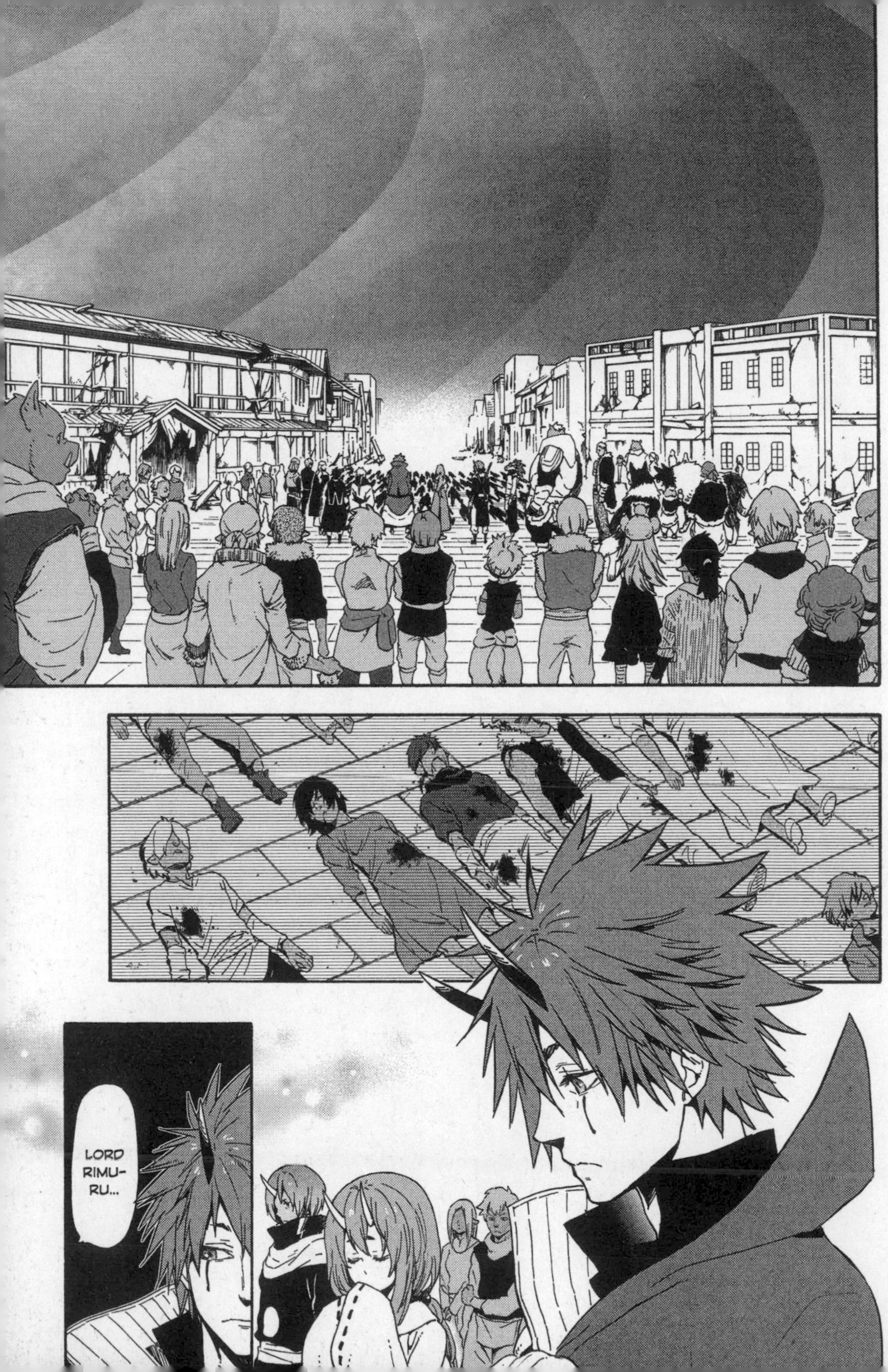
LORD RIMURU...

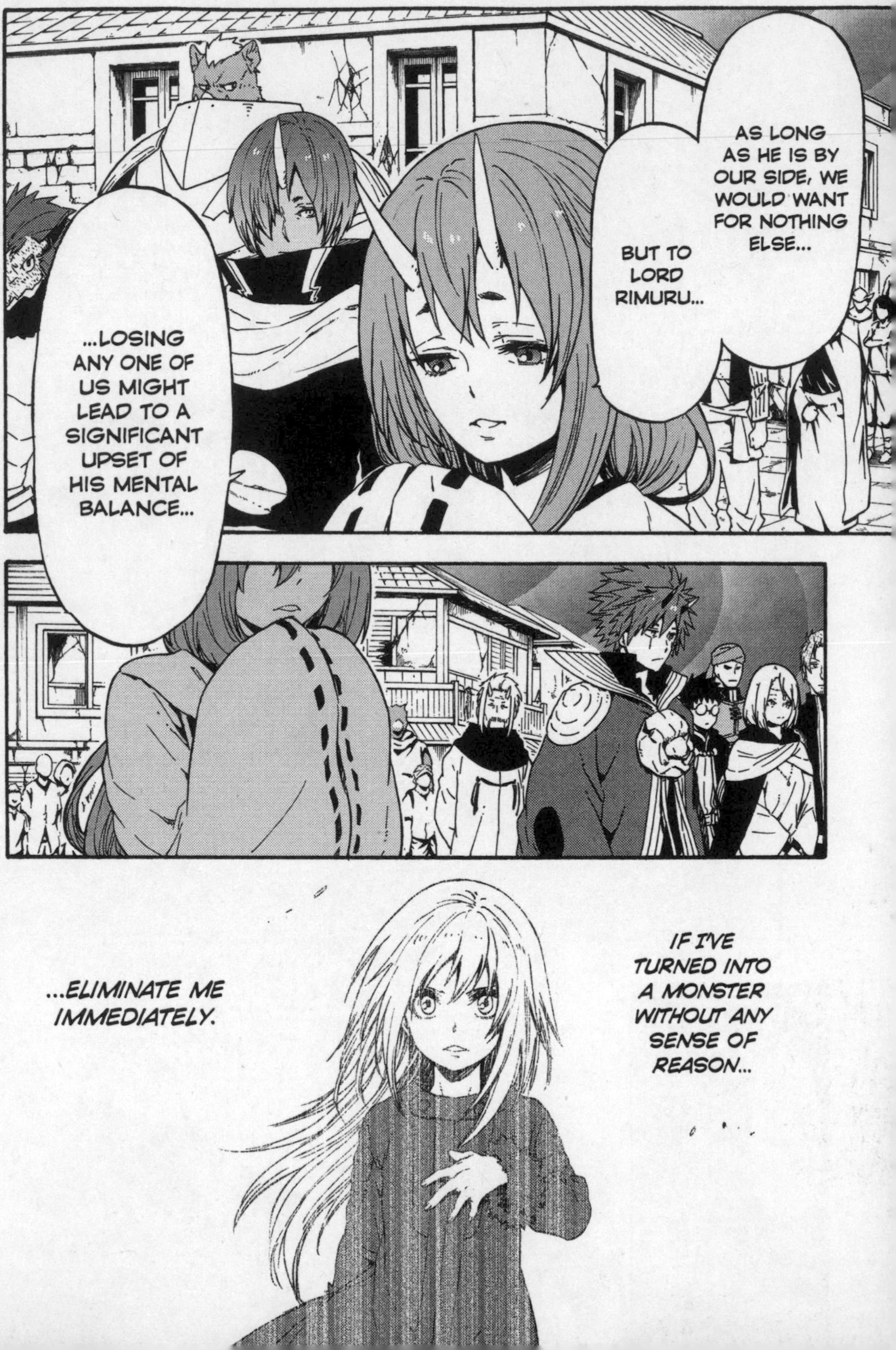
AS LONG AS HE IS BY OUR SIDE, WE WOULD WANT FOR NOTHING ELSE...
BUT TO LORD RIMURU...
...LOSING ANY ONE OF US MIGHT LEAD TO A SIGNIFICANT UPSET OF HIS MENTAL BALANCE...
IF I'VE TURNED INTO A MONSTER WITHOUT ANY SENSE OF REASON...
...ELIMINATE ME IMMEDIATELY.

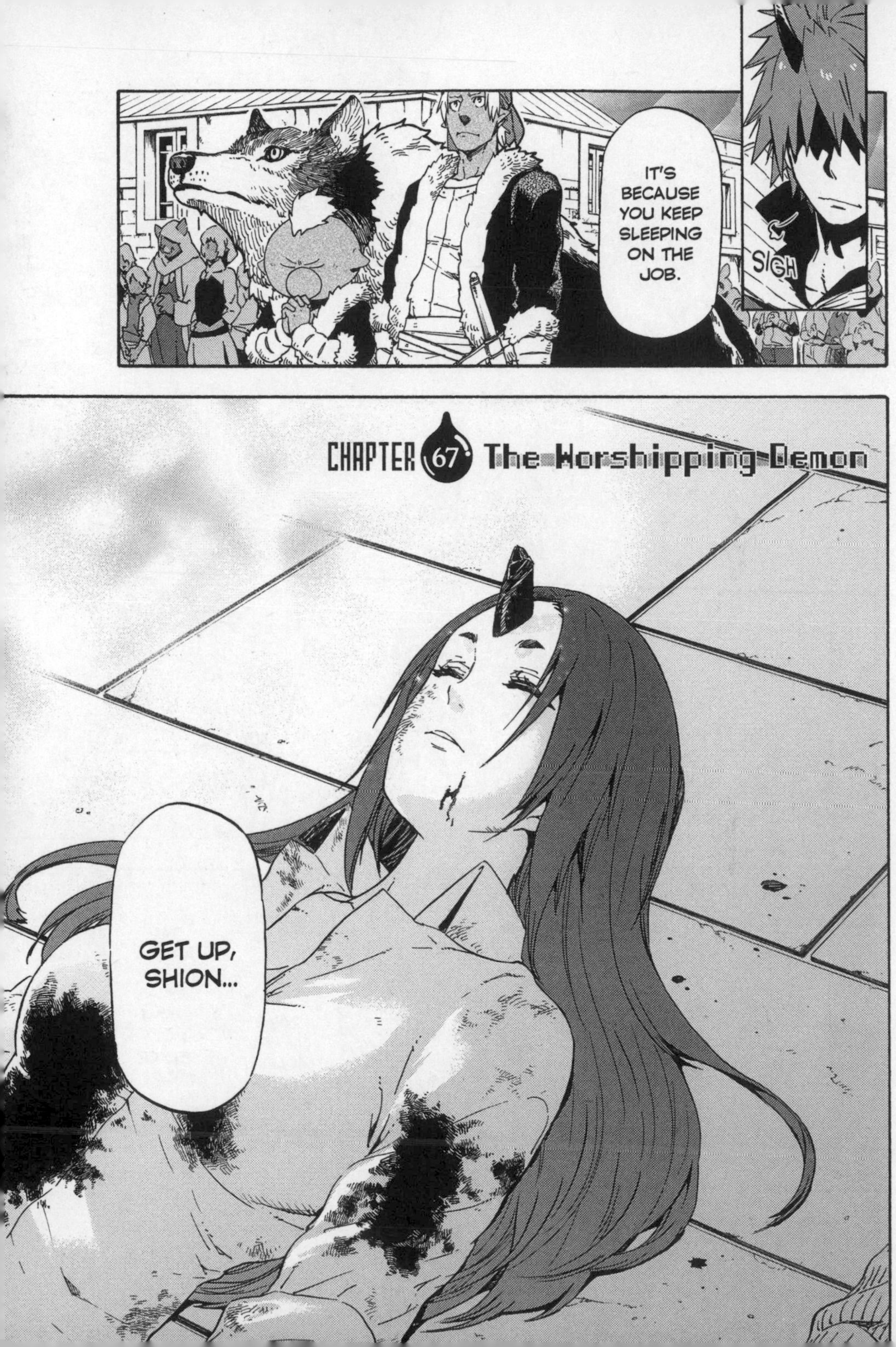
SIGH
IT'S BECAUSE YOU KEEP SLEEPING ON THE JOB.
CHAPTER 67 The Worshipping Demon
GET UP, SHION...

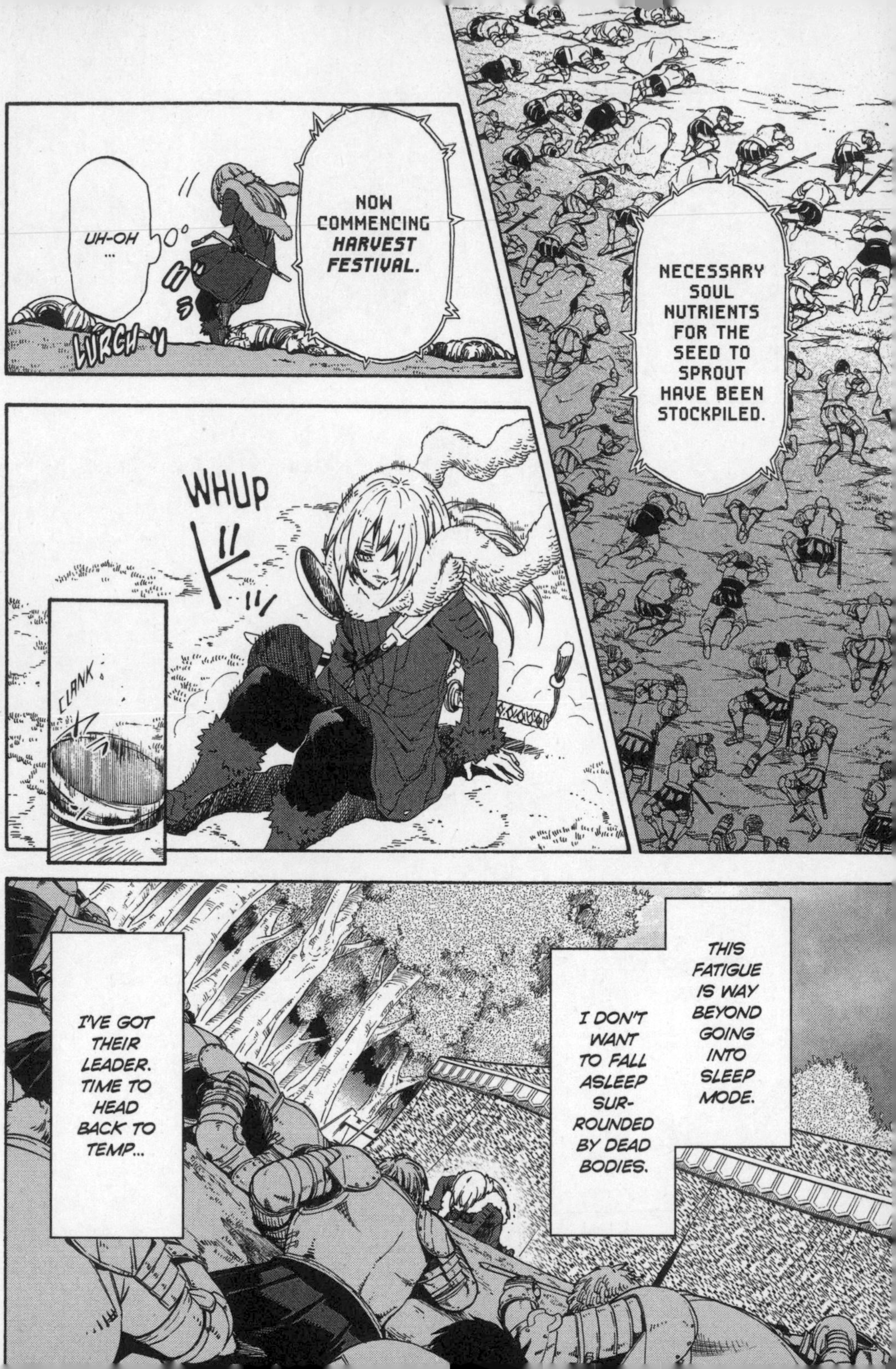
NECESSARY SOUL NUTRIENTS FOR THE SEED TO SPROUT HAVE BEEN STOCKPILED.
NOW COMMENCING *HARVEST FESTIVAL*.
UH-OH ...
LURCH
WHUP
CLANK
THIS FATIGUE IS WAY BEYOND GOING INTO SLEEP MODE.
I DON'T WANT TO FALL ASLEEP SUR-ROUNDED BY DEAD BODIES.
I'VE GOT THEIR LEADER. TIME TO HEAD BACK TO TEMP...

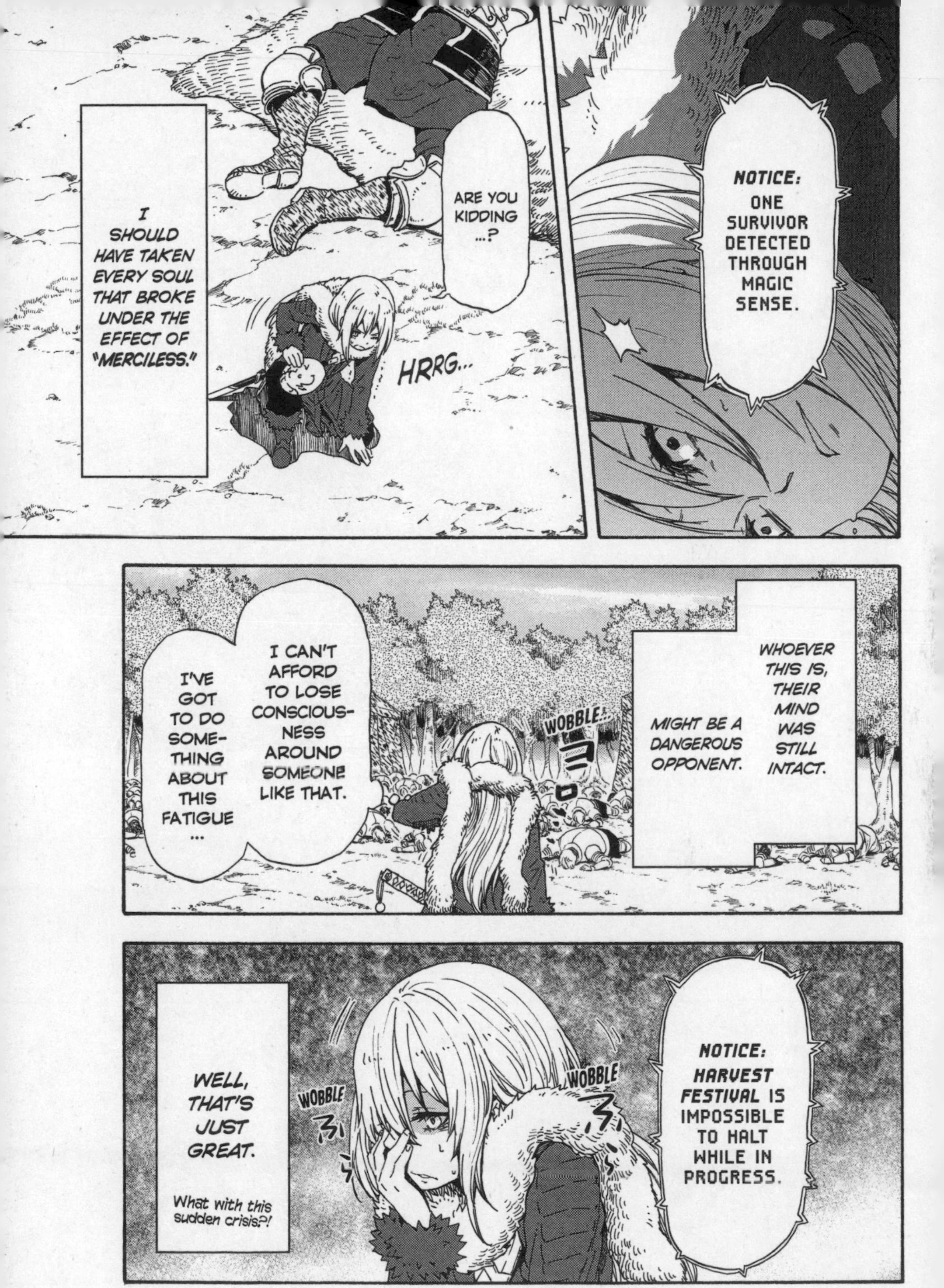
NOTICE: ONE SURVIVOR DETECTED THROUGH MAGIC SENSE.
ARE YOU KIDDING ...?
HRRG...
I SHOULD HAVE TAKEN EVERY SOUL THAT BROKE UNDER THE EFFECT OF "MERCILESS."
WHOEVER THIS IS, THEIR MIND WAS STILL INTACT.
MIGHT BE A DANGEROUS OPPONENT.
WOBBLE...
I CAN'T AFFORD TO LOSE CONSCIOUSNESS AROUND SOMEONE LIKE THAT.
I'VE GOT TO DO SOMETHING ABOUT THIS FATIGUE ...
NOTICE: HARVEST FESTIVAL IS IMPOSSIBLE TO HALT WHILE IN PROGRESS.
WOBBLE
WOBBLE
WELL, THAT'S JUST GREAT.
What with this sudden crisis?!

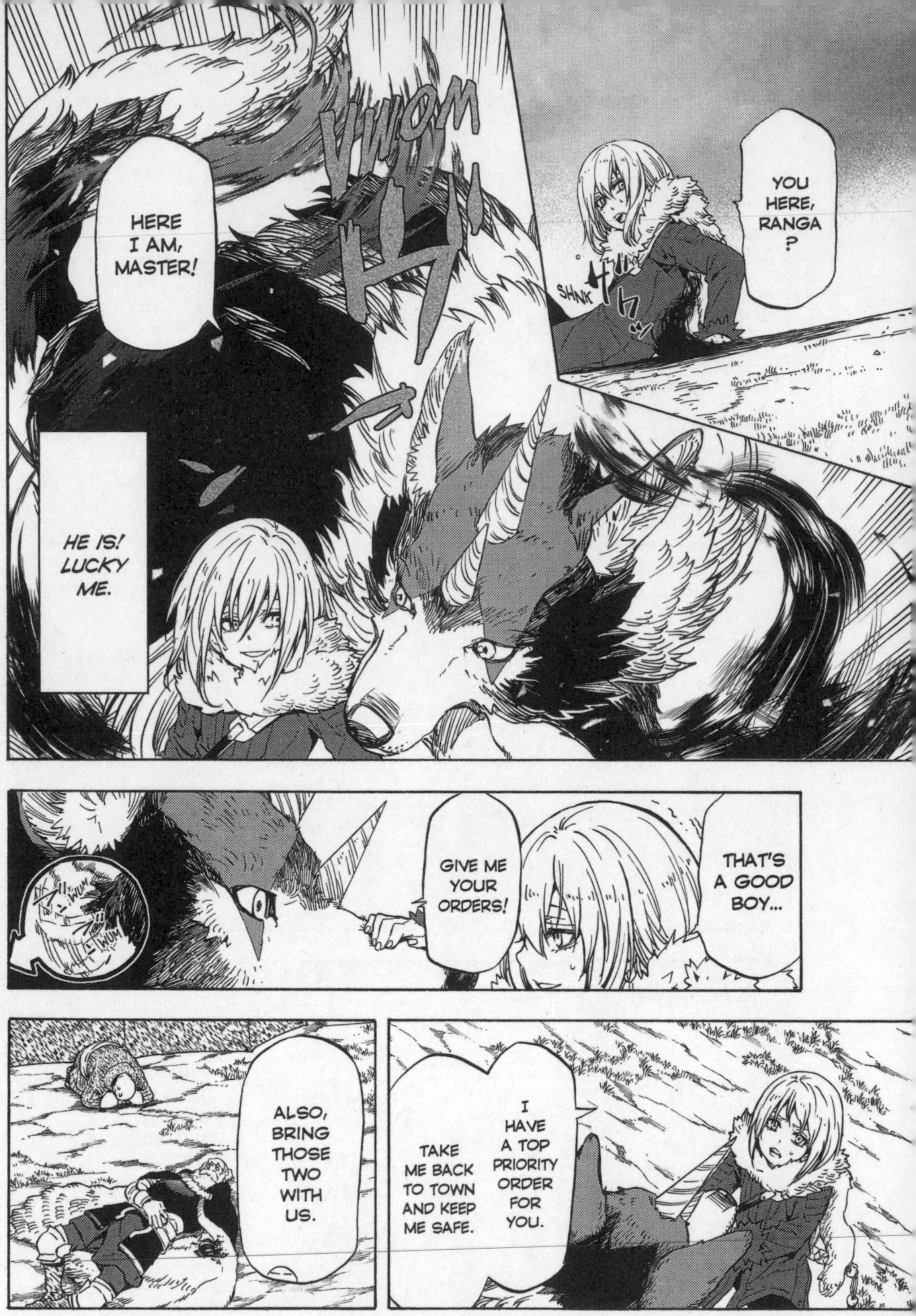
YOU HERE, RANGA?
SHNK
VWOM
HERE I AM, MASTER!
HE IS! LUCKY ME.
THAT'S A GOOD BOY...
GIVE ME YOUR ORDERS!
WUM
WUM
I HAVE A TOP PRIORITY ORDER FOR YOU.
TAKE ME BACK TO TOWN AND KEEP ME SAFE.
ALSO, BRING THOSE TWO WITH US.

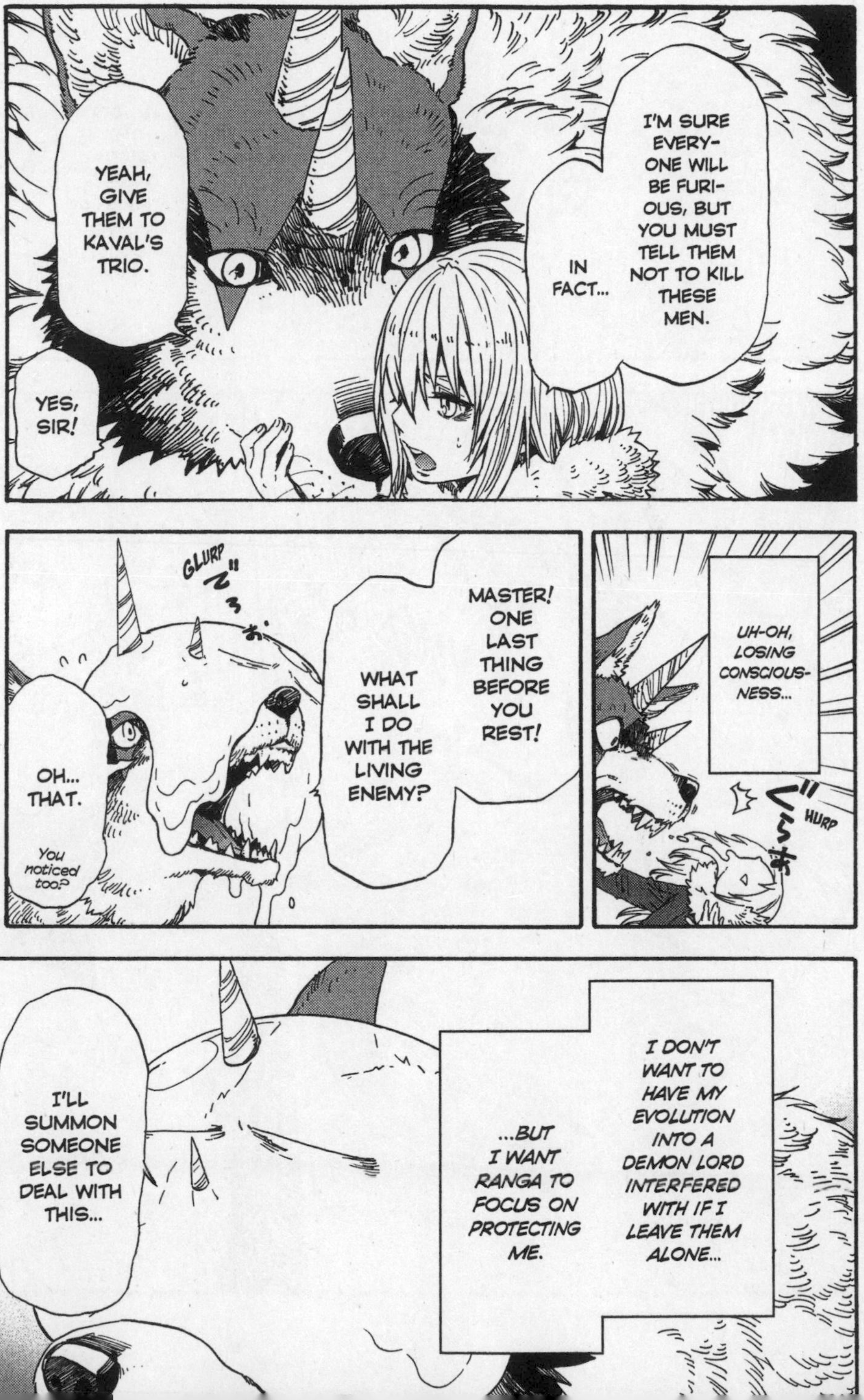
I'M SURE EVERY-ONE WILL BE FURI-OUS, BUT YOU MUST TELL THEM NOT TO KILL THESE MEN.
IN FACT...
YEAH, GIVE THEM TO KAVAL'S TRIO.
YES, SIR!
UH-OH, LOSING CONSCIOUS-NESS...
HURP
MASTER! ONE LAST THING BEFORE YOU REST!
GLURP
WHAT SHALL I DO WITH THE LIVING ENEMY?
OH... THAT.
You noticed too?
I DON'T WANT TO HAVE MY EVOLUTION INTO A DEMON LORD INTERFERED WITH IF I LEAVE THEM ALONE...
...BUT I WANT RANGA TO FOCUS ON PROTECTING ME.
I'LL SUMMON SOMEONE ELSE TO DEAL WITH THIS...

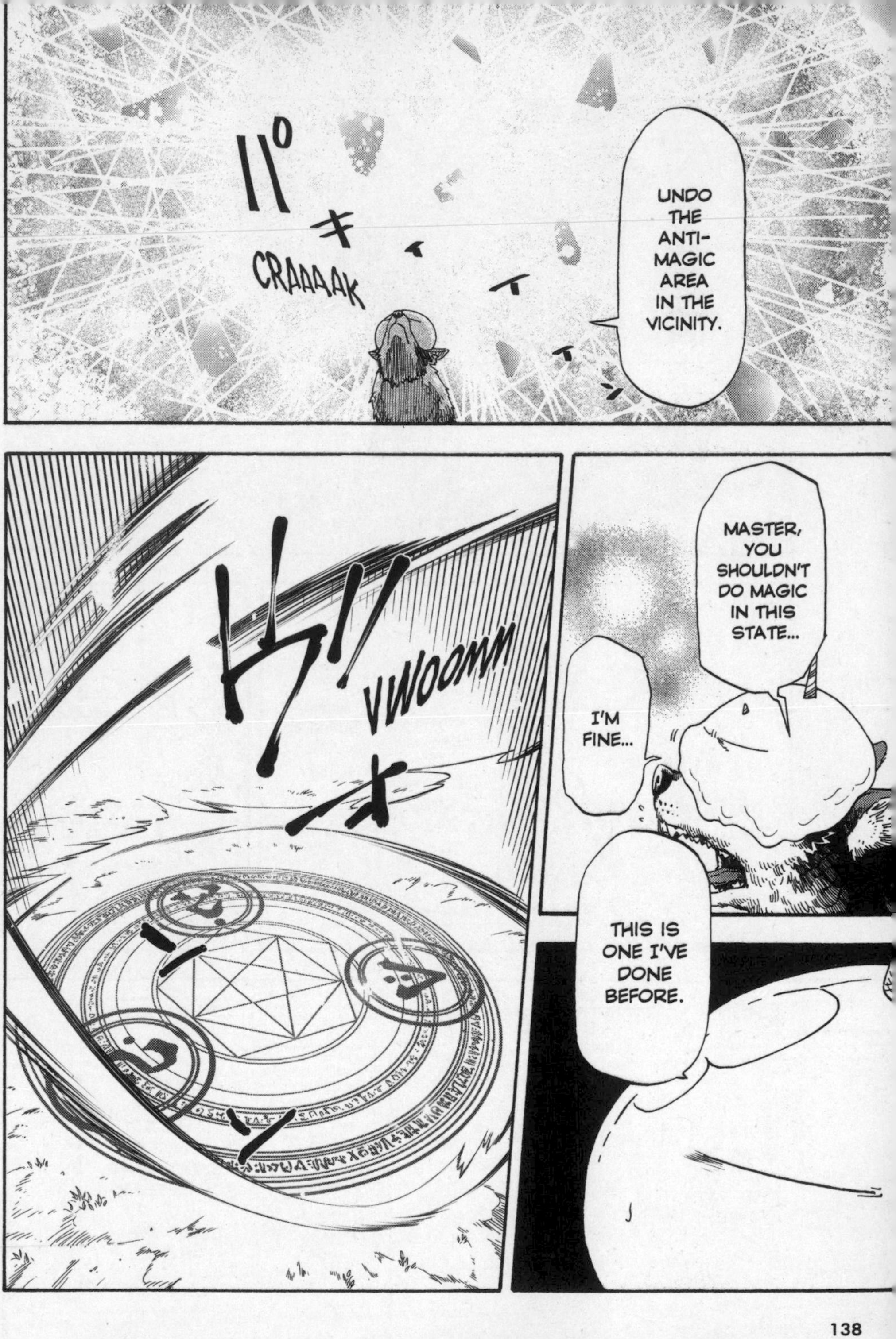
CRAAAAK
UNDO THE ANTI-MAGIC AREA IN THE VICINITY.
MASTER, YOU SHOULDN'T DO MAGIC IN THIS STATE...
I'M FINE...
THIS IS ONE I'VE DONE BEFORE.
VWOOMM

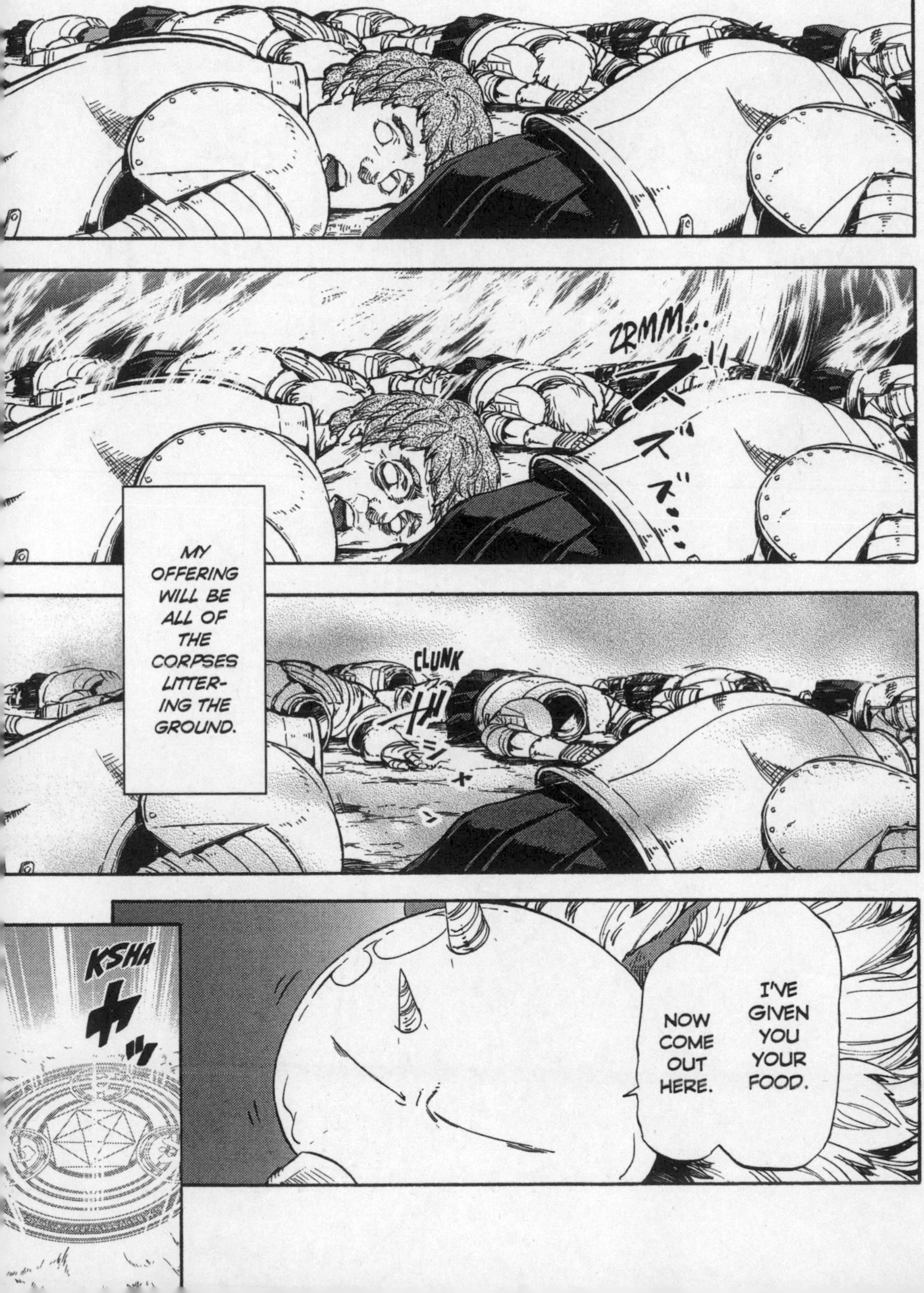
ZRMM...
ズズズ...
MY OFFERING WILL BE ALL OF THE CORPSES LITTERING THE GROUND.
CLUNK
I'VE GIVEN YOU YOUR FOOD.
NOW COME OUT HERE.
KSHA

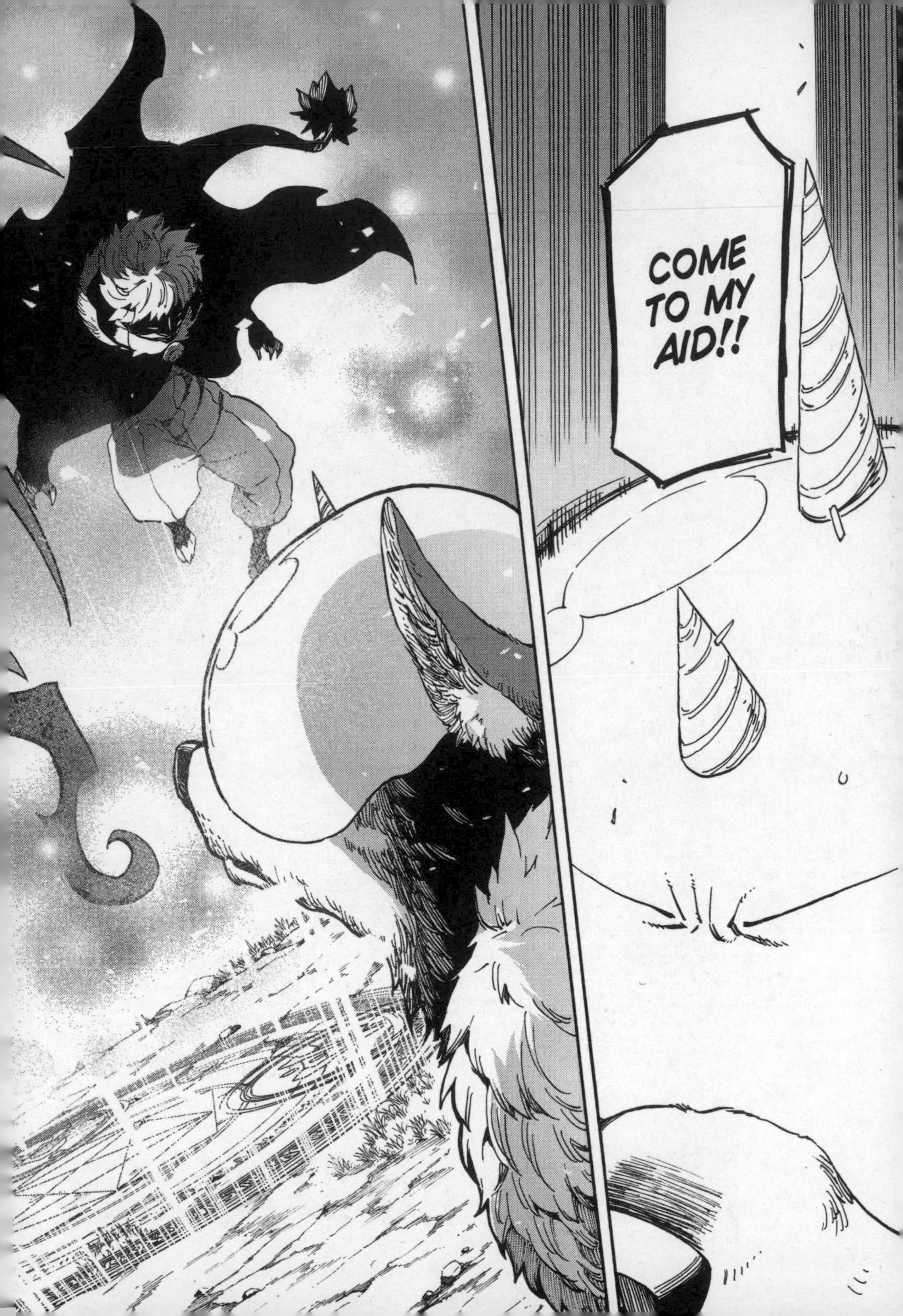
COME TO MY AID!!

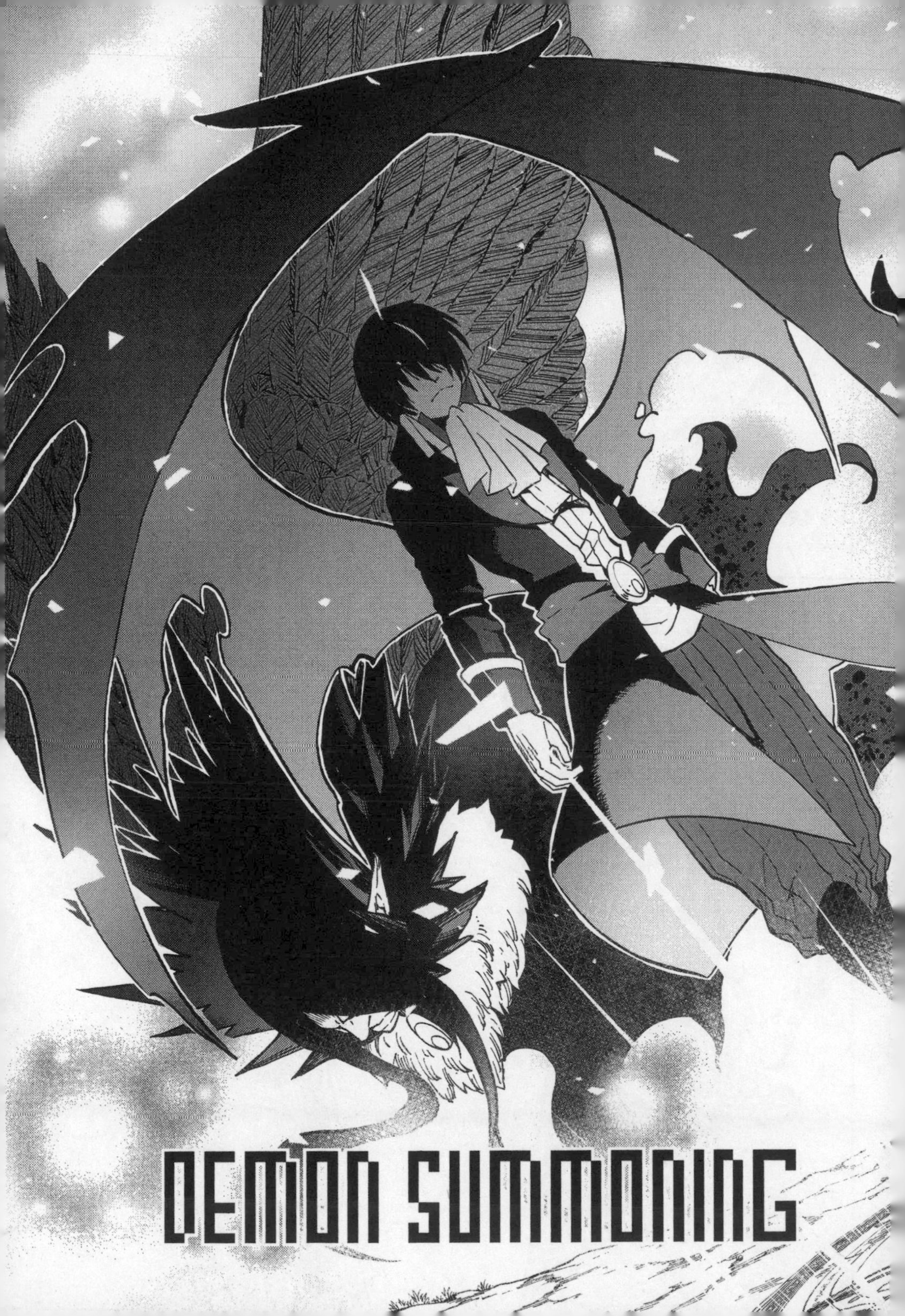
DEMON SUMMONING

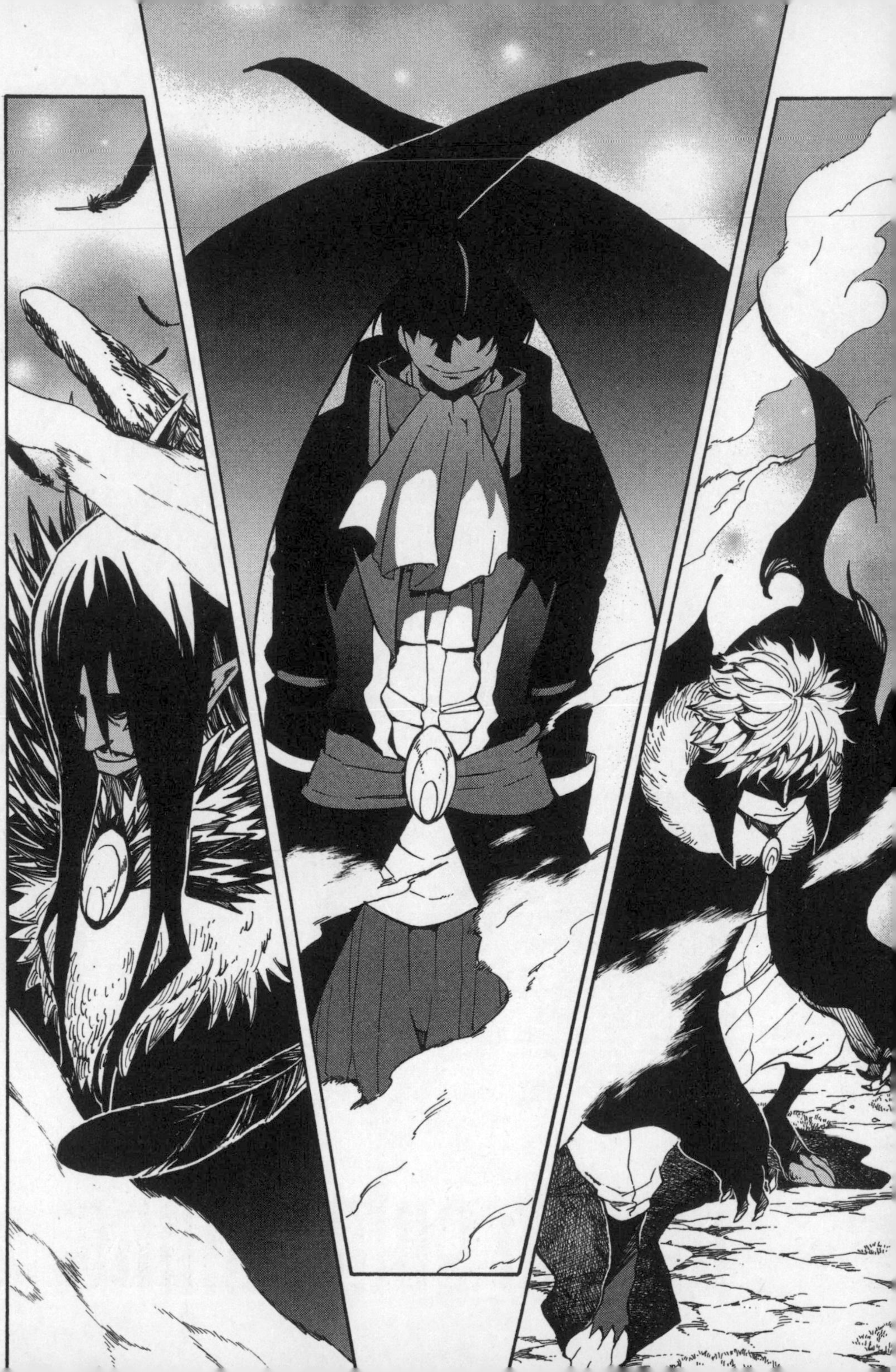

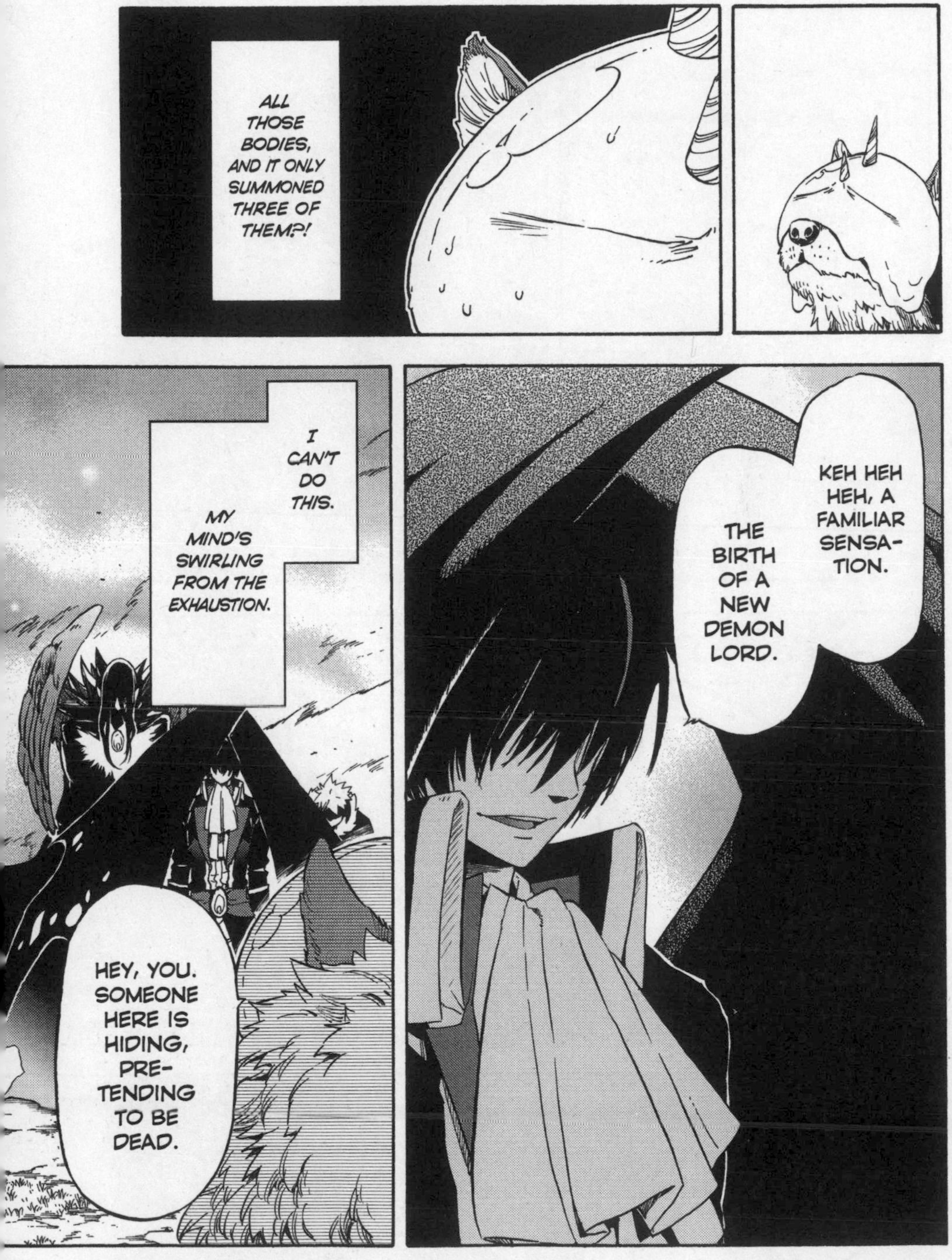
ALL THOSE BODIES, AND IT ONLY SUMMONED THREE OF THEM?!
KEH HEH HEH, A FAMILIAR SENSATION.
THE BIRTH OF A NEW DEMON LORD.
I CAN'T DO THIS.
MY MIND'S SWIRLING FROM THE EXHAUSTION.
HEY, YOU. SOMEONE HERE IS HIDING, PRETENDING TO BE DEAD.

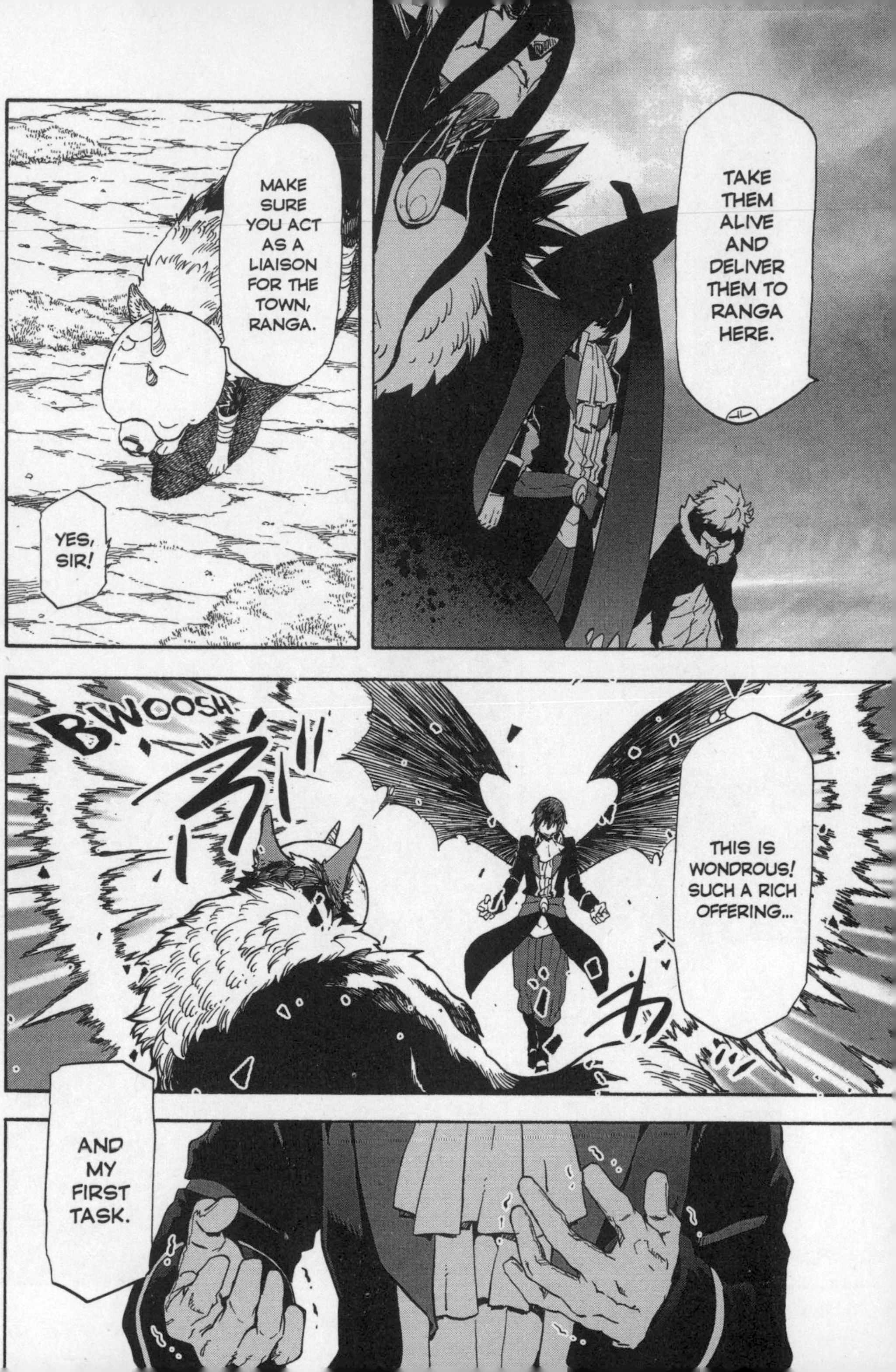
TAKE THEM ALIVE AND DELIVER THEM TO RANGA HERE.
MAKE SURE YOU ACT AS A LIAISON FOR THE TOWN, RANGA.
YES, SIR!
BWOOSH
THIS IS WONDROUS! SUCH A RICH OFFERING...
AND MY FIRST TASK.

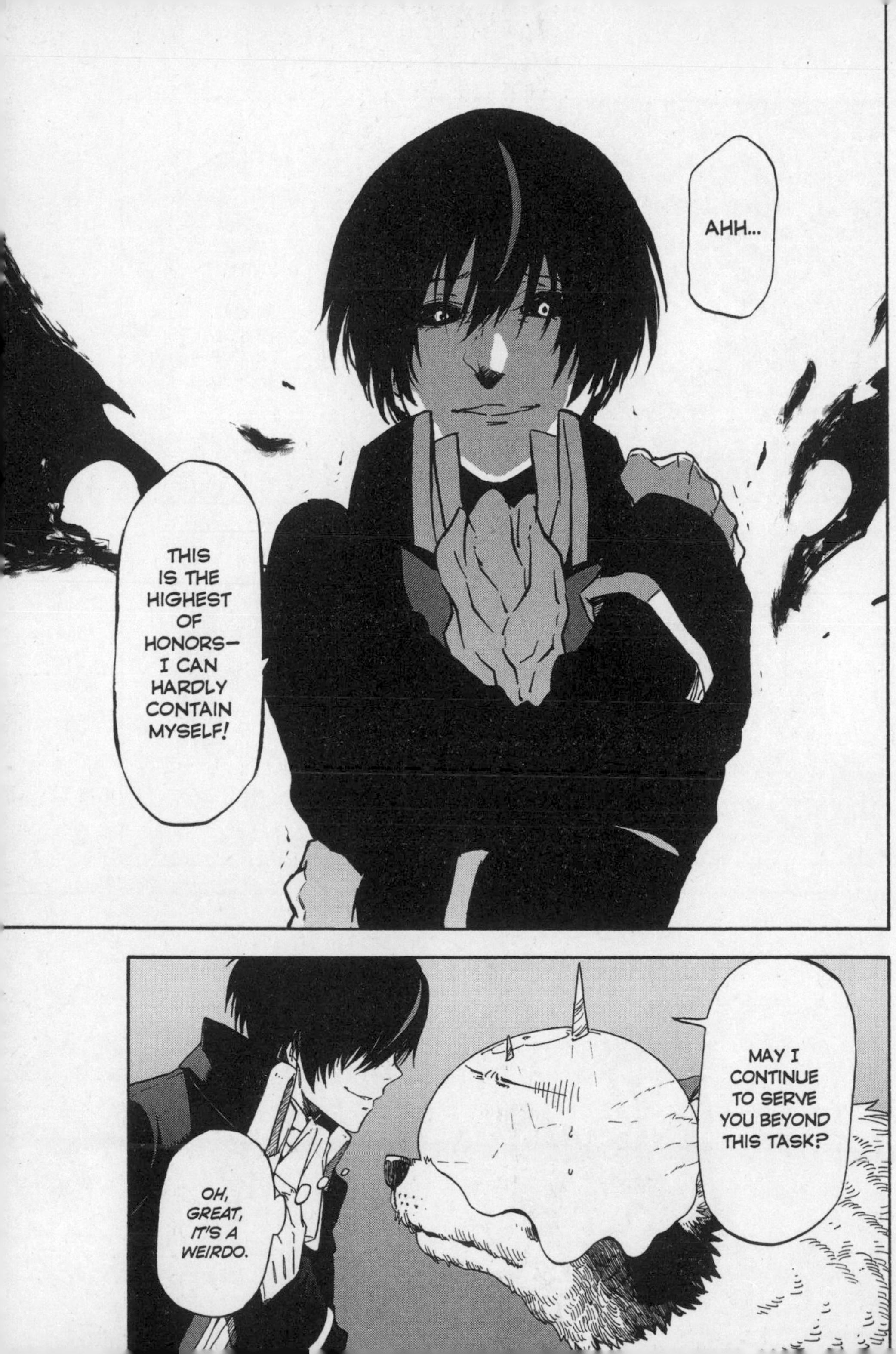
AHH...
THIS IS THE HIGHEST OF HONORS— I CAN HARDLY CONTAIN MYSELF!
MAY I CONTINUE TO SERVE YOU BEYOND THIS TASK?
OH, GREAT, IT'S A WEIRDO.

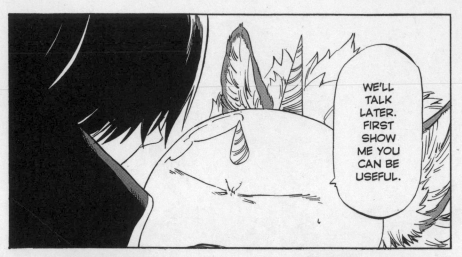

WE'LL TALK LATER. FIRST SHOW ME YOU CAN BE USEFUL.

CONSIDER IT DONE.

BE AT EASE AND REST...

GRIN

...O GREAT MASTER.

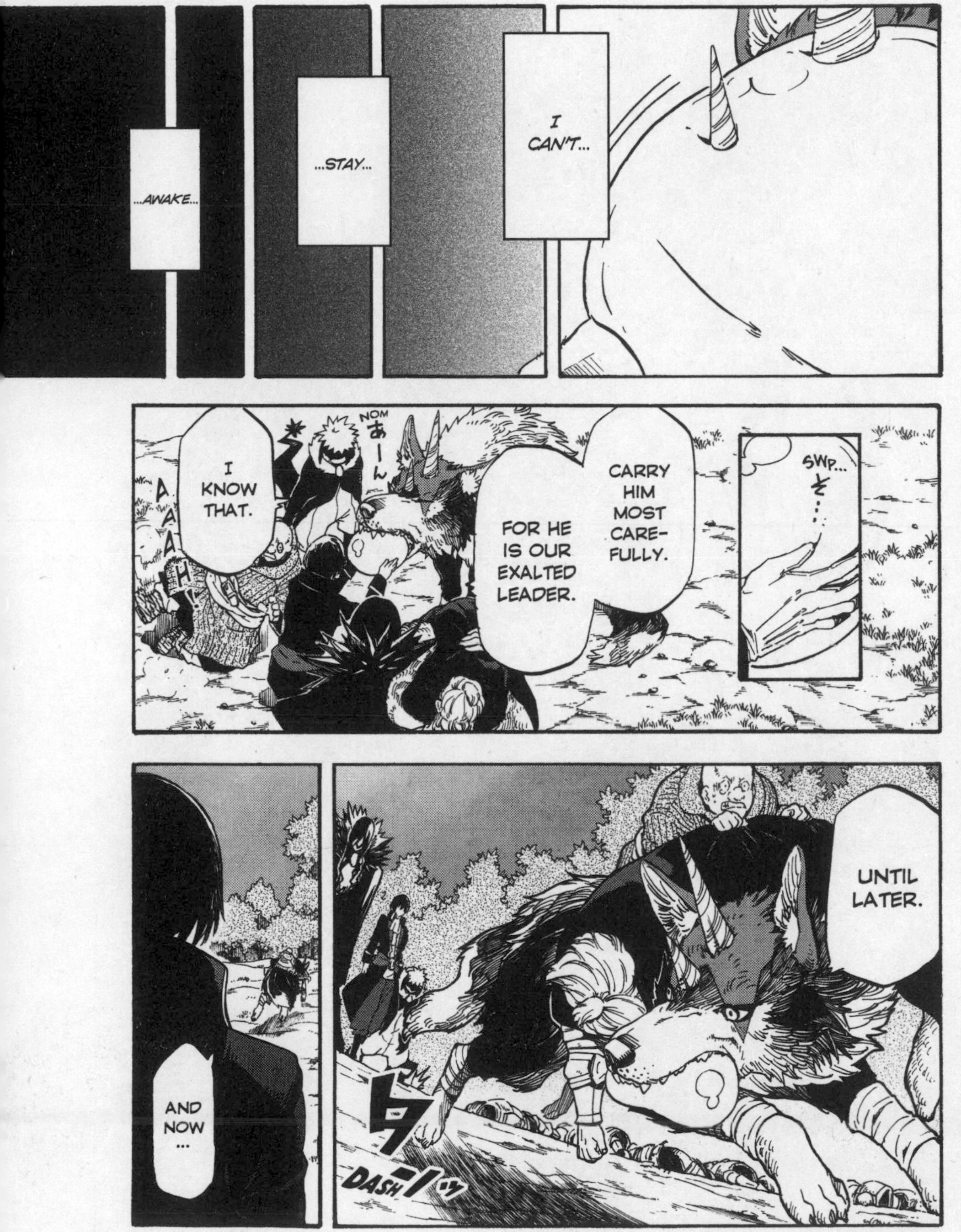
I CAN'T...
...STAY...
...AWAKE...
SWP...
CARRY HIM MOST CARE-FULLY.
FOR HE IS OUR EXALTED LEADER.
NOM
あーん
I KNOW THAT.
AAAH!
UNTIL LATER.
DASH
AND NOW ...

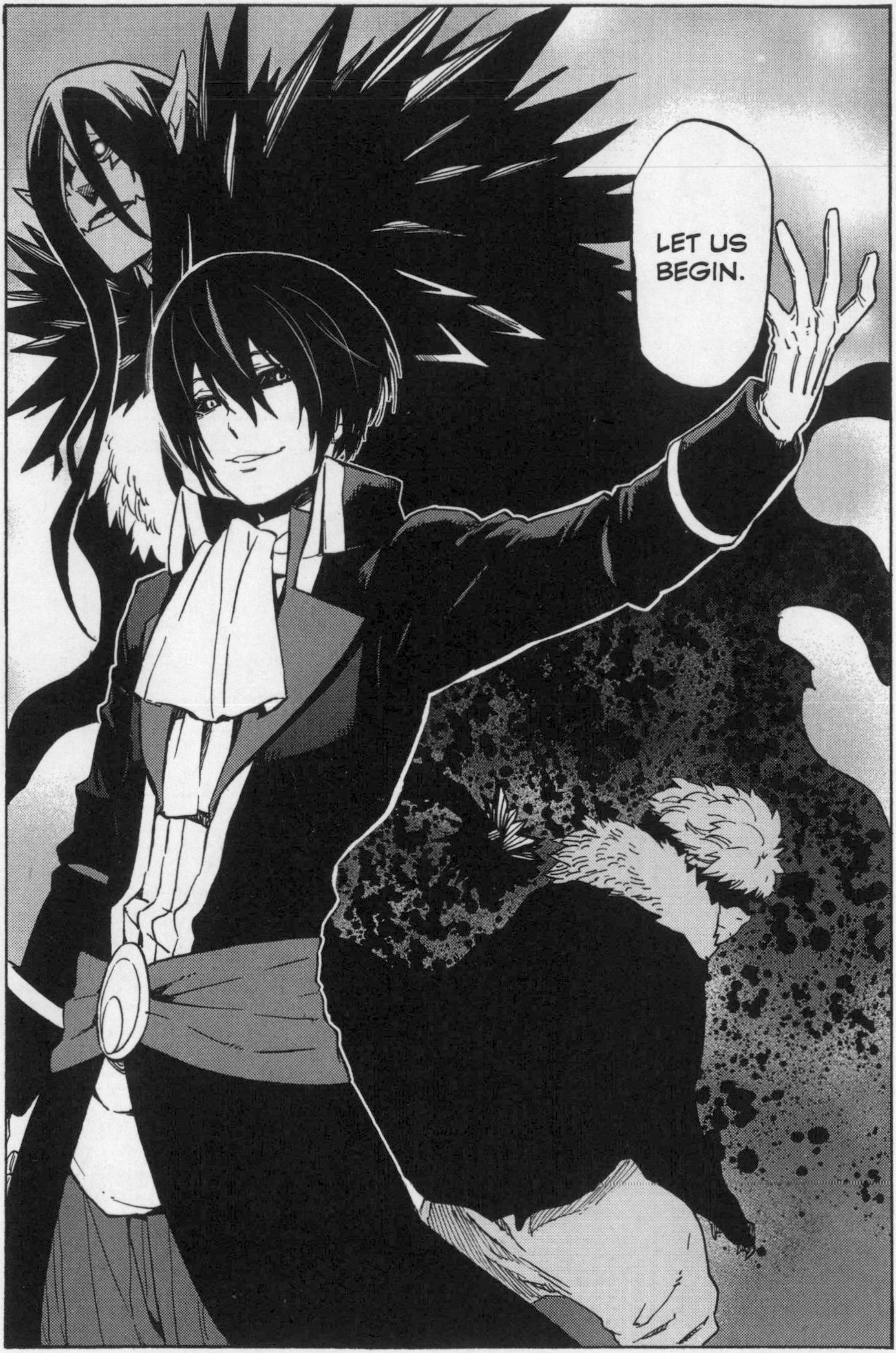
LET US BEGIN.

IT IS MY FIRST TASK... I WISH TO BE PRAISED FOR A PERFECT EXECUTION.

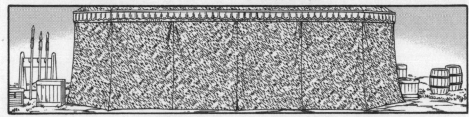

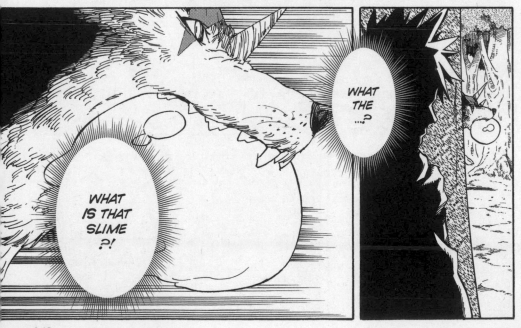

WHAT IS THAT SLIME ?!

WHAT THE ...?

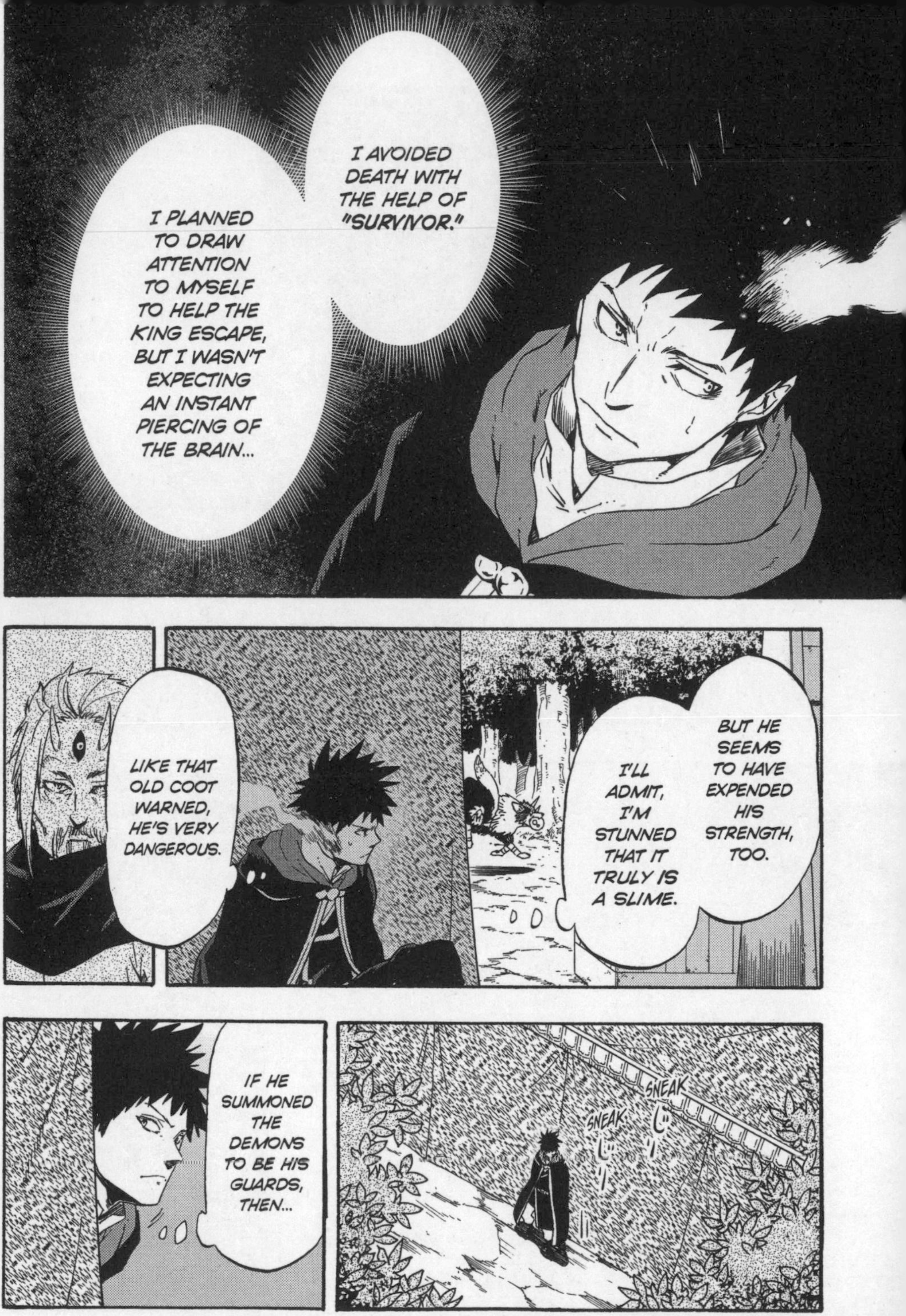
I AVOIDED DEATH WITH THE HELP OF "SURVIVOR."
I PLANNED TO DRAW ATTENTION TO MYSELF TO HELP THE KING ESCAPE, BUT I WASN'T EXPECTING AN INSTANT PIERCING OF THE BRAIN...
BUT HE SEEMS TO HAVE EXPENDED HIS STRENGTH, TOO.
I'LL ADMIT, I'M STUNNED THAT IT TRULY IS A SLIME.
LIKE THAT OLD COOT WARNED, HE'S VERY DANGEROUS.
SNEAK
SNEAK
IF HE SUMMONED THE DEMONS TO BE HIS GUARDS, THEN...

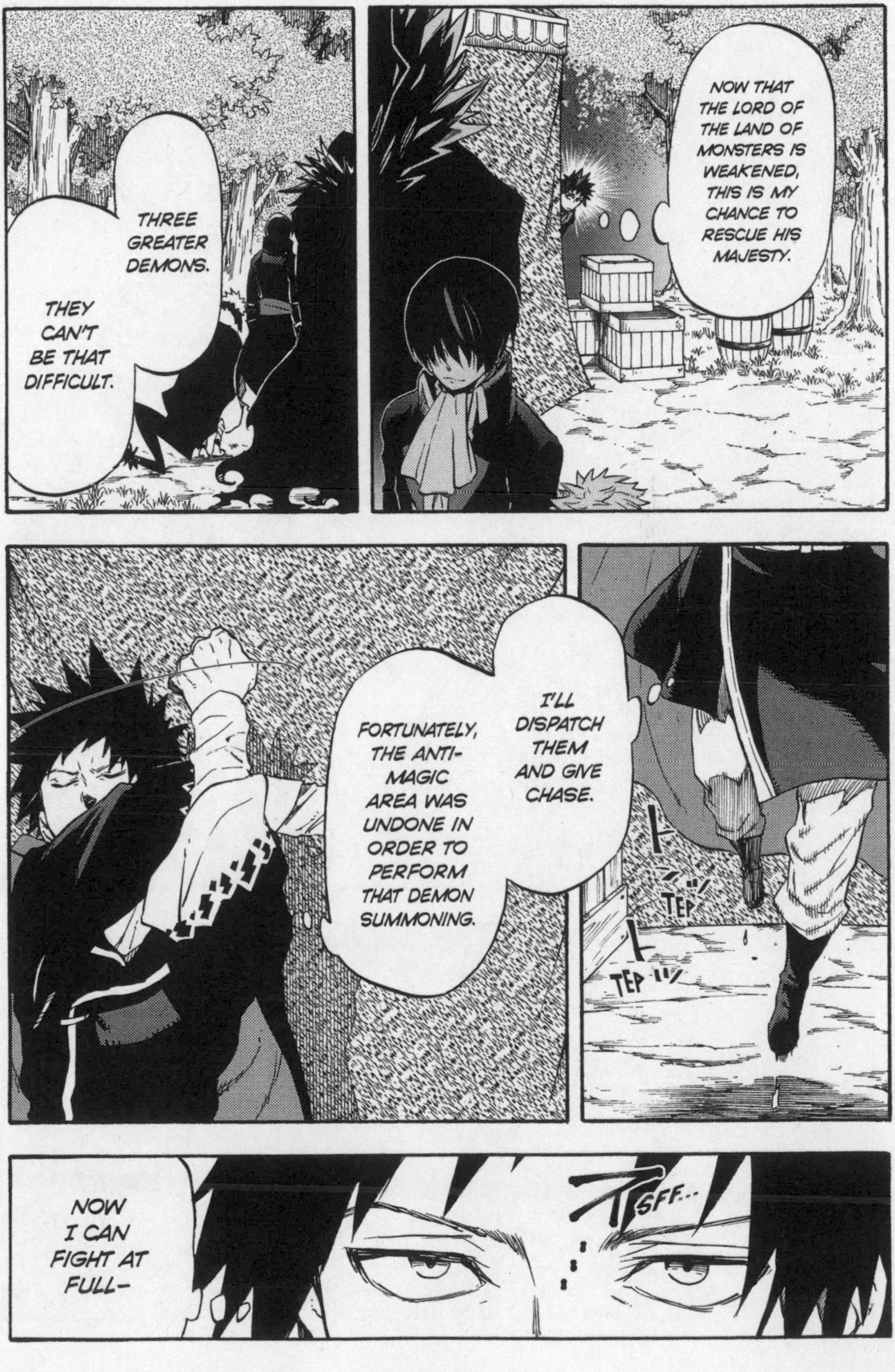

NOW THAT THE LORD OF THE LAND OF MONSTERS IS WEAKENED, THIS IS MY CHANCE TO RESCUE HIS MAJESTY.
THREE GREATER DEMONS.
THEY CAN'T BE THAT DIFFICULT.
TEP
TEP
I'LL DISPATCH THEM AND GIVE CHASE.
FORTUNATELY, THE ANTI-MAGIC AREA WAS UNDONE IN ORDER TO PERFORM THAT DEMON SUMMONING.
SFF...
NOW I CAN FIGHT AT FULL-

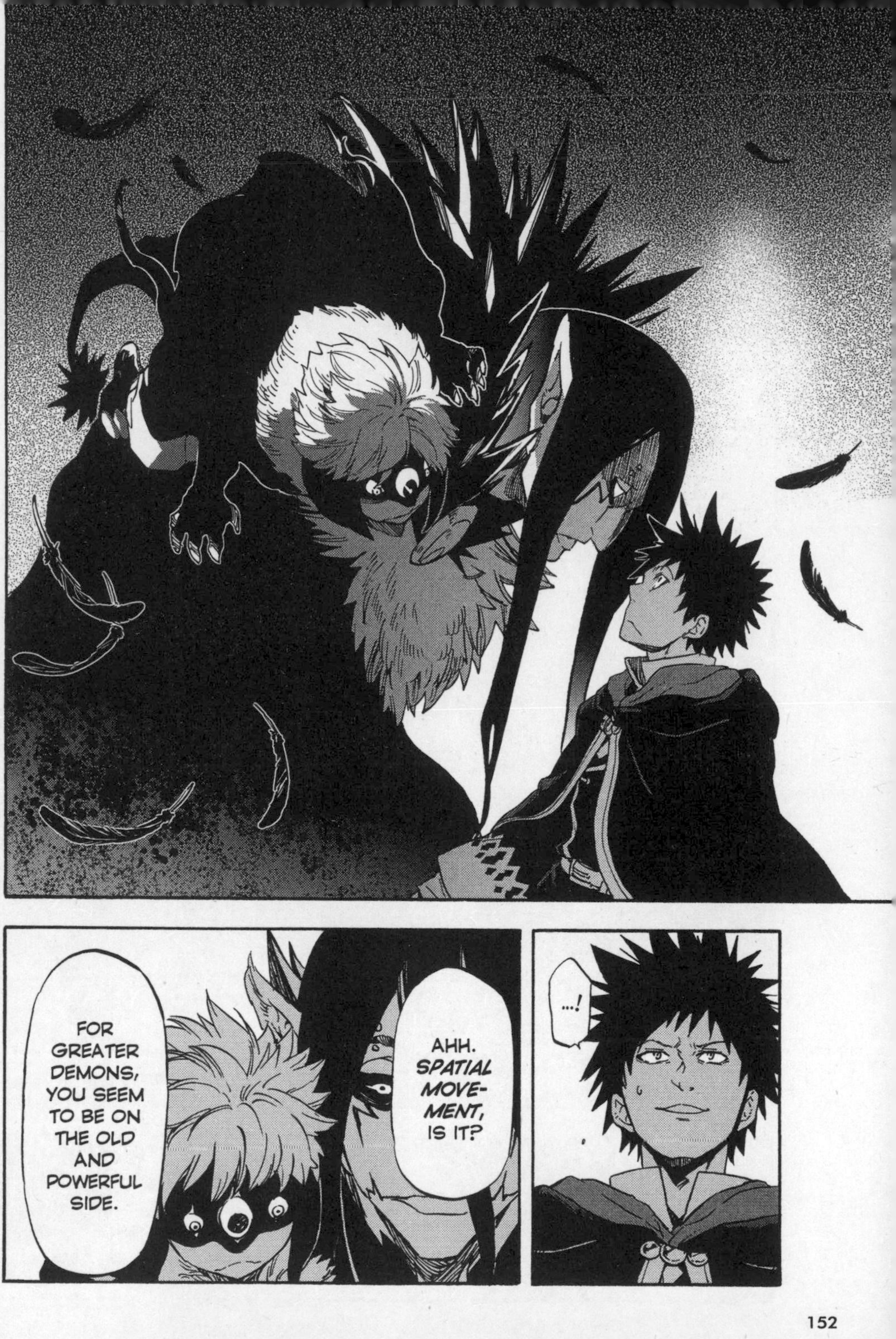
...!
AHH. SPATIAL MOVEMENT, IS IT?
FOR GREATER DEMONS, YOU SEEM TO BE ON THE OLD AND POWERFUL SIDE.

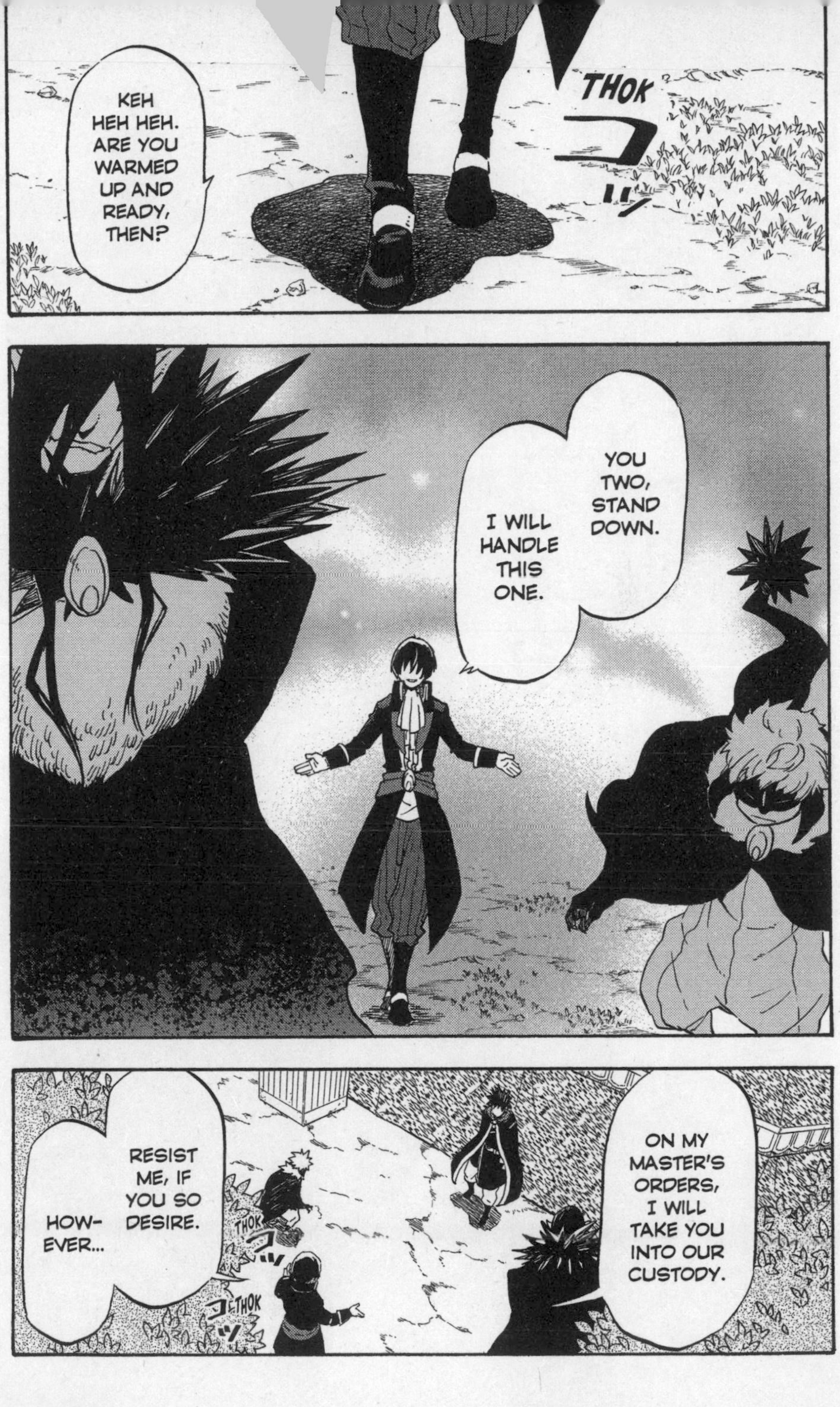
KEH HEH HEH. ARE YOU WARMED UP AND READY, THEN?
THOK
YOU TWO, STAND DOWN.
I WILL HANDLE THIS ONE.
ON MY MASTER'S ORDERS, I WILL TAKE YOU INTO OUR CUSTODY.
RESIST ME, IF YOU SO DESIRE.
HOW-EVER...
THOK
THOK

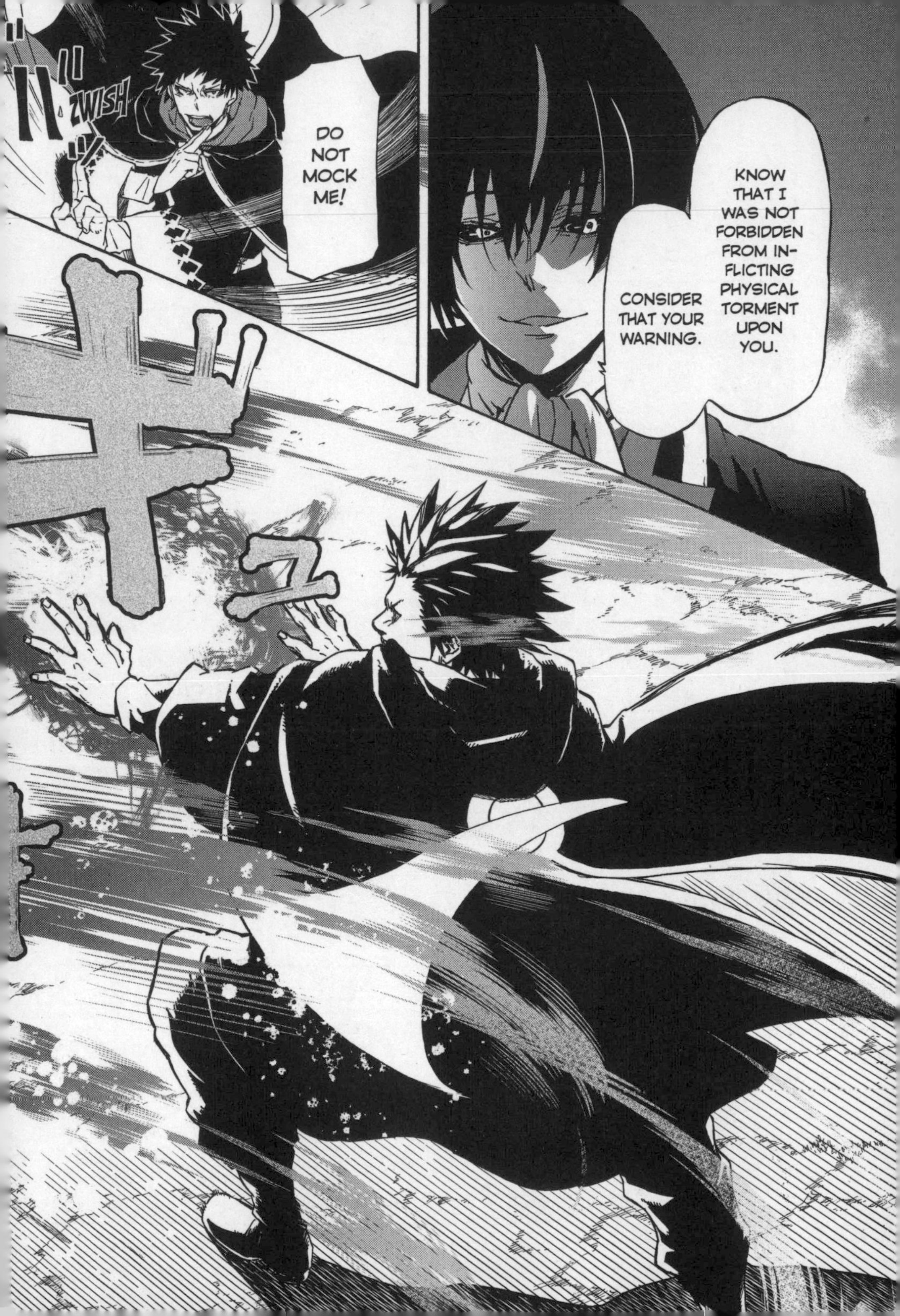
KNOW THAT I WAS NOT FORBIDDEN FROM IN-FLICTING PHYSICAL TORMENT UPON YOU.
CONSIDER THAT YOUR WARNING.
ZWISH
DO NOT MOCK ME!

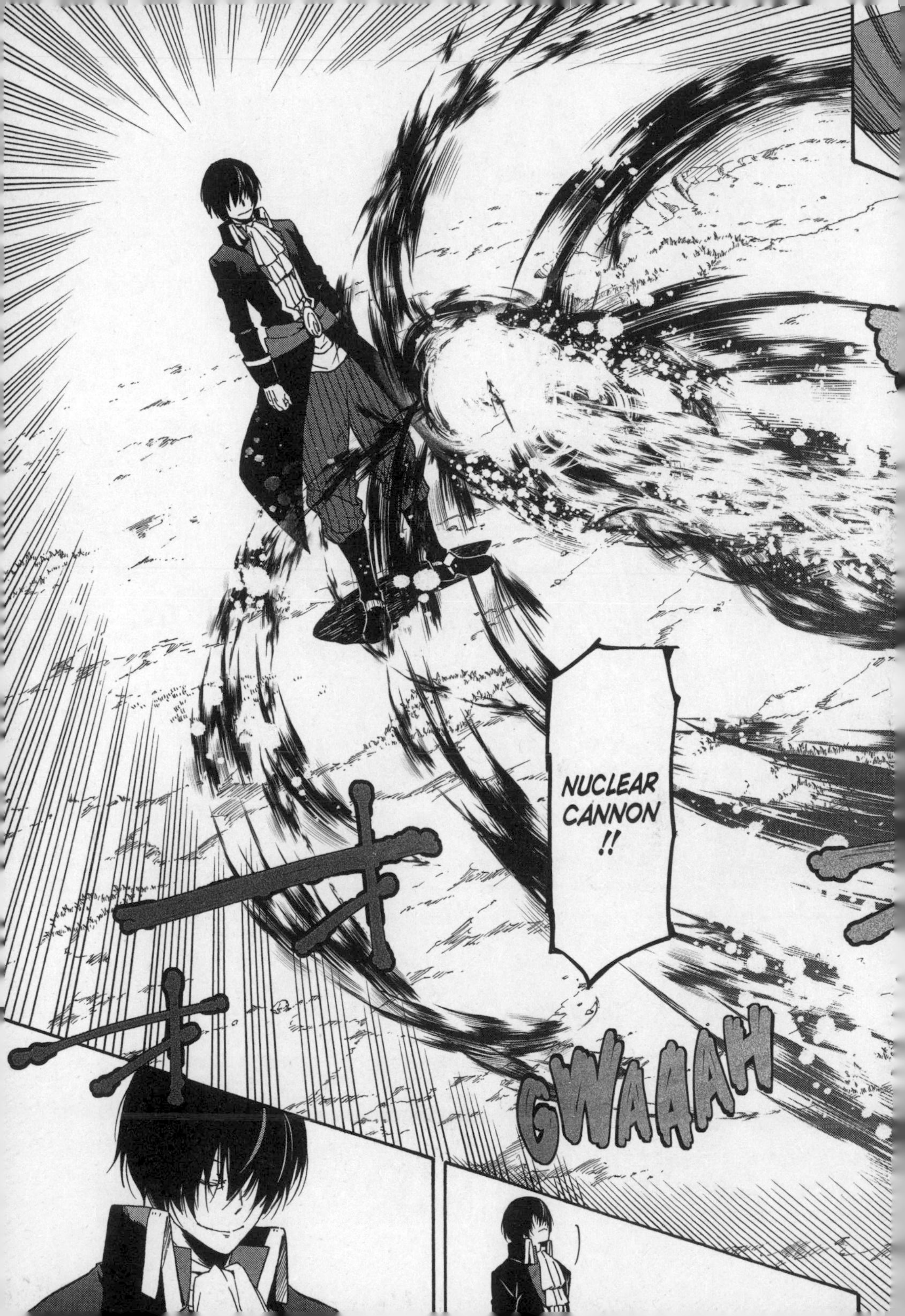
NUCLEAR CANNON !!
GWAAAH

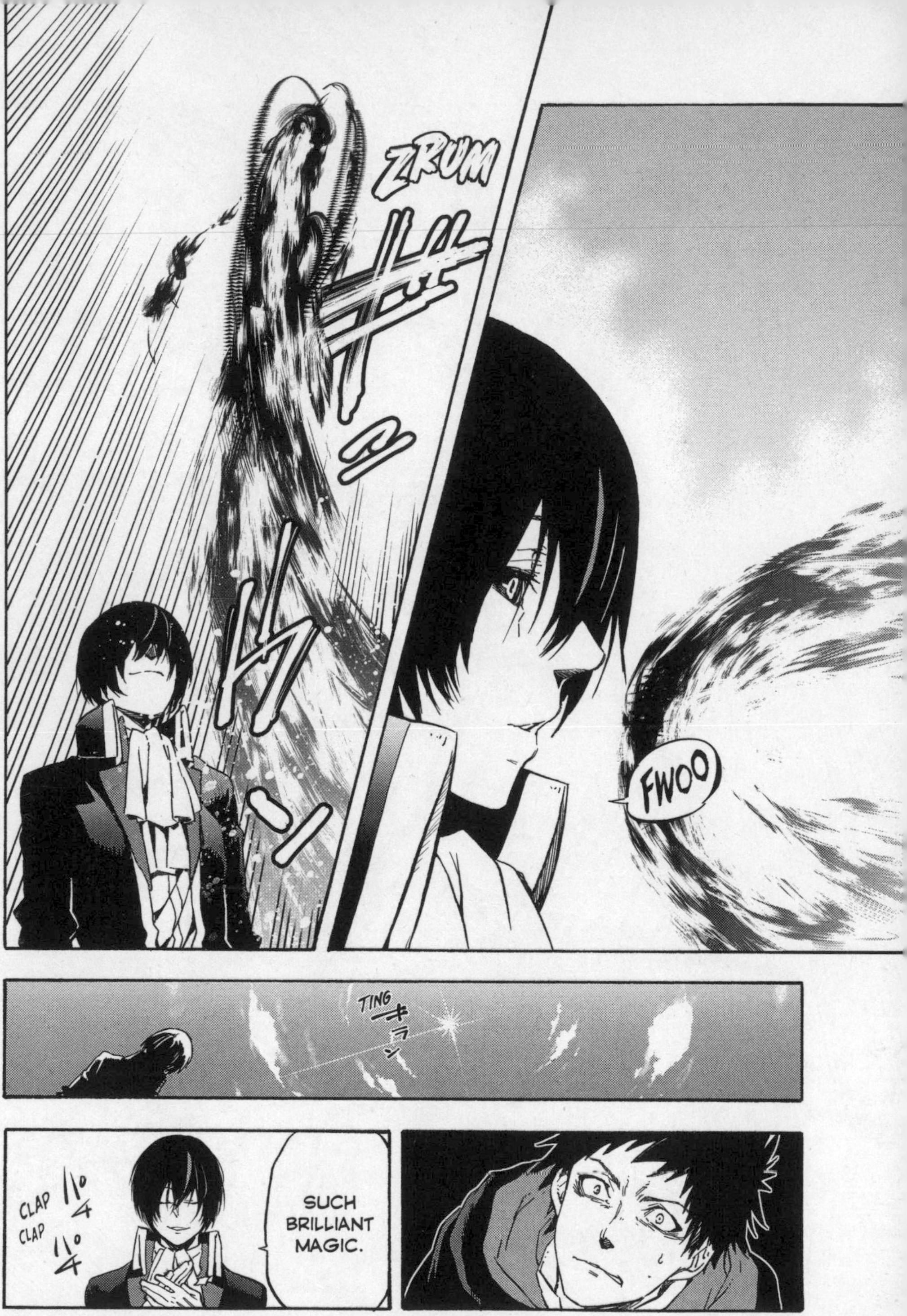
FWOO
ZRUM
TING
SUCH BRILLIANT MAGIC.
CLAP
CLAP

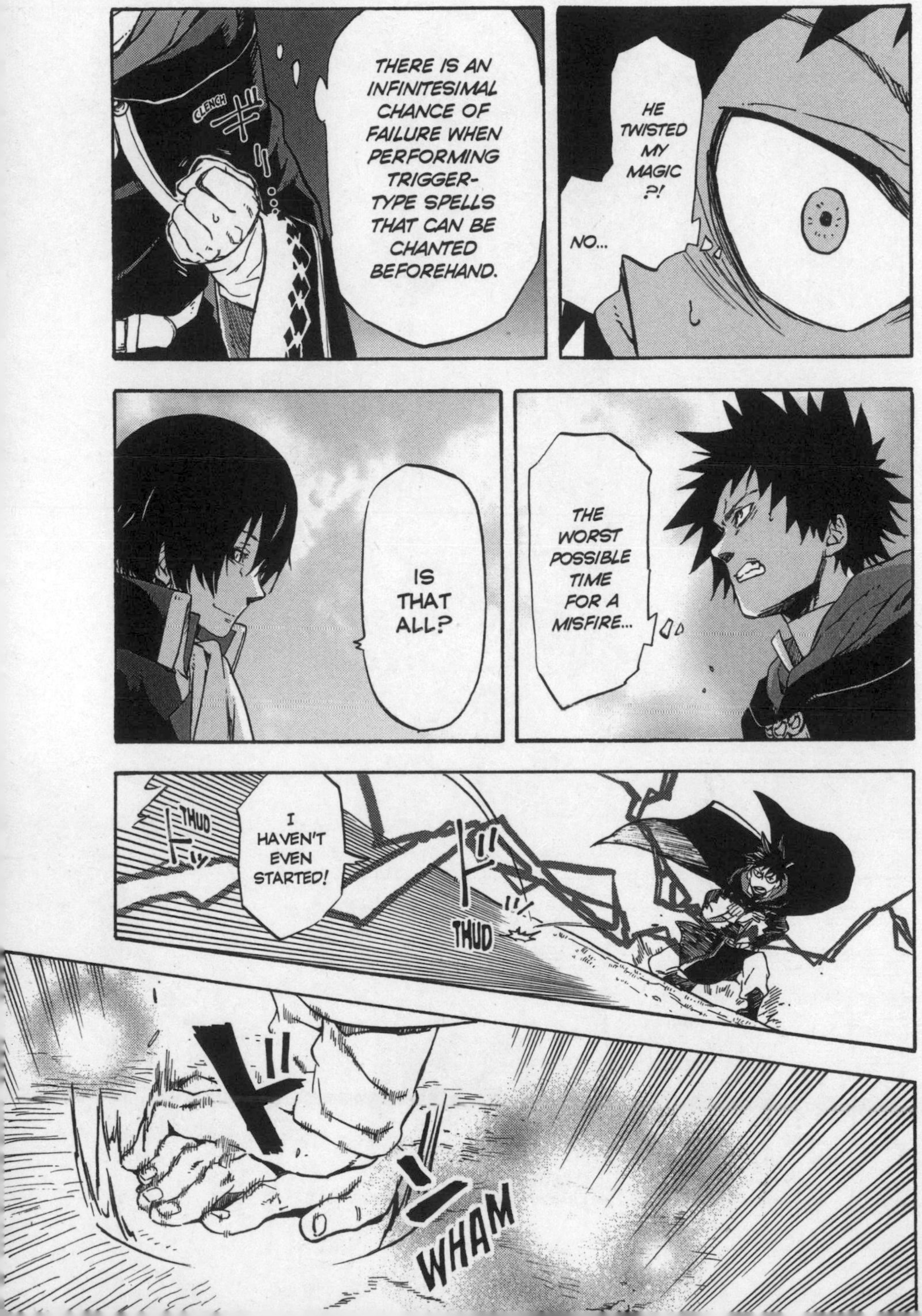
HE TWISTED MY MAGIC ?!
NO...
CLENCH
THERE IS AN INFINITESIMAL CHANCE OF FAILURE WHEN PERFORMING TRIGGER-TYPE SPELLS THAT CAN BE CHANTED BEFOREHAND.
THE WORST POSSIBLE TIME FOR A MISFIRE...
IS THAT ALL?
THUD
I HAVEN'T EVEN STARTED!
THUD
WHAM

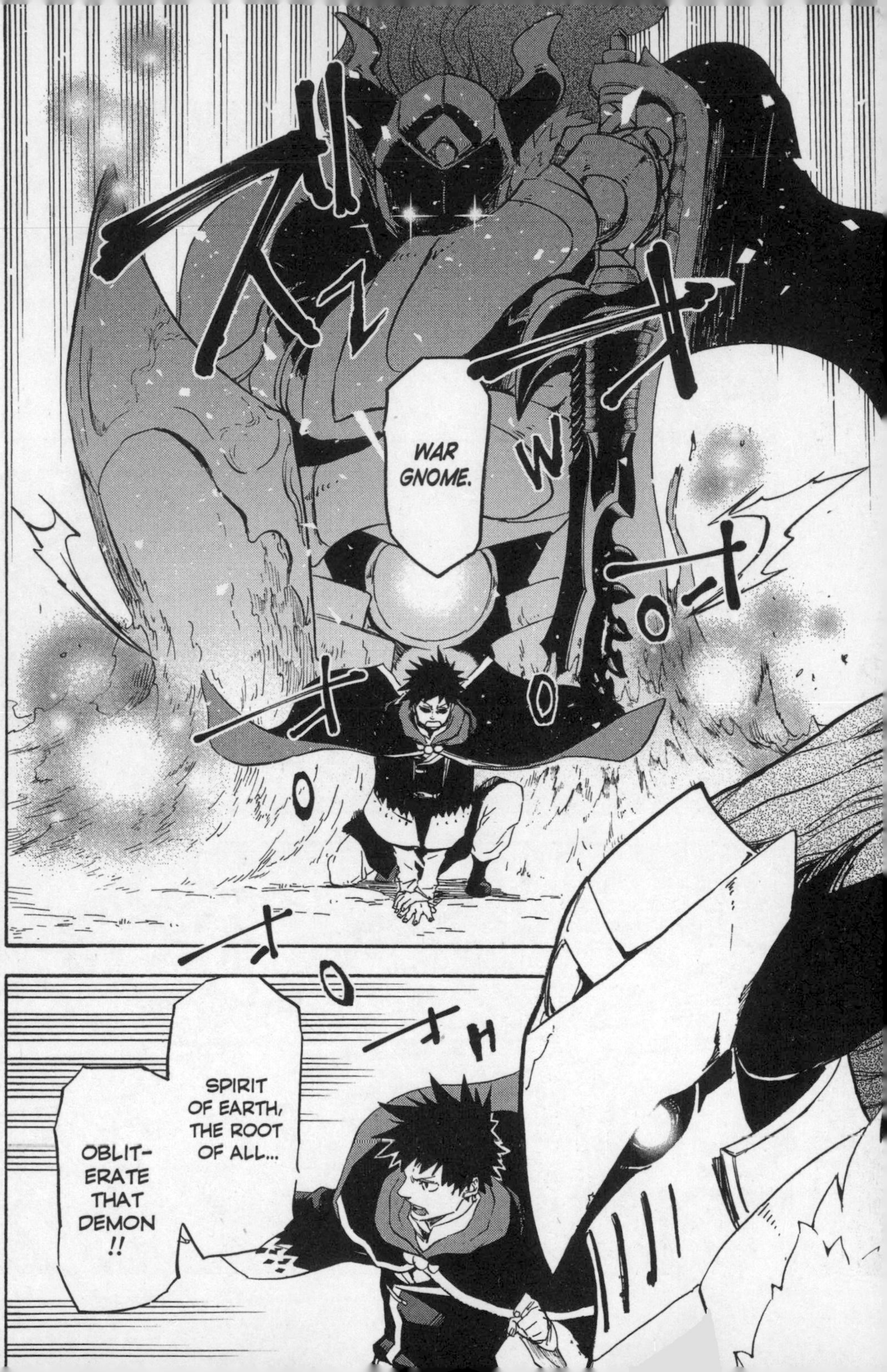
WAR GNOME.
SPIRIT OF EARTH, THE ROOT OF ALL...
OBLIT-ERATE THAT DEMON!!

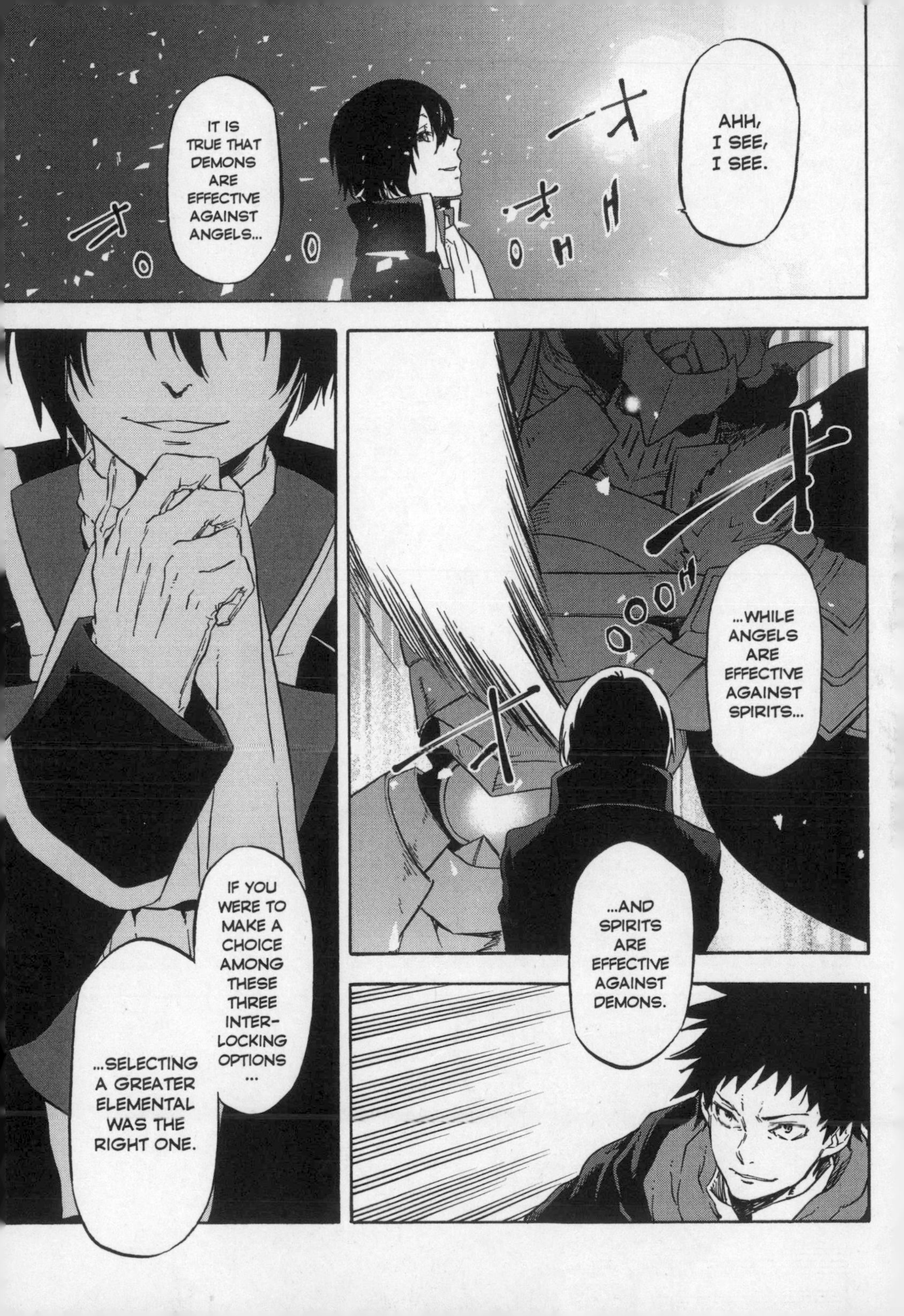
AHH, I SEE, I SEE.
IT IS TRUE THAT DEMONS ARE EFFECTIVE AGAINST ANGELS...
...WHILE ANGELS ARE EFFECTIVE AGAINST SPIRITS...
...AND SPIRITS ARE EFFECTIVE AGAINST DEMONS.
IF YOU WERE TO MAKE A CHOICE AMONG THESE THREE INTER-LOCKING OPTIONS...
...SELECTING A GREATER ELEMENTAL WAS THE RIGHT ONE.

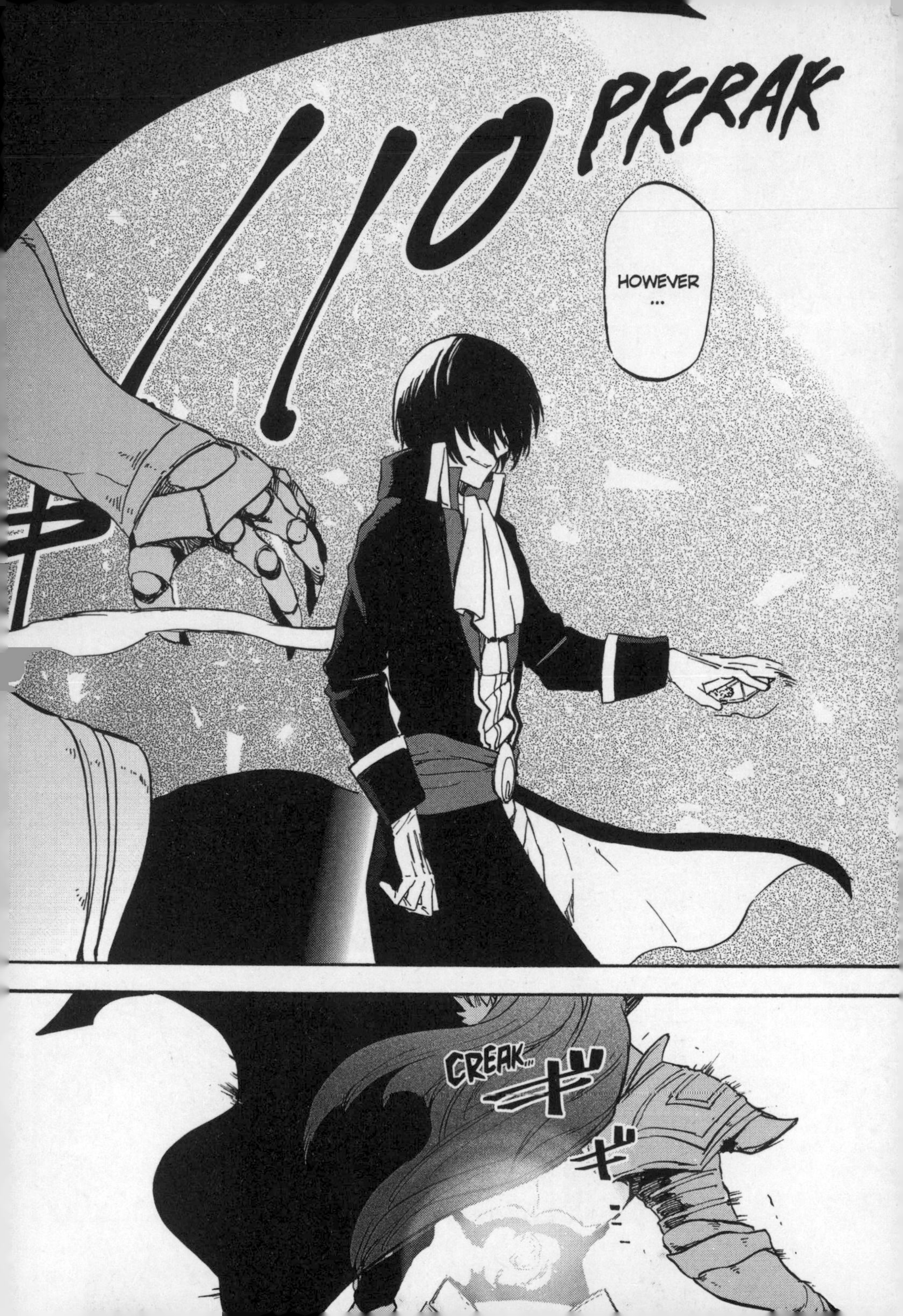
PKRAK
HOWEVER ...
CREAK...

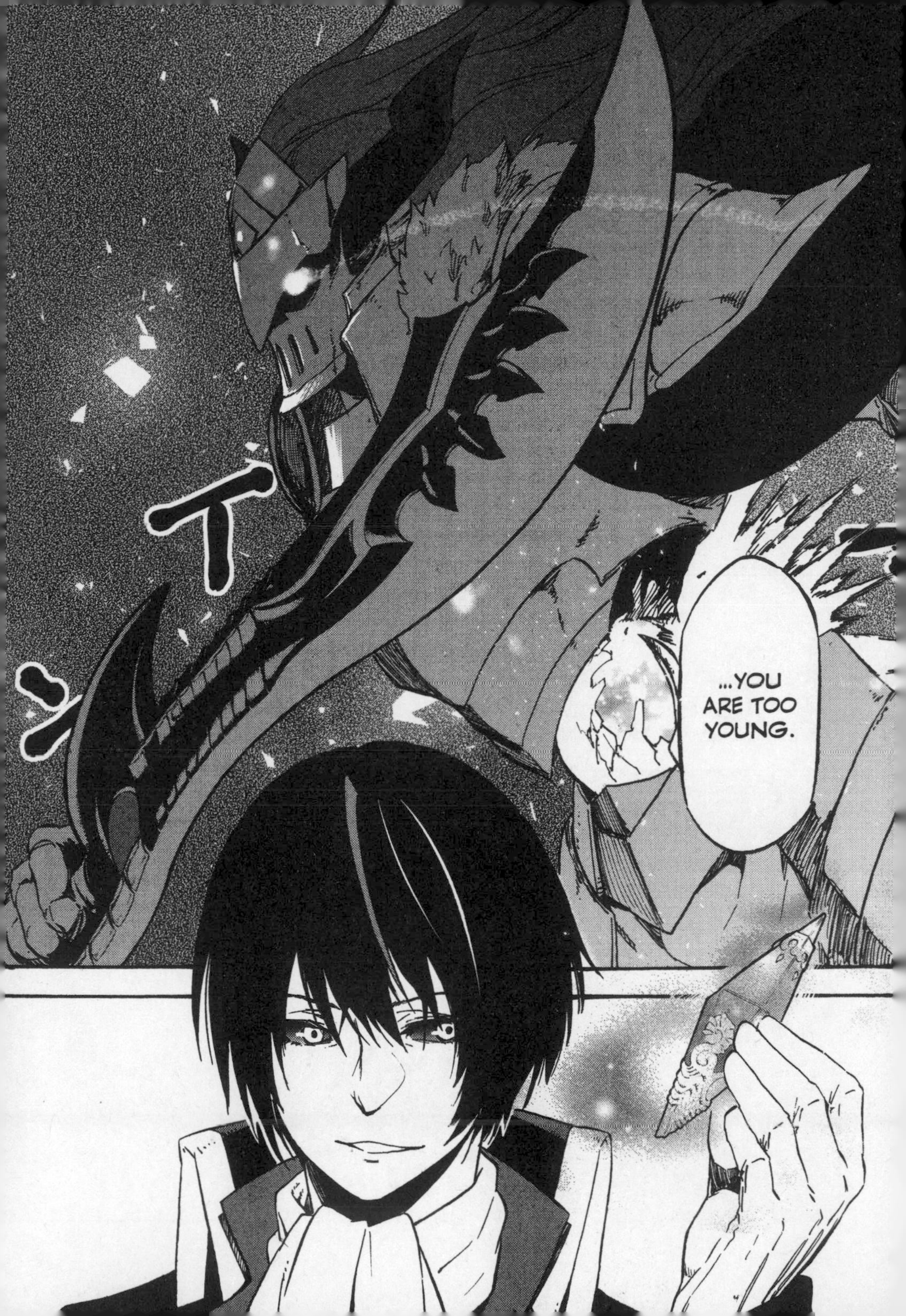
...YOU ARE TOO YOUNG.

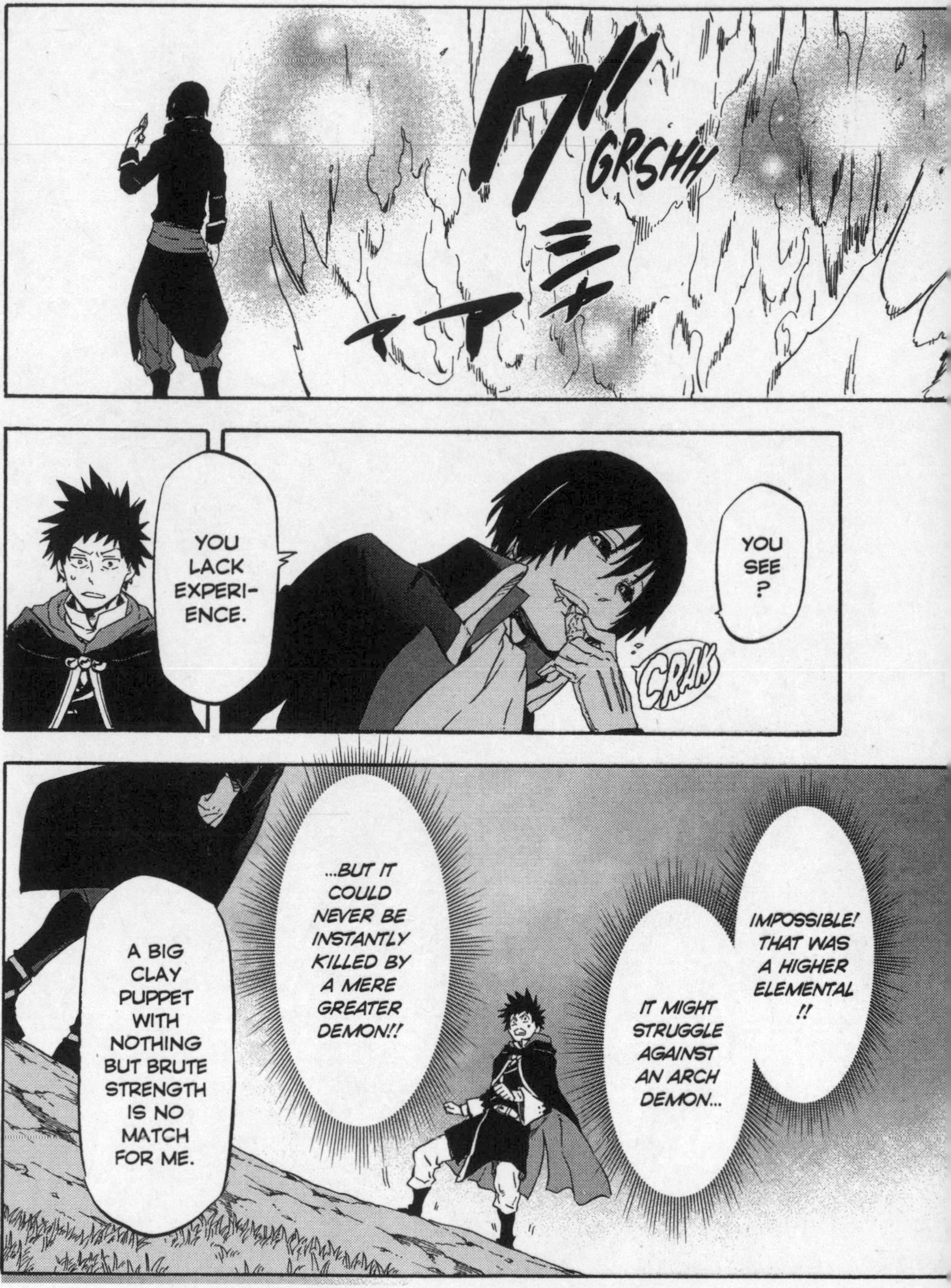
GRSHH
YOU SEE?
CRAK
YOU LACK EXPERIENCE.
IMPOSSIBLE! THAT WAS A HIGHER ELEMENTAL!!
IT MIGHT STRUGGLE AGAINST AN ARCH DEMON...
...BUT IT COULD NEVER BE INSTANTLY KILLED BY A MERE GREATER DEMON!!
A BIG CLAY PUPPET WITH NOTHING BUT BRUTE STRENGTH IS NO MATCH FOR ME.

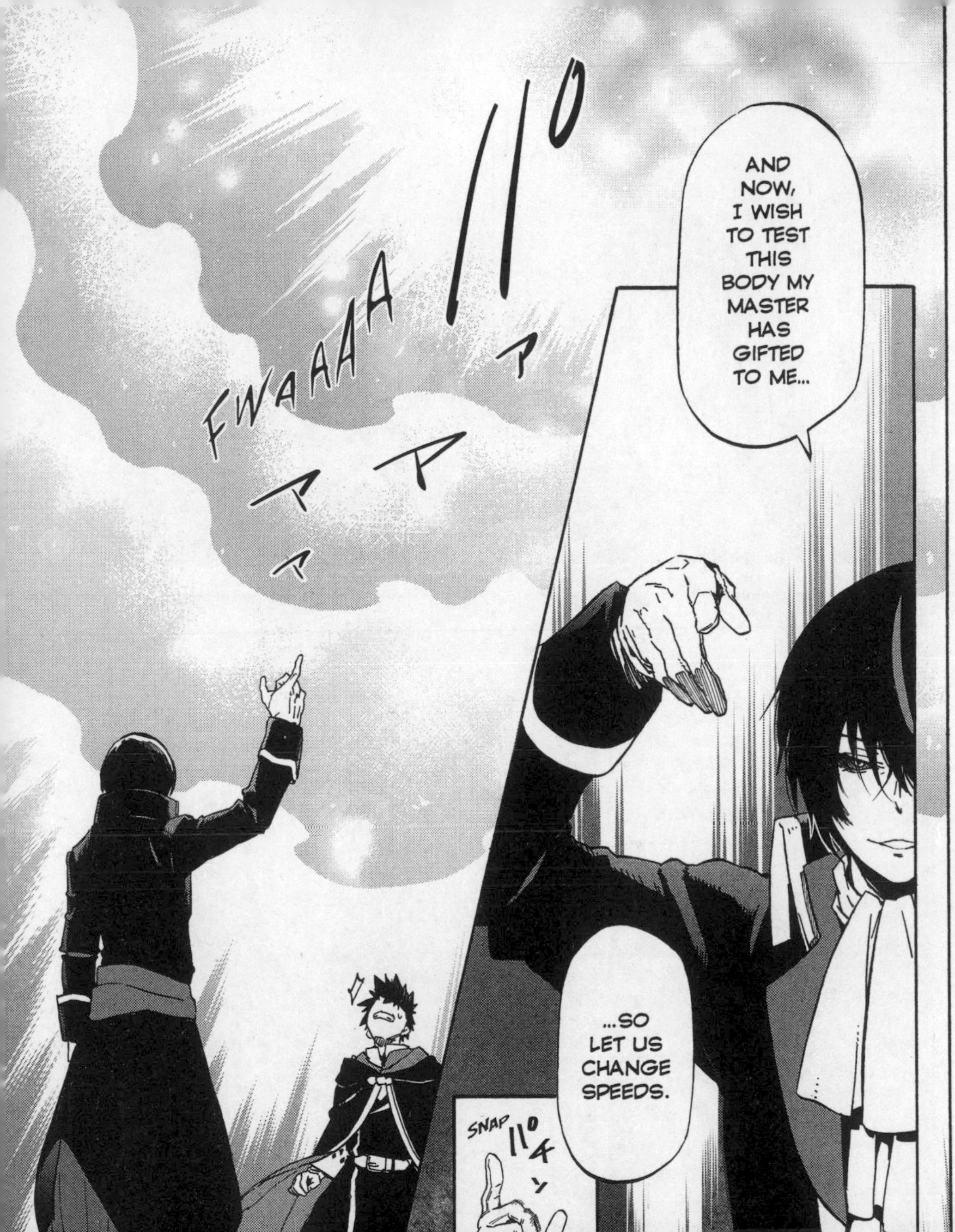
AND NOW, I WISH TO TEST THIS BODY MY MASTER HAS GIFTED TO ME...
...SO LET US CHANGE SPEEDS.
SNAP
FWAAAA

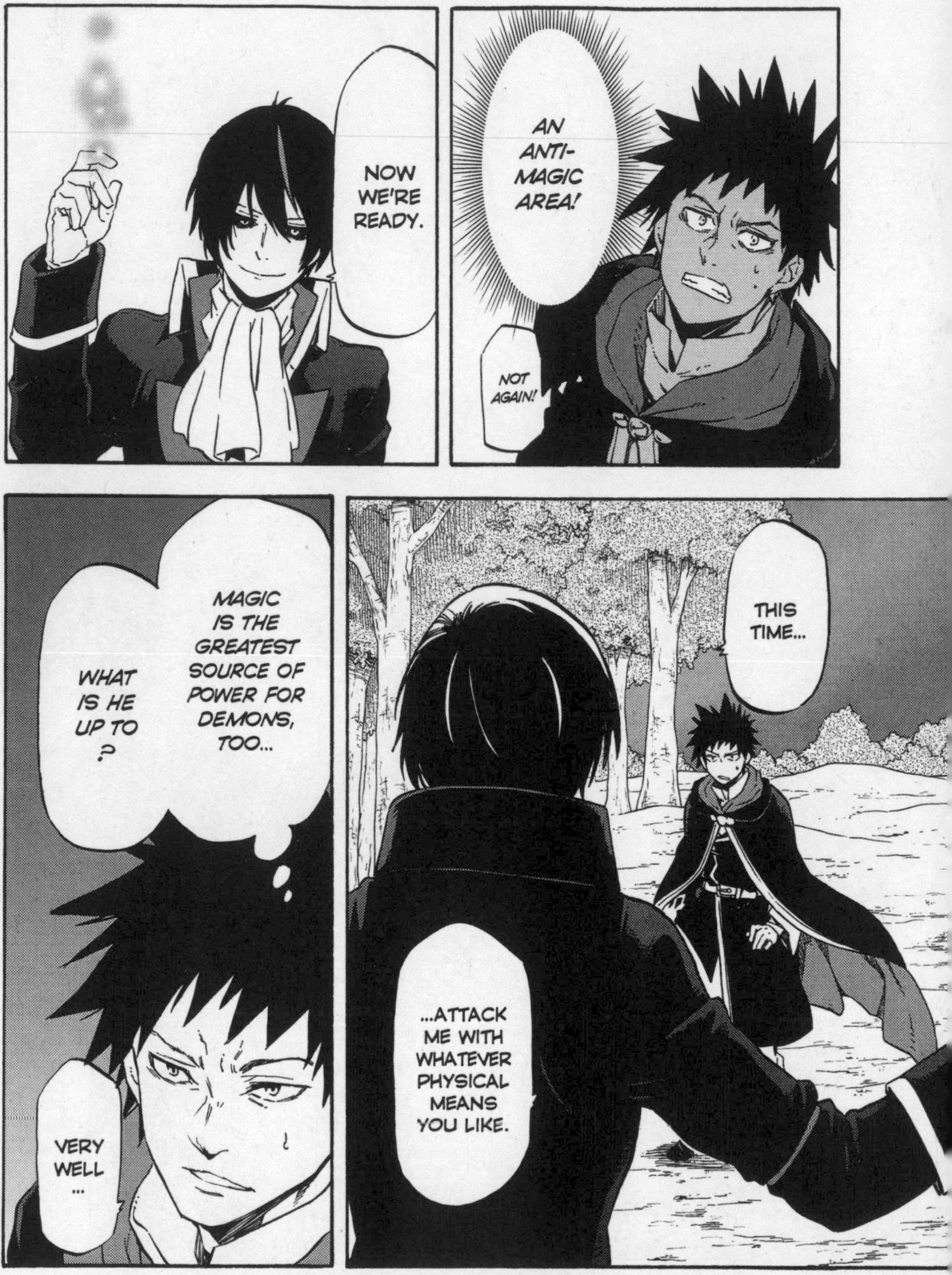
AN ANTI-MAGIC AREA!
NOT AGAIN!
NOW WE'RE READY.
THIS TIME...
...ATTACK ME WITH WHATEVER PHYSICAL MEANS YOU LIKE.
MAGIC IS THE GREATEST SOURCE OF POWER FOR DEMONS, TOO...
WHAT IS HE UP TO?
VERY WELL...

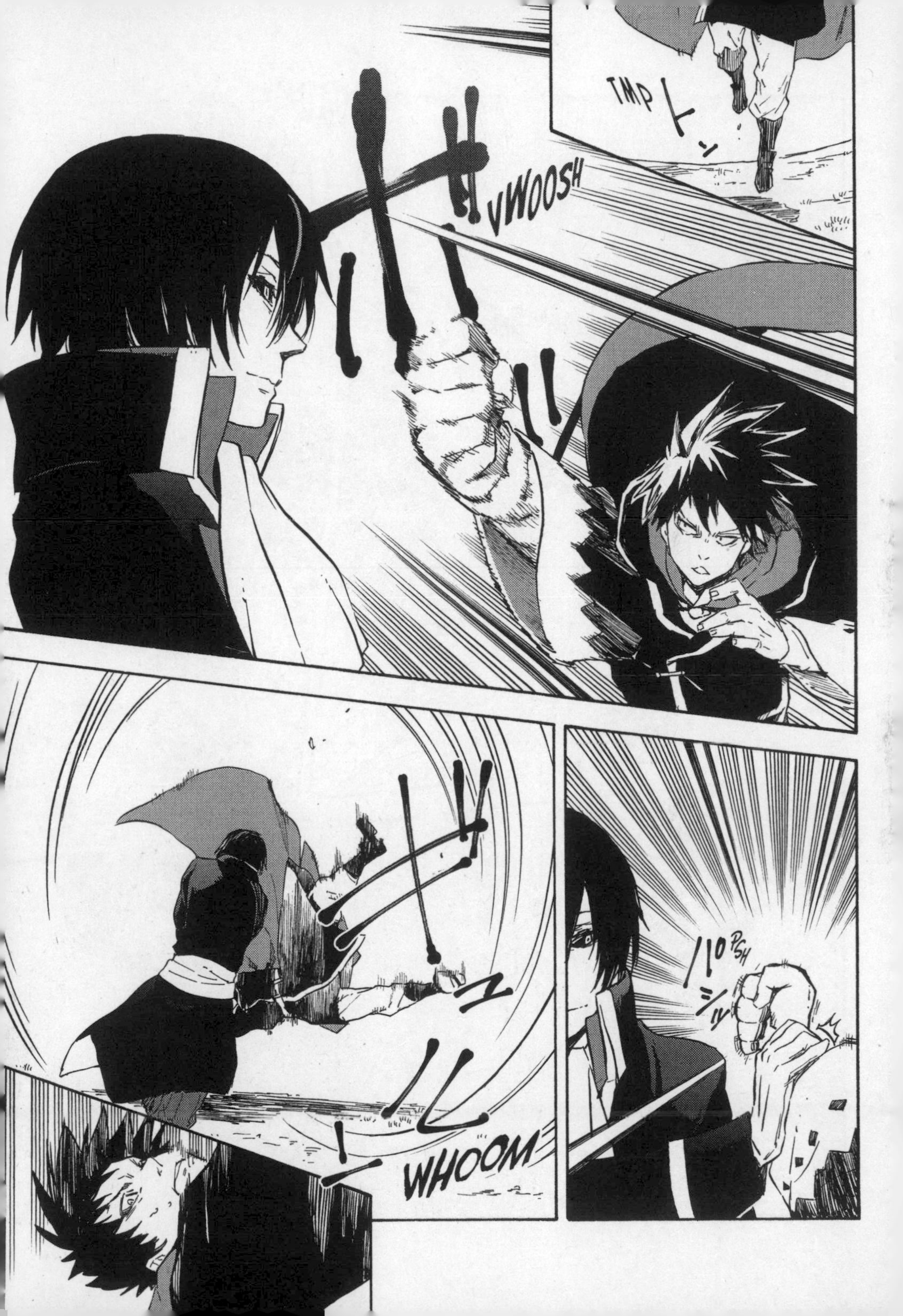
TMP
トン
VWOOSH
PSH
パシッ
WHOOM

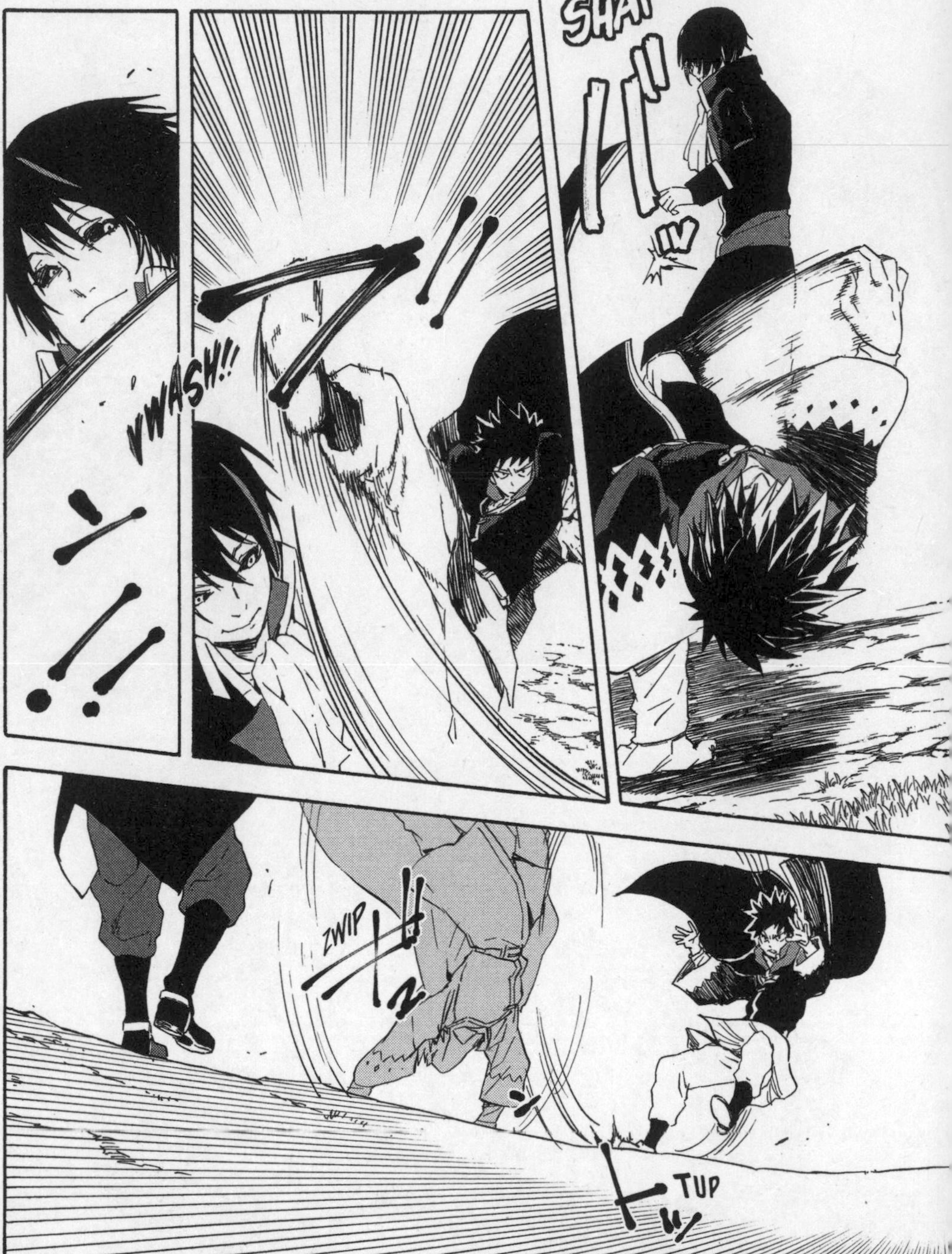
SHAP
VWASH!!
ZWIP
TUP

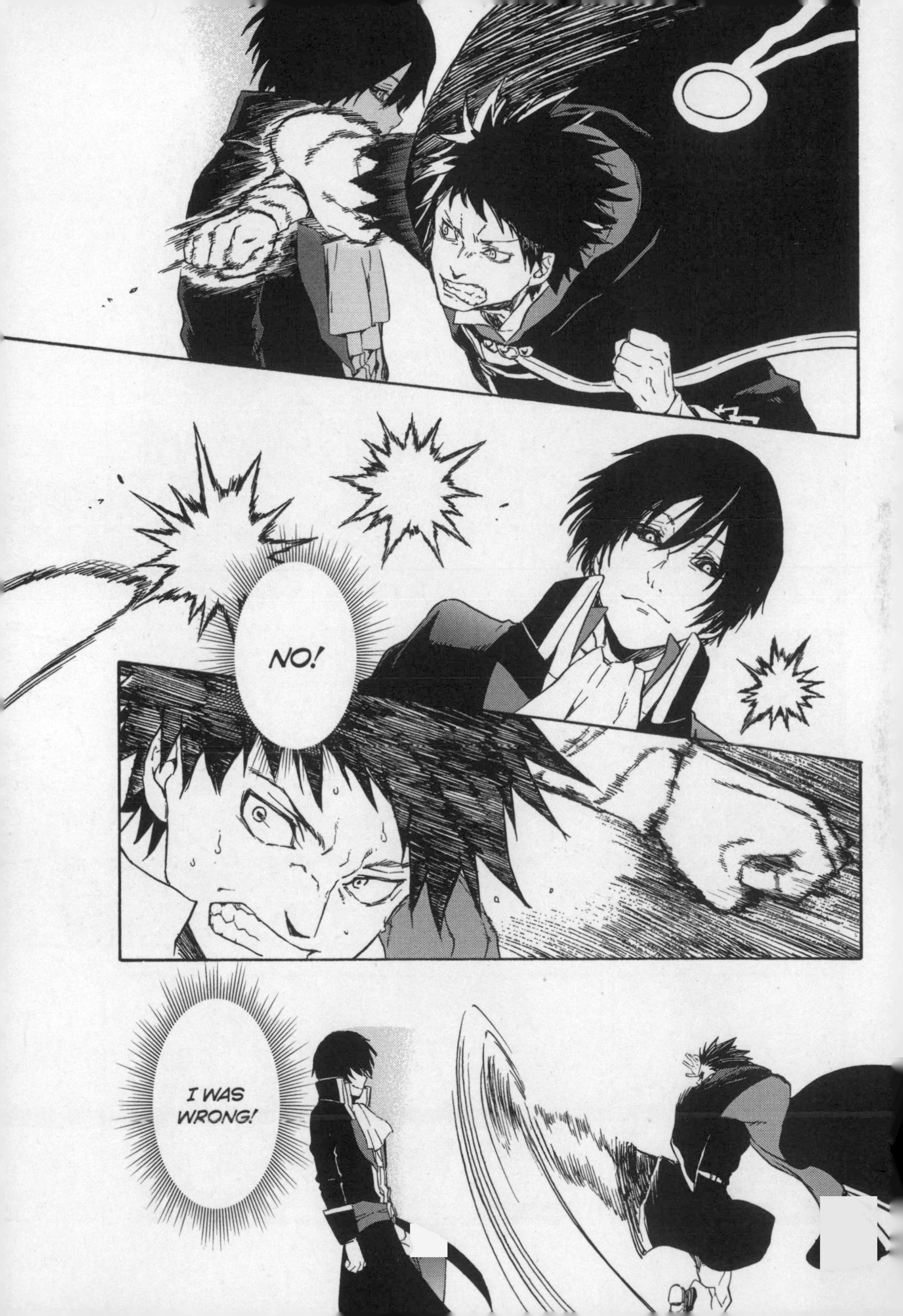
NO!
I WAS WRONG!

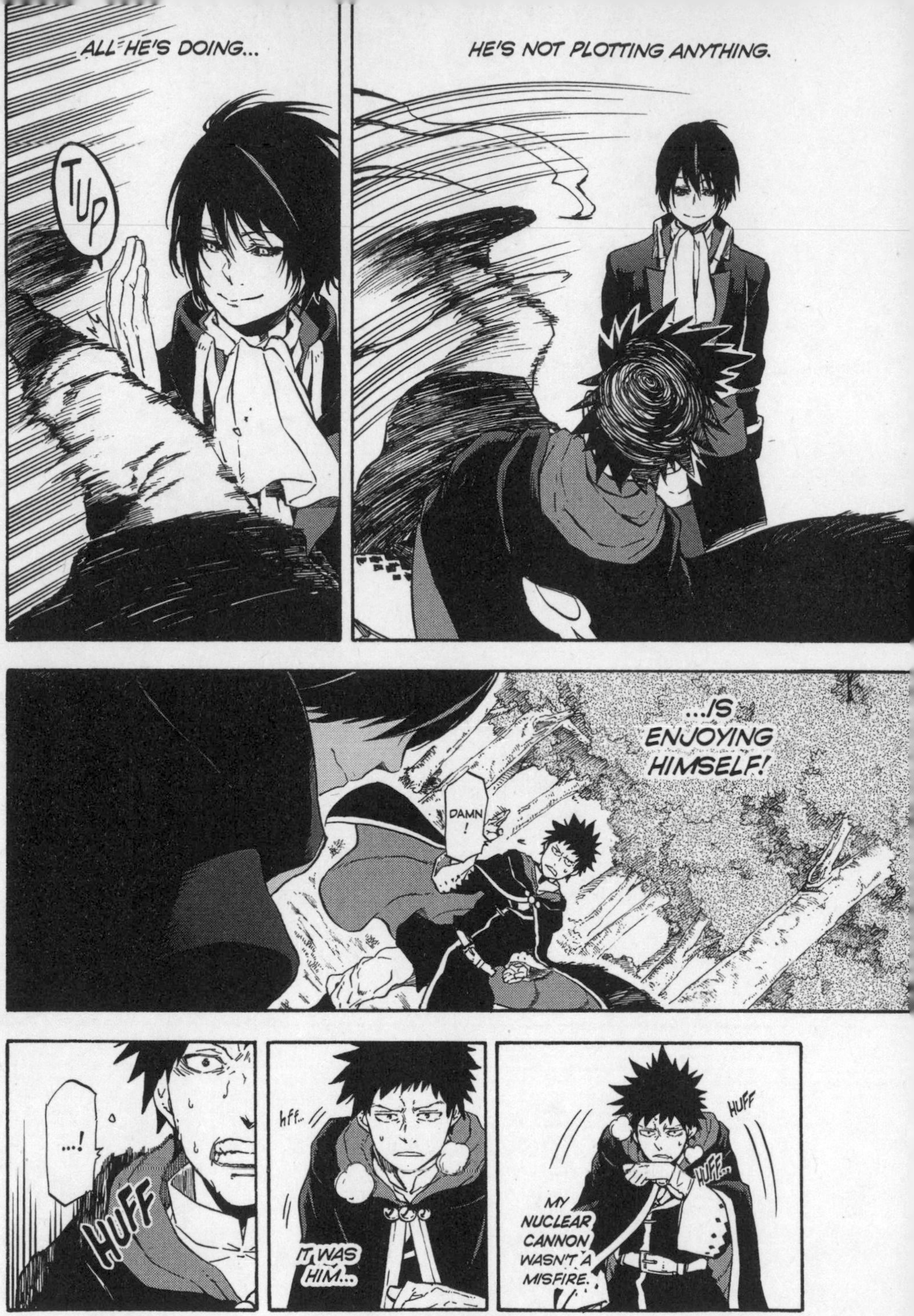
HE'S NOT PLOTTING ANYTHING.
ALL HE'S DOING...
TUP
...IS ENJOYING HIMSELF!
DAMN!
HUFF
HUFF...
MY NUCLEAR CANNON WASN'T A MISFIRE.
hff...
IT WAS HIM...
...!
HUFF

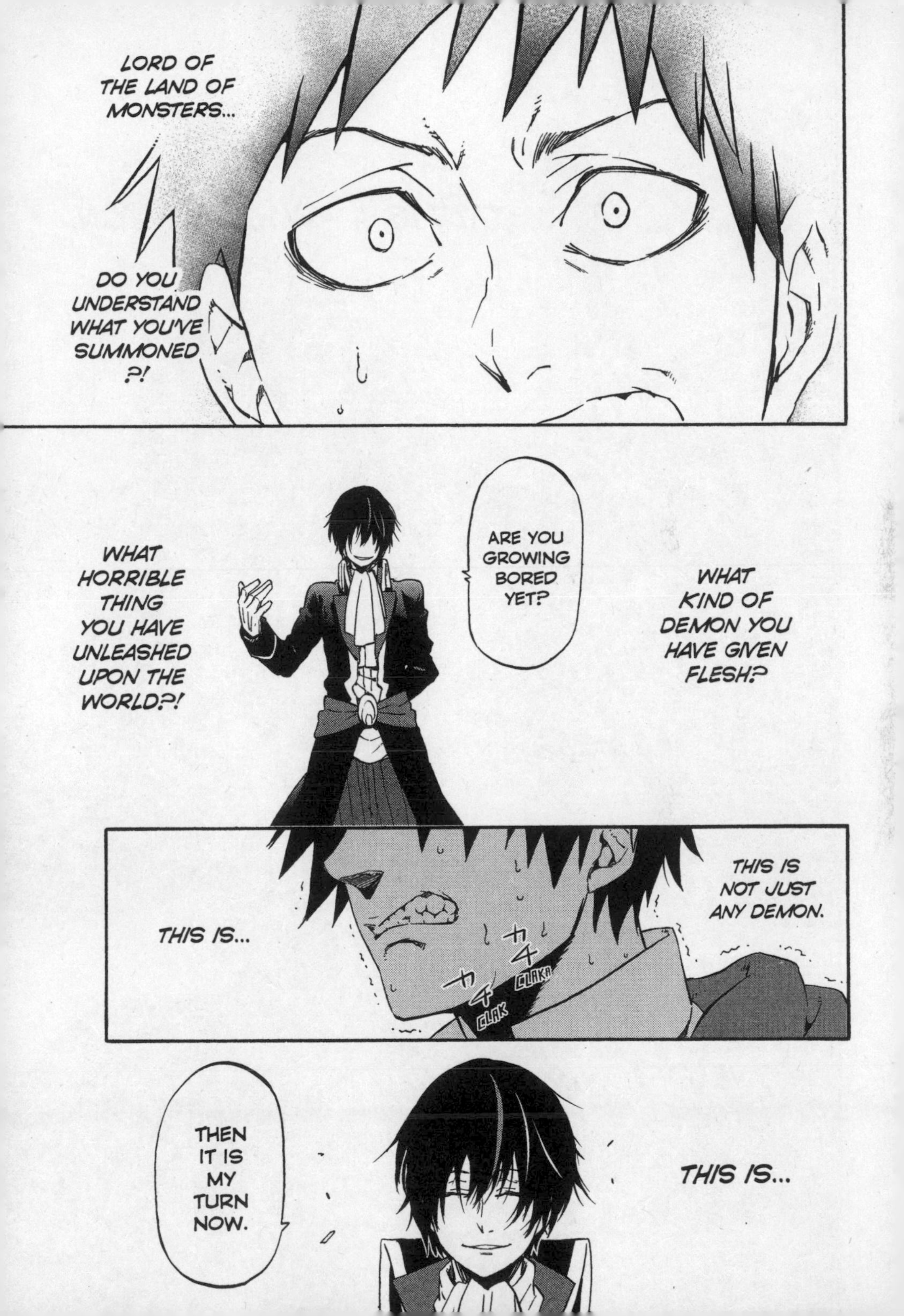
LORD OF THE LAND OF MONSTERS...
DO YOU UNDERSTAND WHAT YOU'VE SUMMONED ?!
WHAT KIND OF DEMON YOU HAVE GIVEN FLESH?
ARE YOU GROWING BORED YET?
WHAT HORRIBLE THING YOU HAVE UNLEASHED UPON THE WORLD?!
THIS IS NOT JUST ANY DEMON.
CLAKA
CLAK
THIS IS...
THIS IS...
THEN IT IS MY TURN NOW.

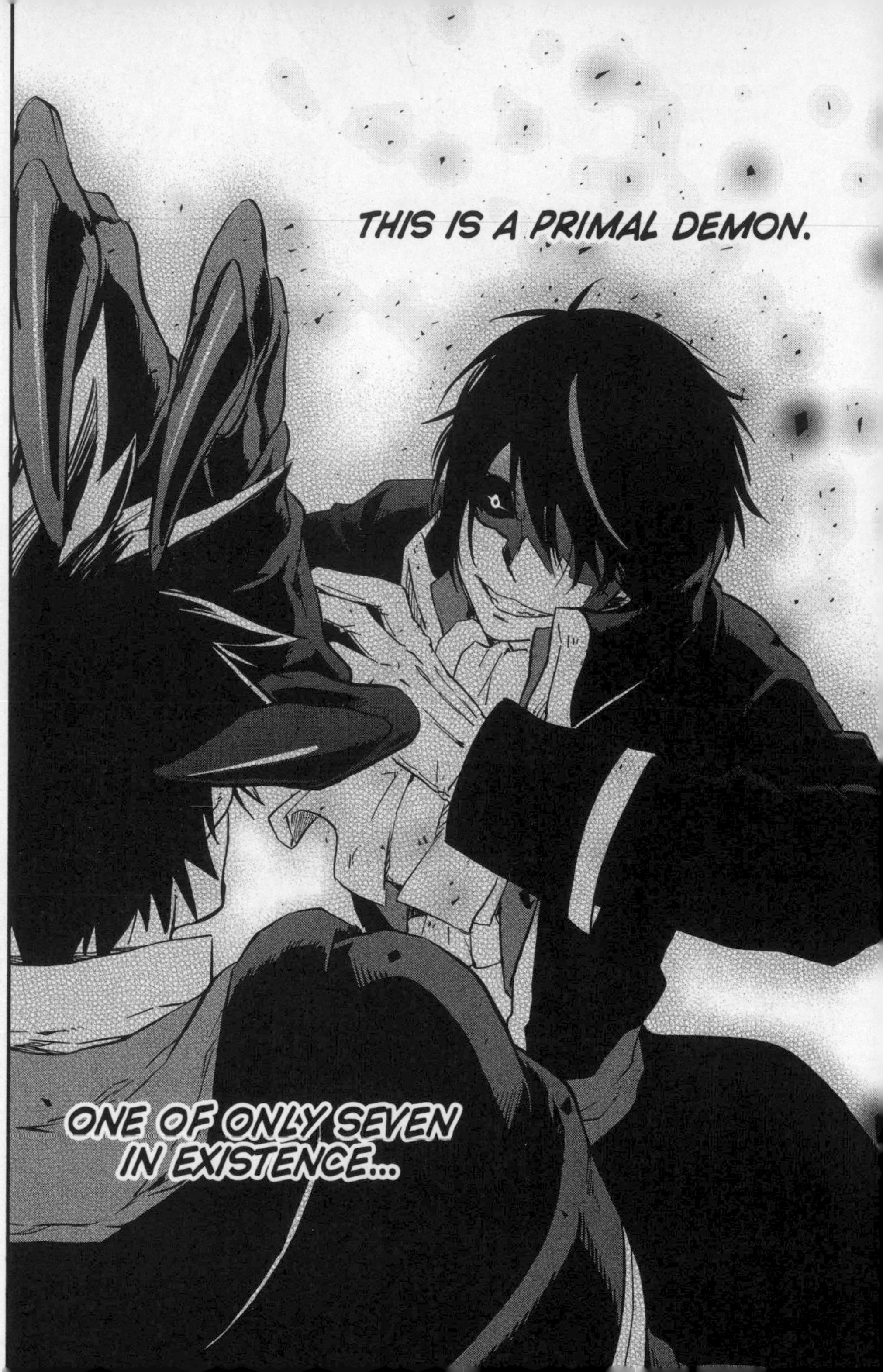
THIS IS A PRIMAL DEMON.
ONE OF ONLY SEVEN IN EXISTENCE...

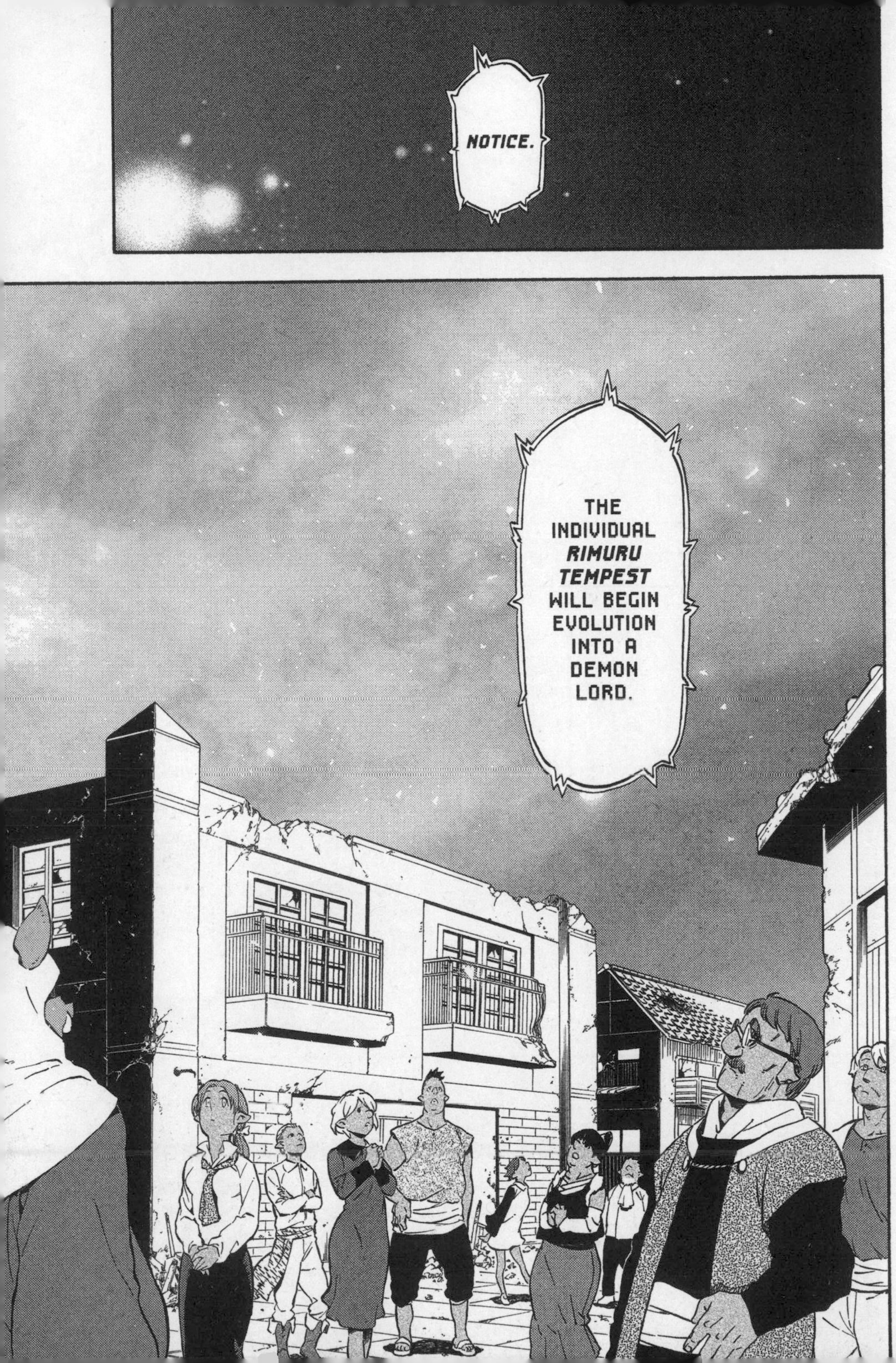
NOTICE.
THE INDIVIDUAL RIMURU TEMPEST WILL BEGIN EVOLUTION INTO A DEMON LORD.

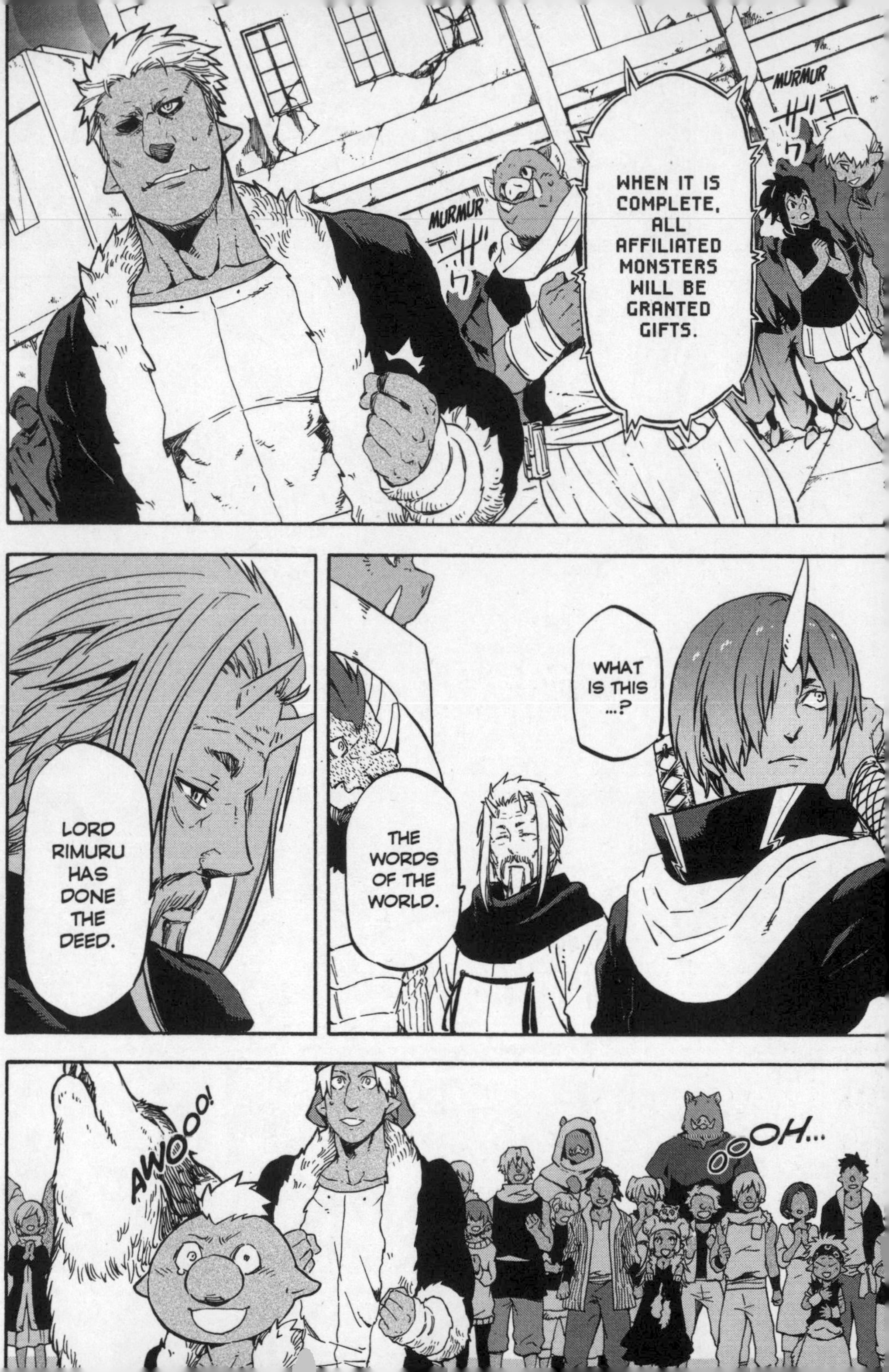
MURMUR
WHEN IT IS COMPLETE, ALL AFFILIATED MONSTERS WILL BE GRANTED GIFTS.
MURMUR
WHAT IS THIS ...?
THE WORDS OF THE WORLD.
LORD RIMURU HAS DONE THE DEED.
OOOH...
AWOOO!

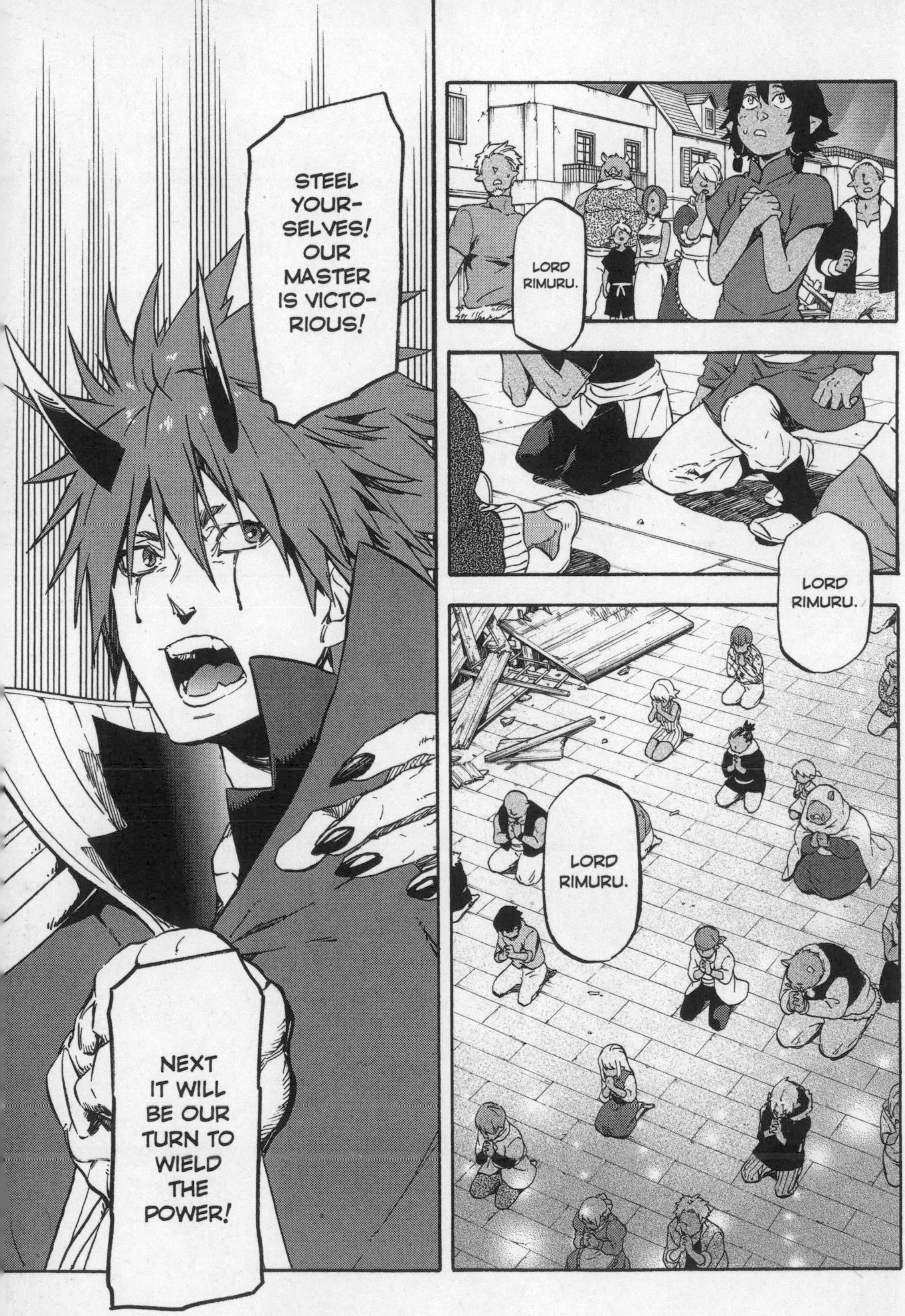
LORD RIMURU.
LORD RIMURU.
LORD RIMURU.
STEEL YOURSELVES! OUR MASTER IS VICTORIOUS!
NEXT IT WILL BE OUR TURN TO WIELD THE POWER!

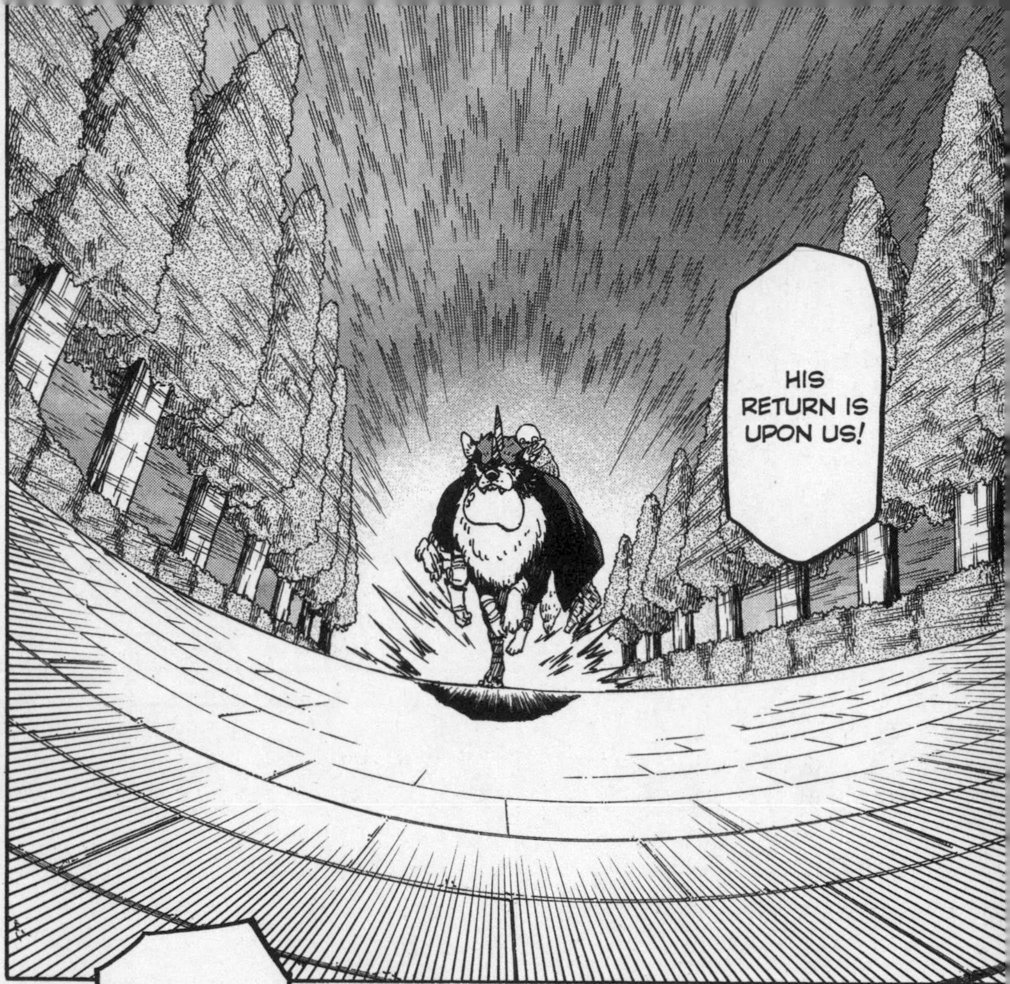
HIS RETURN IS UPON US!
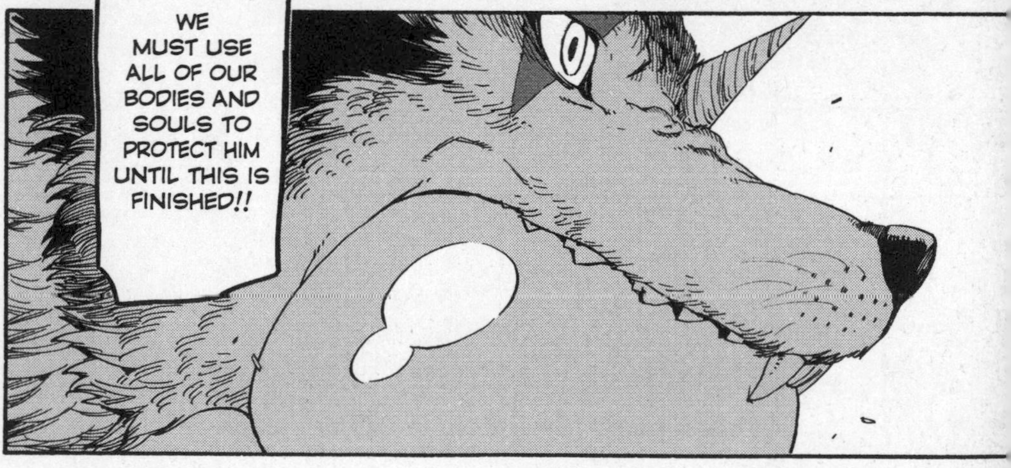
WE MUST USE ALL OF OUR BODIES AND SOULS TO PROTECT HIM UNTIL THIS IS FINISHED!!

Reincarnate
in Volume 15?

→YES

NO

Bonus Short Story

Veldora's Slime Observation Journal

~COUNTERATTACK~

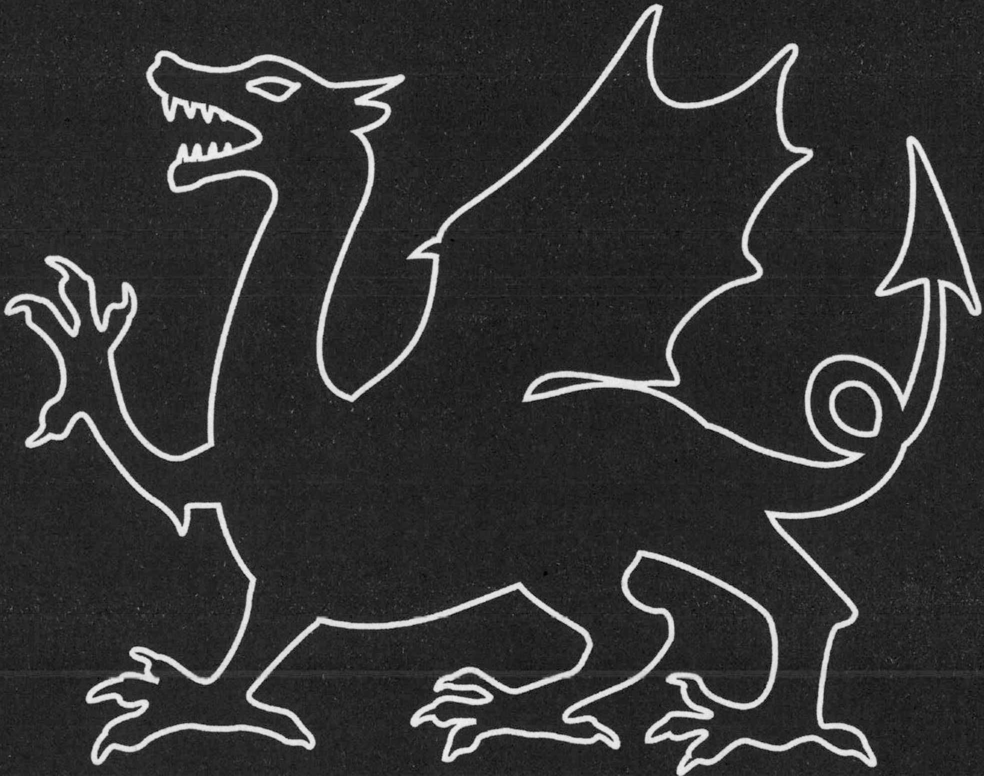

Veldora's Slime Observation Journal
~COUNTERATTACK~

◆DIFFERENCE IN CLASS◆

The counterattack has begun at each location.

The atmosphere itself trembles, pulsing with Rimuru's rage.

The rage of his companions was also startling. Even those who are normally placid are exhibiting an anger never seen before.

And then there are his words: "If I've turned into a monster without any sense of reason, I want you to lead whoever can still fight and eliminate me immediately."

It was a cruel request Rimuru made of Benimaru.

"I would not accept this order," I said.

"I agree. Perhaps in the past, but now things are different. That said, I am not capable of leading monsters, nor could I hope to legitimately stop Lord Rimuru."

"That is also true. Rimuru would not ask the impossible, so this is a sign to Benimaru that he has trust in him. I am even a little envious."

I would refuse that order, absolutely. And yet a part of me was envious of Benimaru that he was considered worthy enough to be asked.

"Well, I cannot imagine that Rimuru will give his companions cause to mourn. He will awaken as a Demon Lord, we can be sure of that."

"Of course. Let us trust in him."

With the two of us in agreement, Ifrit and I watched the subsequent events with bated breath.

Rimuru leapt into action.

It was the start of an absolute trampling.

His first act was to deploy an anti-magic area.

"So, Rimuru, you learned the magic that Mjurran used."

"That comes as no surprise to me now, but why would he utilize magic of that caliber?" asked Ifrit. An excellent question.

Looking down from above, a massive magic circle completely surrounded all of the Kingdom of Falmuth's military forces. Within that 50-kilometer wide circle, all magic was prohibited.

What was the purpose? After much thought, I arrived at one conclusion.

"To prevent escape, perhaps?"

"...Ah, I see. Even the aspectual magic 'Warp Portal' is prevented from activating. That will make escape from this place much more difficult."

Precisely.

An anti-magic area is exactly what the name suggests.

Magic activates by using magicules to overwrite the laws of the world. But activating an anti-magic area spell prevents those laws from being overwritten within its range of effect.

In other words, one must follow the laws of physics there. Meddling with space, such as teleportation, is completely impossible. The only way to escape is on foot.

But certain extra skills like "Gravity Control" can still work. Since it is merely making use of natural gravity waves, it does not need to overwrite the laws of physics. It is dangerous, because its effects cannot be fine-tuned, but one can surely learn to wield it under the circumstances.

These are the distinct differences between magic and skills. Magic is both a skill and an art. While it has two such facets, it has greater effect over the laws of the world as a skill.

But if you had deep understanding of magic, and were more skilled at breathing magicules than breathing air, let us say, you might be able to affect individual events selectively, rather than interfering with the universal laws. It might be indistinguishable from magic, but such an ability would be free from the interference of an anti-magic field, I would expect.

What I am saying if that if you wish to truly master magic, it is crucial to have an innate understanding of what you can and cannot do within an anti-magic area.

Of course, my unique skill "Inquirer" reveals most things to me, so I need not expend the effort! But this is not the time for boasting, so I shall not say so. Let the previous words be unsaid!

Instead, I am focusing quietly on Rimuru.

"Look at that, Master Veldora!" said Ifrit, but I did not need the help. I am already aware that Rimuru has played his next move.

"Now die! Scorched by the flames of God's wrath… Megiddo!!"

My expectations were correct. Rimuru unleashed a most withering attack from the outside of the circle toward the inside.

It was the beginning of a nightmare from which the Falmuth army would never awaken.

◆MERCILESS◆

Light danced wildly upon the battlefield.
The beams were beauteous and terrifying weapons of death.

"Impossible!! What is happening here?! Light magic within the anti-magic area?!" Ifrit howled. I cannot fault his ignorance.

One must be as wise and brilliant as I to understand what it is that Rimuru is doing.

"It is spiritual magic. Rimuru is calling upon spirits to perform it," I said, describing what I saw.

But Ifrit was skeptical. "No, I cannot accept that, Master. With a force that size, the enemy army's legion magic must be of exceptional quality. Their defensive barrier is not so weak that an individual's magic could break it; even a higher elemental like myself would be inadequate. Not even Lord Rimuru has the power to create such powerful thermal beams!! The Falmuth army must have been caught unprepared..."

Ifrit never doubts my wisdom. Is this the beginning of a rebellious phase?

Regardless, I kindly corrected Ifrit's mistake.

"Incorrect, Ifrit. They are not fools, and they were not unprepared. This is exactly why he utilized the anti-magic area."

"...!!"

"Indeed. First it removed the effect of the enemy's defensive magic, giving Rimuru an advantage. And from there, he surpassed their imagination."

"What do you mean by that, exactly?"

"You see, what Rimuru just displayed was a way to utilize spiritual magic that differs from common wisdom."

"Do you mean, summoning multiple higher elementals at once, to avoid the effects of the anti-magic field?"

"Not that, either. What he summoned was lower to middle water elementals. Normally, one uses spiritual magic to ask the spirits to overwrite the physical laws, but Rimuru's orders to them were actually quite simple."

"What was it...?"

"Just look," I said, supposing that witnessing it firsthand would be more comprehensible than a worded explanation. Instead, I would add a description while we observed what was happening.

There are water droplets floating around Rimuru in the air. And above him, water elementals are transformed into convex lenses.

Rimuru is using those lenses to catch the sunlight, reflecting it into one condensed, collected beam--and directing it toward the enemy soldiers upon the ground.

The water lenses near the ground evaporate, unable to withstand the incredible heat, but they execute their job admirably, instantly piercing the enemy soldiers and killing them. And simply by producing more water droplets, the spirits make it possible to dispatch the beams consecutively.

As long as the sun is in the sky, the light will fall mercilessly upon his foes.

It is the light of death.

"How terrifying... To think that merely focusing the sunlight could have such power..."

"Do you remember what I told you before, Ifrit? Your Flare Circle is a deadly flame attack that incinerates everything within its range with thousands of degrees of heat. But it had no effect on Rimuru, who possesses Thermal Fluctuation Resistance. That was because your heat was not focused enough. If you could have condensed the heat of your Flare Circle into a single point, you would have been able to defeat Rimuru in your confrontation."

"...Yes, I do remember that."

"In that case, you should understand how terrible this attack of Rimuru's truly is, shouldn't you?"

"The fear I feel has carved it into my mind..."

The level of power is determined by the amount of energy focused, so one must be aware of just how much concentrated temperature is contained within a thermal beam capable of penetrating through such a tiny hole.

Very low cost for such a great effect. And the speed with which it can be executed repeatedly makes it easy to use, as we have just witnessed. The only trick is that making it work requires a level of computational ability that an ordinary individual cannot reach.

If the angle of reflection is even slightly incorrect, all of that energy will disperse instead.

He called it Megiddo, another name for Armageddon. Truly the act of a merciless and angry god.

Kindhearted Rimuru, he who avoided harming others so diligently, now kills enemy soldiers without hesitation. He chooses the most efficient means of killing, executing the best possible move to achieve his arms.

I must admit that his determination gives me chills.

So I certainly cannot blame Ifrit for being frightened.

I understand that the warmer and more generous a person, the greater their wrath when angered.

I learned that from the holy manga texts, but I did not think the effect would be so frightening. "I forbid you from ever angering Rimuru, Ifrit."

"I wouldn't dream of it, Master."

Don't look at me like you're annoyed I would even suggest it!

At any rate, the two of us learned about a new side of Rimuru on this day.

And that means that the fate of those who incited his anger was sealed.

Rimuru's attacks from the edge of the area reached the enemy's base at last. In a location slightly to the rear of the center, as viewed from the front line of combat, was a much larger and more elaborate tent.

After marching down roads built and maintained by Rimuru's people, the enemy had set up camp where a little roadside town was in the planning stages. They even looted the stockpiled materials there for their own devices. The scavengers!

But these actions only poured oil upon the flames of Rimuru's rage. I can only shake my head at the stupidity of the Falmuth army.

At this point, a knight emerged from the tent in ostentatious armor. As tiny as humans are, this one seemed to be rather powerful--but Rimuru's Megiddo knocked him clean out in an instant!

"Did you see that?"

"I did..."

"I don't know who that man was, but he was fairly mighty."

"I expect so. In recent days I've grown sharper at appraising others, and to my eye, he seemed to have no weaknesses to exploit," said Ifrit.

It is true. It would be cruel to say this, but in fact, he was about as powerful as Ifrit is. And Rimuru mercilessly destroyed him in a single strike.

He could have at least let the man introduce himself, but considering what Falmuth has already done, Rimuru's treatment is probably the best course of action.

In any case, some more very haughty-looking men followed the first one outside.

"Ah!" Ifrit gasped in surprise. I was of the same mind.

Rimuru dispatched one of them again, though he seemed even more powerful than the man before.

By my estimation, he was of a level above even the Orc Disaster. And it was over in an instant…

Just being on the level of Ifrit, the higher elemental, would make him one of the most powerful individuals of a great nation. To vanquish such men in a single blow speaks to just how vast Rimuru's powers have grown.

A big part of that is that Megiddo can kill instantly. It travels at close to the speed of light. While there is a slight degradation of speed, it is not an attack that a human can visually identify and evade in time.

Which is to say that affinities and characteristics make quite a difference. An Orc Disaster would likely have the healing power to survive such an attack. In other words, the key to every different kind of attack is in how you utilize it.

Having removed these obstacles, Rimuru does not seem particularly intent on killing the two haughtiest of the group that remain. Apparently, he would rather take them alive and have them answer for their crimes.

"He is rather calm, isn't he?"

"He is. I would not bother with such measures, though. I would simply slaughter the whole lot."

"But if you think about it, that would only lead to more trouble down the line. Falmuth will be marshalling more forces to rescue their king, but if he's been killed, their entire army will mobilize for the sake of their dignity and pride. And the Western Holy Church will not sit idly by, either. Lord Rimuru's choice may have been the correct one to avoid a continuation of war."

"Hrm. It is a difficult matter. But while he might not kill the man, he will not be merciful, either," I said, just after Rimuru cut off the arrogant human's hand.

But that was the man's fault. Despite his tremendous disadvantage, he attempted to throw around his weight as though he were in control.

"I would have squashed him like a bug, but Rimuru is more patient."

"He has great willpower. And that is the right decision, anyway."

The man, as it turned out, was King Edmaris of Falmuth. He was the leader of the enemy army, so as one would say during the famous strategic board game, this is "check."

However!

"Unfortunately, the necessary number of souls to awaken as a True Demon Lord has not yet been met."

Ah, yes, of course. There was one overarching purpose for this battle, after all.

King Edmaris made some sort of excuse at this point, but Rimuru ignored him.

In the next instant, a dreadful phenomenon occurred: the surviving soldiers of the Falmuth army all lost their lives at once.

I could sense that Rimuru had done something, but I do not know what.

Megiddo was unfathomable in and of itself, but this is something else entirely...

The king of Falmuth fainted, unable to bear the fear. This is the correct response for a human, but not for a supposedly wise king. He should have interacted with Rimuru differently before it came to this.

But the fate of the king of Falmuth was of little consequence.

At this point, Rimuru took the lives of twenty thousand Falmuth soldiers. And the result...

"Notice: The necessary soul nutrients for the seed to sprout have been stockpiled. Now beginning Harvest Festival--the process of evolving into a Demon Lord."

The "Words of the World" rang loud and heavy.

This was a gospel.

Rimuru had achieved his goal.

◆THE WORSHIPPING DEMON◆

Rimuru is in an odd state, perhaps because of the evolution commencing.

"Lord Rimuru is unsteady on his feet."

"Indeed. I have never experienced it for myself, but I must imagine this Harvest Festival process is a very strenuous one."

"But that means..."

"You noticed it, too? The other man is still alive."

"Yes, Master. I'm sure Lord Rimuru will be fine, but I can't help but worry."

Indeed. Under more typical circumstances it would not be a problem, but Rimuru is in no state to fight right now.

I was concerned for what might happen next, but then he summoned Ranga.

Ah, of course. Once again, I am impressed by his thoroughness.

Ranga would not fall in battle to that man. I am not sure if he would win, but he would certainly protect Rimuru until he awakens—but this is not Rimuru's intent, it seems. Instead, he said to Ranga, "Take me safely back to town, and bring those two with us."

And he means to leave the survivor up to someone else. So he would rather put his trust in Ranga and choose safety, then.

Who does he mean to pit against the surviving man?

"Me, perhaps?"

Do not look so excited, Ifrit!

If that were true, though, I might even be a little jealous.

Instead, Rimuru summoned demons.

"That's too bad…"

"Kwaaa ha ha ha! Don't feel too down, Ifrit!"

Rimuru began the demon-summoning rite, and though I pitied Ifrit, I couldn't help but laugh. However, once again, I noticed that something was not quite right. Rimuru's demon summoning produced…

"What's this? Just three greater demons…? That's it?"

He offered twenty thousand dead as a sacrifice. But when the bodies disappeared into a black mist, what appeared was merely a trio of greater demons.

There is no sense in this.

With that total, there should have been at least a hundred demons. So why…?

"Keh heh heh, a familiar sensation. The birth of a new Demon Lord…" said one of the summoned demons with great delight.

Yes, something is wrong.

It was strange that he should be trembling with joy at being summoned by Rimuru.

"This is wondrous! Such a rich offering, and my first task.

Ahh...this is the highest of honors—I can hardly contain myself! May I continue to serve you beyond this task?"

Well, with one human corpse offered as a sacrifice, a greater demon can take form for several days. With twenty thousand split between just three of them, that would represent quite a lot of time.

But to a demon, that is a reward.

In this case, once finished with Rimuru's orders, he would be able to act freely—so choosing to bind himself to a master in this case is something that would never happen.

Rimuru is tiring, and his thoughts are dulling. So I took it upon myself to assess this demon.

Hrrm?!

As I suspected, this one is no ordinary demon.

"That must be an arch demon."

"Huh? But that summoning circle is only capable of calling greater demons," observed Ifrit. And he is right.

It was a greater demon summoning that Rimuru performed. It should be one hundred percent impossible for an arch demon to appear instead.

But there is no denying the reality before us.

If there is any explanation for this phenomenon, perhaps it is that they heard the call, and chose to come of their own volition? But that would mean arch demons with free will...

"That is undoubtedly an arch demon. And not a freshly-born babe, but the dangerous kind that has survived epochs."

"You mean...?"

"Ifrit, as a higher elemental, you are superior to demons. Yet you cannot view his full power, can you?"

"No, Master. He just looks like a simple greater demon to me."

So Ifrit is unable to sense the true nature of the demons Rimuru summoned. My observation tells me that the one in the middle is an arch demon, however. That would be evidence that he is capable of mimicking the lower level to disguise himself.

An eccentric demon that comes when he is not called. The ability to hide his arch demon presence in the shell of a mere greater demon. And most curious of all to me, a lifespan beyond even what I can sense.

Has he been alive for longer than me...?

No, that cannot be true.

It is merely because I am locked in this space. My "Inquirer" skill cannot view him properly.

But the basic fact is that a demon beyond measure has been summoned to this place. And one common fact of demons is that many will betray their master when they sense weakness.

Was this truly what Rimuru wanted? I was worried, but it turned out that I needn't have been.

"We'll talk later. First show me you can be useful," Rimuru ordered calmly.

"Rimuru isn't bothered," I said.

"It's almost as though he meant for this to happen."

The demon accepts Rimuru as his master. Based on his attitude, it would seem his honeyed words are not meant to be a deception, but his honest, true feelings.

That is a relief, then.

This demon is powerful. The man earlier was very impressive, for a human, but is no match for the demon.

I suppose Rimuru knows that as well. He's already gone to sleep.

The next time he wakes up, the world will welcome a new Demon Lord. The future was all but certain to me.

To be reincarnated in Volume 15!

MAJOR TROUBLE ELSEWHERE

Mmm! Yummy muffin!
AT THE MOMENT THE THREE DEMONS WERE SUMMONED NEAR THE CAPITAL CITY OF RIMURU...
...BERETTA HAD SENSED THEIR PRESENCE.
IS THAT... WHO I THINK IT IS...?
Be... ret... ta...
LADY RAMIRIS ?!
GASP
Muffin... stuck...
I'LL MAKE SOME TEA RIGHT AWAY!!
ULP
BUT THERE WERE BIGGER PROBLEMS AT HAND.
BLUB BLUB

LIST OF ACKNOWLEDGMENTS

AUTHOR:
Fuse-sensei

CHARACTER DESIGN:
Mitz Vah-sensei

ASSISTANTS:
Muraichi-san
Daiki Haraguchi-san
Masashi Kiritani-sensei
Taku Arao-sensei
Takuya Nishida-sensei

Everyone at the editorial department

AND YOU!!

Probably a little hard when it's cold out

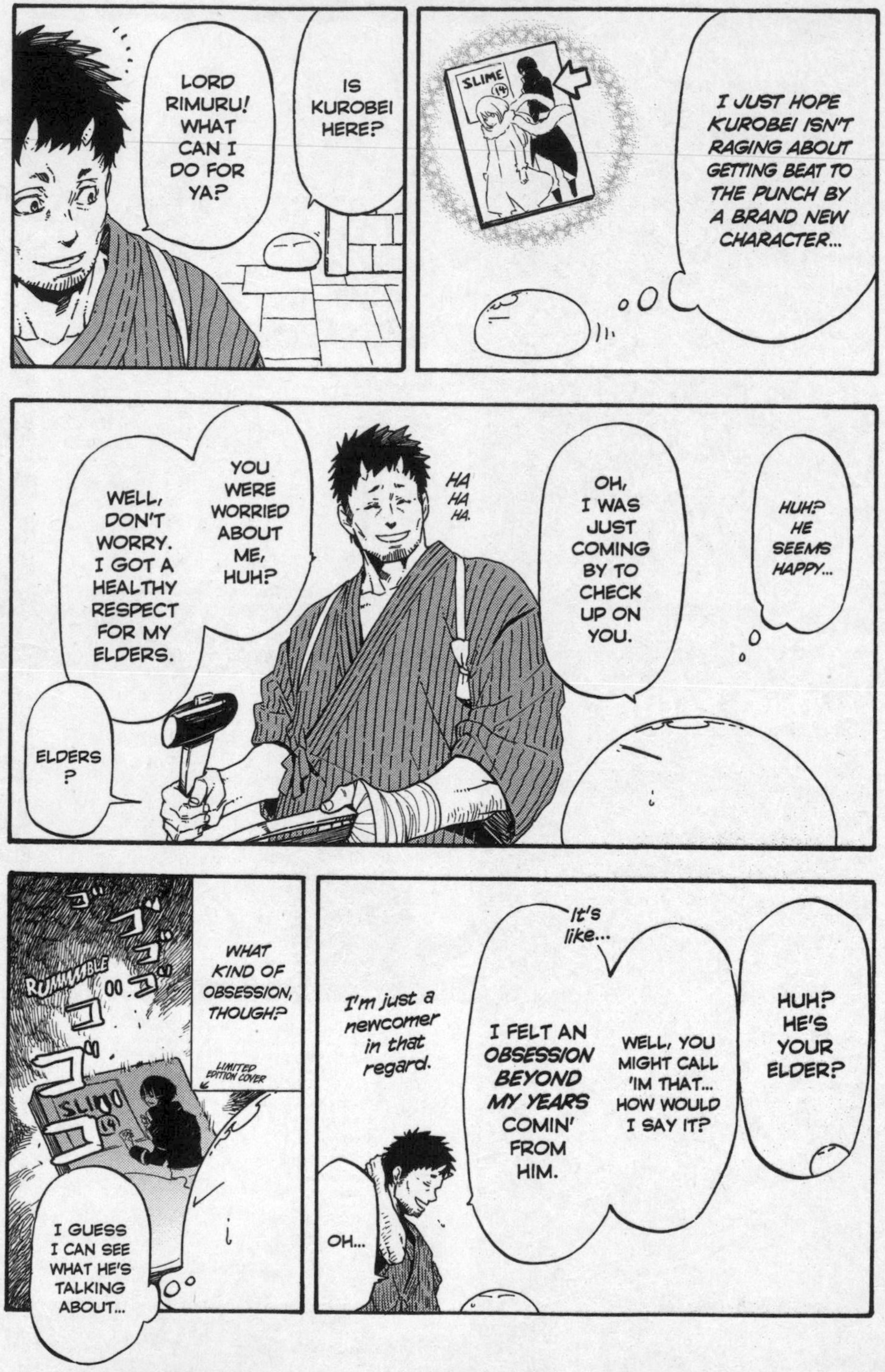
SLIME
I JUST HOPE KUROBEI ISN'T RAGING ABOUT GETTING BEAT TO THE PUNCH BY A BRAND NEW CHARACTER...
IS KUROBEI HERE?
LORD RIMURU! WHAT CAN I DO FOR YA?
HUH? HE SEEMS HAPPY...
OH, I WAS JUST COMING BY TO CHECK UP ON YOU.
HA HA HA.
YOU WERE WORRIED ABOUT ME, HUH?
WELL, DON'T WORRY. I GOT A HEALTHY RESPECT FOR MY ELDERS.
ELDERS?
HUH? HE'S YOUR ELDER?
It's like...
WELL, YOU MIGHT CALL 'IM THAT... HOW WOULD I SAY IT?
I FELT AN OBSESSION BEYOND MY YEARS COMIN' FROM HIM.
I'm just a newcomer in that regard.
OH...
WHAT KIND OF OBSESSION, THOUGH?
LIMITED EDITION COVER
RUMMMBLE
I GUESS I CAN SEE WHAT HE'S TALKING ABOUT...

Sakura Mochi
Slime Cakes

Tempest version

Young characters and steampunk setting, like *Howl's Moving Castle* and *Battle Angel Alita*

Beyond the Clouds © 2018 Nicke / Ki-oon

A boy with a talent for machines and a mysterious girl whose wings he's fixed will take you beyond the clouds! In the tradition of the high-flying, resonant adventure stories of Studio Ghibli comes a gorgeous tale about the longing of young hearts for adventure and friendship!

SAINT ☆ YOUNG MEN

A LONG AWAITED ARRIVAL IN PREMIUM 2-IN-1 HARDCOVER

After centuries of hard work, Jesus and Buddha take a break from their
heavenly duties to relax among the people of Japan, and their adventures in this
lighthearted buddy comedy are sure to bring mirth and merriment to all!

"Brilliant…the physical comedy
and facial expressions will
make you literally LOL."
—Sam Humphries
(host of *DC Daily*;
writer, *Green Lanterns*,
Legendary Star-Lord)

THE SWEET SCENT OF LOVE IS IN THE AIR! FOR FANS OF OFFBEAT ROMANCES LIKE *WOTAKOI*

Sweat and Soap © Kintetsu Yamada / Kodansha Ltd.

In an office romance, there's a fine line between sexy and awkward... and that line is where Asako — a woman who sweats copiously — meets Koutarou — a perfume developer who can't get enough of Asako's, er, scent. Don't miss a romcom manga like no other!

PERFECT WORLD

Rie Aruga

A TOUCHING NEW SERIES ABOUT LOVE AND COPING WITH DISABILITY

An office party reunites Tsugumi with her high school crush Itsuki. He's realized his dream of becoming an architect, but along the way, he experienced a spinal injury that put him in a wheelchair. Now Tsugumi's rekindled feelings will butt up against prejudices she never considered — and Itsuki will have to decide if he's ready to let someone into his heart...

"Depicts with great delicacy and courage the difficulties some with disabilities experience getting involved in romantic relationships... Rie Aruga refuses to romanticize, pushing her heroine to face the reality of disability. She invites her readers to the same tasks of empathy, knowledge and recognition."
—Slate.fr

"An important entry [in manga romance]... The emotional core of both plot and characters indicates thoughtfulness... [Aruga's] research is readily apparent in the text and artwork, making this feel like a real story."
—Anime News Network

KC
KODANSHA
COMICS

Knight of the ICE

Yayoi Ogawa

Knight of the ice ©Yayoi Ogawa/Kodansha Ltd.

SKATING THRILLS AND ICY CHILLS WITH THIS NEW TINGLY ROMANCE SERIES!

The adorable new odd-couple cat comedy manga from the creator of the beloved *Chi's Sweet Home*, in full color!

Sue & Tai-chan
Konami Kanata

Sue is an aging housecat who's looking forward to living out her life in peace... but her plans change when the mischievous black tomcat Tai-chan enters the picture! Hey! Sue never signed up to be a catsitter! *Sue & Tai-chan* is the latest from the reigning meow-narch of cute kitty comics, Konami Kanata.

KC KODANSHA COMICS

A SMART, NEW ROMANTIC COMEDY FOR FANS OF *SHORTCAKE CAKE* AND *TERRACE HOUSE*!

A romance manga starring high school girl Meeko, who learns to live on her own in a boarding house whose living room is home to the odd (but handsome) Matsunaga-san. She begins to adjust to her new life away from her parents, but Meeko soon learns that no matter how far away from home she is, she's still a young girl at heart — especially when she finds herself falling for Matsunaga-san.

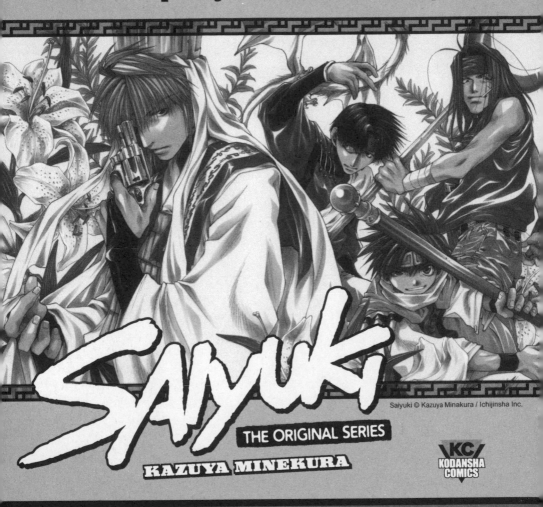

Magus of the Library

Mitsu Izumi

MITSU IZUMI'S STUNNING ARTWORK BRINGS A FANTASTICAL LITERARY ADVENTURE TO LUSH, THRILLING LIFE!

Young Theo adores books, but the prejudice and hatred of his village keeps them ever out of his reach. Then one day, he chances to meet Sedona, a traveling librarian who works for the great library of Aftzaak, City of Books, and his life changes forever...

KAMOME SHIRAHAMA

Witch Hat Atelier

A magical manga adventure for fans of Disney and Studio Ghibli!

Witch Hat Atelier © Kamome Shirahama/Kodansha Ltd.

The magical adventure that took Japan by storm is finally here, from acclaimed DC and Marvel cover artist Kamome Shirahama!

In a world where everyone takes wonders like magic spells and dragons for granted, Coco is a girl with a simple dream: She wants to be a witch. But everybody knows magicians are born, not made, and Coco was not born with a gift for magic. Resigned to her un-magical life, Coco is about to give up on her dream to become a witch…until the day she meets Qifrey, a mysterious, traveling magician. After secretly seeing Qifrey perform magic in a way she's never seen before, Coco soon learns what everybody "knows" might not be the truth, and discovers that her magical dream may not be as far away as it may seem…

KC KODANSHA COMICS

That Time I Got Reincarnated as a Slime 14 is a work of fiction. Names, characters, places, and incidents are the products of the author's imagination or are used fictitiously. Any resemblance to actual events, locales, or persons, living or dead, is entirely coincidental.

A Kodansha Comics Trade Paperback Original
That Time I Got Reincarnated as a Slime 14 copyright © 2020 Fuse / Taiki Kawakami
English translation copyright © 2020 Fuse / Taiki Kawakami

Published in the United States by Kodansha Comics, an imprint of Kodansha USA Publishing, LLC, New York.

Publication rights for this English edition arranged through Kodansha Ltd., Tokyo.

First published in Japan in 2020 by Kodansha Ltd., Tokyo as *Tensei Shitara Suraimu Datta Ken*, volume 14.

ISBN 978-1-64651-074-0

Original cover design by Saya Takagi and Ayaka Hasegawa (RedRooster)

Printed in the United States of America.

www.kodanshacomics.com

9 8 7 6 5 4 3 2 1
Translation: Stephen Paul
Lettering: Evan Hayden
Editing: Vanessa Tenazas
Kodansha Comics edition cover design by Phil Balsman

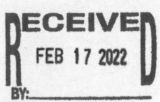

RECEIVED FEB 17 2022 BY:

Publisher: Kiichiro Sugawara

Director of publishing services: Ben Applegate
Associate director of operations: Stephen Pakula
Publishing services managing editor: Noelle Webster
Assistant production manager: Emi Lotto, Angela Zurlo